Sri Krishna Prem:

A Wing and a Prayer

by Jon Chapple

With a Foreword by
Dr Karan Singh

Blazing Sapphire Press
715 E. McPherson
Kirksville, Missouri 63501
2024

ISBN 978-1-952232-88-6

Library of Congress Control Number: 2024950827

Published by:
Blazing Sapphire Press
715 E. McPherson
Kirksville, Missouri 63501

Available at:
Nitai's Bookstore
715 E. McPherson
Kirksville, Missouri, 63501
Phone: (660) 229-2997
Email: ndelmoni@gmail.com

Sri Krishna Prem:

A Wing and a Prayer

What Readers are Saying:

Jon Chapple's work on Sri Krishna Prem (1898–1965) brings light to a little-known spiritual giant of the 20th century. Ronald Nixon left his native England for India after traumatic service as a fighter pilot in World War I. After serving as a professor of English at Lucknow and Banaras Hindu Universities, he established the still-active Mirtola Ashram with his guru Monica Chakrabarti (Sri Yashoda Mai) in the Himalayas. This remarkable biography reads like Gurdieff's *Meetings with Remarkable Men.* Krishna Prem met with Sri Aurobindo, Ramana Maharshi, and Timothy Leary. His interests in India began through his study of Buddhism with Christmas Humphreys, founder of the London Buddhist Society, and with the Theosophists. In Lucknow he embraced the Vaisnava faith without losing sight of insights from other traditions. This book traces his spiritual path in the context of key historical moments that shaped the 20th century, including the end of colonialism in India and the rise of the counter-cultural and cross-cultural movements, making for compelling, edifying reading.

By truly evoking the life and path of a seeker in technicolor, this book rivals the groundbreaking work of Romain Rolland on Ramakrishna and Vivekananda, and perhaps even Isherwood on Swami Prabhavananda. Filled with anecdote and insight, it is a must-read for all persons interested in India's spiritual past and present.

—Christopher Key Chapple, Doshi Professor of Indic and Comparative Theology at Loyola Marymount University (He is not related to the author.)

Sri Krishna Prem, an Englishman, had experiences as a pilot in the First World War which led him to visit India in search of the meaning of life, and guided him to Lucknow University, where he taught English. Extraordinarily, he landed auspiciously at the feet of his future guru, Monica Chakrabarti, the wife of the Vice Chancellor, a Bengali grand dame figure, at home equally in the glitter of high society and in privately treading the inner path of spiritual enquiry. In fulfilment of a longstanding desire to build a temple to Lord Krishna and Radha Rani, Monica renounced the householder's life to become Sri Yashoda Mai and decamped to the Kumaon Himalaya along with her English disciple, Professor Ronald Nixon, renamed Sri Krishna Prem, whom she called "Gopal," indicating that she regarded him as her son.

He had been given initiation on the condition that he would stick to the path revealed by the guru. To free him of his British cultural conditioning, Yashoda Mai enforced on him the strict code of Vaishnav orthodoxy. After the passing of Yashoda Mai—and liberated from both Western and Eastern perceptions of divinity—Krishna Prem's soul blossomed into a rare combination of Radha-Krishna, Christ and the Buddha, attracting to the Mirtola Ashram serious seekers of all faiths.

Jon Chapple's detailed research into Gopalda's steady voyage to become one with compassion as the goal of life beautifully portrays a man whom Dr Karan Singh, along with dozens of others who knew Gopalda, confidently asserts, "Of all the men I have ever met, he was the greatest."

—Bill Aitken, travel writer and student of Sri Krishna Prem

Most residents of Western countries have by now encountered the orthodox form of Gaudiya Vaishnavism [in the form of] the Krishna Movement. Few, however, have heard the remarkable story of an earlier convert, the Englishman Ronald Nixon, known as Krishna Prem.

Unlike the [1960s] countercultural context that featured the breaking of norms and welcomed Eastern spirituality, Nixon's conversion took place in colonial India itself, where Western norms are upheld even more rigorously than in the homeland. Coloniality in general must resist too much 'fraternizing with the natives,' lest sympathies be diverted from English interests. So one can only imagine how shocking the spectacle of a World War I veteran and university professor's complete adoption of a Gaudiya lifestyle and worldview would have been in most British social circles. And this is not a conversion into one of the modern, intellectualized faces of Hinduism which could find Western interlocutors; Nixon's was a complete submersion into the ... emotionally extravagant world of Krishna and his *gopī* lovers. Indeed, characterizations of Bengali Krishna devotionalism had a long and frowned-upon history in British representations of Hindu licentiousness and theological perversion.

After years of painstaking research, Jon Chapple's masterful narrative of Nixon's spiritual odyssey makes for fascinating reading. The very fact that his guru was a female renunciate from a noble family is unconventional even within pre-modern Gaudiya communities. It is the sort of captivating and unexpected information one encounters in every chapter of this biography. Chapple has avoided the tendency ... to veer towards hagiography; this is a historical document, even as it astonishes and fascinates. The book is very well written, free of both academic jargon and the coinages of High Street spiritualities, and so engrossing that one is hard-pressed not to read the entire account in one sitting. Indeed, *Sri Krishna Prem: A Wing and a Prayer* is one of the best reads in this genre of East/West spiritual biography.

—Edwin Bryant, Professor of Hindu Religion and Philosophy at Rutgers University

Researching the histories and philosophies of lesser-known thinkers and spiritualists is often difficult for authors attempting to locate reliable published sources, access unpublished archives, and include the living memory of those who knew the persons being researched. Chapple has done all three ... with several ounces of good humour and drops of healthy scepticism about the nature of the spiritual search and the required temperament of the seeker.

He has synthesised–in a volume with more than 1,000 well-researched and detailed footnotes–a new and previously unpublished presentation of Krishna Prem's complete philosophy, with details of his early life, upbringing, and emergence as a Vaishnava. Chapple has created this work by fusing the few published sources by and about Krishna Prem with an unpublished book draft written by Sri Madhava Ashish (another Briton and Krishna Prem's principal disciple), and with interviews, letters and email correspondence with Mirtola folk and other knowledgeable individuals.

Moreover, Chapple's personal imprint is present throughout. The germs were born during prevalent world events in 2021, and are associated with his own illness and related upheavals. That [this book] has seen the light of day is a singular accomplishment.... That it appears as a nexus of academic history, individual journeying, and meditation on those who have trodden the path is even more impressive. Chapple's words, thoughts, stories of Krishna—the Divine—and Krishna Prem—the person—and his offerings of love should be a welcome and jolly good read to anyone engaged on the spiritual course. This work should appeal to those who love good pilgrimage stories, whether connected to India or not.

—Joshua Nash, Editor, *Some Islands: A Journal of Linguistics and Art*

Contents

Foreword by Dr Karan Singh v

Preface vii

Introduction xiii

I Pūrvāśrama 1

1: Early Life 3

2: Mythmaking 11

3: Kingsman 21

4: "A Hindu Englishman" 27

5: 'Ma' 35

II Vaiṣṇava 45

6: Initiate 47

7: Vairāgī 63

8: Brajavāsī 81

9: The Whole Hog 99

10: Pūjārī 115

11: Yogī 133

12: "Mirtola Teaching" 155

13: War 167

14: Flying Solo 177

15: New Faces 183

16: Down South 193

17: All That Glitters 203

18: Pilgrims 213

III Universalist 221

19: "Attainment" 223

20: Opening Up 239

21: De-structuring 255

22: Legend of a Mind 267

23: Freedom 277

24: Setting Sail 291

Foreword by Dr Karan Singh

Let me start telling you how I came to know Sri Krishna Prem, affectionately called Gopal da. I read about him first in a book, *Among the Great*, by his dear friend Dilip Kumar Roy, in his essay on Sri Aurobindo, along with four other reputed intellectuals—Rabindranath Tagore, Mahatma Gandhi, Romain Rolland and Bertrand Russell. I wrote to Dilip for more information and he sent me his next book, *Sri Aurobindo Came to Me*, in which there was a full chapter on Sri Krishna Prem. To get his address I approached the then Governor of Uttar Pradesh, the eminent scholar and freedom fighter Dr K.M. Munshi, and once I got it I started corresponding with him and Ashish da. A few years later began what became an annual visit to Mirtola. I have described this in detail in my *Autobiography* (Oxford University Press).

Sri Krishna Prem was a truly remarkable person. Born in England and trained as a fighter pilot, he came to India looking for a guru. He joined the Lucknow University as Professor of English and it turned out that the devout wife of the Vice-Chancellor, Yashoda Mai, became his guru. He took *sannyās* and travelled with her through the mountains of Uttarakhand until she discovered Mirtola and decided to build her ashram there. It is an idyllic setting for the small Radha–Krishna temple that she built, and there was enough space for several cottages to be built by devotees in the years to come. Many of us have written about Sri Krishna Prem in bits and pieces, but what was required was a detailed full-length biography of this great scholar/guru/teacher.

This gap has now been filled by Jon Chapple, who has painstakingly put together a great deal of valuable and largely unknown material on Gopal da. He has described at length Sri Krishna Prem's teachings, so I will not try and encapsulate them in this Foreword. But what I would like to do is to commend Jon on this work, which will be of great interest not only to all those directly connected with Mirtola but to the general public who are interested in understanding the subtlety and profundity of Hinduism, cutting across all barriers of cast and creed, race and religion, expounded by this great man, born and brought up in England, who absorbed Hindu teachings and interiorised them in his own life.

I myself had the privilege of visiting Sri Krishna Prem in Mirtola from 1957 all the way up to 1964. It was a joy to sit with him and Ashish da through the long winter nights talking about every topic under the sun while he cooked delicious potatoes over the open fire. During our conversation Sri Madhava Ashish would join in from time to time so effortlessly that it almost appeared as if I was talking to a single mind divided into two bodies. Keen intellectual perception combined with deep emotional empathy enabled them to analyse my life situation in a manner no one had ever done before. And even more eloquent than their words were their silences, when their eyes would lock into a flow of power so tangible that I hardly dared breathe lest it be disturbed.

A special feature of Sri Krishna Prem's writings is his many references to parallel texts in the Western gnostic tradition, which greatly enrich his work. In this book Jon has also brought in other actors in Gopal da's life – his guru Yashoda Mai, her irascible daughter Moti Rani, his early friend and disciple Hari Das, and, of course, his close associate and successor Ashish da. This gives us a wider picture of Gopal da's life and teachings. I warmly congratulate Jon Chapple for this long-awaited book about a person I consider to be the most enlightened among the many remarkable people I have met in the course of my 92 years.

Karan Singh
New Delhi
October 2023

Preface

If writing a biography is a largely impersonal experience—an extended, ego-defying exercise in inhabiting a personality often very different to one's own—composing the preface to that biography is, by contrast, one of self-reflection, with the author forced to confront their motivations for embarking on (and persevering with) a project which will, in many cases, consume years of their life with no promise of obvious reward.

As I meditate on my own reasons, selfish and otherwise, for choosing to write this book, I can't help but be reminded of the words of the Indian guru Sri Aurobindo,[1] whose dismissive attitude towards spiritual biographies was well known. His withering rebuke of one writer, that "no one can write about my life because it has not been on the surface for man to see," should stop in their tracks any would-be chroniclers of the lives of religious personalities, particularly those of us now several generations distant from the subject—and, given the antipathy with which he regarded other writers' attempts (notably his friend Dilip Kumar Roy's) to immortalise life at Mirtola or codify his system of belief, it is difficult to imagine Krishna Prem thinking otherwise. I hope, however, that he would at least recognise the spirit in which this book has been written—one of great love and respect for its subject— even if he were suspicious of the motives of the self-seeking outsider responsible for it.

I became acquainted with Sri Krishna Prem in January 2021, when, unable to get a handle on spiralling cases of Covid-19, the British government had imposed a third stay-at-home order (lockdown) on the long-suffering people of England. Embarrassed by accounts of the great works of art and literature produced during the last major pandemic, the Spanish flu of 1918, and with a growing sense that the virus was here to stay, I resolved to create something substantial that could, I hoped, serve as my own humble pandemic legacy. Working an increasingly depressing day job reporting on the gloom of endless lockdowns, failing businesses and worrying new viral variants, I wanted to prove I could still find pleasure in telling a human story.

It was into this environment that Krishna Prem first appeared to me, bearing the gift of a fascinating—and fortuitously under-chronicled—life that promised to be the cure to my Covid-era malaise. As an amateur historian with a long-standing interest in the Krishna-worshipping religion known as Gaudiya Vaishnavism, the story of the so-called 'first Western Vaishnava' whose daring, apparently divinely assisted escape from the jaws of death seemed to have been ripped straight from the pages of an adventure novel immediately appealed, and I also felt some kinship with the man himself—another tall, spiritually inclined, follicularly challenged Englishman with an affinity for India and a connection to Cheltenham (my mum lives nearby)—despite our vastly different backgrounds. I had never intended to write a biography, but the synchronicity seemed too powerful to ignore. I set to work.

The existing literature, particularly Roy's *Yogi Sri Krishnaprem* and the published works of Sri Madhava Ashish, provided a solid foundation for early research, but it was my making contact with the 'Mirtola circle'—the self-designation of the community, mainly grand-disciples of Krishna Prem, that keeps alive the memory of the ashram he co-founded—and finding them receptive to the idea of a new biography of the man they call Gopalda that kickstarted the undertaking that grew into *Sri Krishna Prem: A Wing and a Prayer*. As we exchanged emails (and later WhatsApp messages and phone calls) and I was welcomed tentatively into the group, it became apparent that the records held by the ashram—especially the manuscript of an unfinished history of Mirtola by Madhava Ashish, Krishna Prem's successor, which the managing committee eventually agreed to share—could form the backbone of a new, comprehensive retelling of the Krishna Prem story drawing on the hitherto unpublished experiences of those who were there. The journalist in me was delighted: an exclusive!

In addition to helping to flesh out the chronology and personalities of Mirtola before 1965, I found that this manuscript, along with letters, photographs and personal reminiscences kindly supplied by various members of the 'circle,' shed new light on the human side of Sri Krishna Prem, the Cambridge intellectual and strictly observant monk, whose affection, open-mindedness, willingness to offer counsel, and role as a father figure to the children of seekers[2] meant as much to his many devotees as his acumen or spiritual credentials. Krishna Prem's words, particularly those dealing with his own mortality, also seemed to speak directly to me; having been diagnosed with advanced cancer in January 2022, I appreciated being reminded that my destiny, as all others, is "in the hands of Sri Bhagavān, and that peace lies in His Will, not in ours." (Indeed, much of the book you are about to read was conceived and written while undergoing treatment, sitting propped up in a hospital bed or, on occasion, lying dead still inside an MRI or CT scanner.)

These first-hand accounts also explore the huge changes that swept over Mirtola in the 1950s and '60s, as Krishna Prem and his protégé Madhava Ashish embarked on the "great clear-out" that transformed this (comparatively) traditional Vaishnava ashram into one with a universalist, proto-New Age outlook—a piece of history only hinted at, or even actively contradicted, in previously published materials (one popular encyclopaedia claims, to the contrary, that Mirtola "began and has continued to be aligned with strict orthodox Vaishnavism").

As an author, I found this era—during which disciples were encouraged to seek for themselves the timeless truth, as Krishna Prem saw it, that lies behind the symbols and archetypes of the Krishna myth—the most difficult to digest, understand and chronicle (a challenge compounded by the abrupt end, some 15 years before Krishna Prem's death, of Madhava Ashish's manuscript, which was cut short by his own passing in 1997). My own spiritual identity developed along personal-theistic lines—I grew up praying nightly to God the Father ("If I should die before I wake, I pray the Lord my soul to take") and as a young adult found my religiosity rekindled by Vaishnava *bhakti* and the intense devotionalism of records such as George Harrison's *All Things Must Pass*—and so the idea of a personal God had always seemed to me natural and logical. If, as the *Hitopadeśa* teaches, *dharma* (religious duty) is the "chief distinction" of humans, without which we are "no different from animals",[3] why wouldn't these divine creatures resemble their creator (and vice versa)? The American Vaishnava Hayagriva Das (Howard Wheeler) has written that the *Advaita Vedānta* of Śaṅkara, with its view that the "Self, the intangible, impersonal *ātman* within everyone, is supreme," once appeared to him "more logical than saying that a cowherd boy named Krishna is supreme."[4] For me, however, the idea that the absolute truth is a human-like figure has always made far more sense.

As I learnt more about these changes—which had as their basis a rejection of the trappings of the "Krishna cult" which, in the words of Madhava Ashish, had become "a safe channel for [Krishna Prem's] feelings"[5]—I felt a resistance build as my own 'safe' assumptions about the nature of the divine were similarly challenged. For all my presumed universalism, I had never seriously considered that a non-theistic approach, which instead recognises man as the supreme personality, could lead one to the same liberation as that promised by the worshippers of a personal God. Although I am, I confess, still "under the spell of name and form", as Krishna Prem once put it, I am now also more certain than ever that my own path is but one of an infinite number comprising that single great road to eternity, travelled by seekers of all stripes since time immemorial.

As the book progressed, and my contact with Krishna Prem's spiritual children and grandchildren increased, the nature of the project also changed. What had at first seemed like a purely selfish exercise (one that would give me something to do while the coronavirus was still considered a threat) felt like it had transformed, subtly but surely, into something more like an offering: to the Mirtola circle, to the Absolute, and (illogical as it may seem) to 'Gopalda' himself. I came to see the process of researching and writing as an act of meditation, and found I identified as never before with the bliss that comes with the surrendering of the self—and the consecrating of one's work and activities—in the service of the divine. "Self-surrendering to the spirit," Krishna Prem once explained, "is the surrender of love;" now, I better understood what he meant.

It is, then, this circle—particularly Chitra Iyer, the current *pūjārī* and custodian of the Mirtola ashram—to whom I am most indebted; without their support and generosity, and that of Krishna Prem's entire spiritual family (including Dr Karan Singh, Bill Aitken, Promila Chitkara, P. Niroop, Pervin Mahoney, Madhu Tandan, Satish Datt Pandey, the Shah family and others I've no doubt overlooked), this book could not have been written.

Thanks are also due to Nathan Hartley, whose *The Hare Krishnas in Britain* served as my introduction to the Sri Krishna Prem legend; John Nixon, Krishna Prem's nephew and the unofficial historian of the Nixon family; John Brown of Taunton School, for his invaluable insight into Krishna Prem's schooldays; Brian Mooney, for his advice on how a journalist might approach writing a full-length book; and a publicity-shy Facebook friend for his encyclopaedic knowledge of Gaudiya Vaishnava history in the West. My gratitude, too, to Sri Shrivatsa Goswami, Chris Russell-Jones, Tony Foster, Sarah Donovan, Omprakash Gupta, Joshua Nash, Martin Buckley, Andrew Chen, Tor Scott, Chris Chapple, Ken Winkler, Betsy and Neal Delmonico (Nitai Das), Neil Steinert (Nityananda Das), Steven Rosen and the late Jan Brzezinski (Jagadananda Das), as well as friends and family too numerous to mention, for other help, guidance and encouragement.

Finally, I offer my *praṇām* to Sri Madhava Ashish for compiling the manuscript that forms a significant part of this book and to all the other authors whose works are quoted and cited in the 100,000-odd words that follow, without whom this book would be very empty indeed. May their words provide strength, illumination and entertainment for all treaders of the "razor-edged path."

With love,

Jon Chapple
London
Summer 2023

Notes

[1]A contemporary and sometime correspondent of Sri Krishna Prem, as well as a fellow alumnus of King's College, Cambridge (1892).

[2]Abha Shah, daughter of Krishna Prem's disciples Jagdish and Rambha Shah, has written of how she and her younger sisters, Amala and Arati, "grew up playing on Gopal Da's lap and clambering onto his shoulders."

[3] Andrea Gutiérrez, 'Embodiment of Dharma in Animals', in Patrick Olivelle and Donald R. Davis Jnr (eds), *Hindu Law: A New History of Dharmaśāstra* (Oxford: Oxford University Press, 2018), 468.

[4]Hayagriva Dāsa, *The Hare Krishna Explosion (The Birth of Krishna Consciousness in America 1966–1969)* (Moundsville: Palace Press, 1985), 20.

[5]Sri Madhava Ashish, 'Preface', in Sri Krishna Prem and Sri Madhava Ashish, *Man, the Measure of All Things*, 1st US edn (Wheaton: Quest Books, 1969), 9.

Introduction

Almora, Uttar Pradesh, 14 November 1972.

A stream of visitors passes through Kundan House, the Himalayan home of Gertrude Emerson Sen. Throughout the day, Gertrude—the American-born widow of the eminent plant physiologist Basiswar Sen—serves breakfast, mid-morning coffee and afternoon tea to the throng of pilgrims making the 18-mile journey to the Mirtola ashram to mark the anniversary of the *mahāsamādhi* of its late co-founder,[1] Sri Krishna Prem (1898–1965), known locally as the *Tul* ('Eminent') Maharaj,[2] who had died seven years earlier.

Born Ronald Nixon in Cheltenham, England, in the twilight of the 19th century, Krishna Prem moved to India in the aftermath of the First World War, in which his life, he believed, had been miraculously saved by a "power beyond our ken" while serving as a fighter pilot. There, he co-founded a hilltop hermitage dedicated to the Hindu god Krishna, for whose love (*prem*) he was named and to whom he remained singularly devoted for the rest of his life.

That is, at least, according to the popular version of the Sri Krishna Prem myth. In this telling, repeated in many existing biographical materials, Krishna Prem remained to his death a conventional Vaishnava in the Bengali Gaudiya tradition, serving Krishna in divine ecstasy to the exclusion of all other influences and teachers. The true story—much like the man himself—is significantly more complicated, charting a deeply personal spiritual odyssey that incorporated influences from Buddhism, Hindu Vedanta, classical yoga, analytical psychology and the Western mystery tradition alongside Krishna *bhakti*.

One legacy of his idiosyncratic, syncretistic approach to spirituality is that published accounts we have of Krishna Prem's life—particularly those by authors with an affiliation to a particular tradition or sect—tend to emphasise one aspect of his belief system at the expense of others. For many Gaudiya Vaishnavas, Krishna Prem is notable as the first Western guru in their tradition. Steven

Rosen, a disciple of Bhaktivedanta Swami, founder of the Hare Krishna movement, connects Krishna Prem's final words with his guru's journey to America, writing: "[I]n November of 1965, on his deathbed, Śrī Krishna Prem had been documented as saying, 'My ship is sailing.' What he didn't know, of course, was that the sublime 'ship of Śrī Krishna Prem' had, indeed, already set sail, just a few months earlier, headed for Western shores."[3] Similarly, followers of HP Blavatsky speak proudly of Mirtola as a "Himalayan ashram with Theosophical roots,"[4] while the psychologist Timothy Leary writes that his "interest in healing as well as enlightenment defines Sri Krishna Prem as a precursor of the humanist psychology movement that was to sweep America and Western Europe in the 1970s."[5]

Depending, then, on one's interests and/or sectarian allegiance(s), it is easy to construct an idealised version of Sri Krishna Prem's philosophy that minimises unwanted influences or views. However, to do so—particularly by ignoring the universalism and secularism that would characterise his later worldview—is to miss the point, according to Krishna Prem's successor at Mirtola, who was unequivocal that Krishna Prem the Vaishnava *bhakta* represented only a half-formed version of the perfected man he would later become; Sri Madhava Ashish would write later of being "embarrassed by their Krishna Prem," whose life had, he felt, been mythologised to one "of singing and dancing in ecstasy."[6]

Other aspects of the Sri Krishna Prem story also defy easy categorisation. In his personality and manners, Krishna Prem was variously described as being both 'more Indian than the Indians' and giving the impression of an English gentleman in saffron robes; he was a former academic and professor who nevertheless swore to the reality of ghosts, magic and psychic powers; and while some visitors to Mirtola remember being offered warmth and hospitality, others note his well-known resentment towards the intrusion into his life of guests.

Indeed, only four aspects of Krishna Prem's beliefs may be said to have remained consistent throughout his life. The first, and perhaps the most strongly held, was faith in the power of the guru, who, as a physical manifestation of the divine consciousness (which he often, but not always, called Krishna), provides the seeker with a clear path, and serves as a conduit, to that consciousness; the second is a complementary emphasis on looking within (to the 'guru' inside) to realise the divinity inherent in one's heart. He also suggested consistently that there exists a universal religious truth (what Aldous Huxley called the 'perennial philosophy') towards which all spiritual paths lead, and he rejected the traditional Hindu dichotomy between personal and impersonal conceptions of the absolute truth, as underlined by the importance he put on monistic texts such as the *Māṇḍūkya Upaniṣad*, from which he would quote as frequently as from core Vaishnava *shastras* such as the mostly theistic *Bhāgavata Purāṇa*.

However, it is precisely because of these apparently contradictory positions—

Briton and Indian, Hindu and universalist, personalist and impersonalist, intellectual and believer, *bhakta* and *jñānī* (gnostic)—as well as the ever-evolving, hard-to-pin-down philosophy that allowed him to hold to them simultaneously, that Krishna Prem's life continues to hold such fascination for spiritual seekers, religious scholars and students of history alike. Having broken down religio-cultural barriers to be accepted as both an Indian and an authentic Vaishnava, Nixon saw for himself the essential unity of all spiritual paths, as he explains in his *The Yoga of the Kaṭhopaniṣad*:

> There are not half a dozen of these mystical absolutes floating about in the universe. There is not even one true and several false ones. There is just one Reality which has been symbolized in various ways, each symbol expressing more or less inadequately some one particular aspect of it. 'The Real is one; men describe it in many ways' (Rig Veda).[7]

It is in this spirit of unity—and in the hope of providing a deeper understanding of one of the great personages of late British and early independent India—that this biography has been written and is offered to readers. As Sri Krishna Prem reminds us, the spiritual 'path' upon "which all true religions were originally based" is not the property of any race or religion,[8] our lives (irrespective of race, caste or sex) comprising a great "eternal correspondence" by which is revealed "the one and same message of unity in multiplicity," in the words of his friend, the Sikh poet Mohan Singh Diwana.[9] Before continuing, let us, then, shed our preconceptions about this remarkable personality at the feet of the one, indivisible Absolute of which we are all part and parcel.

> *"Just as a man never conceives his own head, hands and other limbs as belonging to anyone else, he who is devoted to Me does not regard his fellow creatures as distant from himself. He who sees no difference between Me (who is the combined form of the Creator, Destroyer and Preserver) and the very selves of all living being attains everlasting peace."*[10]
>
> — Sri Bhagavan (Krishna), *Bhāgavata Purāṇa*

Notes

[1]As described in Girish N. Mehra, *Nearer Heaven than Earth: The Life and Times of Boshi Sen and Gertrude Emerson Sen*, 2nd impression (New Delhi, Rupa & Co, 2007) 691.

[2] Bill Aitken, 'Sri Krishna Prem in the Last Years', in Sri Madhava Ashish, *Where'er Love's Camels Lead: Sri Krishna Prem Remembered* (unpublished), Mirtola, Sri Dev Ashish, 2015, p 265.

[3] Steven J. Rosen, *Śrī Chaitanya's Life and Teachings: The Golden Avatāra of Divine Love* (Lanham, Lexington Books, 2017) 203.

[4] Seymour B. Ginsburg (ed.) and Sri Madhava Ashish, 'Mirtola: A Himalayan Ashram with Theosophical Roots', *Quest* 100.3 (2012): 98–105.

[5] Timothy Leary, *Flashbacks – A Personal and Cultural History of an Era: An Autobiography* (New York, GP Putnam's Sons, 1990) 217.

[6] Sri Madhava Ashish, Letter to Andrew Rawlinson, c. April 1988.

[7] Sri Krishna Prem, *Initiation into Yoga: An Introduction to the Spiritual Life* (Wheaton, Quest Books, 1976) 66.

[8] Sri Krishna Prem, *The Yoga of the Bhagavat Gītā* (London, John M. Watkins, 1948) xvi.

[9] Dr Mohan Singh MA, PhD, DLitt, *New Light on Sri Krishna & Gita*, vol.1, 1st ed. (Lahore, S. Sher Singh, 1944) 68.

[10] Adapted from CL Goswami and MA Shastri (trans.), *Śrīmad Bhāgavata Mahāpurāṇa*, part I, 4.7.53-54, 11th rpt (Gorakhpur, Gita Press, 2010) 322.

PART I

PŪRVĀŚRAMA

1: Early Life

"We must not, as elders always do, express surprise at the way children outgrow the clothes we have made for them."[1]
— Sri Krishna Prem and Sri Madhava Ashish, *Man, the Measure of All Things*

Sri Krishna Prem was born Ronald Henry Nixon on 10 May 1898, the eldest of three children of Thomas Christopher and Effie Marion (Heard) Nixon.

The 1890s were a particularly fertile decade for Indian gurudom, with a who's who of 20th-century Hindu leaders—including the father of the Hare Krishna movement, AC Bhaktivedanta Swami Prabhupada (1896–1977), the Bombay beedi seller-cum-Vedanta master Nisargadatta Maharaj (1897–1981), the Bengali mystic Anandamayi Ma (1896–1982), and Paramahamsa Yogananda (1893–1952), whose *Autobiography of a Yogi* became a fixture of every hippie bookshelf—all appearing in India within a few years of Nixon's birth in England. As Triloki Nath Dhar, a biographer of another—the Kashmiri saint Bhagwan Gopinath (1898–1968)—observes: "Obviously there was something celestial about the last decade of the 19th century."[2]

Thomas Nixon (1866–1951), known as 'Christo',[3] was a successful glass and porcelain merchant who owned a "splendid china shop"[4] at 72 The Promenade in Cheltenham, Gloucestershire. Christo appears to have been a pillar of the community—surviving borough council minutes show regular donations to Cheltenham Art Gallery and Museum, including a "carved stone head from Egypt" (1922),[5] a loan of a "collection of fine modern china" (1935)[6] and a "Spode soup plate, c. 1820" (1946)[7]— but had little interest in religious life; Sri Madhava Ashish, Krishna Prem's disciple and successor as head of the Mirtola ashram, relates that Thomas "liked nothing better on a Sunday morning than to walk across the fields to a local country church, ... sleep through the sermon and return in time for lunch."[8]

Effie (1872–1961), by contrast, was well known locally as a devotee of Christian Science, a religious movement emphasising healing through prayer which had been founded by Mary Baker Eddy in 1879. Effie served as both a Christian Science practitioner[9]—a full-time healer certified by the movement's mother church, the First Church of Christ, Scientist,[10] to pray on behalf of others—and a reader, or lay minister, for the Cheltenham branch of the Christian Science Society.[11]

In a testimony printed in the 1 September 1906 issue of the *Christian Science Sentinel*, Effie describes how she cured a recent cycling injury by 'treating' it with prayer, as well relating how Christian Science enabled her to give birth to her second child, Ronald's younger brother Roger (1904–1988), without painkillers:

> I can no longer delay the acknowledgment of my gratitude for Christian Science. Some months ago my baby was born without medical attendance. The nurse was a Christian Scientist and the birth was perfectly harmonious and painless. Last summer my husband and I were cycling in Germany, and one morning I awoke with a sharp attack of pain. Very shortly the pain yielded to treatment and I slept for an hour, when I felt perfectly well, without even the slightest trace or sense of anything having been wrong. We were on our cycles in another hour and had a ride of over sixty miles that day. Before I knew about Christian Science I have had similar attacks and have felt weak and ill for days afterwards.
>
> I cannot tell how grateful I am for these and all other proofs of the power of divine Love, and the understanding that "if man is governed by the higher law of divine Mind, his body is in submission to everlasting Life and Truth and Love" (*Science and Health*, p. 216).[12]

Such was Effie's apparent success with her Christian Science practice—which "as time went on ... absorbed all her attention," to the detriment of her marriage (Ashish, 21)—that she came to attract a circle of admirers who helped her with the cooking and domestic chores around the Nixons' Cheltenham homes, The Briars and Coney Gree. Like the disciples of Indian mega-gurus such as Bhaktivedanta Swami, Maharishi Mahesh Yogi and Rajneesh, these acolytes also bought Effie a car (Ashish, 22), a red MG, with which she was said to have terrified anyone unfortunate enough to accept a lift. John Nixon, Roger's son, recalls that his grandmother drove "like the clappers,"[13] while Bob Alexander, Ronald's Cambridge University friend, said she treated the road as if were "hers by inalienable right" (Ashish, 22).

When not behind the wheel, however, Effie was "very controlled",[14] and her unruly eldest son chafed against what he viewed as her unnatural emotional detachment; later, he would say he wished his mother "would have chased him around with a rolling pin, like other boys' mothers".[15] Madhava Ashish elaborates:

> Mrs Nixon never got angry. ... Ronald felt deprived; it wasn't natural to be so unruffled. It seems to have been the same lack of emotional expression that led a Cambridge friend to say of the household, 'It's very nice. But it's rather hygienic.' The children were not clouted or spanked. They were barely scolded. They were sent to their rooms or made to read from Mary Baker Eddy ... .(Ashish, 16)

In his essay 'A Cross-cultural Adventure: The Transformation of Ronald Nixon,' the scholar of Vaishnavism, David Haberman, contrasts Nixon's lack of attachment to his "'controlled' biological mother" with his "deep attraction to his 'wild' spiritual mother", his guru, Sri Yashoda Mai.[16] However, while 'Ma', as he called the latter, seemed a better candidate for the role of hot-tempered matriarch, even she was found guilty of giving special treatment to her favourite disciple: "She treated Krishna Prem with such consistent gentleness that he complained she was making things too easy for him. He had seen her treatment of others."[17]

Interestingly, despite Christo's apparent lack of inclination towards the 'path,' it was he, not Mrs Nixon, who was the more spiritual of the pair, according to Gyanendra Nath Chakravarti, Yashoda Mai's husband and guru. "So far as the three children were concerned, if there were any spirituality in the family it lay with their mother," recounts Madhava Ashish. "It was therefore to their intense surprise that many years later, when Dr Chakravarti visited their parents, he remarked to his wife that Mr Nixon was a very spiritual person" (Ashish, 15).

Though he forged his own spiritual path, Nixon's biological parents seem to have nevertheless played an important role in the development of his religious life, Madhava Ashish crediting the stuffiness of the Nixon family home with partially inspiring his guru's rejection of traditional married life. "It was this sterile atmosphere, accentuated at the breakfast table, that made Ronald decide, 'If this is marriage, then I don't want it'" (Ashish, 17).

Comparatively little is known about Krishna Prem's formative years, given that he rarely spoke about his *pūrvāśrama*, or life prior to becoming a Vaishnava *vairāgī* (ascetic). Haberman notes that as "Nixon later took *sannyāsa* [a vow of renunciation] and was thereby dead to his former life, he spoke little of and published nothing on his early years",[18] while Krishna Prem's disciple Narendra Nath Kaul writes: "He was a great teacher, but never projected himself as such. He hardly wrote or talked about himself, and whatever is known about his life is very sketchy."[19] "Sri Krishna Prem was a very private person in that he considered the ego and all 'I-ness' as the great enemy on the Spiritual Path," confirms the Theosophist AEI (Ted) Falconar, "so he did not speak of himself."[20]

He did, however, divulge enough about his former life to Sri Madhava Ashish (1920–1997), his foremost disciple and confidant, for the latter to be able to write a biographical 262-page manuscript which, though unfinished, provides invaluable information about his youth and the early years of the ashram, as well as about Madhava Ashish's own first five years at Uttar Brindaban (1946–1951).[21] [The unpublished *Where'er Love's Camels Lead: Sri Krishna Prem Remembered*, is cited with in-text references throughout this book.] The book, as the author explains (Ashish, 11), consists chiefly of "stories I heard from Krishna Prem and Moti" (Rani, Yashoda Mai's daughter). It contains numerous stories about Nixon the angelic-looking but mischievous child who enjoyed pulling pranks on figures of authority: carrying his parents' furniture out into the garden while they were at a Sunday-morning Christian Science meeting (Ashish,16); putting treacle on their housekeeper's chamber pot (Ashish, 18); and taunting the local stationmaster by blowing a railway whistle "at just the wrong moment" (Ashish, 16), for example. However, the author notes that Nixon had "little to say" about his schooldays at Taunton School in Somerset, though he admitted an aptitude for science.

Nixon entered the junior section of Taunton School in January, 1908, aged nine, and would have moved into his senior boarding house, Wills East, at around the age of 14, according to John Brown, the school's long-serving archivist. Brown notes that Nixon served as a house prefect in his final year and was "clearly an academic," having gained his Oxford and Cambridge Higher Certificate in July 1915 and passed the Cambridge University entrance examination the following year (one of three boys from Wills East to win an Oxbridge exhibition, or scholarship, in 1916[22]).

In addition to his academic prowess, Nixon was a skilled athlete—a profile in *The Tauntonian* magazine notes that he had, by his final year, been awarded sporting colours for "rugger and sports" (rugby and athletics) and represented his house in shooting and signalling, helping Wills East win the inter-house shooting cup in 1915—and was a member of the school's Officers' Training Corps (OTC) unit, which had been established in 1913.

As well as giving Nixon his first taste of military life, the Taunton cadet force (one of the 166 junior OTC contingents formed to train new officers in the aftermath of the Boer War[23]) also provided a showcase for the musical ability for which he would later gain recognition in India. "Apart from being a good shot, he must also have been musical," explains Brown, "as his promotion on 27 January 1916 was from corporal to band sergeant, and in a contemporary OTC magazine report we read: 'As regards the musical department of the Contingent, the enthusiasm of the Band, under Sergeant Nixon, is if anything greater than ever.'"[24]

Perhaps given its militaristic overtones and his own later pacifism, Krishna Prem does not seem to have looked back on his schooldays fondly, especially when compared to his university experience. Madhava Ashish says he "later held the view that no intelligent man looks back on his public school with pleasure," and that his guru never "mention[ed] his having had friends at school, at least not of the sort whose friendship survives school. At Cambridge he definitely did" (Ashish, 19).

Ronald's younger brother, Roger, was also sent to Taunton, where he, too, excelled in marksmanship as a member of the OTC (later the Combined Cadet Force). After leaving Birmingham University with a bachelor of commerce degree, Roger set out for Africa in July, 1926, having secured a job with the Sudan Plantations Syndicate. His son, John Nixon, writes:

> Roger's job was encouraging and managing the development of cotton growing on farms owned by the indigenous Sudanese. He covered a vast area frequently on horseback, vast enough that, so say, his nearest white colleague lived some 200 miles distant. Come the Second World War, he sought to enlist at Khartoum but was turned down with instructions to continue to grow cotton for the war effort. The stories I remember were about his love of camping, working with the farmers, protecting the villages from marauding elephants, riding his Indian motorcycle, playing polo and, as 'platoon commander,' regularly drilling his syndicate colleagues, who must have travelled to do so. The likely somewhat apocryphal story goes that each platoon member was issued a Lee–Enfield .303 rifle with just six rounds of ammunition with which to defend their 'territory' from Rommel's Afrika Korps![25]

Roger returned to Britain around 1948 upon the birth of his son (John's elder sister, Annie, was taken out to the Sudan but returned, at her mother Margaret's insistence, after contracting dysentery) and—after a spell camping behind a pub, the Air Balloon, in Birdlip, Gloucestershire—moved above the Nixon family shop on Cheltenham's Promenade. "Growing cotton was no career path for life in the UK, so he was always grateful not only for his good fortune in taking over the business from Christo ... but also to Ronald, who wrote a letter clearly expressing he had no desire to inherit any of the Nixon family [assets]," John explains.[26]

Like her eldest brother, the youngest Nixon, Ronald's sister Barbara (1907–1983), went to Cambridge University, where she studied English literature at Newnham College from 1926.[27] Upon graduating she pursued a career in theatre, working alongside Robert Donat and Flora Robson as a member of the Cambridge Festival Theatre company and finding "success in the field despite the underlying connotations of woman actors."[28]

At Cambridge, Barbara met her future husband, the Marxist economist Maurice Dobb. While the Nixons disapproved of Dobb's communist politics—Christo is said to have "enjoyed drawing hostile articles on the Soviet Union" to his daughter's attention—the family supported the relationship,[29] and Barbara is credited with bringing stability to the tumultuous personal life of her eminent husband, a protégé of John Maynard Keynes and "the foremost Marxian economist of his generation in Britain."[30]

Like her brother, Barbara was a "keenly intelligent and a voracious reader"[31] who volunteered for military service, becoming one of the first female ARP (air raid precaution) wardens in London during the Blitz of 1940–41. Previously, "women were expected to make tea and sandwiches or at most answer telephones at the command centre," writes the academic Matthew J. Clarcq, who has chronicled Barbara's career as an air-raid warden. "Such a role was not enough for Barbara Nixon."[32]

Barbara later wrote about her World War Two experiences in a highly regarded memoir, *Raiders Overhead: A Diary of the London Blitz*.[33] In peacetime she resumed her pre-war theatre career, working as an actress, playwright and stage manager, and also briefly held elected office, serving as a London county councillor for the Labour party from 1946 to 1949.

"All three of Christo's children, Ronald, Barbara and Roger, were in some way pioneers and led quite extraordinary lives," notes John Nixon.[34]

Neither Roger nor Barbara visited their brother's ashram (though the latter did meet him in Benares in the winter of 1950–1951, as detailed in chapter 18). Annie Nixon (later Annie Russell-Jones MRCVS)[35], however, initiated a correspondence with her uncle after finding one of his books in a box in her parents' attic[36] and later made multiple visits to Mirtola, albeit after his death;[37] she accepted as a teacher his successor, Sri Madhava Ashish.[38] The Scottish-born travel writer Bill Aitken—a grand-disciple of Ronald/Krishna Prem who lived at Mirtola from 1965 to 1972—remembers Annie (1945–1991[39]), a musician and vet, as an "ebullient" presence who on one visit spayed Shyam and Pari, two Siamese cats gifted to Madhava Ashish by Aitken's late companion, Prithwi,[40] the dowager *mahārāṇī* of Jind State. Annie's son, Krishna Prem's grand-nephew Chris Russell-Jones, is also a self-described "spiritual explorer"[41] and sometime visitor to Mirtola.

Notes

[1] Sri Krishna Prem and Sri Madhava Ashish, *Man, the Measure of All Things*, 1st US ed. (Wheaton: Quest Books, 1969) 124.

[2] TN Dhar 'Kundan', *Saints and Sages of Kashmir* (New Delhi: APH Publishing Corporation, 2004) 309.

[3]Pronounced /ˈkrɪstoʊ/ (and also, coincidentally, a colloquial Bengali rendering of the name "Krishna").

[4]Miss M. Paterson, 'Beneath the Devils Chimney' Part II, *Friends of Leckhampton Hill & Charlton Kings Common Newsletter* 14 (Winter 2003) 5.

[5]*Cheltenham Borough Council Minutes* (Cheltenham, Cheltenham Local History Society, 2018) 25.

[6]*Cheltenham Minutes*, 158.

[7]*Cheltenham Minutes*, 80.

[8]Sri Madhava Ashish, *Where'er Love's Camels Lead: Sri Krishna Prem Remembered* (unpublished), Mirtola, Sri Dev Ashish, 2015, p 15. Future references to this unpublished book, collated by Sri Dev Ashish and other disciples at Mirtola, will be cited parenthetically in the text.

[9]'1939 England and Wales Register', *Ancestry*, Lehi, Ancestry.com Operations, 2018, https://www.ancestry.co.uk/search/collections/61596 (accessed 15 November 2021). Original data: Crown copyright images reproduced by courtesy of TNA, London England.

[10]'Christian Science Practitioners,' *The Christian Science Journal* 38.4 (1920) xxix.

[11]'Christian Science Churches and Societies,' *The Christian Science Journal* 30.12 (1913) iv.

[12]Effie M. Nixon, testimony of healing, *Christian Science Sentinel* 9.1 (1906) https://sentinel.christianscience.com/issues/1906/9/9-1/i-can-no-longer-delay-the-acknowledgment-of-my-gratitude.

[13]John Nixon, conversation with the author, 5 November 2021.

[14]David L. Haberman, 'A Cross-cultural Adventure: The Transformation of Ronald Nixon', *Religion* 23.3 (1993) 218.

[15]*Ibid.*

[16]Haberman, 222.

[17]Sri Madhava Ashish, Foreword: 'Sri Krishna Prem Through the Eyes of a Disciple,' in Sri Krishna Prem, *Initiation into Yoga: An Introduction to the Spiritual Life* (Wheaton: Quest Books, 1976) 24–25.

[18]Haberman, 218.

[19]Narendra Nath Kaul, *Writings of Sri Krishna Prem: An Introduction* (Bombay: Bharatiya Vidya Bhavan, 1980), v.

[20]AEI Falconar, *Sufi Literature and the Journey to Immortality*,[rpt.] (Delhi: Motilal Banarsidass, 1995), 149.

[21]Much of the manuscript was written in the months preceding Sri Madhava Ashish's death in April, 1997. The author's notes were edited and compiled into *Where'er Love's Camels Lead: Sri Krishna Prem Remembered*, by his disciples, Sri Dev Ashish, Anand Jagota and Pervin Mahoney, in 2005. It remains unpublished. The book's title is taken from a Sufi poem, one of Madhava Ashish's favourites, by the Andalusian mystic Ibn Arabi.

[22]In an email to the author, Brown comments: "The house notes in the Dec 1916 edition of the school magazine contain the entry: 'The best of luck to Dyer, Nixon and Newell, who are trying for scholarships at Cambridge this term.' In the next edition we find: 'Heartiest congratulations to Dyer, Newell and Nixon, who have gained exhibitions at Clare College, Cambridge; Jesus College Oxford; and King's College, Cambridge, respectively,'"

[23] 'The Officer Training Corps', Bristol Cathedral – We Have Our Lives, Bristol, Bristol Cathedral, 2014, https://bristol-cathedral.co.uk/we-have-our-lives/event/otc (accessed 16 November 2011).

[24]Brown, email to the author, 15 November 2021.

[25]John Nixon, email to the author, 28 November 2021.

[26]*Ibid.*

[27] Matthew J. Clarcq, 'Barbara Nixon: A Warden's Blitz', in Caroline Litzenberger and Eileen Groth Lyon (eds), *The Human Tradition in Modern Britain* (Lanham: Rowman & Littlefield Publishers, 2006), 201.

[28]*Ibid.*

[29]Timothy Shenk, *Maurice Dobb: Political Economist* (London: Palgrave Macmillan, 2013), 66.

[30]Maurice Dobb, 'Marxism and the Social Sciences,' rpt. *Monthly Review* 53.4 (2001): 38.

[31]Shenk, 66.

[32]Clarcq, 201.

[33](London: Scholar Press, 1980).

[34]John Nixon, email to the author, 28 November 2021.

[35]'Annie Russell-Jones MRCVS' (obituary), *Veterinary Acupuncture Newsletter, Volumes 16-26* (Cornell: International Veterinary Acupuncture Society, 2004?), 4.

[36]Chris Russell-Jones, conversation with the author, 14 May 2021.

[37]Bill Aitken, email to the author, 2 July 2023.

[38]It is not known whether Annie was ever formally initiated.

[39]Chris Russell-Jones, email to the author, 4 July 2023.

[40]Aitken, email to the author, 2 July 2023.

[41]*Ibid.*

2: Mythmaking

"Having seen this war, all that has been written in Mahabharat and in the Ramayan is altogether true."[1]
— Indian *sepoy*, Western Front (1915)

It is unclear when Ronald Nixon left Taunton: while he is quoted as a house prefect in the spring 1917 edition of *The Tauntonian*, his air officer's service begins in March of that year and John Brown believes it is likely he left the school mid-way through term in a desire to enlist in the armed forces.[2] By that time, the British Empire had been at war for nearly three years, and Nixon felt it his duty to volunteer for the war effort when he came of age (Ashish, 24). His place at King's College, Cambridge, to which he had been granted an exhibition in natural sciences,[3] was reserved for when he returned from the front.

Though Nixon wanted to be an airman, he was briefly persuaded to join the land forces instead of the nascent Royal Flying Corps (RFC), which had a reputation for being a particularly dangerous unit, even in the context of the horrific death toll of World War One. Of the 22,000 British pilots trained by the end of the war, more than 14,000—over 60%—lost their lives, of whom 8,000 died while training in the UK. "In other words, more pilots died training at home than were killed by the enemy, a remarkable state of affairs which even reached the ears of Parliament," writes Denis Winter in *The First of the Few: Fighter Pilots of the First World War.*[4]

With British pilots "dying at an alarming rate,"[5] Christo and Effie Nixon convinced their son to instead join the Royal Field Artillery (RFA), whose horse-drawn medium-calibre guns and howitzers were deployed near to, though not on, the front line. Madhava Ashish explains:

> Then a neighbour's son in the Artillery was killed. Thinking how they would feel if they prevented their son from doing what he wanted,

> and he was killed doing what he did not want, they relented. Ronald, who had already had his medical interviews for the Artillery, now changed the R.F.A. to R.F.C. on his forms and reported to the R.F.C. Official demands that he take the special medical tests for the Air Force pursued him throughout his service, but never caught up. (Ashish, 24)

Nixon's career as a pilot thus began in March, 1917, with a posting to Denham Aerodrome in Buckinghamshire with the Officer Cadet Wing of the RFC.[6] He progressed through training rapidly, being commissioned as an officer on 10 May, 1917—his 19th birthday—when he was promoted from a cadet to a temporary second lieutenant (2Lt),[7] and he was confirmed in his rank (equivalent to a pilot officer in the modern RAF) just over two months later, on 13 July.[8] Brown believes it is likely Nixon's involvement with the OTC at Taunton School sped up the already limited pilot training then provided by the RFC.[9]

As a key part of the Krishna Prem legend, Nixon's military service—particularly the miraculous escape from the enemy which is said to have contributed to his decision to go to India four years later—has been widely mythologised, with varying degrees of accuracy. Madhava Ashish noted later that the story was still circulating in "distorted ... versions" in India (Ashish,25), and a cursory internet search shows the process is ongoing in cyberspace, particularly in the Hindu blogosphere, where stories of Nixon being carried to safety by the hands of a blue-skinned god still abound.

A contemporary example of the kind of mythmaking referenced by Madhava Ashish can be found in volume 11 of *Bhārater Sādhak* (*Saints of India*), a 12-part collection of hagiographies written by Shankarnath Roy, a Bengali journalist and writer, and published by Karuna Prakashani in Calcutta between 1948 and 1959. Here, Roy describes how Nixon, finding himself surrounded over enemy lines, is saved by an "unknown force which enters his body," showing him a divine vision of a snow-covered mountain and compelling him to fly his plane "higher and higher into the distant sky" to escape the German fighters. When he comes to in a British military hospital, the story goes, it is with the words "Himalaya" and "*Bharatvarsha*" (India) on his lips and an anxiety to "know the greatness of Indian *sādhana*" (spiritual practice).[10]

A similar story is recounted in *The Saints of Vraja*, first published in Hindi in 1984 as *Vrajake Bhakta*, wherein author OBL Kapoor writes of a "supernatural power that caught hold of [Nixon's] wrist and took the plane high, very high, and turned it backwards",[11] while mystic–activist Vimala Thakar (1921–2009), an acolyte of Jiddu Krishnamurti, told a version that included "two strong pale brown hands and arms [that] had seized his hands, and taken control of the wheel," flying Nixon back to Britain. "Just then the news came through that his colleagues, the other pilots in the other two planes which had been flying with him, had both been shot down and killed," she lectured. "He decided to go to India and find out what were these hands and arms which had saved his life."[12] Recounting the legend for his guru, AC Bhaktivedanta Swami, Hare Krishna *sannyāsī* Jayapataka Swami explained: "[Nixon] was flying over [the] Himalayas ... and he saw Kṛṣṇa in his mind's eye ... And then, when he was shot down, he saw Kṛṣṇa, and then, when he landed, he searched out who he saw...."[13]

Perhaps the most colourful version of the Krishna Prem myth is that of Shantananda Puri (1928–2014), a *sannyāsī* from Tanjore (Thanjavur) in south India who visited Mirtola in 1956. Swami Shantananda, a great-grand-disciple of of the Bengali mystic Ramakrishna Paramahamsa, introduces into the story an ingenious deception on the part of the enemy, who attempts to lure an exhausted Nixon towards his doom by means of a creative paint job:

> One day [Nixon] had to make more than four sorties, and he was extremely tired while returning. He did not feel like returning to his base in England as it was too far. Luckily he found a big airstrip on the way, where there were a number of planes carrying flags with designs of stars and stripes, which was a symbol of the Americans. Nixon was highly delighted as he could now go towards the airstrip and take rest. He turned his aeroplane towards the airstrip and had gone but after a little distance, [when] the wheel of the aircraft suddenly was wrenched away from his hands and the aircraft turned back to its original track by some unseen hands. It took him some time to recover from the shock, and by that time the aircrafts had travelled a good distance towards the [friendly] base. When he reached the base, he found all the officials standing with anxiety writ large on their faces. All the officials came to congratulate him on his clever escape from being foxed by the Germans, who had camouflaged their own strip of land to look like perhaps an American base. Only then did Mr Nixon realise from what a great calamity the unseen hands had saved him, by wrenching away the wheel from his hands.[14]

So popular were these semi-true stories of Nixon's daring escape that they spawned an almost completely fabricated follow-up, as Madhava Ashish explains:

> Some thirty years after this [myth] had started to circulate, a sequel was heard from two Bengali visitors to the ashram who wanted to know whether it was true. In the sequel, after wandering in search of Krishna for many years, Ronald had met a strange sadhu who led him into the jungle where a European dining table was laid out. He was invited to eat his fill. Then he was left alone and Sri Krishna appeared and gave him teachings. After this he went up into the Himalayas to live, and was joined by a man from Bangalore.
>
> We worked out that the man from Bangalore had to be me. In the Indian mind of the time, Bangalore was the first place where aircraft were manufactured. Since I had been an aero engineer, mythological thinking insisted that I must have been in Bangalore. In fact, I have never been near the place. (Ashish, 28)

Those who heard the story from the man himself tend to tell a rather less fantastical version. It does seem, however, that Krishna Prem believed his life had been saved that day by a "miracle [that] had been wrought by a power beyond our ken," as he told his Lucknow friend and colleague, the "sceptic-cum-rationalist-cum-iconoclast" Dhurjati Prasad Mukherji, in 1923:

> He said: "I was, as you know, a pilot in the First World War. So I had to drop bombs over the enemy territory. One day, as I was reconnoitering [sic], I was about to steer to the right, where half-a-dozen fighter planes whirred and zoomed, thinking that they were ours—that is R.A.F. [sic] planes. Just then some force simply caught hold of my wrist and made me veer right round to the left. I was quite bewildered, the more so as the force was too incredible to be doubted. In a few minutes I returned to our base and was told that I had done well to come back so promptly as a number of enemy planes had just come into action. It was then I realised, with a shock of thankful delight, that I had had a miraculous escape.[15]

Probably the most reliable account is the one related by Madhava Ashish—who likely heard the anecdote told by Krishna Prem on a number of occasions. He devotes seven paragraphs of his manuscript to what he calls "something like the true story of Ronald's strange escape from enemy fighter aircraft" (Ashish, 25).

He, too, alludes to a mysterious force which seized control of Nixon's aircraft, saving pilot and rear gunner from certain death:

Ronald was on the usual dawn patrol, which in his case consisted of a flight of two-seater fighter aircraft patrolling the section of the Front Line for which their squadron was responsible. According to what he told me, the British at that period held air superiority on that sector of the front, even though the German single-seater fighters had greater altitude. In the changing patterns of aircraft design and technological development which determined who had air superiority at any moment, the Germans would not attack a flight of two-seater British fighters, because the Observer's backward-firing guns gave the British the advantage over the fixed, forward-firing guns of the German single-seaters. They therefore adopted the tactic of using their superior altitude range to watch British squadrons from their vantage point, and then descend in force to attack British stragglers. In those days of unreliable aero engines, stragglers with engine trouble were many.

As a counter to these enemy tactics, the British had adopted a rule that any plane with engine trouble would fire a Verey light [flare gun] to signal to his flight commander, who would then escort the plane until it reached the safety of the British lines, where it would be covered by British anti-aircraft fire, and would then resume patrol with the remainder of his flight.

On this occasion Ronald's engine started giving trouble, and he fired the required Verey light which, besides informing his flight commander, also alerted the enemy. Unfortunately, Wallace, his flight commander, was at that moment leaning far out of his cockpit, having a shouted conversation with his Observer about some enemy installation on the ground, and did not see the signal. And, since the R.F.C. pilots had refused to have the new wireless sets fitted because the wind-driven generators reduced their air speed, also saying that they heard enough of the squadron leader's voice on the ground without having it in the air as well, the Verey lights were the only plane-to-plane communication.

Within seconds, even in those days of slow-flying aircraft, Ronald and his Observer were on their own, spluttering their way towards the British lines. But they were not alone for long. The Observer banged Ronald on the shoulder and signalled a cross, which was the identification sign carried on the German planes. Ronald started taking evasive action. But without full engine power there was little to be done. His sole advantage lay in his Observer's Lewis guns, which could fire at anything out of range of his fixed, forward-firing guns. A minute or so later his Observer passed him a blood-stained note to say that his guns were shot away and that he himself was wounded.

> So Ronald now had six German fighters on his tail and a malfunctioning engine. The Germans were lining up to attack one by one, as their fixed guns allowed. The plane was being hit, bullets were shattering the instruments on the panel in front of him, and Ronald was wondering to himself whether he would feel the bullet hit the back of his head and then go out, or whether he would simply go out.
>
> Meanwhile, he was watching his attackers over his shoulder. When he judged that the attacking plane was about to open fire, he sideslipped. This manoeuvre is achieved by giving full aileron on the side to which it is wished to slip, and giving opposite rudder. The plane then slides sideways, making a difficult target for a pursuer. Ronald was slipping sometimes this side, sometimes that, each time losing height which he could not regain. The attacking planes were coming so close that Ronald could see the pilots' eyes behind their goggles. The next plane was pushing up close. Ronald began to slip left, when he felt his hand on the control column pushed over to the right. As he slid right, he saw the attacker's tracer bullets flash past just at the place he had expected to be. The Germans had got wise to his tactics.
>
> Except for keeping up a course for home, he could not watch where he was. In fact he had reached the British lines. The British antiaircraft guns opened up. The German squadron sheered off. Ronald landed his plane behind the lines and got his Observer into a Forward Field Hospital where they promptly amputated his shattered leg. (Ashish, 25–27)

Though by far the best known, this ill-fated sortie was only one of at least three incidents involving Nixon's aircraft in his short time in the RFC and RAF.[16] These events led collectively to "Ronald's cracking up," writes Madhava Ashish, and eventual "breaking down under the stresses of active service" (Ashish, 27–28).

According to military records, the incident took place within days of a similar event involving another Bristol F.2 Fighter biplane and the same crew, 2Lt RH Nixon and Lt P. Douglas (presumably the unnamed observer/gunner referred to in Madhava Ashish's manuscript) of №11 Squadron of the RFC. The pair are mentioned in two RFC casualty reports filed just three days apart—both of which required Nixon to make an emergency landing after encountering engine problems.

The first, reported on 7 December 1917, records Bristol Fighter A7128 making a forced landing in a field in Wagnonlieu, near the town of Arras in Pas-de-

Calais, around 75 miles from the Belgian border, after the plane's engine failed while on a 'CO' (counter-offensive) patrol. The second, logged on 10 December, describes Bristol Fighter C4849, again crewed by Nixon and Douglas, suffering engine trouble on a photo-reconnaissance mission over the Arras–Cambrai road, necessitating a forced landing in the commune of Wail.[17] It is likely the first incident is the one that would pass into legend—Wagnonlieu being closer to the enemy lines than Wail, and it involving a full-scale engine failure as opposed to less serious engine "trouble"—though both events resulted in the aircraft sustaining significant damage.[18]

According to the casualty reports, Nixon and Douglas escaped unscathed from the unscheduled landings, though a third incident, on 5 August 1918, near the war's end, would result in a fatality. Madhava Ashish continues:

> Another event which contributed to Ronald's cracking up was an occasion when he returned to land at his aerodrome and found that the C.O. [commanding officer] had set the mower to cut the grass during operations—something that is normally forbidden because of the risks. Ronald did what any inexperienced pilot may be expected to do. In his anxiety to avoid the mower, he kept his eyes on it. This is the best way to ensure that one lands on top of it—which is what Ronald did, killing the driver and smashing everything. Killing one of your own men is peculiarly distressing. (Ashish, 29)

A contemporary newspaper report places the accident at Cudham Lodge in Kent, the predecessor of the famous Biggin Hill RAF station, and the deceased as John Westacott, a 57-year-old farm labourer. Giving evidence to the inquest, Nixon said he believed Westacott must have walked in front of his aircraft at the last minute:

> At about 700ft. [Nixon] saw the deceased to his right and another workman on his left, and there appeared to be plenty of room. He put the machine on a gliding angle, and as he neared the ground it flattened out and collapsed. He then saw the horse pulling away from the front of his machine, and on jumping out saw the body of the deceased lying in the wreckage of the mowing machine. He did not know that he had collided with the deceased until he saw the horses, as the biplane was wrecked. He thought the deceased must have moved across his track.[19]

The inquest jury, which also heard from Nixon's injured passenger, Sergeant Davis, returned a verdict of accidental death.[20]

By this time, the trauma had, according to Madhava Ashish, led to the emergence of psychic abilities in Nixon, who had begun seeing dark shadows over the faces of the men who would not return from their next mission. "In times of great stress, like wartime, latent psychic powers are often activated, but people are shy of mentioning their experiences for fear of being treated as mad," he says (Ashish, 28).

Ultimately, Nixon did find himself in hospital as one of the many 11 Squadron men to break down under the stresses of combat.[21] There, he and his flight commander, Wallace (who had similarly been deemed insane), "tackled the doctor together, convincing him that they were sane but over-stressed. All they needed was a holiday." The pair were soon discharged and allowed to go on a camping trip to Dartmoor (Ashish, 29).

Nixon's experiences in the war left him with a sense of "the futility and meaninglessness of worldly ambitions" and "determined to discover for himself some meaning behind the apparently aimless flow of events," according to Bob Alexander.[22] David Haberman notes that the existential crisis described by Alexander, later Nixon's student, is "strikingly similar to the experience of Larry in W. Somerset Maugham's [1944 novel] *The Razor's Edge*,"[23] and Krishna Prem has been suggested as a possible influence for the character, an American First World War pilot who finds enlightenment in India, along with the novelist Christopher Isherwood, the poet Lewis Thompson and the American-born British MP Henry 'Chips' Channon. (The title *The Razor's Edge* is taken from a verse in the *Kaṭha Upaniṣad*, on which Krishna Prem had published a commentary in 1940.[24])

An article for *Saṅkīrtan* magazine of Meerut, 'The Birth of Sri Krishna'[25] (later included in the 1938 collection *The Search for Truth*), illustrates the drastically changed attitude Krishna Prem, then in his 30s, had towards a war for which he had originally felt it his duty to volunteer:

> We all like to flatter ourselves that we are the good, and that those who oppose us are the wicked. Did not both parties in the late war pray to God utterly to destroy their wicked enemies and to save their righteous selves? It pleases us to think that all our misfortunes are the result of the wickedness of our oppressors and that, if they were destroyed or converted, we should be perfectly all right. But this is an entire delusion. It is not external enemies who oppress us, but we ourselves who oppress ourselves....
>
> He who appears to oppress me from without is but the instrument of my *karma*; his destruction would in no way lessen my sufferings. It is my own evil desires and tendencies that are my oppressors; it is they who cause me to suffer, and it is they who are the wicked who must be destroyed.[26]

In fact, as is evident from his writing in the 1940s, when he had further developed the idea of war as an external manifestation of humanity's darkest inner desires,[27] Krishna Prem would come to oppose warfare in all its forms, and watched with mounting horror as the European powers geared up for another 'war to end all wars' in the preceding decade. Writing in July 1938, he said: "Knowing that 'hatred ends not by hatred; hatred ends by love alone,' we have yet given a reluctant assent to policies of rearmament for the sake of peace...."

"We must," he urged, "shut our ears to the siren voices which assure us that ... peace can be attained by war (even if called a war to end war), that justice can be achieved by armed force (even if termed the force of collective security) and that brotherly love can come through idolatrous worship of our own nation."[28]

Notes

[1] David Olusoga, *The World's War: Forgotten Soldiers of Empire* (London: Head of Zeus, 2014) 107.

[2]Brown, email to the author, 15 November 2021.

[3]'Ronald Henry Nixon' (obituary), *King's College, Cambridge, Annual Report 1966*, (November, 1966) 50.

[4]Denis Winter, *The First of the Few: Fighter Pilots of the First World War* (Athens: University of Georgia Press, 1983), cited in Les Parsons and Samantha Battams, *The Red Devil: The Story of South Australian Aviation Pioneer, Captain Harry Butler, AFC* (Mile End: Wakefield Press, 2019), 50.

[5]*Ibid.*

[6]Air Ministry, Officer's service record: Nixon, Ronald Henry (AIR 76/374/118), The National Archives, Kew, 1918–1919, p 4.

[7]Supplement to *The London Gazette* 30,100 (29 May 1917), 5,309.

[8]Supplement to *The London Gazette* 30,181 (13 July 1917), 7,053.

[9]Brown, email to the author, 15 November 2021.

[10]Shankarnath Roy, 'Krishna Prem' ('কৃষ্ণপ্রেম'), in *Bhārater Sādhak* (ভারতের সাধক), Vol. 11 (Calcutta: Karuna Prakashani, 1958), 282–331.

[11]OBL Kapoor, 'Śrī Kṛṣṇaprema (Ronald Nixon)', in *The Saints of Vraja*, 4th ed (New Delhi: Aravali Books International, 2015), 293.

[12]Christine Townend, *The Hidden Master: From 'I' to 'Itness' on Vimalaji's Teaching'* (Delhi: Motilal Banarsidass, 2002), 263–264.

[13]'760819 – Conversation A – Hyderabad', Vanisource, Mayapur, Vanipedia, 2020, https://vanisource.org/w/index.php?title=760819-Conversation-A-Hyderabad (accessed 30 March 2023).

[14]Shantananda Puri, 'The unseen Hand of Grace', *Swami Shantananda Puri Maharaj* (Tiruvannamalai: Deepti Ahuja, 2013), 1–2. http://swamishantanandapurimaharaj.org/anecdotes/The-unseen-Hand-of-Grace.pdf (accessed 19 November 2021)

[15]Dilip Kumar Roy, *Yogi Sri Krishnaprem*, 3rd edn (Bombay: Bharatiya Vidya Bhavan, 1992), 54.

[16]The Royal Flying Corps was merged with the Royal Naval Air Service on 1 April 1918 to create the Royal Air Force (RAF).

[17] Royal Flying Corps, 'Reports on Aeroplane and Personnel Casualties' (AIR 1/886), 1917, The National Archives, Kew, cited in Andrew Pentland, 'Royal Flying Corps: People index, surnames N–O', *airhistory.org.uk*, Yorkshire, airhistory.org, 2021, http://www.airhistory.org.uk/rfc/files/names-combined-N-O.csv (accessed 19 November 2021).

[18]According to Andrew Pentland, a historian of the RFC/RAF, an RFC casualty report form, designated 'W3347,' would be completed only in the event of serious damage to an aircraft, regardless of whether personnel were injured.

[19]'Killed by a Descending Aeroplane,' *The South Eastern Gazette*, 6 August 1918, p 6.

[20]*Ibid.*

[21]Another young 11 Sqn officer was admitted to hospital in October 1917 in a "mentally-depressed, restless, and unhappy" condition, with "a strong impulse to cut his [own] throat." He was recommended a period of rest for his "purely psychoneurotic" symptoms. As recorded in Lynsey Shaw Cobden, 'The Nervous Flyer: Nerves, Flying and the First World War', *British Journal for Military History* 4.2 (2018): 121–142.

[22]R. D. Alexander, 'A Biographical Note, in *Sri Krishna Prem, The Search for Truth* (Calcutta: Ganesh Chandra Bose, 1938).

[23]Haberman, 'A Cross-cultural Adventure', 218.

[24]Paraphrased in the book as: "The sharp edge of a razor is difficult to pass over; thus the wise say the path to Salvation is hard."

[25]The date of the original (Hindi) article is unknown, though *Saṅkīrtan* began publication in 1932. Krishna Prem's sometime correspondent, Swami Sivananda Saraswati of Rishikesh, was editor in chief for the next five years.

[26]Sri Krishna Prem, *The Search for Truth* (Calcutta: Ganesh Chandra Bose, 1938), 15.

[27]See chapter 13.

[28]Krishna Prem, *The Search*, 125.

3: Kingsman

"The trouble with education ... is that it consists in making us learn to accept substitute questions for the ones we really want to ask."[1]
— Sri Krishna Prem (1943)

Nixon was demobilised in 1919 and left the RAF with the rank of lieutenant.[2] He took up his place at King's College—the University of Cambridge college where one of his great-uncles, the "legendary eccentric ... don"[3] John Edwin Nixon (1839–1916), had twice been dean[4]—in January of that year, initially studying English but later reading the 'moral sciences' (philosophy).[5]

At Cambridge, Nixon's contemporaries included the surrealist painter Roland Penrose, the barrister and judge Christmas Humphreys, the psychiatrist Henry Dicks, the literary scholar Bonamy Dobrée, and his future University of Lucknow colleague John 'Arjava' Chadwick, as well as Mirtola ashramites-to-be Bob Alexander and George Poole.

Humphreys, an early British convert to Buddhism, writes that his enthusiasm for Indian religious ideas, in particular that of reincarnation, was "fortified by conversation with such men as Ronald Nixon of King's College,"[6] who he remembers as a "silent, heavily built man, smoking his eternal *meerschaum* [pipe], and moving on the fringe of the Buddhist-Theosophical activities in which I was then involved."[7] According to the British philosopher Alan Watts, whose *The Way of Zen* helped popularise Buddhist thought in the West, it was through the Theosophical Society that Humphreys (known as Toby), later the president of the Buddhist Society in London, his "fey, Celtic wife," Aileen (known as Puck and caricatured by the group as 'the Airy-fairy Lilian'[8]), and Nixon were exposed to Buddhism, the first spiritual tradition in which Nixon took a serious interest. As Watts puts it:

> [T]oby and Puck were, first of all, Theosophists, disciples of that incredible and mysterious Russian lady Helena Petrovna Blavatsky,

> who founded the Theosophical Society in—of all places—New York City in 1875, thereafter moving off to Madras and London. Her story was that, as a young woman, she had gone into Central Asia and Tibet to become the student of supreme gurus Koot Hoomi and Maurya (which are not Tibetan names, and whose alleged photographs look like versions of Jesus), who thereafter wrote her constant letters by psychokinetic precipitation or telepathic amanuensis in a distinctly Russian style of handwriting. Madame Blavatsky's voluminous works reveal only the most fragmentary knowledge of Tibetan Buddhism, but she was a masterly creator of metaphysical and occult science fiction, as well as being a delightful, uninhibited, and outspoken old lady who spat and swore and rolled her own cigarettes. Perhaps she was a charlatan, but she did a beautiful job of it, and persuaded a goodly number of British aristocrats to consider the *Upaniṣads*, the *Yoga Sūtra*, the *Bhagavad-Gītā*, and the Buddhist *Tripiṭaka*. Those persuaded found them much more interesting and profound than the Bible, especially the Bible interpreted by run-of-the-mill Catholic and Protestant clergy at the end of the nineteenth century.
>
> Thus it was through the work of Blavatsky that these traditions were delivered to Toby when he was a student at Cambridge, in company with psychiatrist Henry Dicks, and Ronald Nicholson [sic], who later became the *sādhu* Sri Krishna Prem. They joined the Cambridge branch of the Theosophical Society, and Toby subsequently founded—in London—an independent Buddhist Lodge of the Society...[9]

The 'TS' also provided Nixon with his introduction to Hindu thought, specifically the *Advaita Vedānta* of the eighth-century scholar Ādi Śaṅkara[10]—a philosophy the young intellectual found well "suited to his developed mind," recalls Christmas Humphreys.[11] Sometimes characterised as the antithesis of the tradition of theistic Vaishnava *bhakti* (devotion to a personal God) into which he was later initiated,[12] *Advaita* (non-dualist) thought—with its emphasis on the non-difference of the individual soul (*Ātman*) and the ultimate truth, or *Brahman*, and on the oneness of all existence—would continue to exert an influence on Krishna Prem's beliefs and practice for the rest of his life. As he explained, quoting Shelley's 'Love's Philosophy,' in *The Yoga of the Kaṭhopaniṣad* (1940):

> [W]hen we perceive things as so many separate entities or events, as in scientific studies or in ordinary common-sense, that is the *mānasik* mode [the analytical mind]. When, on the other hand, we see that:
>
> Nothing in the world is single,

> All things by a law divine,
> In one another's being mingle— ...
>
> [W]e are seeing in the mode of the *buddhi* [the higher intellect].[13]

According to his biographer, James King, Penrose (who would later visit Nixon and Poole in India) had at Cambridge "witnessed the former fighter pilot's sense of meaninglessness,"[14] and then a "strong interest in Buddhism [which served as] a way of distancing himself from the traumas of the war."[15] In this he was by no means alone, suggests Madhava Ashish: "Men who have had the contemplation of death forced upon them by war will often turn to enquiry into the meaning of life. Any psychic experiences of the sort mentioned earlier [shadows on the faces of doomed pilots] add to the incentive"(Ashish, 32).

As his interest in Buddhism grew, Nixon took up the study of Pali, the liturgical language of the Theravada tradition, and filled his rooms at King's with Buddhist paraphernalia: "images of the Buddha, Tibetan Than-kas [religious paintings], incense, and oil lamps."[16] While Christo was supportive of his son's burgeoning interest in Eastern spirituality, having bought Nixon the *thang-ka* (which he described as "depicting *buddhas* and '*budivistas*' [*bodhisattvas*]") to add his to his collection (Ashish 34), Effie was less impressed and preferred to stay in a hotel when she visited Cambridge, declaring Nixon's rooms "too full of confusion" for her Christian Science practice (Ashish, 22).

Though already attracted to the figure of the Buddha, it was a chance encounter with a ceramic sculpture of a *luohan* or *lohan*, a legendary disciple of Gautama Buddha, that solidified the china merchant's son's "dedication to the search" (Ashish, 34). With its stern, serene facial expression and commanding presence, the statue—one of a set of life-size Liao-dynasty (AD 907–1125) stoneware *luohans* sold to European museums in the 1910s—made a deep impression on the undergraduate Nixon. As Madhava Ashish explains:

> Ronald had gone up to London where he loved to browse in the Charing Cross Road bookshops. On this occasion he went to the British Museum where he was confronted by the severe ceramic image of the Lohan Buddha. He knew that this image was made some fifteen hundred years after the Buddha's death, so there was no question of its being a photographic or realistic representation. This being the case, from where did this impressive form and facial expression come which was having so great an impact upon him? It could have come only from the heart of the sculptor, from the heart of a man. 'What comes from the human heart,' argued Ronald to himself, 'can be realised by a man. And what is realisable must at some time have been

> realised. What one man has realised, another can realise.' And so he determined to set out on the journey of the soul. (Ashish, 34–35).

Nixon's fondness for book shopping also led to his introduction to Robert Dudley (Bob) Alexander (1899–1957), a brilliant Cambridge medical student who would go on to become one of the top doctors in northern India, and later still Nixon's godbrother[17] and *sannyāsa* disciple. Alexander—like Nixon a Kingsman, a recently demobilised RAF airman, and a student of Indian philosophy—first met his future guru in a Cambridge bookshop, Bowes & Bowes,[18] where both were looking for a text by HP Blavatsky, the co -founder of the Theosophical Society (Ashish, 32). The college history describes how Alexander "realised in a flash that here, in this freshman scarcely a year his senior, was his Guru, his sage and spiritual teacher" and "the man who was to be his spiritual guide through life."[19] Or, as Madhava Ashish puts it: "'At that moment,' said Bob, 'I felt I had met a man I could follow for the rest of my life'" (Ashish, 32).

Though a brilliant intellect and "ready and ruthless debater,"[20] Nixon was critical of the moral sciences curriculum, feeling that it was "unacceptably lacking in Eastern thought,"[21] and lost interest in his studies, "sacrific[ing] his chance of a First" in favour of "grasping the opportunities for expanding his interests which [Cambridge] University offered."[22] He graduated King's BA (bachelor of arts) in 1921, having taken "seconds" (second-class honours) in the English tripos[23] and in part II of the moral sciences tripos.[24]

Hoping to better understand Buddhism—a tradition into which he had by now been initiated by a senior member of the Theosophical Society[25]—and Hinduism in the land of their birth, as well as to find an explanation for the psychic phenomena he is reported to have continued experiencing while at university,[26] Nixon's mind turned fully towards India, where he hoped to find a guru. "Ronald's intention was to get to India as quickly as possible," confirms Madhava Ashish. "There, he felt, he might find a teacher who could speak from experience and not from books" (Ashish, 36).

Seeking employment in India, Nixon wrote to the Theosophical Society at Adyar in Madras, hoping that his Cambridge degree and Theosophical connections might recommend him for a teaching post.[27] His letter was forwarded to Gyanendra Nath Chakravarti, recently appointed the first vice-chancellor of the new University of Lucknow, and a meeting was arranged in London between Nixon and Bertram Keightley, Chakravarti's disciple and a member of the university senate.

A scion of "one of those wealthy Victorian families who would have considered it extremely bad manners had anyone inquired where the wealth came from" (Ashish, 70), Keightley was an early convert to Theosophy who had helped

Madame Blavatsky edit her 1888 *magnum opus, The Secret Doctrine.* Shortly before her death in 1891, Blavatsky sent Keightley to India, "saying that he would find his Teacher there" (Ashish, 72). There he stayed until his death in 1944. Though he remained "wholly a British Sahib," the eccentric Keightley was well regarded by the average Indian and a devoted student of Chakravarti, with whom he lived and with whose instructions he "would comply without a hint of complaint, even when it was something he normally hated, like travelling to Kashmir in cold weather" (Ashish, 72–73).

The young graduate impressed during his interview and Keightley lent him money to get to Lucknow, then the capital of the United Provinces in northern India, to take up his new role as a reader (associate professor) in English at Canning College[28] (incorporated into the University of Lucknow in 1922). Having been expected to take over the family china business, Nixon's accepting a job 4,000 miles away met with a mixed reaction from his parents, as Madhava Ashish explains:

> Mrs Nixon was not pleased. 'These foreign appointments are all very well for people who have no home ties,' she said. Ronald, on the contrary, felt that it was the very strength of those home ties which were compelling him to get away. His father was more reasonable. In spite of one of his brothers having died while working in Lucknow, he told Ronald, 'When several million people manage to live in India, I see no reason why you shouldn't' (Ashish, 36).

Notes

[1]Kaul, *Writings of Sri Krishna Prem* (Mumbai: Bharatiya Vidya Bhavan, 1980), 92.

[2]Lt RH Nixon was transferred to the unemployed list on 11 January 1919. *The London Gazette*, 31,162 (4 February 1919), 1,801.

[3]LP Wilkinson, *Kingsmen of a Century 1873–1972*, reprint with corrections (Cambridge: King's College, 1980), 312.

[4]Cambridge University Library, 'Collection: Nixon: The Papers of John Edwin Nixon', *ArchiveSearch University of Cambridge* (Cambridge: University of Cambridge, 2003) https://archivesearch.lib.cam.ac.uk/repositories/7/resources/1234 (accessed 24 April 2023).

[5]*King's College, Cambridge, Annual Report 1966*, p 50.

[6]Christmas Humphreys, 'From Branches to the Root,' in Bernard Dixon (ed), *Journeys in Belief*, (London: George Allen & Unwin, 1968), 118.

[7]Christmas Humphreys, 'Initiation into Yoga: An Introduction to the Spiritual Life' (review), *The Middle Way*, 51 (1976–77): 182.

[8]Aileen Humphreys (née Faulkner) is likely the 'Lilian' mentioned in Madhava Ashish's manuscript, which reads: "There was a lady they rudely called 'The Airy-fairy Lilian' who gave the sort of occult teachings which are common to most such groups."

[9]Alan Watts, *In My Own Way: An Autobiography*, 2nd ed (Novato: New World Library, 2007), 74.

[10]Haberman, 'A Cross-cultural Adventure', 218.

[11]Christmas Humphreys, 'The late Sri Krishna Prem,' *The Middle Way* 41 (1966–1967).

[12]Krishna Sharma, 'Towards a New Perspective,' in David N. Lorenzen (ed.), *Religious Movements in South Asia 600–1800* (Oxford: Oxford University Press, 2004) 294.

[13]Sri Krishna Prem, *The Yoga of the Kaṭhopanishad* (Allahabad: Ananda Publishing House, 1940) 135–136.

[14]James King, *Roland Penrose: The Life of a Surrealist* (Edinburgh: Edinburgh University Press, 2016) 78.

[15]King, *Penrose*, 32–33.

[16]*King's College, Cambridge, Annual Report 1966*, 50.

[17]An individual with whom one shares a guru, in this case Yashoda Mai. Also *guru-bhai.*

[18]Ian Stephens, *Monsoon Morning* (London: Ernest Benn, 1966), 134.

[19]'Robert Dudley Alexander (Sri Haridas)' (obituary), *King's College, Cambridge, Annual Report 1957*, (November 1957), 18.

[20]Madhava Ashish, 'Sri Krishna Prem Through the Eyes of a Disciple,' 20.

[21]Gabriel Monod-Herzen, 'Sri Krishna Prem, Yogi et Théosophe', *Le Lotus Bleu* 71 (1966): 75–86. https://www.revue3emillenaire.com/blog/vie-et-oeuvre-de-sri-krishna-prem-par-gabriel-monod-herzen (accessed 15 June 2022).

[22]*King's College, Cambridge, Annual Report 1966*, 50.

[23]A Cambridge University term for the final examinations for a BA honours degree.

[24]RH Bulmer and LP Wilkinson, *A Register of Admissions to King's College, Cambridge, 1919–1958* (London: King's College Association, 1963) 15.

[25]According to Madhava Ashish, "Ronald took a Buddhist initiation from the Theosophical President who was visiting Cambridge and its lively Theosophical Lodges." It is unlikely he is referring to Annie Besant, the president of the Theosophical Society, whom he knew by name; it is possible the "president" in question was Harold Baillie-Weaver, general secretary of the Theosophical Society in England from 1916 to 1921.

[26]These included a thought experiment under the tutelage of 'the Airy-Fairy Lilian,' in which Nixon and his partner 'met' in their "astral bodies" at the Pyramids of Giza, and had an out-of-body vision of the universe—a "vast, roughly egg-shaped mass, glowing with the light of myriads of stars"—in the company of a spiritual 'guide.'

[27]Madhava Ashish records that Nixon "wrote to the Principal of the Theosophical School at Adyar," which is probably the Olcott Memorial High School, founded in 1894 and named after Theosophical Society co-founder Henry Steel Olcott.

[28]'*Bhagavad-Gītā no Yoga* (The Yoga of the Bhagavad-Gītā [sic])' (review of the Gujarati translation by Kishansinh Chavda), *The Aryan Path* 44 (1977), 138.

4: "A Hindu Englishman"

"Become a Buddhist? If that means to turn one's back on all that Krishna stands for, certainly not. Remain a Vaishnava? If that means to ignore all that the Buddha stands for, again, certainly not."[1]
— Sri Krishna Prem (1939)

Nixon sailed for India on 15 September 1921, boarding the *SS Castalia*, an Anchor Line ship running a regular service from Glasgow to Bombay, at Liverpool.[2]

Clive Dewey, in his history of the Indian Civil Service, points out that Nixon was one of many Kingsmen who responded to the call of the East in the final decades of British India. These adventurous exiles, particularly those who went into education, followed the example of the unconventional King's graduates making a mark on the political–economic landscape at home:

> Just as the college reached its academic peak, a stream of alienated intellectuals replaced the normal establishment figures— bishops, judges, headmasters. The most famous Kingsman of the century, Maynard Keynes, destroyed an economic orthodoxy. The highest-ranking politician, Hugh Dalton, was socialist Chancellor of the Exchequer. The best-known schoolmaster was a communist president of the National Union of Schoolteachers. ...
>
> The Kingsmen who went out to India were in keeping with this trend. If they were civilians, they sympathised with the nationalists' desire for independence. ... The Kingsmen who taught at Indian universities took assimilation to extremes. They were drawn to the East, like sixties hippies, by a yearning for spiritual enlightenment. R.H. Nixon can stand for them all.[3]

From his arrival in India, as Dewey observes, Nixon snubbed the stuffy members' clubs and exclusive garden parties of the Anglo-Indian establishment in favour of assimilating into Lucknow's indigenous intelligentsia. He quickly struck up friendships with the Marxist intellectual Dhurjati Prasad Mukerji, his colleague at the University of Lucknow, and Dr Joy Gopal Mukerji, reader in pathology at Lucknow Medical College, as well as an almost familial relationship with GN Chakravarti (who was a similar age to his father) and his wife, Monica. The young professor also socialised and occasionally holidayed with his students—at 23, he was younger than many of them—some of whom were invited to pass the evenings in his rooms at the vice-chancellor's house. "Above all, he made it abundantly clear that he preferred the company of Indians in general to that of his British colleagues," states Madhava Ashish.[4]

Gertrude Emerson Sen, Krishna Prem's friend in Almora (and, according to her biographer, a descendant of the Transcendentalist poet Ralph Waldo Emerson[5]), whose husband was the celebrated agricultural scientist Basiswar 'Boshi' Sen, witnessed the subtle anti-Hindu prejudice common among other Anglo-Indians in the final decades of the British Raj:

> [I]n 1932, she was invited one afternoon to a ladies' tea-party at the home of one of the local English officials in Almora. One of the ladies began to dilate on the Hindu-Muslim theme. "After all, the Muslims are more like us," she remarked. "They have communal worship, and though it happens to be on a Friday instead of a Sunday, they get together and pray to one God, but the Hindus worship hundreds of gods and goddesses!" Suddenly she remembered an alien American in their midst, and turning to Gertrude, remarked almost defensively, "Boshi is a Christian, isn't he?" Gertrude had kept silent, not seeing any point in trying to defend the Hindus in that atmosphere, but to this lady's question she replied, "No, he is a very good Hindu." That put an end to that trend of conversation.[6]

In Lucknow, Nixon had been placed, as was customary for newcomers to the university, in the Chakravartis' guesthouse, an annexe to the "sumptuous mansion"[7] in Kaiserbagh that then served as the vice-chancellor's residence. (The building was the former Kabootar Wali Kothi (Ashish, 42), or Pigeon House, of the final king of Oudh, Nawab Wajid Ali Shah, who used it to house his prized birds.) While this arrangement was intended to be temporary (guests would typically move on as soon as they found lodging elsewhere), Nixon stayed on in the guesthouse, encouraged by Chakravarti himself, as Madhava Ashish relates:

> [Ronald's] preference for Indians was clear to Dr Chakravarti also. When Ronald tackled him on the matter of it being high time that

> he found himself quarters, Chakravarti said: 'What are you going to do with a whole house to yourself? You are not married. You are not associating with your countrymen, so cannot share with one of them. Stay on here in the guest house. And I would like you to meet my wife.'
>
> So Ronald stayed on, met Mrs Chakravarti, and soon became an accepted member of the large family of her own children and the many she had adopted (Ashish, 41).

Nixon's rejection of the informal segregation of the Raj, whose rulers "live[d] in a world of their own creation into which an Indian seldom or never [found] admittance,"[8] is in keeping with his interest in Theosophy, whose Anglo-Indian adherents were among the first Westerners to break ranks with the "complete isolation of the English people in India," as Chakravarti had noted some 16 years earlier.

"While both the rulers and the ruled are working steadfastly for the peace and good government of [India], they understand amazingly little of the inner life, thoughts and aspirations of each other," wrote Chakravarti, then inspector of schools in the United Provinces, in 1905. This segregation, according to Chakravarti, marked the "weakest spot in the otherwise stable foundation of British rule and the consequent peace in India." In contrast, he adds, the "European Theosophist is singularly free from the trammels of the enforced reserve which handicaps official life in India, as also from the overwhelming sense of moral and religious superiority which only too often characterizes the non-official European.... He goes into an Indian home with his heart full of love for the people who are the lineal descendants of the great sages, whose wisdom has brightened his life and whose teachings are his dearest possession. There is no magic more miraculous than the mantra of true sympathy, and it is to be wondered that it proves an 'open sesame' to the heart of the Indian, which opens out to its gentle touch exposing its richest treasures."[9]

While this behaviour naturally did not endear Nixon to the *pukka sahibs* from whom he kept a careful distance—Gertrude Emerson Sen remembers him as "a thorn in the side of the local British officials," most of whom "felt that he had badly let them down by his open and flagrant identification of himself with India and Indians, and especially with Hinduism"[10]—Madhava Ashish points out that his war service, as well as the perceived respectability of the people with whom he surrounded himself, worked in his favour, even after his move to Mirtola:

> He had 'gone native', but done it in such a superior way that no British mud flung at him would stick. He had done his share of fighting in the First World War. He was a successful professor of

> English literature, much loved and admired by his Indian students. His disciple and companion, Major Alexander, was a highly qualified physician in the Indian Medical Service whose premature retirement as Principal of the Lucknow Medical College had upset the Lucknow public. Krishna Prem's guru, Sri Yashoda Mai, was Mrs Chakravarti, wife of the ex-Vice-Chancellor of Lucknow University.[11]

Nixon was also protected in the face of Anglo-Indian disapproval—polite society expected him, and other Britons, to "live British, eat British, join the British club, and pay duty calls on any senior man from the immediate man up to the Governor of the Province"[12]—by the patronage of Chakravarti, who was a personal friend of Sir Harcourt Butler,[13] then the governor of the United Provinces.

Spiritually, Nixon's interests during those first years in Lucknow were similar to those he pursued in England, though he does appear to have taken advantage of the opportunity to play a more active role in organised Buddhist life. Among the groups with which he became involved were the Indian Buddhist Society, the Maha Bodhi Society and the short-lived International Buddhist Union (IBU).

In 1922, an RH Nixon of Lucknow is listed in *The Buddhist Review*, the organ of the Buddhist Society of Great Britain and Ireland, as one of five prominent members of the Indian Buddhist Society who will serve as "honorary correspondents" of the IBU, a new association it was hoped would create a "bond of union ... between all existing societies and individual Buddhists throughout the world."[14] Others included on what Nixon's old Cambridge friend, Toby Humphreys, calls a "remarkable list of representatives in all parts of the world"[15] are the Ceylonese Buddhist revivalist Anagarika Dharmapala, also in India; U Hla Kyaw (James Hla Kyaw) in Burma; Capt. JE Ellam, the *Review*'s editor, in England; CT Strauss, sometimes regarded as the first European Buddhist, in Switzerland; and Ernst Hoffman in Italy. (German-born Hoffman would, like Nixon, end up in Almora, later achieving fame as Lama Govinda, the foremost western expert on Tibetan Buddhism.)

The former Cambridge scholar Andrew Rawlinson, author of *The Book of Enlightened Masters: Western Teachers in Eastern Traditions* (1997), writes about the eclectic make-up of the short-lived but influential IBU:

> This was originally Anagarika Dharmapala's idea in Calcutta and was supported in the West in the early 1920s by Ananda Maitreya, Ernst Hoffman (later Lama Anagarika Govinda), George Grimm, C.T. Strauss, Dwight Goddard and Ronald Nixon (later Sri Krishna Prem). That is:

> a Sri Lankan living in India (Dharmapala) and influenced by an American Theosophist (Olcott) had an idea for a society—an international Buddhist society—that was supported in the West by:
>
> two Englishmen (Ananda Maitreya, who had been a monk in Burma from 1902 until 1914; and Nixon/Krishna Prem, who went on to become a Gaudiya Vaishnava guru in India);
>
> two Germans (Hoffman/Govinda, who went on to become a Theravadin anagarika for a time in Ceylon before entering the Tibetan tradition; and Grimm, author of *The Doctrine of the Buddha* and co-founder of Das Altbuddhistische Gemeinde/Old Buddhist Community in 1921);
>
> a Swiss (Strauss, who was the first Westerner ever to formally become a Buddhist in the West when he took the five lay vows from Dharmapala in Chicago on the occasion of the founding of a branch of the Maha Bodhi Society there in 1893);
>
> and an American (Goddard, who later practised Zen for a while in Japan and tried to establish a Western Buddhist order, based on Zen principles, in America).

> Nothing like this mixture—and I mean a mixture of Sri Lankan, Burmese, Japanese—could be found anywhere in the East. Nor could Dharmapala have found support for the International Buddhist Union in any Theravadin country (or any Buddhist country, come to that).[16]

The following year, Nixon was invited to give an address at Sri Dharmarajika Vihara, the Calcutta headquarters of the Maha Bodhi Society, another organisation founded by Dharmapala. He presented a paper titled 'The Knowledge of the Buddha,' an apologetic work arguing against the common view that the Buddha's "magnificently rational doctrine was marred by the uncritical acceptance of the baseless superstition of re-birth, ... which he is said to have accepted without question from the current stock of then current Brahmanical beliefs."[17]

Nixon's essay is reproduced in two parts in volume 31 of the *Maha Bodhi Journal* (1923) alongside articles by Dharmapala and other leading Buddhist thinkers and supporters of the society, including Lord Ronaldshay, who contributes the sympathetic essay 'Buddhism and Morality.' Ronaldshay (Lawrence Dundas), the former governor of Bengal, would, like Nixon, later graduate from Buddhism to Vaishnavism, becoming in 1934 the first president of the London Gauḍīya Mission Society.[18] The same year, Nixon also engaged in a back-and-forth correspondence with the educationist Frederick Gordon Pearce in the pages of *The Theosophist* (grouped together under the heading 'The Atheism of Buḍḍhism') on the Buddha's non-theism.[19]

It was at this time that Nixon first met and befriended Dilip Kumar Roy, the celebrated composer, poet and yogi. Roy recalls their first meeting—at the Lucknow home of another Bengali poet, Atul Prasad Sen, in early 1923—in his book *Yogi Sri Krishnaprem*, a collection of letters, essays and anecdotes drawn from more than four decades of friendship and correspondence:

> I can still recapture in my memory the radiant face of a young Englishman (of about my age) seated, a pipe in his mouth, on a sofa. The poet [Sen] said to me: "This is Ronald Nixon, Dilip, our brilliant Professor—an English Hindu or a Hindu Englishman, if you like."
>
> We laughed and the person at whose expense we made merry outlaughed us all. I fell in love with him at first sight and, on my return home, told Dhurjati [Prasad Mukerji], the bibliophile, that I had recalled his favourite Marlowe's: "Who ever loved that loved not at first sight?"[20]

Harry Oldmeadow, the author of *Journeys East: 20th Century Western Encounters with Eastern Religious Traditions*, notes that Nixon was one of a number of Westerners for whom the teachings of the Theosophical Society served as a gateway to more traditional Hindu and Buddhist thought:

> The Theosophical movement played no small part in the Theravadin [Buddhist] revival in Sri Lanka and South-East Asia and also gave some impetus to the Hindu reform movements of the late 19th century. ... [M]any Europeans ... were, at least for a time, influenced by Theosophical ideas, these sometimes being an avenue to less adulterated Eastern religious forms. Consider, for starters: W.B. Yeats, Ananda Metteya [Charles Allan Bennett], Krishna Prem, W.Y. Evans-Wentz, René Guénon, Christmas Humphreys, Nyanatiloka Thera [Anton Gueth], Miriam Salanave.[21]

Little information is available on Nixon's professional life in Lucknow. He appears to have spoken seldom about his readership, though contemporary records show he had been promoted to acting professor by 1926[22]—but he is said to have enjoyed the social aspect, at least initially. Madhava Ashish writes that "he liked [his students], got on well with them, organised student theatricals, and generally enjoyed the new life" (Ashish, 37), while Roy recalls tea parties, musical soirées and long evenings when the pair had, "to quote Krishnaprem's quotation, tired the sun with talking and sent him down the sky."[23] In his foreword to Krishna Prem's posthumously published *Initiation into Yoga: An Introduction to the Spiritual Life* (1976), Madhava Ashish recounts that even then, nearly 50 years after Nixon gave up his professorship for the life of a Vaishnava renunciate, "I still meet grey-haired old men whose faces light up when they talk of their Professor Nixon, even though they were members of a class of three hundred science students who attended Ronald's lectures only once a week."[24]

Both men also make frequent reference to Nixon's fondness for powerful motorcycles, which he is said to have delighted in racing at "break-neck speeds through the streets of Lucknow,"[25]

Nixon, as Krishna Prem, would later attribute the hardship in the world to "selfish karma," saying that the substitution of "little islands" for the "traditional give-and-take" of family and community life had led to an increase in the "psychic suffering" of humanity.[26] It was in Lucknow that he first observed what he saw as the contrast between the people of India—where such "separatist tendencies" had not yet taken root—and the individualistic West, noting how happy even the poorest Indians were compared to wealthy people back home. "When I first came to India—that must have been in 1921 or so—the back window of my room in the Lucknow University hostel opened towards poor people's quarters. Even in those days, out of curiosity, I kept on observing their life and found it much more rich than that of the people of comparatively much higher income groups in Europe, or at least in England," he recalled in the 1940s.[27]

As the 1920s wore on, however, Nixon seems to have tired of the city, and particularly the intrigue and gossip of campus life— he told Roy he had run out of patience with "tongue-waggers,"[28] and later said to Madhava Ashish that DP Mukerji was the only one of his colleagues who "genuinely preferred to talk of other things than university politics" (Ashish, 41)—and, guided by his surrogate parents, the Chakravartis, turned his attention wholeheartedly inwards, towards the spiritual quest which had brought him to India in 1921.

Notes

[1]Roy, *Yogi Sri Krishnaprem*, 90.

[2]'UK and Ireland, Outward Passenger Lists, 1890–1960', Ancestry, Lehi, Ancestry.com Operations, 2012, https://www.ancestry.co.uk/search/collections/2997 (accessed 15 April 2022). Original data: Board of Trade: Commercial and Statistical Department and successors: Outwards Pas-

senger Lists. BT27. Records of the Commercial, Companies, Labour, Railways and Statistics Departments. Records of the Board of Trade and of successor and related bodies. The National Archives, Kew, Richmond, Surrey, England.

[3]Clive Dewey, *Anglo-Indian Attitudes: The Mind of the Indian Civil Service*, (London and Rio Grande: The Hambledon Press, 1993), 135.

[4]Ashish, *Where're Love's Camels Lead*, 40

[5]Girish N. Mehra, *Nearer Heaven than Earth: The Life and Times of Boshi Sen and Gertrude Emerson Sen*, 2nd impression (New Delhi: Rupa & Co, 2007), book jacket blurb.

[6]Mehra, *Nearer Heaven than Earth*, 490.

[7]Roy, *Yogi Sri Krishnaprem*, 53.

[8]Gyanendra Nath Chakravarti, *The Influence of Theosophy on the Life and Teachings of Modern India*, 2nd ed, Adyar Pamphlet 35, (Madras: Theosophical Publishing House, 1913), 7.

[9]Chakravarti, *The Influence of Theosophy*, 8.

[10]Gertrude Emerson Sen, Introduction: 'Sri Krishnaprem,' in Dilip Kumar Roy, *Yogi Sri Krishnaprem*, 3rd ed. (Bombay: Bharatiya Vidya Bhavan, 1992), xix–xx.

[11]Ashish, 'Sri Krishna Prem Through the Eyes of a Disciple,' 9.

[12]Ashish, 'Sri Krishna Prem Through the Eyes of a Disciple,' 19.

[13]*Ibid.*

[14]'The International Buddhist Union,' *The Buddhist Review* 12.1 (1912): 3–4.

[15][Toby] Christmas Humphreys, 'The Development of Buddhism in England: A Brief History', in Christmas Humphreys (ed.), *A Buddhist Students' Manual* (London: The Buddhist Society, 1956), 49.

[16]Andrew Rawlinson, *The Book of Enlightened Masters: Western Teachers in Eastern Traditions*, (Chicago and La Salle: Open Court, 1997), 48–49.

[17]Prof. Ronald Nixon, 'The Knowledge of the Buddha,' *The Maha-Bodhi and the United Buddhist World* 31.8 (1923), 290.

[18]Bhakti Vikāsa Swami, *Śrī Bhaktisiddhānta Vaibhava*, ebook ed, (Surat: Bhakti Vikas Trust, 2009), 865.

[19]Ronald Nixon, 'The Atheism of Buḍḍhism: II' and 'The Atheism of Buḍḍhism,' *The Theosophist* 45 (1923–1924): 116–118 and 674–675.

[20]Roy, *Yogi Sri Krishnaprem*, 6–7.

[21]Harry Oldmeadow, *Journeys East: 20th Century Western Encounters with Eastern Religious Traditions*, (Bloomington: World Wisdom, 2004), 66.

[22]Alex Hill (ed.), *Third Congress of the Universities of the Empire, 1926: Report of Proceedings*, (London: G. Bell and Sons, 1926), xviii.

[23]Roy, *Yogi Sri Krishnaprem*, 73.

[24]Ashish, 'Sri Krishna Prem Through the Eyes of a Disciple,' 19–20.

[25]Roy, *Yogi Sri Krishnaprem*, 10.

[26]Kaul, *Writings of Sri Krishna Prem*, 109.

[27]*Ibid*,

[28]Roy, *Yogi Sri Krishnaprem*, 9.

5: 'Ma'

"[I]n the absence of a competent teacher, no inner path can be absolutely devoid of dangerous pitfalls."[1]
—Sri Krishna Prem (1935)

Though Nixon was already familiar with the most important Indian religious texts (Dilip Kumar Roy speaks of listening with "rapt attention when he discussed the Vedas, the [*Bhagavad] Gita*, the *Tantra*, etc."[2] on one of his twice-yearly visits to Lucknow), it was in the person of Monica Chakravarti that he found the living spiritual teacher for whom he'd been searching since Cambridge.

Monica was born in 1882 into a Theosophical family, one of three children (and the only daughter) of Bengali civil servant Gagan Chandra Roy (b. 1848–49). A "noble-minded and pious man,"[3] Roy was president of his local branch of the Theosophical Society (Ghazipore in the United Provinces, now Ghazipur in Uttar Pradesh),[4] as well as a freemason,[5] patron of holy men and travellers, and distinguished public servant who was in 1893 awarded the Rai Bahadur[6] for his services to the Indian Empire, having risen to become chief accounts officer of the opium department,[7] overseeing the famous opium factory at Ghazipur (to this day the largest such facility in the world). He also owned a large *zamindari* (estate) in a "wretchedly poor area" in Bankura, West Bengal (Ashish, 227).

By the time he retired from government service in 1908, Roy, one of that forgotten class of men "who kept the wheels of the Raj turning,"[8] had also attended the coronation of Edward VII in London, as part of a delegation from Calcutta that also included his relative, Maharaja Sir Prodyot Coomar Tagore,[9] and been awarded a certificate of honour at the 1903 Delhi Durbar, which marked King Edward's accession as emperor of India. (Roy's other eminent kinsmen in Bengal included the Nobel laureate Rabindranath Tagore.[10]) A photograph by Sir Benjamin Stone, depicting Roy, with umbrella and crisp white turban, outside the Houses of Parliament for the coronation, sits in the National Portrait Gallery in London.[11]

He is, however, more famous for his association with Swami Vivekananda—the best known of the procession of itinerant saints and *sādhus* who passed through the Roy household in Monica's formative years. Madhava Ashish recounts Roy's first meeting with Vivekananda (another Bengali, born Narendra Nath Datta), who stayed in the Roys' garden house when he visited Ghazipore in 1890 for the *darśan* (appearance) of Pavhari Baba,[12] an ascetic devotee of Krishna who lived in nearly total seclusion in an subterranean hermitage outside the city:

> Walking home from work one day, Gagan Babu [Roy] found a young Brahmachari (a celibate monk) lying exhausted beside the road. He brought him home. This young man was to become the great Swami Vivekananda. His Guru, the famous Bengali saint Ramakrishna, had died, and Vivekananda was wandering the country, perhaps in search of another teacher of equal status. He had come to Ghazipur for Pauhari Baba's darshan.
>
> But when he went to Pauhari Baba's ashram and sat outside the temple door, Pauhari Baba refused to speak to him, no matter how long he sat. So for several weeks he spent his time between Gagan Babu's house and Pauhari Baba's ashram. One of the other things he did was to perform the Kumari Puja,[13] taking ... Monica to represent the [goddess] Devi. Monica also learned some Sanskrit verses from him (Ashish, 56).

The young Monica left a lasting impression on Vivekananda, who would go on to achieve international fame for his powerful, patriotic exposition of India's spiritual heritage, particularly after his seminal speech at the 1893 Parliament of the World's Religions in Chicago. It is said the swami agreed to meet Annie Besant, of the Theosophical Society, in Almora in 1898 "only at the entreaties of Mrs [Monica] Chakravarti ... whom he knew and loved as a little daughter of Gagan Chandra Roy of Gazipur."[14]

The Vaiṣṇava scholar Jan Brzezinski (Jagadananda Das) connects Monica's own experience of Pavhari Baba to her lifelong belief in supernatural phenomena. He writes:

> [S]he had heard that a local yogi, Pawhari Baba was giving free cloth and *kamaṇḍalu* [the *sannyāsī's* water pot] to all monks who came to his cave. Wondering how he could fit the large amounts of cloth, etc., which would be required to make this gift, she disguised herself as a boy and stood in line as the goods were handed out. When it came her turn, she jumped into the small space of his grotto and saw

that it was empty. This act of daring resulted in a strong belief in miracles.[15]

Other notable visitors, most of whom came to Ghazipore on "the boats travelling to and from Calcutta" (Ashish, 54), included Keshab Chandra Sen (1838–1884), the Hindu–Christian syncretist and social reformer who founded his own branch of the Brahmo Samaj, and Swami Rama Tirtha (1873–1906), a Punjabi *sannyāsī* who was inspired by Vivekananda to lecture on Hindu Vedanta in the United States. Another traveller, a Christian bishop who was staying at the Roys' when Monica was born, inspired the child's unusual name after suggesting she be named after Saint Monica, the North African mother of St Augustine of Hippo, about whom he had dreamt the night of her birth (Ashish, 54).

Little is known about Monica's mother, other than that she was born and brought up in the Punjab,[16] though Madhava Ashish notes that she was a Vaiṣṇava who objected to having to cook meat for Narendra Nath Datta (Vivekananda), "a Brahmachari who, in her view, should also be vegetarian" (Ashish, 56). After their mother's death, Monica emerged as a maternal figure to her younger brother, Gyan Chandra (Ashish, 54), her sibling becoming the first of the many dozens of children to whom she would be an adoptive mother over the next five decades.

At the age of 12 (Ashish, 57), Monica's marriage was arranged to Gyanendra Nath Chakravarti (1861-1936)[17], a widower 19 years her senior then working as a lecturer in mathematics at Muir Central College in Allahabad.[18] (She would later opine that man is free to make his own choices—with the exception of birth, death and marriage.)[19] Though Chakravarti "hesitated at first to remarry," having been left "feeling dreadfully alone and desolate" following the death of his first wife,[20] the match was a good one: Chakravarti shared many similarities with his new father-in-law. Like Gagan Roy, he was a civil servant, Theosophist and Freemason.[21] (According to the French esotericist René Guénon, the "Babu Chuckerbutty" mentioned in Rudyard Kipling's panegyric to his own Masonic lodge, 'The Mother-Lodge,' is based on Chakravarti[22].) He was also later awarded the Rai Bahadur—and as husband and wife Chakravarti and Monica were united both by their love for each other and their dedication to matters of the spirit. Madhava Ashish relates that on first meeting his new lodger, Chakravarti told Nixon "that his and his wife's major interest in life was the spiritual path" (Ashish, 37).

Chakravarti had joined the Theosophical Society in Cawnpore (modern Kanpur in Uttar Pradesh) in March 1883,[23] and guests at the couple's wedding in Ghazipore included prominent Indian Theosophists such as Tookaram Tatya and Aditya Ram Bhattacharya, and the future leader of the society, Chakravarti's

English-born disciple Annie Besant.[24] Besant's biographer, Geoffrey West, describes Chakravarti as a "mysterious Brahmin" who "for a number of years ... hovers mysteriously in the background of Theosophical history;"[25] like Bertram Keightley, he was an early student of Helena Petrovna Blavatsky,[26] and—along with the likes of Besant, Anagarika Dharmapala and Theosophical Society co-founder William Quan Judge—was a member of the Theosophical delegation to the Parliament of the World's Religions in 1893. (Though it is Vivekananda's lecture in Chicago that is best known today, Judge's *The Path* magazine notes that Chakravarti was chosen as a "special delegate" to the conference on behalf of Hinduism by "three orthodox Brahmanical [Hindu] Societies" of India—"the first time," to the writer's knowledge, "that Brahmanical religious bodies have done such a thing."[27])

Together, the newlyweds travelled widely on Theosophical business, including to Europe, where stories of Mrs Chakravarti's interactions with the locals have passed into Mirtola lore. Madhava Ashish writes about his *param* guru (guru's guru):

> One of the intriguing stories of Monica's early life is that of her trip to Europe in about 1900–1901, when there was an Exposition in Paris and the Crystal Palace was still new in London. Monica went with her husband and Annie Besant, and there was a Bengali woman (Borodidi) who went with them as Monica's 'companion.' They went via Italy and visited St Peter's in Rome. Monica was wearing a blue *sari* with silver stars embroidered on it. Some Italian peasants who were there saw this dark, big-eyed, beautiful woman in blue and silver and took her for an incarnation of the Virgin Mary. They surrounded her, tearing off bits of her *sari*. Annie Besant hurried her out and into a cab, admonishing her never to wear that *sari* again.
>
> In India Monica was not considered beautiful because her complexion was dark. But in Paris they saw her features and declared her most beautiful. ... When they visited the Exposition, Monica in all her finery and laden with heavy gold ornaments was thought to be the Queen of Madagascar. But then she found the Indian display, which included a copy of Kachauri Gully in Banaras, a narrow street devoted to the production of fresh hot savoury fried *kachauris* [deep-fried wheat snacks]. Banaras men had been brought with all their equipment, and they were delighted to see Monica who they knew as a regular visitor. (Ashish, 61-62)

A further trip to Italy yielded an Italian marble statue which Monica intended to be the main *vigraha* (figure) of Krishna when she achieved her childhood dream of building him a temple (Ashish, 94).

From 12 pregnancies, Monica mothered four biological children—Bhalli, the eldest son; Bulbul, the eldest daughter, who was educated in Paris;[28] Ratan, the youngest son; and Arpita, the youngest daughter—and adopted countless more. According to Madhava Ashish, Monica "adopted, educated and married off some" 40 children, the final two as late as when Chakravarti was vice-chancellor of Lucknow University (1920–1926), when his wife would have been in her late 30s or early 40s (Ashish, 60). Legend has it that Monica's maternal instincts were so powerful that they extended beyond human children: she is said to have personally suckled a litter of orphaned puppies in Lucknow (Ashish, 136).

Remembered by Almora resident Prema Pant as "a warm, motherly person full of affection,"[29] 'Ma' was also known for her temper, which is said to have rivaled even the notoriously cantankerous Madame Blavatsky in its ferocity: Madhava Ashish recalls that Nixon "once asked Chakravarti what sort of woman Blatavsky was. One would have had to know [Blavatsky's] fiery and tempestuous nature to appreciate his reply: 'I have known only one woman like her,' and he nodded towards his wife sitting a few feet away."[30] Though in Mirtola circles it is her youngest daughter, Arpita (known as Moti Rani), who is usually identified with Blavatsky, Monica and 'HPB' also shared a reputation for plain speaking—the former had a "fund of peasant woman's crude sayings that she could use to great effect"[31]—and harsh treatment of their respective disciples. According to Madhava Ashish, Bertram Keightley was "accustomed to being sworn at and called all sorts of names" by Blavatsky (Ashish, 71), while Monica "was capable of [similar] behaviour, though she never used it on Krishna Prem," which "led him to complain that she was taking him on a velvet path" (Ashish, 167). He is said to have observed, concerning the difference between Monica Chakravarti and her husband: "He was the type who would gently push at a door and leave it if it did not open, whereas she would give a shove to a door, and if it did not open would give it a kick" (Ashish, 65).

Both Chakravartis were sought-after spiritual teachers, and it was the elder of the pair, Gyanendra Nath—the high-caste (Brahmin) "theosophicalized Hindu"[32] —to whom many seekers came for initiation and instruction. (Like his wife, he also turned away plenty of prospective disciples, "flatly refus[ing] initiation to several Europeans who applied to him. 'They don't stick,' he said. 'They expect to get something, put it in their pockets, and go back to Europe.'"[33]) Though Chakravarti's "inner life ... was shared with only a small circle of friends,"[34] those who were permitted to peek behind the curtain discovered a deep devotion to his native spiritual traditions that belied his Western-style habits and manners. He had founded a Hindu society, the Yoga Samāj, when posted in Allahabad,[35] and extolled the wisdom of Hindu texts such as the *Bhagavad Gītā*, the Krishna-centred text on which Krishna Prem would write a commentary, and to which he introduced Mirra Alfassa, later the 'Mother' of

Sri Aurobindo Ashram in Pondicherry.[36] His personal *sādhana* included three hours' daily meditation between three and six in the morning.[37]

Sri Aurobindo, who described Chakravarti as a "remarkable *sadhak[a]*", comments on the apparent contradiction between his 'inner' and 'outer' lives, the latter characterised by material wealth and a seeming lack of concern with religious life:

> [H]e was externally a very worldly man, accepting the not very exalted outward personal life and surroundings he had as the milieu given him and not in the least wishing to change it. It was his theory that this was the teaching of the Gita—to feel Krishna within, to have the inner spiritual life and realisation,—the rest was the *Lila* and could be left as it was unless or until the Divine himself in the automatic movement of his play chose to change it. This explains the double character of the impression he conveyed to others. ... Those who had themselves some development or aspire to it could, I suppose, feel the *sadhak* in him; others might see only the worldly man, able, strong, rich, social, successful, accepting, even perhaps drawing to himself enjoyment of riches and power. Others felt both sides, but could understand neither[.][38]

The Chakravartis also made a handful of disciples together, notably in Bareilly (Ashish, 68), a city in modern Uttar Pradesh where Gyanendra Nath had been a professor (of physical science at Bareilly College) in the 1880s.[39]

If Mr Chakravarti could be said to have lived a double life, the same was arguably even more true of Monica, outwardly a "resplendent ultramodern hostess" who was, in the words of Dilip Kumar Roy, "the life and soul of every party she threw in her salon" at the vice-chancellor's mansion.[40] Chakravarti, he writes, was "an extremely hospitable man who kept an open table"[41]. The house in Lucknow "seems to have had a constant stream of visiting Theosophists from England" (Ashish, 64), among them Isabel Cooper-Oakley, the friend and disciple of Madame Blavatsky, and Mary Tibbits (Mrs Walter Tibbits), known for her 1909 book *The Voice of the Orient*. It was only when the guests had departed, however, that Chakravarti's wife could turn her attention to her chief concern in life: the spiritual 'path' on which she had been travelling since her *sādhu*-filled childhood in Ghazipore.

That is, at least to the casual observer. Though Monica had never "hid her own lamp under a bushel of conventionalities"[42]—having "made a habit of meeting anyone with spiritual predilections" (Ashish, 63), she was often seen "hobnobb[ing] with outlandish religious mendicants"[43]—in a social setting she was every inch the glamorous, gregarious vice-chancellor's wife. Roy recalls that this "great lady of birth and breeding with the innate personal charm of a born hostess, aristocratic to her fingertips,"[44] was renowned throughout Lucknow as a *"dame de salon"* of fashionable high society. However, it soon became clear that "behind Mrs Chakravarti's social façade was a woman of outstanding mystical experience,"[45] The Gauḍīya Vaiṣṇava writer OBL Kapoor relates how Nixon noticed that Monica would often, for short periods, retire to her room mid-way through a party, and one day resolved to follow her:

> Her real self could not escape the keen eyes of Nixon ... [who] wanted to know the secret of her sudden disappearance. ...
>
> When he peeped into her room, he saw that she was sitting in a corner, motionless and unconscious. When she came out, after about half an hour or so, her eyes were wet and an inconceivable peace seemed to radiate from her face.[46]

Kapoor quotes Monica telling Nixon about the content of these visions, as well as why they occurred even during social occasions:

> ... Kṛṣṇa is so naughty that time or no time, He pulls me near Him whenever He wishes. At that time a light emanates from His feet, which makes me unconscious of my body and the world outside. I do not do anything. It is He, who pulls me and drowns me in the ocean of His ambrosial presence and company.[47]

It was this sense that in meditation Monica had cultivated a personal relationship with the supreme—that, in the form of Krishna, the "divine hero, alluring god-child, cosmic prankster, perfect lover, and universal supreme being,"[48] she could really see and commune with God—which convinced Nixon he had found the spiritual master to whom he would devote his life.

That Monica had first-hand experience of the object of her devotion was underlined on a family holiday to Almora, in the Kumaon Himalayas, in 1922 or '23, when she began to teach Nixon Hindi from a translation of the *Bhāgavata Purāṇa* (or *Śrīmad Bhāgavatam*), the 12-volume Sanskrit text which contains an account of Krishna's youthful adventures in the pastoral idyll of Vrindavan:

> From learning Urdu, the standard language for beginners in North India, under the tutelage of a Munshi [language teacher], Ronald now began to learn Hindi from Mrs Chakravarti. She taught him by making him read from the *Sukh Sāgar*, a folk version of the *Śrīmad*

> *Bhāgavat* in simple Hindi which tells the story of the life of the Lord Krishna. As he read, she explained and commented. ...
>
> [His] perception was that when Mrs Chakravarti spoke of Sri Krishna, she was speaking of someone who was entirely real. One might not be able to see him, but that was only because he was in the next room.
>
> It was shortly after this that Ronald asked her for initiation, for it was apparent to him that she was teaching from experience (Ashish, 45).

"This Hindi version of *Bhāgawat* awoke the dormant aspiration in Krishna Prem," elaborates the Gujarati writer and politician Kanaiyalal Maneklal (KM) Munshi (1887–1971), "and upon discovering that Monica "had attained 'realization' [he] begged her to initiate him in the Krishna Cult."[49]

With two conditions, Monica accepted Nixon's request to become her formal student. The first condition, that he become a vegetarian, "held no problems for Ronald because he already preferred a vegetarian diet" (Ashish, 46). The second was that—unlike Mr Chakravarti's European Theosophists—Nixon should 'stick' to his guru and the path they had chosen, "and not, like so many would-be *Sādhakas* [spiritual seekers], change his loyalties at each passing whim."[50] This, too, he accepted without hesitation.

Notes

[1]Sri Krishna Prem, review of Paul Brunton, *The Secret Path* in *The Aryan Path* 6.5 (1935): 328.

[2]Roy, *Yogi Sri Krishnaprem*, 8.

[3]Sailendra Nath Dhar, *A Comprehensive Biography of Swami Vivekananda*, Part One, (Madras: Vivekananda Prakashan Kendra, 1975), 264.

[4]*The Theosophist* 30.1–6 (1909): 138.

[5]'United Grand Lodge of England Freemason Membership Registers, 1751–1921,' *Ancestry*, Lehi, Ancestry.com Operations, 2015, https://www.ancestry.com/search/collections/60620 (accessed 27 November 2021). Original data: Membership registers 1751–1921 from the collection of the United Grand Lodge of England held by the Museum of Freemasonry. Images reproduced by courtesy of the Museum of Freemasonry, London. Rights reserved.

[6]Literally "Brave Prince", the highest honorific title awarded to individuals in British India.

[7]'Part VIII: Bengal', in *Who's Who in India, Coronation Edition* (Lucknow: Newul Kishore Press, 1911), 65.

[8]Kusoom Vadgama, *India in Britain: The Indian Contribution to the British Way of Life* (London: Robert Royce Limited, 1984), 77.

[9]'Part VIII: Bengal,' 65.

[10]GD Khanolkar, *The Lute and the Plough: A Life of Rabindranath Tagore* (Bombay: The Book Centre, 1963), 82.

[11]Benjamin Stone, 'Rai Bahadur Gagan Chandra Rai' [picture], https://www.npg.org.uk/collections-/search/portrait/mw13624/Rai-Bahadur-Gagan-Chandra-Rai (accessed 28 November 2021).

[12]Swami Pavitrananda (publisher), *The Life of Swami Vivekananda*, 3rd ed, (Almora: Advaita Ashrama, 1944), 1:221.

[13]A Bengali Hindu ceremony in which an unmarried girl is worshipped symbolically as the Mother Goddess (Devi).

[14]Sankari Prasad Babu (ed.), *Swami Vivekananda in Contemporary Indian News (1893–1902): With Ramakrishna and the Mission* (Calcutta: Ramakrishna Mission Institute of Culture, 1997), 1:58.

[15]Jan Brzezinski, 'Women Saints in Gauḍīya Vaiṣṇavism,' in Steven Rosen (ed), *Vaiṣṇavī: Women and the Worship of Krishna* (Delhi: Motilal Banarsidass, 1996), 78.

[16]Phanindranath Bose, *Life of Sris Chandra Basu* (Calcutta: R. Chatterjee, 1932), 163.

[17]'Part IV: United Provinces', in *Who's Who in India, Coronation Edition* (Lucknow: Newul Kishore Press, 1911), 163.

[18]*Ibid.*

[19]Jagdish Shah, 'Memoirs' (email to the author), 3 May 2023, 6.

[20]Bose, *Life of Sris Chandra Basu*, 154–155.

[21]'United Grand Lodge of England Freemason Membership Registers, 1751–1921', *Ancestry* (accessed 23 December 2021).

[22]René Guénon, *Theosophy: History of a Pseudo-Religion*, 1st English edn (Hillsdale: Sophia Perennis, 2003), 152.

[23]'Faces of Friends', *The Path* 8 (1893–94): 204.

[24]Bose, *Life of Sris Chandra Basu*, 163.

[25]Geoffrey West, *The Life of Annie Besant* (London: Gerald Howe, 1933), 183.

[26]John L. Crow, *Occult Bodies: The Corporal Construction of the Theosophical Society, 1875–1935* (PhD diss., Tallahassee: Florida State University, 2017), 226.

[27]'Faces of Friends', 205.

[28]Ravinder Kumar and DN Panigrahi (eds), *Selected works of Motilal Nehru*, Vol. 1 *(1899–1918)* (New Delhi: Vikas Publishing House, 1982), 96.

[29]Joshi, 'My Memories of Mussoorie.'

[30]Madhava Ashish, 'Sri Krishna Prem Through the Eyes of a Disciple', 21.

[31]*Ibid.*

[32]Ashish, 'Sri Krishna Prem Through the Eyes of a Disciple,' 20.

[33]Ashish, 'Sri Krishna Prem Through the Eyes of a Disciple,' 22.

[34]Ashish, 'Sri Krishna Prem Through the Eyes of a Disciple', 20.

[35]Guénon, *Theosophy*, 152.

[36]Sri Aurobindo, 'Talk of 13 December 1940,' *Mother India* 39 (1986): 340, cited in 'Archival Notes: Sri Aurobindo, the Mother and Paul Richard 1911–1915', *Sri Aurobindo: Archives and Research*, 13.1 (1989): 114.

[37]Ashish, 'Sri Krishna Prem Through the Eyes of a Disciple', 20.

[38]Sujata Nahar, Michel Danino and Shankar Bandyopadhyay (eds), *Sri Aurobindo to Dilip*, Vol. 1 (1929–1933), *The Mother & Sri Aurobindo* (Mysore: Hari Krishna Mandir Trust, 2003), 188, https://web.archive.org/web/20160321131242/http://aurobindo.ru/workings/sa/to-dilip/vol-1-e.-htm (accessed 9 April 2023).

[39]Supplement to *The Theosophist* 7.73 (1885): xxxv.

[40]Roy, *Yogi Sri Krishnaprem*, 64.

[41]Roy, *Yogi Sri Krishnaprem*, 53.

[42]Ashish, 'Sri Krishna Prem Through the Eyes of a Disciple', 21.

[43]Ashish, 'Sri Krishna Prem Through the Eyes of a Disciple', 21.

[44]Roy, *Yogi Sri Krishnaprem*, 54.

[45]Madhava Ashish, 'Preface,' in Krishna Prem and Madhava Ashish, *Man, the Measure of All Things*, 7.

[46]Kapoor, 'Śrī Kṛṣṇaprema,' 296.

[47]Kapoor, 'Śrī Kṛṣṇaprema,' 297.

[48]William K. Mahony, 'Perspectives on Kṛṣṇa's Various Personalities' (reviews of Noel Sheth, *The Divinity of Krishna*, and James D. Redington, *Vallabhācārya on the Love Games of Kṛṣṇa*), *History of Religions* 26.3 (1987): 333.

[49]KM Munshi, *Janu's Death and Other Kulapati's Letters* (Bombay: Bharatiya Vidya Bhavan, 1954), 55.

[50]Madhava Ashish, 'Sri Sri Krishnaprem Vairagi,' in Jyotsna Singh (ed), *Letters from Mirtola (Written by Sri Krishnaprem and Sri Madhava Ashish to Karan Singh)* (Mumbai: Bharatiya Vidya Bhavan, 2004), 88.

PART II

VAIṢṆAVA

6: Initiate

"The voice of the Masters is always in the world; but only those hear it whose ears are no longer receptive of the sounds which affect the personal life."[1]
— Mabel Collins, *Light on the Path*

Even before it was common knowledge that Nixon had taken Monica as his guru, it was clear the professor—whom she had taken to calling 'Gopal' (literally "protector of cows," Krishna in the form of an impish, butter-stealing child)—had fallen under Mrs Chakravarti's spell. Dilip Kumar Roy, visiting the Chakravarti family in Lucknow shortly after Nixon's initiation in 1924, recalls:

> I noticed ... how reverently Krishnaprem gazed at her and prostrated himself before her every time she greeted him as her *Gopal*, heart's darling (the name by which Krishna's Mother, Yaśodā Rāṇī, called her little son). I was no less impressed when I saw that in her presence the leonine intellectual turned in a moment into a docile lamb![2]

As Nixon became Monica Chakravarti's 'Gopal,' to him she was simply 'Ma' ("Mother"). These names stuck, even after the founding of the Mirtola ashram, where Sri Krishna Prem was called 'Gopalda' ('elder brother Gopal') by everyone except Moti Rani, Monica's youngest daughter, "who stuck to her 'Chhotoba' ('little father')" (Ashish, 100). (Moti Rani, who became Krishna Prem's disciple in the 1930s, was five—"a little girl in a pink frock" (Ashish, 76)—when he moved into the Chakravartis' house in Lucknow.) Satish Datt Pandey, a disciple of Madhava Ashish, explains: "Ma called him Gopal (the fond, household name of Krishna) and, thus, in the Mirtola 'family' he is referred to as Gopal Da ('Da' literally means elder brother, a form of address common both in the Bengali society from which Ma came, and in Kumaon where the ashram is located)."[3] As Krishna Prem's successor, Sri Madhava Ashish went by the similar 'Ashishda.' He explained: "Da ... means 'big brother.' It is a way for my pupils to name me without becoming overly absorbed in the niceties of addressing a Hindu holy man. ..."[4]

It is notable that during this period Nixon continued to express an interest in Buddhism, writing 'An Outline Sketch of Buddhist Philosophy' (1925)[5] as a follow-up to 'The Knowledge of the Buddha' and 'The Atheism of Buḍḍhism', despite the Hindu form of initiation he had received from Mrs Chakravarti.

In the figures of the Buddha, the ascetic renunciate whose example had made such an impact on him as a younger man, and Krishna, the playful god whose dalliances with the village girls of Vrindavan, as detailed in the *Bhāgavatam*, had more recently caught his imagination, Nixon saw how spiritual realisation could manifest in different ways, says Madhava Ashish:

> In the Buddha image he had seen the attainment represented as a poised withdrawal from life. Now, in the Kṛṣṇa legend, he saw the same attainment, but here held intact by a figure who did not hesitate to act meanwhile as a statesman, warrior, friend, or lover.[6]

It should be noted here that Nixon's conception of Krishna, as he is said to have appeared some 5,000 years ago, as an *avatār* or enlightened human teacher comparable to the Buddha or Christ, runs contrary to the mainstream Krishnaite view, which considers that "statesman, warrior, friend [and] lover" to be *Svayam Bhagavān*, the supreme truth and source of all reality. In Gauḍīya Vaiṣṇavism, Krishna as Govinda—the adolescent, flute-playing "cowherd-Cupid"[7] of Vrindavan—is regarded as the source of the impersonal (*Nirguṇa*) Brahman from which all else derives, whereas for followers of 'classical,' Upanishadic (700–500 BC) Hinduism, and Ādi Śaṅkara's later *Advaita Vedānta*, the "One True Reality (Brahman) is primary and original, while the many real things are derivative from Brahman."[8] As is evident from his writing and correspondence, Nixon continued to hold to his position even after his initiation into Krishnaite Vaishnavism; see, for example, his commentary on the *Bhagavad Gītā* (see chapter 11) and his letters to Roy in the 1930s, in which he distinguishes between the 'human' Krishna and the eternal 'One' who may be referred to by the same name: "Knowledge of Him [God] alone gives immortality. Know Him through Christ, through Krishna or through Buddha, *but know Him somehow or other.*"[9] This distinction is also evident in 'The Yoga of the Gita,' a 1935 essay which precedes the similarly named book, in which Krishna Prem differentiates between "the eternal Krishna"[10] and the Krishna who "appeared on earth in a human form and wore a yellow Dhoti" at the "end of Dwapara Yuga"[11] (3,102 BC).

He would soon witness the same 'attainment' he had seen in the "human" Krishna even closer to home, in the person of another unconventional Gauḍīya Vaiṣṇava: his new spiritual master, Monica Chakravarti.

It was early one morning in 1924, the year of Nixon's initiation and his fourth in India, that he received a note in his room at the vice-chancellor's house. Written in Hindi, it read simply: "What you are seeking, that I have found" (Ashish, 48).

The previous night, Monica said, she had received her most profound vision to date: a deeply affecting mystical experience characterised by Sri Madhava Ashish as a "an overwhelming vision of the unity of being."[12]

What this vision looked like in practice is known only to Monica, who did not document it, though Madhava Ashish writes that the event marked "what would be called the final attainment" (Ashish, 48) and says she considered the experience the "culmination of her life's dedication to the spiritual path."[13] He also "discreetly described" this mystical experience to many of his own disciples, explaining that their *paratpara* guru (guru's guru's guru) had been given a "vision of the unity of being."[14]

Sy Ginsburg, a student of Madhava Ashish and follower of the teachings of Russian mystic George Ivanovich Gurdjieff (the 'Work'), relates the experience in similar terms, writing that Monica had been given the "unitive vision"[15]—the sight of the world as observed from the perspective of the higher 'self,' as distinct from the personality or ego (the lesser self). Ginsburg notes that Krishna Prem also called this greater self 'the Light:'

> [Krishna] Prem wrote eloquently of "the pure Consciousness itself dwelling in the heart of every living being and particularly that Light ... [which] dwells in all beings and speakers (that is why some traditions have termed it the Logos, the Word) in our hearts with the voice of conscience; though only too often we confuse its voice with various other voices that speak with louder accents." In all of us, said Krishna Prem, there dwelt, beyond the flux of daily thought and endeavor, this Light, this Self—the higher Self.[16]

Madhava Ashish notes that he describes the vision as "overwhelming" because Monica could not immediately make sense of it, though he adds that it was a factor in her eventual decision to relocate to Almora. "I put it in that way because it took her many years to integrate the content of that vision into her being, as is the case in general with people whose attainment is marked by this sort of sudden enlightenment" (Ashish, 48). This, he explains, is a "notoriously difficult process ... for the fact of a vision does not necessarily change one's capacity to conceptualise or to change one's viewpoint."[17] Indeed, Monica was purportedly able to induce the vision in other people, including Nixon's Lucknow University colleague Cecil Roy, though not the enlightenment that had for her, a veteran spiritual seeker, accompanied it:

> It is evident that Mrs Chakravarti had been wanting to show Ronald the vision that had marked her attainment. While it should be obvious that she could by no means give the attainment, for no one can 'give' the attainment of liberation to someone else, the visionary component could be reproduced. But it seems that Ronald was not sufficiently receptive, for one day when Cecil was present he suggested to Mrs Chakravarti that Cecil was able to 'see,' so why not try it on him. Both were agreeable, and the experiment was made. When it was over, Cecil remarked, 'How interesting. How do you do it? By hypnosis?' The awe-inspiring vision which had accompanied Mrs Chakravarti's liberation, taken by itself, was nothing more than 'interesting' to a person like Cecil. (Ashish, 47)

Though in Monica the experience characterised her "final attainment" after a lifetime of Vaiṣṇava *bhajana* (worship), such visions may also kickstart a seeker's spiritual journey, as in the case of Bill Aitken. He writes about his first "out-of-the-body" experience, when he realised "all is One and One is all:"

> It completely opened my eyes: life is not what we are taught it is—it isn't the rat race ... we are taught by people who don't know what it is. They mean well, they haven't seen, that's all. The scales dropped from my eyes: I saw what a glorious thing human existence is; I experienced this engine of the cosmos beating by the crude force of Eros and there is nothing to be ashamed of. ... I knew I had to find [this state] again. ... This tantalizing glimpse, call it divine—it was real [and] changed my life. ..."[18]

In fact, Aitken's experience is the more common one, as a glimpse of the 'unitive vision' rarely marks the end of the road, explains the author Madhu Tandan, who, with her husband Rajeev, lived for seven years at Mirtola. She quotes Madhava Ashish:

> The work never ends. You've experienced something enormous. The question is—can you live up to it and integrate it into your ordinary life? It is one thing to have this experience in an altered state and quite another matter to live by it for the rest of your life. For,

> remember, when you come out of that experience all your desires, compulsions and hang-ups don't automatically vanish. You have to work at it by being ruthlessly honest in trying to bridge the gap between what you've seen and what you are.[19]

Madhava Ashish himself recalls once being "given an overwhelming vision of Radha–Krishna, shining in all their glory," which he took initially to mark the culmination of his spiritual journey. "[W]ithin a few days," however, he was "shown that this was the view of an immature boy. It was by no means the end of the path, as it had seemed to be, but only the beginning of a new stage on the road to the completion of the human task."[20]

Some clue as to Monica's conclusions can be found in her book *Punarāvartin*, published in Hindi in 1937 and translated into English by Krishna Prem as *The Homeward Journey*. In the book, which often more resembles a treatise on classical *jñāna yoga* than a *bhakti* text, she writes extensively about the concept of the higher self or soul (here called the 'Divine Self' or left untranslated as the Sanskrit *Ātma[n]*) and the goal of realising that self in order to achieve union with the supreme, variously referred to as God, Sri Krishna, the Supreme Self, the 'great Magician,' and the One (the Neoplatonic term for the source of all existence).

On the ego, or lesser self, she writes: "As long as there is consciousness of 'I,' the separate self, there can be no consciousness of the Divine Self. Where the latter is, all self entirely dies."[21] Once this 'I-consciousness' has been eliminated, the result is a new way of seeing in which the *sādhaka* (spiritual practitioner) becomes aware of the universal consciousness which pervades all creation:

> When anyone really attains that Divine Self he sees all beings as limbs of the One Self, just as a man sees his fingers and toes as limbs of his one body.[22]

Monica (by now known as Yashoda Mai) also hints at personal experience of the *paramātman*—God in the form of the indwelling 'supersoul' that resides in the hearts of all living things—the need to attune to which is also a frequent motif in Krishna Prem's writing:

> The one Paramatman, Sri Krishna, is the Self in all beings, and shines like the sun in the hearts of all. ... The ego ... asserts its separateness and that of others but, when at last the vision of Krishna is attained, then it sees that He is One in all and it subdues itself before Him, recognising that it, itself, is but a play of His.[23]

In order to give formal initiation (*dīkṣā*) to Nixon, Monica had herself taken an initiating guru: her husband, Gyanendra Nath Chakravarti, whose piety and learning she felt to be greater than any of the *sādhus* he had been inviting to meet his increasingly spiritually minded wife. Having "persuaded him to allow her to meet as many as possible of the spiritual figures of the day in pursuit of her own search," Monica "had ended by asking initiation from him because, she said, she had found no one his equal."[24]

The French physicist and Theosophist Gabriel Monod-Herzen, a friend of Dilip Kumar Roy's who made multiple visits to Uttar Brindaban, notes that while "extremely rare," the initiation of a wife by her husband is "regarded in India as an exceptionally happy circumstance."[25]

Although his wife was inclined towards Vaiṣṇavism, the veneration of Viṣṇu or Krishna, Gyanendra Chakravarti came from a family of Śāktas, who worship the goddess Śakti (also called Devī) or her various incarnations as the divine mother. (The identity of Chakravarti's own initiating guru is not known: Geoffrey West records that he was known to Theosophists as being a "*chela* [student] of one of the numerous Yoga systems in India,"[26] while William Quan Judge writes that Chakravarti, to whom he was hostile,[27] was, at the time of the Parliament of the World's Religions, a "Chela of a minor Indian Guru."[28]) Śāktism is popular among Bengalis like the Chakravartis—a well-known saying holds that "every Bengali is half Vaiṣṇava and half Śākta."[29] In fact, several famous Vaiṣṇavas were at one time Śāktas, including Ramakrishna Paramahamsa[30] (who, while chiefly remembered as the neo-*Vedāntin* guru of Vivekananda, was initiated as a Vaiṣṇava[31] and cultivated *mādhurya bhāva*,[32] the sentiment of romantic or erotic love for Krishna) and the Gauḍīya Vaiṣṇava revivalist Bhaktivinoda.[33] The politician, philosopher and one-time prince regent of Jammu and Kashmir, Karan Singh, was also initiated into Śāktism prior to taking Vaiṣṇava initiation from Madhava Ashish.[34]

Because "her guru was not authorised to give" the desired Vaiṣṇava *dīkṣā*,[35] Monica's first initiation was a Śākta one, in which she received from her guru the *mantra* (sacred sound) "of a *sattvic* form of Devi" (Ashish, 63)—a form of Śakti imbued with the quality (*guṇa*) of goodness, or *sattva* (the other two *guṇas* being passion, *rajas*, and ignorance or darkness, *tamas*). She was, however, soon offered an initiation more in keeping with her own background when the same goddess appeared in a vision and bestowed on her a Vaiṣṇava *mantra* (Ashish, 63).

Monica in turn accepted 'Gopal' as her initiated disciple, setting tongues wagging among the gossips of Lucknow, as Dilip Kumar Roy recalls:

> He had confided to me that he had taken a Guru, but as he seemed rather reticent, I left it at that. But the professors wagged their tongues freely, the more so as many a rich father with nubile daughters went on inviting him under all sorts of transparent pretexts which could fool nobody. They did think him eccentric, but his bright personality and brilliant lectures attracted many a lady student and so Dame Gossip had a field day with her speculations.[36]

In 1926, after six years as vice-chancellor of the University of Lucknow, GN Chakravarti retired to Benares (modern Varanasi), the ancient pilgrimage city 200 miles south-east of Lucknow on the banks of the holy Ganges where he had earlier been pro (deputy)-vice-chancellor of Banaras Hindu University (BHU).[37] Determined to stay close to his spiritual teachers, and particularly his guru of two years, Mrs Chakravarti, Nixon wrote to Madan Mohan Malaviya, co-founder of the BHU and its vice-chancellor from 1919 to 1938, seeking employment at the university—to the horror of his colleagues in Lucknow:

> Malviya [sic] was delighted when Ronald asked for employment in Banaras Hindu University, but pointed out that he lacked funds and would be able to pay Ronald only a little over one half of his current salary. Ronald's colleagues in Lucknow called him a fool for even considering such a move. He now had an assured career ahead of him, and his salary would soon be increasing. But Ronald was not happy. (Ashish, 49)

Though the Chakravartis refused to influence his decision on whether to relocate, Mr Chakravarti had given Nixon the following advice: "Whenever I have to make a major decision in my life, I try to follow what I think to be highest in myself. I have not always succeeded. When I have, I never had occasion to regret it. When I have not, I have always regretted it."[38] "That," says Madhava Ashish, "was enough for Ronald and he went to Benares."[39]

According to Roy, Nixon dropped the "bomb-shell" news that he was leaving for Benares at a tea party attended by University of Lucknow colleagues:

> It was then that his learned friends conferred together and decided that it had ceased to be a laughing matter.
>
> "You must persuade him, Dilip, at any cost," they appealed to me in a deputation, in deep alarm. "A professor of the Hindu University

> gets only about Rs 300/– per month,[40] whereas he is getting here already Rs 800/– and it will increase, in due course, to Rs 1,200/– or even more. He may even come to flower out into a vice-chancellor with his brilliant gifts, not to mention his popularity...."[41]

Having accepted a teaching post in the English department of the Central Hindu College,[42] part of Banaras Hindu University, Nixon joined the Chakravartis at their new house in the Nagwa area of Benares, named *Radha Vilas* ('Radha's Pastimes') after Krishna's favourite consort and feminine counterpart, as well as the family's previous home in the city.

The filmmaker and author Satyajit Ray, who made the second Feluda film, *Joi Baba Felunath* (1979), in Varanasi, used the house for the residence of the Ghoshal family, who have tasked the detective with investigating the attempted theft of a valuable Ganesh idol. Ray describes the house, which by the 1970s was owned by the wealthy Dalmia family of industrialists:

> A long driveway led from the front gate to the house, which was hidden behind a number of trees. It was a large mansion. No one lived there now. Its massive compound bore evidence of its past grandeur. ... The river was not far, but the plinth of the house was so high that even during the monsoon there was no fear of flooding. Apparently, the land had once belonged to an English lady. Soon after she came to know Gyan Chakravarty, she dreamt one night that he had been her own child in a previous life. Having lived in Varanasi for many years, this lady had been influenced by Hindu beliefs and had started to believe in reincarnations. The upshot was that, as a result of her dream, she left all the land and her other assets to Mr Chakravarty. ...
>
> There was a remarkable view of the city of Varanasi from the roof. The river stretched beyond the railway bridge in the far distance, its banks spread out like the blade of a giant sickle.[43]

A palatial detached bungalow (in the Indian sense) set out over three stories, in extensive gardens, and equipped with electric lighting,[44] Radha Vilas II nevertheless fell short of Monica's expectations for her new home. In addition to lacking separate entrances for "the inevitable sweeper to enter the bathrooms" (Ashish, 49), the high columns that raised the house over the flood waters from the Ganges a mere 200 yards away meant Monica, then in increasingly ill health, had to climb a steep stairway to access the property from ground level (Ashish, 49). Worst of all, the house lacked a *pūjā* room for the ceremonial worship of the beloved family deities, which in addition to the marble Krishna from Italy included an idol (*mūrti*) of the elephant god Gaṇeśa (Ashish, 63). Though a small temple was hurriedly constructed above the house's portico, Monica was, writes Madhava Ashish, "too unwell to tackle the steep staircase up to the roof to see what the promised temple was like" (Ashish, 66) and the *mūrtis* were forgotten.

As Jan Brzezinski observes, "Yaśodā Mā had a deep emotional attachment to her deities in the parental mood,"[45] or *vātsalya-rasa*—one of the principal relationship types (*rasas*) between Krishna and his devotees, along with *śānta-rasa* (neutrality), *dāsya-rasa* (servitude), *sakhya-rasa* (friendship) and *mādhurya-rasa* (lover and beloved)—and it wasn't long before the concerned mother ordered the images rescued from their rooftop exile, where they were being exposed to the elements, over the protests of her husband. Madhava Ashish writes:

> Shortly after moving in she had a disturbing dream. The marble image of Ganesh she had in her puja room was cuddling up to her and shivering because he was feeling cold, behaving as if he were a little child. In the morning she insisted on climbing upstairs to have darshan of her Thakurs (the figures of the deities). A temple had been built on the roof, as promised, but the temple itself had no roof. Her Thakurs were unprotected from the weather, and the images themselves were wet with dew. She promptly ordered all the images removed to her own room where she could look after them—and never mind the orthodox objection, voiced by her husband, that a bedroom was not the proper place for the Lord's images. (Ashish, 67)

Nixon, meanwhile, felt immediately at home in Benares. Living in this sacred city—famous for its riverfront *ghāṭs* (the imposing stone staircases used for *pūjā*, ritual bathing and cremation); its thousands of temples, most dedicated to Benares's patron deity, Shiva; and its daily *Gaṅgā ārati* (the sunset offering to the Ganges which attracts its celebrated local *sādhus*, hair matted and heads painted in brightly coloured *tilak*)—seems to have given a boost to Nixon's yogic practice, as well as inspired him to give spiritual discourses of the kind that later became central to evening life at Mirtola. Roy writes:

> [I]t was there [Benares] Krishnaprem began his Yoga[46] assiduously, or, shall I say, with his native "British doggedness," as Sri Aurobindo once put it. My informant told me that in the holy atmosphere of Varanasi, Krishnaprem's very soul seemed to have flowered out under the aegis of his guru, Yasoda Ma. He related a revealing repartee of Krishnaprem's:

> "What on earth have you found to adore, sir, in this drab city of dust and din?" heckled an ultra-modern, as Krishnaprem was giving a discourse on the symbol of Varanasi and Shiva's aura.
>
> Krishnaprem replied with a radiant smile: "Gold-dust, my friend, and the music of the Ganga."[47]

Adding to that dust and din was Nixon's motorbike, which had come with him from Lucknow. Writing in 1972, a former student, AN Banerji, described how BHU alumni "still discuss among ourselves the following picture which is still vivid in our memory: Prof. Nixon coming to the University campus from Shri Chakravarty's house on his motor cycle at a *terrific* speed—the red dust of the *kutcha* [dirt] road, raised by his motor cycle swirling and trailing far behind him. We used to enjoy this sight almost every day from the verandah of the College."[48]

It was also in Benares that Nixon met Hanuman Prasad Poddar, the writer, publisher and Indian independence activist, for the first time. Poddar was in the city soliciting articles for a special issue of his Hindi magazine *Kalyan*, titled *Bhakta-Ank* (the *bhakta* edition), to which Nixon contributed the article '*Bhakti aur gyan*' ('*Bhakti* and *jñāna*').[49] It was published in 1928. Nixon, now Krishna Prem, wrote later to Karan Singh that he had "loved" his time in Benares, which was "full of happy memories. When one stands on Dasashwamedha Ghat and gazes on the flowing Ganga (especially in the quiet of the night) and then realizes that nearly all the *Mahātmas* of India must, sometimes or other, have stood in that very spot gazing on the same flowing stream, one is thrilled by the sense of the eternal that is there, shining as it were just below the surface bustle of the day."[50]

In addition to its religious life, Nixon was impressed by the people of Benares, particularly those residing in the villages around the city. Staying with his friend Biren Banerji in the city of Calcutta in the late 1940s, Krishna Prem recalled: "How is it that in Banaras I saw village people walking down the street, carefree, laughing and relaxed, whereas here in Calcutta I see strained faces, tense smiles, and if anyone laughs it is a nervous laugh?" (Ashish, 188)

The first of the two Cambridge friends who had resolved to follow Nixon to India, Bob Alexander, finally arrived in 1927,[51] having chosen to continue his medical training in Britain after Nixon left for Lucknow.

Born on 14 August 1899[52] into an aristocratic family, Alexander was the youngest son of Colonel Harvey Alexander,[53] an officer of the 10th Royal Hussars who was awarded the Distinguished Service Order for his service in the Boer War of 1899–1902, in which he was wounded twice.[54] Through his mother, Mildred Maria (née Prideaux-Brune), Alexander was also a direct descendent of Edward III,[55] king of England from 1327 to 1377.

Like Nixon he entered King's College from the RAF, though the war ended before he could see active service (Ashish, 84). Leaving King's with a bachelor of medicine (MB) degree,[56] Alexander continued his studies at St Thomas' Hospital in London, qualifying as a doctor in 1924,[57] and then joined the Indian Medical Service (IMS) to be close to his old friend and future godbrother (Ashish, 32).

Roy notes that Alexander, of whom he was fond, was distinguished both by his devotion to Nixon, whom he "idolised,"[58] and his skill as a doctor, being "respected by all for his ... his competence as a surgeon."[59] He was also admired by Jawaharlal Nehru, the first prime minister of India, who praised him as an "eminent surgeon,"[60] while his King's College obituary relates how on arriving in India he "quickly made a name for himself as a first-rate, and indeed a brilliant young doctor; 'such doctors,' men said, 'don't come to India.'"[61]

The young Dr Alexander's arrival in India came as Monica Chakravarti, the woman he would accept as his guru, finalised her plans to step away from married life in Benares and retire to the hills as a *vairāginī*, or Vaiṣṇava renunciate. In addition to her long-held desire to build a temple dedicated to Krishna and her dislike of the new house, Monica struggled with several long-term health conditions. Alexander, on examining the "fibroid tumours, gall stones, and numerous other ailments" (Ashish, 136), such as pleuritis (Ashish, 93), "which had been with her since early days" (Ashish, 136), gave her six months to live as early as 1930. These factors contributed to her decision to leave the family home. Madhava Ashish writes:

> It will have been at about the time of Chakravarti's retirement from Lucknow and the move back to Banaras that Monica began to feel increasingly the conflict between what she had understood of the spiritual nature of the universe, and the daily affairs of her household. Her own illness exacerbated these feelings, and her husband was also ill with high blood pressure from the strains of his work. Ronald had observed Chakravarti's ability to withdraw into himself in the middle of a long and boring meeting, and to emerge obviously rested, yet this could not compensate for the tensions he had to absorb.
>
> It is therefore not surprising that Monica began to think in terms of

> leaving the family, taking *sanyas,* and building the Krishna temple she had dreamed of since childhood. (Ashish, 65—66)

By this time the Chakravartis' youngest daughter, Arpita, was 12 years old and surrounded by "a bevy of adult women to look after her besides her father" (Ashish, 94). According to Madhava Ashish, Gyanendra Nath had already given his blessing to Monica's plan to found a temple and ashram away from their family. Moreover, Mr Chakravarti could not accompany his wife to the Himalayas due to high blood pressure, while she had been strongly advised by her doctors against spending another hot summer in the Indian plains (Ashish, 93).

For Nixon, meanwhile, the decision to accompany Monica to her new home "as her first [live-in] disciple had been taken when he left Lucknow" nearly two years earlier (Ashish, 94). This was easier said than done—the young professor had, after all, recently taken a job at BHU, and no sooner had he left Benares than was he "pursued by two-page telegrams from Malaviya," the vice-chancellor, "begging him to return" (Ashish, 93). A solution came in the form of a second Cambridge friend, George Poole, who arrived in India in late 1928.[62] Having agreed to take on the teaching assignment, Poole was duly furnished with a grateful Nixon's library of English literature (Ashish, 94).

Notes

[1]Mabel Collins, *Light on the Path: A Treatise* (Los Angeles: United Lodge of Theosophists, 1920), 47.

[2]Roy, *Yogi Sri Krishnaprem,* 55.

[3]SD Pandey, *Guru by Your Bedside: The Teachings of a Modern Seer* (Gurgaon: Penguin Books, 2003), 7.

[4]Seymour B. Ginsburg, *The Masters Speak: An American Businessman Encounters Ashish and Gurdjieff,* 1st Quest ed, (Wheaton: Quest Books, 2001), 13.

[5]Sri Madhava Ashish, 'The Guru as Exemplar of and Guide to the Term of Human Evolution,' in Satish Datt Pandey, Seymour Ginsburg, Seán Mahoney and Pervin Mahoney (eds), *What is Man?: Selected Writings of Sri Madhava Ashish* (Gurgaon: Penguin Books, 2010), 66.

[6]Ashish, 'Sri Sri Krishnaprem *Vairagi,*' 88.

[7]Dr. GP Bhatt (ed.), *The Padma-Purāṇa,* Part VI, (Delhi: Motilal Banarsidass, 2013), 1,996.

[8]Loyal Rue, *Religion is Not About God: How Spiritual Traditions Nurture Our Biological Nature and What to Expect When They Fail* (Piscataway: Rutgers University Press, 2005), 256.

[9]Roy, *Yogi Sri Krishnaprem,* 179.

[10]Shri Krishna Prem Bhikhari, 'The Yoga of the Gita,' *Kalyana-Kalpataru or The Bliss* (*Gita* Number) 2.1 (1935): para 11, https://gitaseva.org/kalyanskalpataru/gita-number-year-2-part-1 (accessed 13 August 2023).

[11]Krishna Prem, 'The Yoga of the Gita,' para 16.

[12]Ashish, 'Sri Krishna Prem Through the Eyes of a Disciple', 22.

[13]Ashish, 'Sri Krishna Prem Through the Eyes of a Disciple,' 22.

[14]Pandey, *Guru by Your Bedside*, 26.

[15]Ginsburg, *The Masters Speak*, 18.

[16]Sri Krishna Prem, *Initiation into Yoga: An Introduction to the Spiritual Life* (Wheaton: Quest Books, 1976), 35–36, cited in Ginsburg, *The Masters Speak*, 21.

[17]Sri Madhava Ashish, Letter to Andrew Rawlinson, 22 June 1988.

[18]Malcolm Tillis, 'Bill Aitken, Landour, Mussoorie, 20th December 1980,' *New Lives* (Shrewsbury: Malcolm Tillis, 2006), http://www.newlives.freeola.net/interviews/7-bill-aitken.php (accessed 2 April 2023).

[19]Madhu Tandan, *Faith & Fire: A Way Within* (Gurgaon: Harper Collins, 1997), 222.

[20]Madhava Ashish, *An Open Window: Dream as Everyman's Guide to the Spirit* (New Delhi: Penguin Books, 2007), xix.

[21]Rajeev Tandan, 'Metaphors and Quotes of Yashoda Mai' (summary of Sri Krishna Prem [trans.], *The Homeward Journey* [unpublished]), (Mirtola: Thakurji Sri Sri Krishna Trust, 2019), 4.

[22]*Ibid.*

[23]Tandan, 'Metaphors and Quotes of Yashoda Mai,' 3.

[24]Ashish, 'Sri Krishna Prem Through the Eyes of a Disciple,' 21.

[25]'Sri Krishna Prem,' in Gabriel Monod-Herzen and Jacqueline Benezech, *Qui est ton Maître? suivi de Notre ami Kédar* (France: Courrier du livre, 1977), http://www.monod-herzengabriel.fr/pdf/Qui%20est%20ton%20maitre2.pdf (accessed 17 January 2022).

[26]West, *The Life of Annie Besant*, 183.

[27]Judge held Chakravarti, whom he accused of being an agent of "Black Magicians" and of having "magnetized" (hypnotised) Besant, responsible for what he claimed were her deviations from the teachings of 'HPB' and the *Mahātmas*. The Theosophical Society split in 1895, with Besant remaining head of the original TS in Adyar and Judge leading the newly independent 'American Section.'

[28]William Q. Judge, *By Master's Direction*, (Blavatsky Study Center, 2000), para. 18, https://www.-blavatskyarchives.com/judgebmd1894.htm (accessed 18 April 2023).

[29]Jeffrey J. Kripal, *Kali's Child: The Mystical and the Erotic in the Life and Teachings of Ramakrishna*, 2nd ed, (Chicago: University of Chicago Press, 1998), 55.

[30]Jeffrey J. Kripal, *Serpent's Gift: Gnostic Reflections on the Study of Religion* (Chicago: University of Chicago Press, 2007), 103.

[31]Swami Prabhananda, *Journeys with Ramakrishna* (Chennai: Sri Ramakrishna Math, 2001), 51.

[32]Prabhananda, *Journeys with Ramakrishna*, 65.

[33]Charles Brooks, 'Gauḍīya Vaiṣṇavism in the Modern World,' in Steven J. Rosen (ed), *Vaiṣṇavism: Contemporary Scholars Discuss the Gauḍīya Tradition* (New York: FOLK Books, 1992), 152.

[34]Raghav Verma (ed), *Essays and Reflections by Karan Singh*, ebook ed, (Noida: HarperCollins, 2019), Part 4 ('Essays'), ch. 1, para. 44.

[35]Madhava Ashish, letter to Andrew Rawlinson, 22 June 1988.

[36]Roy, *Yogi Sri Krishnaprem*, 8–9.

[37]Mohita Tewari, 'How a Two-Room Memorial School Turned into a 225-Acre Lucknow University,' *The Times of India*, 11 November 2019, https://timesofindia.indiatimes.com/city/lucknow/how-a-two-room-memorial-school-turned-into-a-225-acre-lucknow-university (accessed 1 March 2022).

[38]Madhava Ashish, 'Sri Krishna Prem Through the Eyes of a Disciple', 22.

[39]*Ibid.*

[40]300 rupees.

[41]Roy, *Yogi Sri Krishnaprem*, 9.

[42]*Handbook of Indian Universities*, no 2, (Cawnpore: Inter-University Board, 1928), 56.

[43]Satyajit Ray, *Childhood Days: A Memoir* (New Delhi: Penguin Books India, 1998), 141.

[44]Roland Penrose, letter to Alec Penrose, 18 March 1933, Roland Penrose collection, Scottish National Gallery of Modern Art Archive, Edinburgh, RPA370.

[45]Brzezinski, 'Women Saints in Gauḍīya Vaiṣṇavism,' 78.

[46]In *Initiation into Yoga*, Krishna Prem defines *yoga* as "the method by which man can unite his finite self with Infinite Being."

[47]Roy, *Yogi Sri Krishnaprem*, 57.

[48]AN Banerji, letter to Sri Madhava Ashish, 6 June 1972.

[49]Bhakta Ramsharan Das Pilkhuva, स्त्य एवं प्रेरक घटनाएँ (*Satya Evaṃ Prerak Ghaṭanāeṅ*), 3rd ed, (Gorakhpur: Gita Press, 2015), 121.

[50]Singh, *Letters from Mirtola*, 32.

[51]'Robert Dudley Alexander (Sri Haridas)', 18.

[52]'England & Wales, Civil Registration Birth Index, 1837–1915,' *Ancestry*, Lehi, Ancestry.com Operations, 2006, https://www.ancestry.co.uk/search/collections/8912 (accessed 18 June 2023). Original data: General Register Office. *England and Wales Civil Registration Indexes*. (London, England: General Register Office). © Crown copyright.

[53]Hugh Montgomery-Massingberd (ed), *Burke's Irish Family Records* (London: Burke's Peerage, 1976), 15, cited in Darryl Lundy, 'Person Page – 25947' *The Peerage* (Wellington: Darryl Lundy, 2008), http://www.thepeerage.com/p25947.htm (accessed 15 March 2022).

[54]*Who's Who 1919: An Annual Biographical Dictionary with which is Incorporated "Men and Women of the Time"* (London: A&C Black, 1919), 27.

[55]The Marquis of Ruvigny and Raineval, *The Plantagenet Roll of The Blood Royal: The Clarence Volume, Containing the Descendants of George, Duke of Clarence* (London: TC & EC Jack, 1905), 516.

[56]*List of the Fellows, Members, Extra-licentiates and Licentiates of the Royal College of Physicians of London, and of Holders of the Diploma in Public Health, Granted Conjointly by the Royal Colleges of Physicians and Surgeons* (Cambridge: Cambridge University Press, 1956), 406.

[57]'Robert Dudley Alexander (Sri Haridas),' 18.

[58]Roy, *Yogi Sri Krishnaprem*, 74.

[59]*Ibid.*

[60]G. Parthasarathi (ed), *Jawaharlal Nehru: Letters to Chief Ministers*, Vol 2 (1950–1952), (New Delhi: Jawaharlal Nehru Memorial Fund, 1986), 561.

[61]'Robert Dudley Alexander (Sri Haridas),' 18.

[62]'UK and Ireland, Outward Passenger Lists, 1890–1960', *Ancestry*, Lehi, Ancestry.com Operations, 2012, https://www.ancestry.co.uk/search/collections/2997 (accessed 31 March 2022). Original data: Board of Trade: Commercial and Statistical Department and successors: Outwards Passenger Lists. BT27. Records of the Commercial, Companies, Labour, Railways and Statistics Departments. Records of the Board of Trade and of successor and related bodies. The National Archives, Kew, Richmond, Surrey, England.

7: Vairāgī

"Professor Nixon? Oh, he died long ago."
— Sri Krishna Prem

With both guru and disciple released from their material responsibilities, the pair set about finding a suitable location for a temple to Krishna. They had decided on Almora, the site of numerous previous family holidays (including the formative trip with Nixon around five years prior) and where the Chakravartis had friends; they originally moved into a rented bungalow on the edge of town while they looked for a site for the temple (Ashish, 93). The house, called Chilkapita, was later home to the writer and tantrika Barry Long, who stayed for six months in 1965,[1] and musician Chris Jagger, the younger brother of Rolling Stone Mick. Chris Jagger remembers Chilkapita as standing "alone, looking out across a steep valley that dropped to a river below. It was surrounded by pine trees that were robbed of their vigour by the practice of gashing the trunk to bleed sap into a waiting cup. Life went on much as it had for centuries. Our firewood was carried there on the backs of strong Sherpas and, without electricity, all was peace and quiet."[2]

After the disappointment of Radha Vilas, Monica wasted no time in establishing a proper *pūjā* room in the new house dedicated to Krishna, represented by the Italian marble statue she had brought from Benares. Though initially the only idol at Chilkapita, Krishna was soon joined by Monica's other *mūrtis*; after she heard that the home temple she had left behind was again being neglected in her absence, she "promptly ordered Ronald to go down and bring all the images up to Almora" (Ashish, 94).

With Monica overseeing spiritual matters, Nixon set to work making Chilkapita into a suitable temporary home for the pair. Though he "could be derisive about the 'nuts and bolts' conversations held between mechanically or technically minded people"—which Madhava Ashish says he called "'talking about sproglets,' an invented word" (107)—Nixon was good with his hands. Monica was delighted with a bookcase he made for her out of thin packing-case planks, and brought it to Mirtola in 1930 (Ashish, 108).

The seat of the medieval kings of Kumaon, the town of Almora is located at an altitude of around 5,500 feet (1,640m) on a ridge at the southern edge of the Kumaon Himalayan range, where it serves as capital of an eponymous district of the modern state of Uttarakhand. In the first half of the 20th century it was, like neighbouring Ranikhet and Naini Tal, part of the United Provinces of British India, but attracted a crowd very different from other Kumaoni 'hill stations' developed by British officialdom as summer resorts or military cantonments.

Ian Melville Stephens, the editor of the *Statesman* of Calcutta, who stayed at Kundan House (the Almora home of Boshi and Gertrude Emerson Sen) in 1943, describes Almora as a "socially extraordinary" place a world apart from towns such as Simla, Murree, Dalhousie and Ranikhet, which "lacked character and seemed half-smothered by officialdom," and Mussoorie, with its objectionably "raffish 'palais de danse' atmosphere."[3] "Visitors from Europe perhaps unkindly wrote them all off as mere projections into the Indian scene of the British suburbia you'd find near Aldershot or Chatham," Stephens writes,

> made the more absurd by being set in Himalayan landscapes so stupendously big and beautiful. An outstanding exception, however, was Almora: like the rest of them indeed partly military in origin and it had some Gurkhas still, but in the 1930's and early '40's so socially extraordinary, attracting to itself painters and scientists, musicians, ballet-dancers, mystics, Orientalized Westerners who'd become Hindus or thought they had. ...[4]

Other Westerners who made Almora their home included the American painters Earl and Achsah Barlow Brewster, the German-born Tibetan Buddhist Anagarika Govinda (Ernst Hoffmann) and his Indian Parsi wife, Li Gotami (Ratti Petit), and the eccentric Danish mystic Alfred 'Sunyata' Sorensen, a "cross between a Hindu *sannyāsi* and a Buddhist *bhikku*"[5] whose stone hut bore a sign reading "NO VISITORS, SILENCE."[6] The Sens, meanwhile, served as Almora's "social hub; the solid axis round which its various eccentrics revolved."[7] Most of these artists, writers and spiritual seekers lived on the pine-covered Kasar Devi ridge, above the town proper, in an area nicknamed 'Cranks' Ridge' (later 'Hippie Hill'[8]) on the way to the ancient Kasar Devi temple. "The inmates in and around the Ridge lead solitary lives," observed Sunyata, who was close to Monica and called her his foster mother.[9] "They are friendly but inclined to avoid social mix-up. Attuned to silence, they do not favour listening to the radio. They study Sanskrit, yoga, abstract painting and indulge in other spiritual pursuits."[10]

The British traveller Anne Marshall, who stayed in a house formerly occupied by 'Omraam' Mikhaël Aïvanhov, of the esoteric Universal White Brotherhood, recalls that the first person she met when she arrived in Almora "was a South American in a grey suit and topee, who solemnly assured me that Jesus Christ still lived, and that every June he visited him in his mountain retreat. He was even now on his way. This Jesus was a beautiful, red-haired person who looked perennially youthful."[11] She also befriended Sunyata, "by far the most sociable person on the ridge and a great one for dropping in at tea-time,"[12] and his terrier, Wuji, the goats' bells around whose throat could be heard from his house a mile away.

Bill Aitken attributes the town's unique atmosphere to its "orthodox brahminical culture," which was "so secure in its own esteem that it did not see these exotic outsiders as any threat to local *dharma* [the moral-religious order]."[13] He explains: "Almora is unique for its '*lumbi dhoti*' brahmins—those families entitled to wear long cotton nether wraps, and possessed of extraordinary intellect. They were sought as prime ministers of princely states for their administrative acumen. ... The great thing about the Almora pundits [Hindu scholars] is their open mindedness. Secure in their own beliefs and unafraid of missionaries of any faith, they open are to exchange with other seekers."[14]

Though famous for its contingent of Western eccentrics, Almora, points out KM Munshi, had been attracting indigenous "great men in search of the Spirit"[15] since at least Shankara's time (eighth century AD), including, in modern times, Gandhi, Tagore, and Swamis Vivekananda and Rama Tirtha.[16] One visiting soldier, a Captain Bhattacharya (the aide-de-camp to Munshi, then the governor of Uttar Pradesh), said that during his three-day visit in 1952 he met more *sādhus* "than in all his life.... They talk about Kailas"—the snowy Himalayan peak believed to be the abode of the Hindu god Shiva—"as if it was their back yard," he marvelled.[17]

Although Cranks' Ridge was briefly considered as a potential location for the Krishna temple, Monica, writes Madhava Ashish, "wanted quiet and privacy" (Ashish, 95) of the kind that could not be had living amid a burgeoning bohemian colony. Monod-Herzen elaborates:

> Sri Yashoda Maï already enjoyed a reputation for holiness, and one can imagine the curiosity added to this by the presence of an English disciple with her! Within a short time, two hundred requests for horoscopes and talismans arrived daily at their "retreat," so Sri Yashoda Maï decided to leave Almora for a more secluded location.[18]

Additionally, the new temple would have shared a spring with Kasar Devi, "where troops from the Gurkha regiment in Almora would wash after performing animal sacrifice—a state of affairs that could not be tolerated in a Vaiṣṇava temple. Besides, it was so conveniently close to Almora that people out for an evening stroll would constantly be dropping in" (Ashish, 95).

As a *brahmachārī*, or celibate student, Nixon was expected to beg for food[19] for himself and his guru in Almora, with the goal of learning "humility and self-abasement."[20] This, as Madhava Ashish records, he did for a year.[21] Meanwhile, the search for land for the temple continued.

Before leaving for Almora, Nixon had met with John Albert Chadwick (1899–1939), an old colleague also preparing to swap his British academic's robes for those of an Indian *sādhu*. Chadwick's life to this point in many ways resembled Nixon's—he had also served in World War One, studied moral science at Cambridge, and taught at the University of Lucknow, where he was professor of philosophy from 1927 to 1929[22]—and Chadwick had been inspired by Nixon to seek out a guru of his own, as his godbrother Dilip Kumar Roy explains:

> He had been profoundly stirred by Krishnaprem's pure and one-pointed aspiration for the Grace of the Guru, the more so as he also had longed, like Krishnaprem, to accept a Guru. Happily for me, he came to be swept off his feet by Sri Aurobindo, whom he accepted, once and for all, as the keeper of his soul, insomuch, that, after his surrender to Sri Aurobindo, he never once looked back...[23]

Both men also shared a deep distrust in what Roy calls the "materialistic civilisation of the West,"[24] with Chadwick, characterised by other residents of Sri Aurobindo Ashram as "stiff but polite,"[25] having been similarly affected by his time in the military; his friend, the philosopher Charlie Dunbar Broad, writes that this "man of singular beauty and refinement"[26] had been left with "scars on his spirit" by the "horrors of war" and "the stupidity and malevolence of the subsequent peace."[27]

Nixon did not see Chadwick again after 1928, though he did write the foreword to his posthumously published book of poetry, *Poems by Arjava* (1941), whose title features the name Chadwick received from Sri Aurobindo, Arjavananda (Arjava for short), meaning the "joy of straightforwardness."[28] Suffering from "a complex of illnesses which were mysterious in origin and a nightmare to diagnose for Nirodbaran [Talukdar], the Ashram doctor, but which were very concrete in their ravaging effects,"[29] Arjava died in 1939—but not before undergoing what Nixon (now Krishna Prem) describes favourably as a "profound psychic transformation in his nature [that is] clear from the fact that he, whose language had hitherto been limited to the arid propositions of intellectual philosophy, became a poet:"[30]

> It must be now twelve years since Chadwick and I sat together on the banks of the Ganges at Benares, talking far into the night of dreams that lay close to our hearts, dreams that had brought us together as they had brought us both to India. ...
>
> Once more we met in a university bungalow at Lucknow, a background that we both felt to be an utter irrelevance, and then we departed, I to the North and he to the South where he had found his Guru in Sri Aurobindo. There, in the Ashram at Pondicherry, he lived for the past ten years, shedding at the feet of his Guru the burden of all that the world counts valuable in order to find the hidden treasure for which most men have no eyes.[31]

Just as Chadwick had been "profoundly stirred" by Nixon's Vaishnava initiation and his acceptance of Monica as his spiritual master, for Roy it was the news, delivered by a mutual friend in Lucknow, that "Krishnaprem had 'gone the whole hog and actually taken to begging for his food in Almora'"[32] that began the process of his abandoning the life of a secular musician for that of a *sādhaka* (spiritual seeker), devotional composer and, later, a guru in his own right.

> It affected me so vitally because it involved a kind of psychological shame of feeling that, do what I would, I dare not go to this length. ... I could not, indeed, help admiring his courage and *audace*, but nevertheless I felt sad to imagine him actually going a-begging for his daily food. Neither could I dismiss from my mind his young wistful face which shone, mirroring his luminous soul. To think that the robust intellectual who used only the other day to drive on a motorcycle at a break-neck speed through the streets of Lucknow, with me in his side-car, should be literally going about now from house to house begging for a bare handful of rice and possibly turned away by some irate householders who looked upon such vagrants as definitely harmful parasites of society! And then, everything in Lucknow reminded me of him: his friends and mine, the University grounds where we had strolled together arm-in-arm, the tea-parties which I had to attend now without him, the musical soirées where I had to sing without his dear, eager presence—in short, every scene rebuked

> me sternly for having stopped short where he had taken a leap into the dark, trusting to the Divine Compassion alone to see to his safe landing. In the end, his absence began to haunt me so much that it would hardly be an exaggeration to claim that what he had achieved at one bound gave me just that decisive push which I needed to go over the edge staking everything that does not matter for the one thing which does.[33]

By November 1928, Roy—scion of an aristocratic, artistic family, graduate of Presidency College, Calcutta, and Cambridge University, and "one of the leading lights of the Indian Renaissance"[34]—had also joined Sri Aurobindo Ashram in Pondicherry, south India, where he remained until 1952. In the words of the poet and ashram resident KD Sethna, "it was through the pointing finger of this Indianised Westerner that Dilip Kumar Roy the Westernised Indian first turned his eyes towards Sri Aurobindo who is the perfect synthesis of East and West."[35]

Other notable figures for whom Nixon's example served as an inspiration for their own spiritual quests include Bede Griffiths, the British-born Christian *sannyāsī*,[36] the Indian yoga guru Swami Rama, who spoke of being inspired by Nixon (now Krishna Prem)'s love for his guru,[37] and Shivanath, the scholar of the Dogri language of Kashmir, who wrote that his meeting with Krishna Prem in 1952 "rekindled my interest in spirituality and devotion."[38]

Back in Almora, the hunt for a more secluded spot for the temple had by 1930 led 'Ma' and 'Gopal' to focus their attention on the smaller villages and settlements away from the town proper. "The longer they hunted, the more difficult it seemed to become, and they covered quite a lot of ground" (Ashish, 95—96). Binsar, the lofty former summer capital of Kumaon's Chand dynasty rulers where Bertram Keightley now owned a house, was rejected as too British, while a promising property supposedly located in Panuanaula was actually deep in a valley below, where malaria was rife and the climate uncomfortable (Ashish, 96). Deflated, they made the serendipitous decision to push on from Panuanaula to visit the ancient Shiva temple complex at Jageshwar, a route that took them past the village of Mirtola. Madhava Ashish continues the story:

> On the way the local men who had been hired to carry Yashoda Mai's dandi or carrying chair told them there was land for sale just above the bridle path on which they were travelling. They climbed up about

> one hundred feet through pine forest and came out onto a (by hill standards) large flat field, with the hill stretching out in a semi-circle above them. There was water in the ravine a hundred yards ahead. 'This is it,' she said. ...
>
> Then began a prolonged and ultimately successful negotiation to obtain possession of the land. (Ashish, 96—97)

Now accessible by a motor road which brings pilgrims to the ashram with which it's become synonymous, Mirtola in 1930 was reachable only by a nearly 30km bridle path which served to place "an effective barrier between them and all but the most determined traveller."[39] At that time, the village "consisted only of a large double-storeyed hill house and a smaller building nearby," explains Aitken:

> Strategically sited on a steep hill on the main bridlepath between Almora and the Nepal border, the hill house became a Post Office for the surrounding villages. In splendid isolation the smaller building was rented out by the low-caste owners as a lodging for high-caste administrators and colonial shikaris [hunters] for dirty weekends off the beaten track.[40]

The temple was ultimately constructed some 200 feet higher than the field first identified by Monica, closer to the centre of the estate's farmland (Ashish, 107), as Madhava Ashish describes:

> The site finally chosen for the temple is at just about 7,000 feet above sea level and with a south-west aspect. The hill rises behind it for another 200 to 500 feet, so the morning sun reaches it late but, as a compensation, it is protected from the north and gets any sun there is from around nine in the morning till it sets on the western horizon some fifty miles away. To see the great Himalayan snow peaks one must walk two miles up the hill, and then, if one is fortunate, one has a view of the range stretching from horizon to horizon, with the magnificent peak of Nanda Devi in the middle. (Ashish, 106—107)

The day Monica found the place she would call home for the next 14 years—"twenty miles away by bridle path on the other side of a deep valley" from Kasar Devi, "a white spot high up on a wooded hill"[41]—after a nearly two-year search, was naturally considered an auspicious one, and the decision was made that day to initiate 'Gopal' as a *vairāgī*, a Vaiṣṇava renunciate (Ashish, 97). Monica "had a long history of interaction with the temple Goswamis [hereditary Brahmin priests] at Radha-Raman" Temple in Vrindavan[42]—the pilgrimage town where, in the 16th century, Vaiṣṇava saints such as Chaitanya, Hit Harivansh and Vallabhacharya 'rediscovered' the sites of Krishna's childhood pastimes and identified them with Vraja,[43] the idylic pastoral playground described in the *Bhāgavata Purāṇa*. Monica had herself recently been given *vairāgya* initiation (the word literally means a state devoid of attachment, or *rāga*, for worldly desires or things) by her guru/husband Gyanendra Chakravarti (Ashish, 96), who had been acting under the guidance of one of the Vrindavan temple's hereditary priests, Bal Krishna Goswami. In addition to authorising the somewhat unorthodox ceremony—with large families, both men were 'householders' and not renunciates, and so would usually be considered unqualified to initiate a new *vairāginī*—Bal Krishna also established the form of worship for Sri Krishna Vilas, the new Radha–Krishna temple at the heart of the Mirtola ashram (Ashish, 64), aka the new Vrindavan.

Despite his health problems and advancing years, the then 69-year-old Chakravarti personally made the 500-mile journey from Benares to Almora to invest his wife with the saffron robes he had been given by Bal Krishna for the occasion. "Bal Krishna Maharaj at Brindaban ... had himself given her the gairik vastra [ochre robes]," writes Madhava Ashish, "though it was agreed that Chakravarti as her original Guru would actually dress her in the cloth. Chakravarti had intended to stay at least a fortnight in Almora, but the altitude (almost 6,000 feet above sea level) caused him so much trouble from blood pressure that he hurried away after performing the ceremony" (Ashish, 96).

Monica was given the name Sri Yashoda Mai (or Ma),[44] after Yashoda, Krishna's mother (*ma[i]*) in Vraja,[45] while Ronald Henry 'Gopal' Nixon became Sri Krishna Prem[46] (literally "Love of Krishna" in Sanskrit[47]) in a ceremony performed "in the jungle below the site" chosen for the temple (Ashish, 97). In a Mirtola context, the honorific title 'Sri,' denoting prosperity and beauty, was affixed to the names of renunciates:[48] For example, as a *brahmachārī* Sri Madhava Ashish was named Dev Ashish, while Bob Alexander, prior to becoming Sri Haridas, was known as Ananda Priya.

In existing histories of Mirtola, Krishna Prem's *vairāgya* initiation is usually referred to as his taking *sannyāsa*, and the terms are often used interchangeably (the male gurus, for example, are more usually described as *sannyāsīs* rather than *vairāgīs*, and Yashoda Mai and Moti Rani as *sannyāsinīs* and not *vairāginīs*).

However, as Madhava Ashish clarifies: "The Vaiṣṇava form of Sannyas, Vairagya (detachment), differs from the Dasnami (Shankaracharya) form which can be given only by a Sannyasi. Properly the Vaiṣṇava form is not called Sannyas. It is called Vairagya, and the recipient is a Vairagi (feminine Vairagini). As in Christianity where a priest takes the cloth, so the Vaiṣṇava takes Vesha (the cloth)."[49]

Additionally, unlike the classical *daśanāmī* (ten-name) tradition of renunciation described by Madhava Ashish (which involves initiation into a formal 'Order of Swamis' rather than a loose category of Viśṇu/Kṛṣṇa-worshipping ascetics), Vaiṣṇava *vairāgīs* or *bābājīs* traditionally wear white, rather than *gairik vastra* [ochre]—and, unlike *sannyāsīs*, are not required to conduct their own death ceremony as part of the initiation, which would render them as "untouchable as a dead body and therefore unfit to perform puja or yagna"[50] (fire sacrifice).

It is clear, then, that Monica, having already headed to the hills with the blessing of her unorthodox initiating guru—the Westernised, meat-eating, Shakta–Theosophist Gyanendra Nath Chakravarti—desired for her final years a kind of lifestyle which did not fit neatly into any existing tradition of Hindu renunciation.

This is confirmed by Shrivatsa Goswami, the current *acharya* of the Radha-Raman Temple, who says Yashoda Mai's *vairāgya* ceremony would not have involved the awarding of *sannyāsa* proper (complete with mock funeral ceremony) as her initiator was not himself a *sannyāsī*. "Yashoda Mai and Krishna Prem lived an ascetic life without taking official *sannyāsa*," says Goswami, who belongs to a 450-year-old familial lineage established by the disciples of Gopal Bhatta Goswami, a direct disciple of the founder of the Gauḍīya Vaiṣṇava tradition, Chaitanya Mahaprabhu (1486-1533). Bal Krishna might, he says, have established a novel "system of *vairāgi-dīkṣā*" for the pair "that he called *sannyāsa*," and which involved the awarding of certain *mantras*, and ochre or yellow robes,[51] but could not have given them formal *sannyāsa*.[52]

Madhu Tandan was initially mystified by the ashram's conception of *sannyāsa*, which, she writes, she had associated with "wandering mendicants with matted hair and ash-smeared bodies, bound by a religious tradition which had little regard for the progress being made by mankind."[53] She explains that her guru had redefined the *sannyāsa aśrama*, the final of the traditional four stages of life in Hinduism, as the period when the

> ego is slowly withdrawn from activity as the individual ponders over the purpose of experience and accepts a phase of quiet withdrawal. Built around actualizing its capacity, the ego must at this stage be sieved and distilled as the individuality pursues a more in-turned

> principle. For that is what life is about—the development of the ego and then offering it to a principle larger than itself. When that is done then *sanyas*, or the ochre cloth, is donned. ... "Initiation, the disciple asks for, but *sanyas* (the robe) the guru has to offer you," [Ashishda] had said.[54]

Funeral rites or not, Krishna Prem treated his first 'death' as very real, according to his friend Gertrude Emerson Sen, in that it marked the end of one life and the beginning of another. She relates the following anecdote:

> Once someone came up to [Krishna Prem] in a street and, obviously guessing his identity, inquired pointedly if he could tell him where "Professor Nixon" was. He merely turned away, answering casually, "Oh, he died long ago."[55]

While the exact details of Yashoda Mai's, and in turn Krishna Prem's, *vairāgi-dīkṣā* ceremony are known only to the three people involved, there are certain rules traditionally followed by Vaishnava *vairāgīs*, as laid down in the *Samskāra Dīpikā*, a manual for aspiring renunciates, putatively written by Bal Krishna's antecedent, Gopal Bhatta Goswami (1503–1578):

> He must spend time at Brindāban, and consort only with Vaishṇavas. ... He must not take water from a non-Vaishṇava, or receive anything which has not been offered to Kṛishṇa. He must not take food offered to any other god, and must not swear in Hari [Krishna]'s name even if his life be at stake! He is required to observe ... in all things the practices of an ekāntin [devoted] Vaishṇava, i.e. one who has forsaken all other gods except Kṛishṇa. He must rid his mind of all ideas of possession, and adjust himself to the life of a vairāgī.[56]

Melville Kennedy, writing from his position as warden at the Calcutta YMCA in 1925, points out another text, the *Bhekāśrita Tattva Grantha*, in which he finds specific rules for a *vairāgī* living as a mendicant, as Krishna Prem did for a year in Almora:

> Whatever is received without begging is considered best of all; that which is begged from door to door is next in value; while that which is obtained by begging from the rich is of least value. Begging should not take place on fast days, or on days of new and full moon; it is likewise prohibited on the banks of or on the Ganges, or any river, in the

> market, or in a desert place. Land, silver, rice, cloth or gold should not be received. Food offered at the śrāddha ceremony [rites for the dead] is taboo. The village priest, a wine merchant, a Chaṇḍāla [untouchable], or other low-caste person, and a *Mleccha* [foreigner] should not be approached.[57]

Kennedy also notes, however, that Vaiṣṇava *vairāgī* is also to be distinguished from classical Hindu *sannyāsa* in that there are no caste restrictions on taking *vairāgya*: even the lowest in society—including, in Krishna Prem's case, a *mleccha* (non-Indian) with no caste at all—"are entitled to enter the ascetic life. This is essentially different from the various *sannyāsī* orders into which no *Śūdra* [member of the labouring class] may enter."[58]

Krishna Prem's own thoughts on *vairāgya* can be found in an article on Shankara's 'Fourfold Path' ('*Sadhanā Chatustaya*' [sic]) for spiritual seekers which he contributed to *Kalyana-Kalpataru*, an English-language periodical published by Gita Press of Gorakhpur, in 1936, and which was later collected in *The Search for Truth* (1938). Writing about the second of these four practices, also called the 'four means of salvation' (the others being *viveka*, the power to discriminate between the real and the unreal; *Ṣaṭ-sampatti*, the six aspects of mental control; and *mumukṣutva*, the desire for liberation), Krishna Prem speaks of his conception of *vairāgya* as an essentially inner detachment which may or may not be accompanied by the outer trappings often associated with Indian renunciates:

> *Vairāgya*, detachment, is a word which conjures up in our minds the picture of ascetics, naked and perhaps smeared with ashes, filled with disgust for the world, leaving wife and children to go and dwell in burning grounds or remote Himalayan caves. But this is to confuse *vairāgya* with one of its occasional manifestations. *Vairāgya* does not mean disgust for the world nor an abandonment of duties and responsibilities, but detachment from the world and a detached performance of duties, and it can be as highly developed in the busy householder as in the carefree wandering ascetic. ...
>
> True *vairāgya* consists, not in the contemplation of decaying corpses and such like sights but in an inner detachment from all things that are temporary, from pleasant things no less than from painful ones. The *vairāgī* is one who sees that both pleasure and pain are feelings which serve certain purposes in evolution and who refuses to allow his inner self to be attracted or repelled by them.[59]

He elaborates on this idea in *The Yoga of the Bhagavat Gita* (1938), where he explains that the *vairāgi(nī)* is a yogi who has taken the "desire-prompted actions of the worldly, the enthusiasm and zest of youth and the tireless energy of the ambitious" and "transmuted [them] into something higher."[60] "The true '*vairāgī*,'" then, "is not a dull, dried-up, 'holy' person of the type that has made the very name of religion a thing of nausea to so many of us, but a tireless fountain of joyful and inspired life based on the eternal *ānanda* [bliss] of the *Brahman* [ultimate reality] which overflows into creation out of Its own inherent fullness."[61]

Having completed a "prolonged and ultimately successful negotiation to obtain possession of the land" for the ashram (Ashish, 97), Yashoda Mai gave orders to move:

> They had come to Almora in 1928 and it was now 1930. The day the proceedings were completed, ... [t]hey set out in pouring rain with the image of Sri Krishna carried in a Palki (palanquin or sedan chair). The town hardly knew they had gone, but by the time they reached open country at the upper end of the town the weather cleared and the deity's eighteen-mile journey was accomplished in style, with shankhs [conches] blowing and gongs ringing. (Ashish, 97)

The idol of Krishna was installed temporarily in the veranda of an old two-storey house, renamed the post office, while Yashoda Mai and Krishna Prem took up residence in a "newer but rather badly built single room 'bungalow' with a tin roof which the previous owner had built for the entertainment of officials on tour" (Ashish, 98). To construct the temple building, which she named Sri Krishna Vilas, Yashoda Mai recruited a Eurasian engineer, a Mr Rochefort (known as 'Engineer Sahib') from Mukteswar, near Naini Tal, whose British father had sent him to the engineering college at Roorkee (now the Indian Institute of Technology). "Whether he had learned anything there is another matter," writes Sri Madhava Ashish, "for in later years massive beams of reinforced concrete have had to be removed from the temple building, sometimes because they were cracking in the middle, and it was found that all the reinforcement was at the top of the beam where it adds little or nothing to the strength (Ashish, 98)."

> However, he was certainly able to call up masons, carpenters and other skilled workers from all over the place. Without him it is doubtful if the work could ever have been done within the limited range of

> funds at Yashoda Mai's and Krishna Prem's disposal. All the personal money they had went into the formation of the Trust under which the temple and ashram were to run, and the entire lot was spent by the time the temple was completed. (Ashish, 98)

Yashoda Mai afterwards received 300 rupees per month from Chakravarti and, later, from her husband's estate (Ashish, 98—99).

There were, Madhava Ashish continues, further "minor excitements during the year it took to build the temple: a new quarry of building stone being opened, deodar [cedar] planks and beams arriving from the Jageswar forest, men making lime from local limestone with fire blown by a primitive bellows of a whole buffalo hide. And some workmen attempted to rob the money from the wall almirah [cupboard] where it was kept by cleverly digging away the rubble wall behind it" (Ashish, 99—100). However, Krishna Vilas was completed, and in 1931 Yashoda Mai gave orders for consecrating the temple and installing the deity.

She entrusted this task to Badrinarayan Acharya, a Hindu priest from Ghazipore whom she had known as a child. Despite being so ill she "believed she might die that day" (Ashish, 104), she had given instructions that if she did, news must not reach Badrinarayan at the temple, as the *pratiṣṭhā* ceremony invoking Krishna in the *vigraha* would have been called off. In the event, the ceremony was cancelled after the Krishna statue, the soft Italian marble rescued from the Banares *pūjā* room, lost a finger, and the priest was unwilling to wait for a replacement (Ashish, 104). "[T]he breaking of a finger," relates Madhava Ashish, "was interpreted to mean that the Lord wished to be to worshipped in the dual form" (Ashish, 105)—Krishna alongside his lover, Radha, chief of the gopis (milkmaids) of Vraja—and George Poole was sent to Vrindavan to obtain new images of the divine couple. The new deities, cast in eight-metal *aṣṭadhātu* (gold, silver, copper, lead, zinc, tin, iron and mercury) were named Thakurji Sri Sri Krishna Sri Sri Radhika Mohan, or Radhikamohanji[62] for short. (*Ṭhākur*, roughly 'Lord', is a common Bengali name for Krishna; Mohan is another name for Krishna meaning attractive or charming, while Radhika is a name of Radha.) The deities were installed by Krishna Prem himself (Ashish, 105) in a ceremony also attended by, among others, Shanti Lal Trivedi, a Gandhian activist "who [had] the reputation of having organised all the wool spinning and weaving in the Kumaon" (Ashish, 260). The marble icon of Krishna was placed in Yashoda Mai's *samādhi mandir* (memorial shrine) after her death in 1944.[63]

Having completed the remaining 18 months of his (originally Krishna Prem's) teaching contract at Banaras Hindu University, George Poole became one of the first residents of the ashram that developed at Mirtola, which was named

Uttar Brindaban, or the Northern Brindaban (Vrindavan). (The 'other' Vrindavan is located in India's northern plains, around 100 miles south-east of Delhi.) Both Poole—"a handsome scholar and artist"[64] whose articles appeared in the Theosophical journal *The Aryan Path* alongside Krishna Prem's[65] and who studied painting with the Brewsters in Almora—and Bob Alexander became students of Yashoda Mai (though Alexander would not join the ashram until 1938). Poole also helped Krishna Prem tutor Moti Rani in English and philosophy, the youngest Chakravarti having spent much of the school holidays at Uttar Brindaban prior to moving to the ashram permanently after her father's death.

Other early residents of the makeshift ashram at Mirtola included Sushil Maharaj, a Bengali *brahmachārī* disciple of Yashoda Mai, and Radharani Devi, one of the Chakravartis' disciples in Bareilly, who built a small stone cottage (later occupied by Moti Rani) at Uttar Brindaban before returning to a temple in the plains, to live as a *vairāginī* in more familiar surroundings (Ashish, 78).

In addition to the full-time ashramites, the congregation included a number of peasants from the neighbouring village, who considered themselves "lay disciples" of Yashoda Mai and offered their services to the ashram.[66] (Between "friends and disciples ... the distinction was not always very clear," reflects Madhava Ashish.[67])

While 'Ma,' having renounced family life, did not want the responsibility of managing a large estate, "the privacy and independence she did want could not be had without the fifteen acres of cultivable land that came with Mirtola village," writes Madhava Ashish, "and its forty-five acres of pasture and forest which fed the one perennial spring," fitted with a hydraulic ram by Krishna Prem (Ashish, 115). She resigned herself to taking on once again some of the responsibilities of a housewife, including stocking a store room with Bengali-style food for residents and visitors (after the food was offered to Radha–Krishna and consecrated as *bhoga*). A first-aid dispensary (with Yashoda Mai offering homoeopathic preparations and Alexander, on his frequent visits to Mirtola, dispensing modern medicine), as well as a school for local boys, completed the picture.

Notes

[1]Barry Long Foundation, 'Chilkapita, near Almora, India,' *Barry Long Bulletin* [blog], 28 June 2014, https://barrylongbulletin.tumblr.com/post/90142608660 (accessed 1 April 2022).

[2]Chris Jagger, *Talking to Myself*, ebook ed, (Berlin: BMG Rights Management, 2021), ch. 10: 'Mother Ganga,' sec.: 'Mountain Life,' para. 2.

[3]Stephens, *Monsoon Morning*, 131.

[4]Stephens, *Monsoon Morning*, 131–132.

[5]Anne Marshall, *Hunting the Guru in India*, (London: Victor Gollancz, 1963), 144.

[6]Rawlinson, *The Book of Enlightened Masters*, 529.

[7]Stephens, *Monsoon Morning*, 132.

[8]Bill Aitken notes that later Western visitors were less welcome than the original residents of the ridge: "The personalities and lifestyle of the foreign characters on Cranks' Ridge [were] perceived by the locals as respectful of their religion, especially as Yashoda Mai [through GN Chakravarti], Gopalda and Bob [Alexander] had academic status; the reverse of the later hippie onrush in search of *marihuana* growing wild on Almora's municipal rubbish heaps."

[9]Gurubaksh Rai, 'A Short Biography', in *Sunyata, Dancing with the Void: The Innerstandings of a Rare-born Mystic*, 1st Indian ed, (Delhi: New Age Books, 2004), xxx.

[10]Rai, 'A Short Biography,' xxxiv.

[11]Marshall, *Hunting the Guru in India*, 140–141.

[12]Marshall, *Hunting the Guru in India*, 143.

[13]Bill Aitken, *Footloose in the Himalayas* (Delhi: Permanent Black, 2003), 42.

[14]Bill Aitken, email to the author, 24 June 2021.

[15]Munshi, *Janu's Death and Other Kulapati's Letters*, 53.

[16]Munshi, *Janu's Death and Other Kulapati's Letters*, 54.

[17]*Ibid.*

[18]Monod-Herzen, 'Sri Krishna Prem, Yogi et Théosophe.'

[19]"The *Brahmachari* after *upanayana* [sacred thread ceremony] is required 'to beg alms according to the prescribed rules' (Manu II.48-50)." B. Kuppuswamy, 'Concept of Begging in Ancient Thought,' *Indian Journal of Social Work* 39.2 (1978), 188.

[20]Falconar, *Sufi Literature and the Journey to Immortality*, 150.

[21]Madhava Ashish, 'Sri Sri Krishnaprem Vairagi,' 88.

[22]CD Broad, 'John Albert Chadwick, 1899–1939,' *Mind* 49.194 (1940), 130.

[23]Roy, *Yogi Sri Krishnaprem*, 60.

[24]*Ibid.*

[25]Georges Van Vrekhem, *The Mother: The Story of Her Life* (Site of Sri Aurobindo's & Mother's Yoga, 2014), Part 9, Ch. 3, https://www.aurobindo.ru/workings/other/van-vrekhem-mother.htm (accessed 30 November 2022).

[26]Broad, 'John Albert Chadwick, 1899–1939,' 131.

[27]Broad, 'John Albert Chadwick, 1899–1939,' 129.

[28]Amal Kiran (KD Sethna), 'The Inspiration and Art of John A. Chadwick,' *Mother India* 69.7 (2016), 522.

[29]Van Vrekhem, *The Mother*, Part 9, Ch. 3.

[30]Sri Krishna Prem, Foreword, in JA Chadwick, *Poems by Arjava*, (London: JM Watkins, 1941), cited in Roy, *Yogi Sri Krishnaprem*, 61–62.

[31]Roy, *Yogi Sri Krishnaprem*, 61.

[32]Roy, *Yogi Sri Krishnaprem*, 10.

[33]Roy, *Yogi Sri Krishnaprem*, 10–11.

[34]Dr Amrita Paresh Patel, *A Lover of Light Among Luminaries: Dilip Kumar Roy* (Ahmedabad: LD Institute of Indology, 2002), 3.

[35]KD Sethna, *The Indian Spirit and the World's Future* (Pondicherry: Sri Aurobindo Ashram Press, 1953), 281.

[36]Thomas A. Forsthoefel, 'Bede Griffiths and the Gītā,' *Journal of Vaiṣṇava Studies*, 16.1 (2007), 79.

[37]Swami Rama, *Living with the Himalayan Masters*, 18th printing (Honesdale: Himalayan Institute Press, 2007), 367.

[38]Shivanath, *Mosaic of Life (Award-winning Collection of Dogri Essays)* (New Delhi: Sahitya Akademi, 2014), 33.

[39]Madhava Ashish, 'Sri Sri Krishnaprem Vairagi,' 89.

[40]Aitken, email to the author, 2 July 2023.

[41]Madhava Ashish, 'Sri Krishna Prem through the eyes of a disciple,' 9.

[42]Charles R. Brooks, *The Hare Krishnas in India*, (Princeton, Princeton University Press, 1989), 99.

[43]"Vraja" and "Braj" are alternative renderings of the same word. In this book, the former spelling is used to denote the mythical land of Krishna's *līlās*, while "Braj" means the region around the town of Vrindavan (Brindaban) in modern Uttar Pradesh.

[44]As can be seen from her letters to 'Gopal,' Chakravarti spelt her *vairāginī* name 'Yashoda Mai' when writing in English. Other transliterations include 'Yasoda Mai,' 'Yashoda Ma,' 'Yaśodā Mā' and 'Jasoda Mai.'

[45]In Hindu myth, Yaśodā is technically Krishna's foster mother, the divine child having been born to Devaki in a prison cell in Mathura. However, because in Chaitanyaite theology Krishna never leaves Vrindavan, Gauḍīya Vaiṣṇava commentators have emphasised the role of his 'real' mother, Yashoda, who is said to have attracted the lord by dint of her devotion (*bhakti*)—see, for example, the 16th-century *Krishna-sandarbha* Anuccheda 149, verses 3 and 16, wherein Jīva Goswamī, the famed grand-disciple of Chaitanya, describes how "Kṛṣṇa became the son of Nanda and Yaśodā. He was not the son of anyone else."

[46]Also Krishnaprem, Kṛṣṇaprema, etc.

[47]Patel, *A Lover of Light Among Luminaries*, 34.

[48]"The *Sri* is not used in a *brahmachārī* name." Dev Ashish (David Beresford), email to Brian Mooney, 19 May 2010.

[49]Madhava Ashish, letter to Andrew Rawlinson, c. April 1988.

[50]*Ibid.*

[51]Acharya Sri Shrivatsa Goswami, conversation with the author, 23 June 2021.

[52]A formal order of saffron-clad Chaitanyaite *swamis*, inspired by the Sri Vaiṣṇava *sannyāsīs* of south India, had been created by the controversial Gauḍīya Vaiṣṇava revivalist Bhaktisiddhanta Saraswati in the 1920s; the Mirtola gurus, however, are not in his lineage and there is no evidence that Yashoda Mai was influenced by, or even aware of, Saraswati's reforms.

[53]Tandan, *Faith & Fire*, 254.

[54]Tandan, *Faith & Fire*, 255.

[55]Sen, 'Sri Krishnaprem,' xix.

[56]Melville T. Kennedy, *The Chaitanya Movement: A Study of the Vaishṇavism of Bengal*, (Calcutta: Association Press [YMCA], 1925), 164–165.

[57]Kennedy, *The Chaitanya Movement*, 165.

[58]Kennedy, *The Chaitanya Movement*, 162.

[59]Krishna Prem, *The Search for Truth*, 53–54.

[60]Sri Krishna Prem, *The Yoga of the Bhagavat Gita*, (London: John M. Watkins, 1948), 25–26.

[61]Krishna Prem, *The Yoga of the Bhagavat Gita*, 26.

[62]Haberman, 'A Cross-cultural Adventure,' 219.

[63]Shivanath, *Mosaic of Life*, 32.

[64]MS Randhawa, *The Art of EH Brewster and Achsah Brewster*, (Allahabad: Kitabistan, 1944), 48.

[65]See, for example, GH Poole, 'The Archetypal Struggle: Euripides Interpreted,' *The Aryan Path*, 9.10 (1938), 498.

[66]Gabriel Monod-Herzen, Appendix C: 'On Sri Krishnaprem,' in Dilip Kumar Roy, *Yogi Sri Krishnaprem*, 3rd edn, (Bombay: Bharatiya Vidya Bhavan, 1992), 309.

[67]Madhava Ashish, 'Preface,' in Krishna Prem and Madhava Ashish, *Man, the Measure of All Things*, 9.

8: Brajavāsī

The rainbow-lilts of eternal Brindaban
I still recall, I still recall again:
O Prince of loveliness, Light's darling Son,
Touching to radiant joy our nights of pain! –
I still recall and call to thee again."[1]

— Dilip Kumar Roy, 'Brindabaner lila'

Having established the temple and the beginnings of an ashram at Mirtola, in early 1931 'Ma' and 'Gopal' travelled to Vrindavan (Brindaban), where they met with Bal Krishna Goswami and other members of the local Vaiṣṇava community. It was Krishna Prem's wish that he be formally inducted into an established Vaiṣṇava *sampradāya*, or lineage of gurus and disciples. Though Bal Krishna, a Gauḍīya Vaiṣṇava, had sanctioned her *vairāgya* initiation, it was Gyanandra Nath Chakravarti who performed the ceremony and the giving of robes—and they lived for weeks at one of the city's many *ghāṭs* while Krishna Prem searched "the entire town for the best teacher, regardless of sectarian affiliation."[2]

It was not the pair's first trip to Vrindavan—the Chakravarti family, including the adopted Nixon, had visited the holy city, where they had "toured the temples and other sacred sites which were identified with the Krishna Līlā,[3] watched the Līlā acted out by troupes of small boys who played Krishna and the Gopīs, sat with the Goswamis and discussed philosophy and Vaiṣṇava theology, and generally enjoyed the orthodox religious life," when they lived in Lucknow (Ashish, 100–101). However, this was their first trip not as spiritual tourists, but as dedicated seekers, as well as their debut outing in the saffron garb of the renunciate. This visit "created much excitement among people in Vṛndāvana, because he was the first European they saw in the form of a Vaiṣṇava, wearing *mālā* [necklace] of *tulasī* beads and *tilaka* [sacred mark on the forehead] and chanting Harinama [the names of Krishna]," records OBL Kapoor.[4] (Later, when questioned as to why he wore beads of *tulasī*, or holy basil, a plant considered sacred by Vaiṣṇavas, Krishna Prem responded by asking the inquisitor why they wore a watch. "That reminds me of the time," was the reply, to which came the rejoinder: "And this reminds me of eternity."[5])

Both Sri Madhava Ashish, Yashoda Mai's *praśiṣya* (grand-disciple), and P. Niroop, a present-day trustee of Uttar Brindaban, are of the opinion that Yashoda Mai—though herself unconcerned with external formalities—supported this search for yet another guru in order to make life easier for Krishna Prem when she was no longer present. Niroop, a senior advocate at the Supreme Court of India, explains: "Sri Yashoda Ma, being what she was, would not need any initiation from anyone except the Lord himself. But she was too conscious of the problems that Sri Krishna Prem would face if he was not formally launched into the Sampradaya, in a rigid tradition- and-sectarian-bound Vaishnav society."[6] Confirms Madhava Ashish:

> Yashoda Mai ... had the confidence to carry it off without external affiliations, but she was concerned with what Krishna Prem might suffer after her death if he could not, as it were, show that he came from a respectable lineage.[7]

According to Jagdish Lal Goswami, the son of Bal Krishna, the tall, fair-haired, blue-eyed Englishman found himself in high demand in the spiritual capital of the Vaishnavas, where Krishna is believed to have spent his youth during his most recent descent to Earth. "Every sampradāya was after him. All the gurus and fake gurus came also," he recalls.[8] Ultimately, however, it was Bal Krishna Goswami who Krishna Prem felt "had the best answers to his questions,"[9] and the former man recalls being equally impressed by Krishna Prem, who, he notes in his diary, was "very humble and wore a necklace of tulsi and gopi-chandan [the V-shaped clay marking worn by Vaishnavas] on his forehead. Balkrishna records that upon meeting Krishnaprem he became very joyful."[10]

David Haberman describes the relationship that blossomed between Bal Krishna and Krishna Prem, whom he called the "European sadhu," in February 1931:

> During the next several days Balkrishna spent much time with Krishnaprem, Concerning their talks he notes that 'the thoughts of Krishnaprem are in accord with the philosophy of the Goswamis.'[11] Krishnaprem was asked to speak publicly in Vrindaban about his experiences as a Vaishnava. After much hesitation he agreed, and was introduced by Balkrishna Goswami himself. During this speech he

> said that he believed that Vaishnavism was the best of all religions and that faith had become so weak in modern Christianity that it is like a dry tree which is easily blown over in the face of a storm. When he finished speaking he was presented with a garland of flowers and an honorary degree by the Madhva-Gaureshvar Pith, a local religions [sic] institution. Krishnaprem attracted the attention of many of the residents of Brindaban over the following days of his stay.[12]

Though Yashoda Mai requested another (*dīkṣā*) initiation for Krishna Prem to cement his ties with the Radha-Raman Temple and Gauḍīya *sampradāya*, he considered this poor etiquette,[13] since he had already been given *dīkṣā* by 'Ma,' a Vaiṣṇavī in good standing. Instead, it was decided that Bal Krishna Goswami would give Vaiṣṇava initiation to Yashoda Mai (a disciple of a non-Vaiṣṇavite guru, her Śākta husband GN Chakravarti), who would then formally initiate her European disciple into the Chaitanya Vaiṣṇava tradition. This "indirect initiation ritual"[14] made Bal Krishna Goswami Krishna Prem's *param guru*—his guru's guru—and therefore someone from whom "he could legitimately take instruction," notes Charles R. Brooks in his *The Hare Krishnas in India.*[15]

The actual ceremony took place not in Vrindavan, but in Mirtola, on 21 June 1932.[16] Bal Krishna Goswami, who had arrived at Uttar Brindaban on 12 June after "a long journey by foot and mule,"[17] initiated Yashoda Mai with the sacred Gopal and Gayatri *mantras,*[18] marking her official induction into the tradition.[19] She in turn, as part of the same ceremony, gave these *dīkṣā mantras* to her disciple, Krishna Prem. Bal Krishna also presented Krishna Prem with the three strands of the *tulsi* (holy basil) beads worn around the neck by initiated Chaitanya Vaiṣṇavas.[20]

Bal Krishna stayed until 25 July, during which time the two men "passed their days walking in the mountains discussing the philosophy of the particular branch of Vaiṣṇavism known as Gauḍīya Vaiṣṇavism. Balkrishna also instructed Krishnaprem about the Vaiṣṇava form of worship."[21] Bal Krishna records in his diary that the features of the area surrounding Uttar Brindaban in which they walked had been named after sites in Braj—the region that includes Vrindavan and the city believed to be Krishna's birthplace, Mathura. He also notes being impressed with Krishna Prem's singing and drumming abilities on the *tabla.*[22]

The spiritual movement called Gauḍīya Vaiṣṇavism, after the Gauḍa region of Bengal, or Chaitanya Vaiṣṇavism, after its founder, the 16th-century mystic

Chaitanya Mahāprabhu, is a relatively recent addition to the wider Vaiṣṇava tradition, the largest branch of modern Hinduism, which worships Viṣṇu, or his various *avatārs* and incarnations, as the supreme God. Finding its scriptural basis in ancient texts such as the *Bhāgavata Purāṇa* and *Bhagavad Gītā*, as well as the writings of Chaitanya's early followers, Gauḍīya Vaiṣṇavism emphasises the personal nature of God (Krishna) and the path of *bhakti yoga*, the yoga of love and devotional service, as a means of attaining union with the supreme.

Inspired by the ecstatic *saṅkīrtan* parties of Chaitanya, the tradition also encourages the communal chanting of the names of God, known as *saṅkīrtan* or *harināma*, often in the form of the 16-word Hare Krishna '*mahā-mantra*' ("great *mantra*")—Hare Krishna, Hare Krishna, Krishna Krishna, Hare Hare / Hare Rama, Hare Rama, Rama Rama, Hare Hare—first found in the *Kali-santaraṇa Upaniṣad* of the *Yajurveda* (1,200–800 BC).[23]

Michael Sudduth, the professor of philosophy and religion, outlines the main features unique to the Chaitanyaite form of Vaiṣṇavism:

> the belief that (i) Krishna is the original form of the Godhead, not merely an avatar (or incarnation) of the Supreme Being Vishnu, (ii) bhakti, properly cultivated, results [in] intimacy with God, the highest form of which is the ecstatic enjoyment of conjugal love (madhurya rasa), (iii) Radha, the highest devotee of Krishna in the Krishna narrative, is herself God in the mode of sacrificial love, (iv) although God manifests in many different forms, Caitanya is the manifestation of Radha-Krishna (lover and beloved) in one body, expressing the highest form of bhakti for this age as the chanting and singing of the holy names of God, and (v) the relation between God and the individual soul is an inconceivable simultaneous difference and non-difference (acintya bhedabheda tattva).[24]

Today, the legacy of Chaitanya—also known as 'Gaura' or 'Gauranga' ("golden-complexioned") on account of his fair skin, said to resemble Radha's—can most easily be seen in the saffron-clad devotees of the International Society for Krishna Consciousness (Iskcon), a splinter group from the reformist Gauḍīya Maṭh (1920–1937), a missionary monastic order, and their *saṅkīrtan* parties in cities around the world. While initiated Chaitanya Vaiṣṇavas in the Gauḍīya Math/Iskcon lineage (also called the *Sāraswata* line, after the Gauḍīya Maṭh's founder, Bhaktisiddhanta Saraswati) are in the majority in the West, *dīkṣā* in Gauḍīya Vaiṣṇavism was traditionally given by a representative of one of several hereditary lineages (known as *parivārs*, literally "families"), all of which can trace their origin to Chaitanya's companions. They include the Nityānanda *parivār* (originated by Nityānanda, Chaitanya's closest friend and disciple, and his wife Jāhnavā

Mā), the Advaita *parivār* (promulgated by two sons of Advaita Āchārya, an elder companion of Chaitanya and ancestor of Dilip Kumar Roy's) and the Gopal Bhaṭṭa *parivār* (established by Chaitanya's South Indian disciple Gopal Bhaṭṭa Goswami), to which Yashoda Mai and Krishna Prem belonged by virtue of their initiation by *parivār* member Bal Krishna Goswami.

Despite requesting initiation from Bal Krishna, Krishna Prem was, from the outset, an unconventional Gauḍīya Vaiṣṇava who seems initially to have found it difficult to accept the central tenet of the Chaitanya Vaiṣṇnava tradition—that Chaitanya is Krishna incarnate, or Radha and Krishna combined—according to both Haberman and Kapoor. The former describes how, several days after his and Yashoda Mai's Gauḍīya initiations, Chaitanya had appeared to Krishna Prem in a dream and revealed his divinity. "Krishnaprem told Balkrishna that he now considered himself a dedicated follower of Chaitanya."[25]

Kapoor elaborates on this dream, writing that Krishna Prem required a sign from Krishna himself before he would accept Chaitanya's divinity:

> Kṛṣṇaprema did not regard Gaurāṇga Mahāprabhu as an incarnation of Śrī Kṛṣṇa. He had pledged that although he was initiated into Mahāprabhu's *saṃpradāya*, he would not accept Mahāprabhu as identical with Kṛṣṇa until Kṛṣṇa Himself made him do so. Kṛṣṇa, who always dances to the tune of a sincere devotee, told him in a dream, "Śrī Caitanya Mahāprabhu is the same as I."[26]

The Mirtola ashram would also diverge from traditional, male-dominated Gauḍīya Vaiṣṇavism in its attitude towards women, in terms of both its leadership and philosophy. Chaitanya, as a *sannyāsī*, forbade his renunciant disciples from mixing with women (the *Chaitanya Charitamrita*, a hagiography of Chaitanya, relates how one disciple, known as Junior Haridas, committed suicide after being ostracised for begging rice from a female devotee) and his successors, the *Goswamis* of Vrindavan, "with [their] strong emphasis on asceticism, [appear] to have followed the Puranic traditions regarding women as found in the *Bhāgavatam*, with its many clearly mysogynistic [sic] statements."[27] While practising Gauḍīya Vaiṣṇavas usually aspire to a female spiritual body (*siddha-deha*) in which to serve Radha, who occupies a pre-eminent place in Chaitanyite theology, in the afterlife, women play a subordinate role in most Gauḍīya Vaiṣṇava groups to this day:

> Vaishnavism teaches that all people are, in essence, equally pure, blissful perfect eternal souls. But on another level, Gaudiya literature and discourse broadly define and depict women as honoured or reviled according to two typecasts: a wife who produces sons or a seductress.[28]

Bill Aitken notes that "both gurus"—Krishna Prem and Madhava Ashish—recommended having a female guru "because, her mind being subservient to her gut, she is a natural knock-out artist—and each time her pupil picks himself up he is a little wiser than before."[29]

After rendezvousing with Bal Krishna in Aligarh, some 40 miles north-east of Vrindavan, where Krishna Prem gave "several public talks which were attended by large crowds," the pair returned to Vrindavan in late 1932 for the Sharad Purnima festival,[30] which marks the start of the holy month of Kartik. On 13 October, Bal Krishna had taken Krishna Prem into the Radha-Raman Temple for a special Sharad Purnima *darśan* (viewing) of its famous *mūrti* of Krishna, Sri Radha Raman, and then presented him with a garland of *tulsi* and invited him to sing devotional songs (*bhajans*) in the temple.[31]

Though "no one said anything at the time,"[32] several days later Bal Krishna was told that he had been "excommunicated by the temple authorities, the consensus being that rules of ritual purity had been violated"[33] by his allowing a non-Indian to enter the temple. The matter was put to a *panchayat* (a council of the Radha-Raman Temple *Goswamis*), which asked Bal Krishna to sign a formal statement admitting his 'error' and asking for their forgiveness, which he did under pressure from temple authorities, who had threatened to expel him if he refused.[34]

However, when Krishna Prem next returned to Vrindavan, in January 1933, his cause was taken up by another temple priest, Sridhar Goswami, who, remarkably, told the *panchayat* he would go on a hunger strike unless they agreed to reconsider the case of the European *sādhu*.[35] Ultimately, a compromise was reached in which Krishna Prem and "'others like him'" would be allowed to behold (have *darshan* of) the deity from a small doorway at the rear of the temple—though Haberman notes that, after visiting Vrindavan again later that year and preaching to a large crowd at the historic Govind Dev temple, "the doors of the Radharaman temple were opened to [Krishna Prem] completely."[36]

According to Kapoor—who like Haberman and Brooks had access to Bal Krishna Goswami's diaries—shortly thereafter the local Vaiṣṇavas even organised, perhaps by way of apology, an event feting Krishna Prem, during which he was awarded a special title: "[W]hen they came to know that Kṛṣṇaprema was truly as devout a Vaiṣṇava as anyone else in Vṛndāvana … the Vaiṣṇavas organized a meeting in his honour under the presidentship of Sri Banamali Lala

Gosvami and conferred on him the title, 'Gaura-prema-nidhi,' (ocean of love for Sri Gauranga [Chaitanya] Mahaprabhu).[37]

The *Goswamis'* decision on access to the Radha-Raman *mandir*—"that if an individual met required standards of knowledge and cleanliness, he could be admitted to the temple"[38]—set a precedent for attitudes towards the Western Vaiṣṇavas who followed in later decades, particularly benefitting the Iskcon devotees who began arriving in the late 1960s. Charles R. Brooks observed in 1989:

> [T]he reaffirmation of the underlying principle of noncasteism already implicit in the Chaitanya religion set the foundations for this temple's future attitude toward the foreign Vaishnavas of ISKCON. Other sects in the town have also adopted this precedent established by the Radha-Raman priests as the basis for their own policy. As Jagdish [Lal Goswami] put it, "Krishna Prem had intellectual capacity for understanding the knowledge, and he was so careful about his purification habits also. Only in such cases can we accept, so it is person to person only. ... With Indian persons the same is also. The person-quality, that is what counts." ...
>
> While there are few people in Vrindaban willing to make any personal comparisons between the devotees of ISKCON and Krishna Prem, his example is often cited as a precedent for their acceptance today.[39]

"[A]ll Western Vaishnavas owe a debt of gratitude to both Swami Krishna Prema and Bal [Krishna] Goswami," confirms one of these Western Vaishnavas, Bhaktivedanta Parivrajak, an Italian-born disciple of Swami BR Sridhar of Navadwip. "Swami Krishna Prema was undoubtedly the most important historical precedent for the Western Vaishnavas."[40]

While Sri Krishna Prem is sometimes described as the "first Western Vaishnava," including by the aforementioned Swami Parivrajak,[41] that distinction—depending on one's definition of "Western" (and "Vaiṣṇava")—probably belongs to Heliodorus, an ambassador of the Indo-Greek king Antialcidas (c. 130–120 BC), whose inscription on the pillar that bears his name identifies him as a devotee of "Vāsudeva, the god of gods," a deified hero of ancient Braj whose cult contributed significantly to the development of Krishnaite Vaishnavism.

('Vāsudeva,' meaning son of Vāsudeva, is also a name of the modern Kṛṣṇa.) Later candidates include the East India Company officer Charles 'Hindoo' Stuart (c. 1758–1828), noted for his collection of Hindu *mūrtis*, his daily baths in the Ganges, and for greeting Indians with the salutation "*Jay Sittaramjee*"[42] ("glory to Sita and Rama," respectively *avatārs* of Lakshmi and Vishnu), and the Swedish businessman Hjalmar Pontén-Möller (1884–1943), who was initiated into Vaiṣṇavism[43] and later studied tantric texts with Atal Bihari Ghose, a collaborator of another Hindu convert, the English-born orientalist Sir John 'Arthur Avalon' Woodroffe (1865–1936).

Though, as Brooks notes, Krishna Prem's initiation, via Yashoda Mai, by Bal Krishna Goswami "is the first instance of a Westerner being accepted as a disciple, albeit indirectly, by any traditional Vrindaban guru,"[44] he is also pipped to the post for the honour of first Western Gauḍīya Vaiṣṇava by one of a handful of American converts, of whom the most prominent are the American followers of Premananda Bharati (1858–1914), a Bengali convert to Chaitanya Vaiṣṇavism who at one time claimed to have 5,000 disciples, most of them female, in Los Angeles.

The son of a wealthy magistrate, Premananda was born Surendra Nath Mukherjee into an influential Brahmin family in Dacca (now Dhaka in Bangladesh) in January, 1858, during the great Indian Rebellion (Sepoy Mutiny) of 1857–58. The Mukherjees were members of colonial Bengal's Westernised upper middle class, the *bhadraloks*, and Surendra Nath was fluent in English and educated to degree level at the University of Calcutta. Post-graduation, Mukherjee, much like Ronald Nixon, seemed destined for a comfortably non-history-making life of mostly secular intellectual pursuits, working on English-language newspapers by day and hobnobbing with Calcutta's Hindu intelligentsia by night. His religious awakening came aged 26, not in the seat of an aircraft but in a Calcutta theatre, where he reported being deeply affected by a play depicting the life of Chaitanya. In an article for the *New York Herald* in 1902, he recalls:

> [J]ust at this time my religious instinct started to assert itself, and very soon it overcame my passion for journalism. I was witnessing a performance of "Chaitanya Lila" at the Star Theatre. Chaitanya was an incarnation of Krishna, the Form Manifestation of the Hindoo's [sic] absolute deity.
>
> He was born a little more than 400 years ago, in Bengal, at Nuddia [Nadia] on the Ganges, about 100 miles above Calcutta. He preached Krishna, the seed and the soul of the purest love, and of the universe, and while preaching he would burst forth into song in praise of Krishna, his Master, Friend, Father, and Lover. Thus singing, he would be filled with ecstasy and in the fullness of joy within him

> perform the most graceful dance the world has ever seen, his arms and whole-body waving and quivering with the heaving billows, as it were, within his heart. He was like an ocean of divine love and streams of water from many fountains would flow from his eyes in the shape of tears. And in those tears, streaming straight from his eyes to the ground, all those who sang and danced around him in ecstatic motion would be liberally bathed.
>
> This indescribable, wondrous scene made a profound impression upon me. I had at last found my religion of love so hazily understood in boyhood, and resolved to give my life to it. With this awakening all attraction for things material left me, and in the depth of my heart flowed a stream of nectar which every moment thrilled through my being. "Krishna, my beloved!" I exclaimed to myself, "I am thine forever. Thou art the mystery of love, the universe is its expression, and Chaitanya their most merciful explanation. Merciful, O Lord, because thou art thy Chaitanya thyself, thou comest again as thy own devotee to teach us the way to thee.[45]

Mukherjee soon set to work extricating himself from his old life as a newspaperman in order to become a full-time devotee of Krishna. In 1890 he took *sannyāsa* initiation from Brahmananda Bharati, a disciple of the famous *jñāna yogī* Lokenath Brahmachari (reported to be seven feet tall, and by then more than 160 years old), taking the name Baba Premananda Bharati, and later became a follower of Prabhu Jagadbandhu, another Bengali Vaiṣṇava whose disciples considered him Chaitanya incarnate.

By 1900, 'Baba Bharati' was living as a hermit at Radha Kund in Vrindavan when he received from Chaitanya himself an order to go west. Writing in 1910, he described the divine vision:

> The whole room was really filled with the golden light, which deepened as I sat up and tried to peer through it. Soon in front of me a face began to form and as I looked on its wondrous beauty it developed into a whole figure—the figure of Sri Chaitanya, the full incarnation of Sri Krishna, The Lord whose servant of servants I was, whom I worshipped with all the strength of my being. ... The Lord's lips seemed to move and it struck me that he was saying something. Attuning my ears to that most musical voice, I heard him say—"Beloved, thou hast to go to the Far West to America, to spread the Name of Krishna there. Thou shouldst have no fear. I'll keep thee protected with My embrace and carry thee in My bosom.[46]

The idea of spreading the cult of Sri Krishna Chaitanya among the *mlecchas* of Europe and America was not a new one. The Gauḍīya Vaiṣṇava reformer Kedarnath Datta Bhaktivinoda—the father of Gauḍīya Maṭh founder Bhaktisiddhanta Saraswati—had written in the 1880s of his dream that people in "England, France, Russia, Prussia and America" would "take the name of Chaitanya Mahaprabhu again and again in their own countries, and raise the waves of *saṅkīrtana*." In 1896, he sent copies of his book *Śrī-gaurāṅga-līlā-smaraṇa-maṅgala-stotram*[47]— a collection of Sanskrit verses summarising the teachings of Chaitanya which also included a 47-page English introduction titled *Sri Chaitanya Mahaprabhu, His Life and Precepts*–to scholars across the British Empire, including the Oxford University professor of Sanskrit, Monier Monier-Williams. While the book did find its way into academic libraries in London, Montreal and Sydney, the response in the West was decidedly muted and Bhaktivinoda received only a "few polite letters of appreciation" for his work.[48] In 1898, the first volume of full-length work by his fellow *bhadralok*, the journalist, Indian independence activist, occultist and Chaitanyaite, Shishir Kumar Ghose, came out. This two-part English biography titled *Lord Gauranga or Salvation for All* was generally well received.[49] It earned positive reviews in the *Hindustan Review*,[50] *Bhavan's Journal*[51] and *The Theosophist*,[52] though it similarly failed to achieve the hoped-for breakthrough in Europe and North America.

While Premananda clearly credited Krishna himself, in the form of Chaitanya, with inspiring his mission to North America, a number of contemporary Vaiṣṇavas also claimed to have had some influence on his decision to head west, including the followers of Jagadbandhu.[53] Whatever the truth, within two years Baba Bharati was en route to New York, his first port of call in the United States, the latest Indian holy man on a mission to save the Americans from themselves. ("The trouble with America is that it is building on a material plane," he wrote in a typical contribution to *The New York Herald*. "It is making tremendous progress in all things material, but we of the Orient understand the spiritual. ... Your much-vaunted progress counts for naught."[54])

As one of the countless Indian gurus who flocked to America in the years following the 1893 World's Parliament of Religions in Chicago (where GN Chakravarti represented Theosophy), Premananda, when he arrived in the US in October, 1902, was able to benefit from his relationship with Swami Vivekananda, the fellow Bengali whose addresses to the 1893 conference are often credited with introducing Hinduism to America. While Premananda by that time had little in common philosophically with Vivekananda—preaching devotion to a personal God over the latter's nontheistic Neo-Vedanta—the two had been acquaintances in Calcutta, both having been part of a group of young intellectuals who gathered around Vivekananda's guru, Ramakrishna.[55]

After lecturing in New York and Boston and publishing a book, *Sree Krishna:*

The Lord of Love, through his New York-based Krishna Samaj (Krishna Society), Premananda accepted an invitation to speak at the Venice Assembly—a 'World's Parliament' incorporating 'nine great Congresses,' including a Chicago-style Congress of Religion[56]—being held in Venice, Los Angeles, in July and August, 1905; he thereafter made his home in California. In Los Angeles, he established a Radha–Krishna temple and ashram, the Krishna Home, at 730 West 16th Street, and began publishing a journal, *The Light of India* (later called *East and West*), with his disciple, the novelist Rose Reinhardt Anthon, as editor. A contemporary newspaper article by Anthon and David St Clair, another American follower, describes the familiar-sounding scene at Krishna Home:

> Rādhā, Kṛṣṇa, and Caitanya enshrined; disciples singing the Song to the Lord at evening *āratī*, waving the light in the twilight, listening to the Baba read Kṛṣṇadāsa Kavirāja's *Caitanya Caritāmṛta*, and teaching the devotees step by step "the devotion by which he can find the way that leads to the depth of the heart."[57]

Accompanied by five American disciples, Premananda Bharati returned to India in 1907, "after which services at the Krishna Home continued for some months under the direction of two of the Baba's disciples, Elizabeth Delvine King and C. P. Neilsen, a California artist, but then ceased."[58]

In 1910, he returned briefly to the United States, leaving Anthon in India, but his ailing health put paid to attempts to establish a new, larger Vaiṣṇava temple at 1240 Dana Street in south-east Los Angeles. In 1912, Premananda returned to India, via London and Paris (where he "received far less newspaper coverage than he had in America"[59]); he died of complications from diabetes on 24 January 1914.[60] The Krishna Samaj was shut down later that decade.[61]

While his American 'Krishna Homes' were short-lived, Baba Bharati holds the distinction of opening the first Krishna temple in the West, as well as being the author of the "the first full-length Gauḍīya Vaiṣṇava theological treatise in English" with *Sree Krishna*.[62] His writings also influenced several esoteric groups in California, including the Aum Temple of Universal Truth and the Order of Loving Service. (An Order member, Maud Lalita Johnson, dedicates her 1934 novel *Square* to "Baba Premanand Bharati, who by his love, patience and continued watchfulness has led me out of darkness into Light, out of weariness into Rest, out of confusion into Understanding, out of continuous striving into Perfect Peace".[63]) As Premananda's biographer, Gerald Carney, demonstrates, "there were still some who identified themselves as 'disciples' of Baba Bharati ... in Chicago and New York more than twenty years after his passing," speaking to "some lasting impact."[64] Rose Reinhardt Anthon, Premananda's closest American disciple, returned to Chicago in 1914 and died in 1951.

While the true number of Premananda's disciples was likely far less than the 5,000 he claimed, it has been suggested that the Baba's limited success at converting young Americans to Vaiṣṇavite Hinduism had a more lasting impact—being a factor in the passing of the Immigration Act of 1917, which prohibited immigration to the US from a "barred zone" encompassing British India, the Pacific islands, most of south-east Asia and the Middle East. Those able to successfully mobilise public support for the act included nativist intellectuals such as the Oriental scholar Elizabeth Armstrong Reed[65]—whose polemical *Hinduism in Europe and America* (1914) directly attacks *Sree Krishna: The Lord of Love*[66]—and homegrown occultists and "mages (like 'Admiramled'[67]) who urged people to support their local gurus and 'Buy American.'"[68]

Other pre-Krishna Prem converts to Gauḍīya Vaiṣṇavism include a Mrs GB Adams of Chicago, aka Nityananda Dassee,[69] who in 1908–1909 finds mention in the *Hindu Spiritual Magazine* of Shishir Kumar Ghose[70] as a "pious American lady ... who has adopted Vaiṣṇavism as taught by the Lord Gauranga"[71] and who is "trying to spread the faith."[72] Another Chicago-based associate of Ghose, Lucy E. Adams, seems to have achieved some fame independently as a teacher of Hindu philosophy; she is recognised as a "great spiritualist" (in the older sense meaning *sādhaka*, rather than a spirit medium) by the author of *Lord Haranath* (a hagiography of the Vaiṣṇava saint Pagal Haranath, regarded by his followers as Chaitanya reborn), while the *Modern Review* of Calcutta, (vol. 3, 1908) records how "[e]very Indian student in or about Chicago looks upon her as 'Mother'" (396). There was also one Professor Osman, another American devotee introduced in Haripada Adhikary's *Unifying Force of Hinduism: The Harekrsna Movement* (2012). According to Adhikary (an ophthalmologist and amateur historian of Hinduism), Osman established a "Chaitanyasamaja" (Chaitanya Society) somewhere in the US in "about 1897,"[73] making him "the first recorded Vaisnava disciple in the West,"[74] though no further information is given.

The French-born *sannyāsinī* Marie Louise (Swami Abhayananda), the first female disciple of Swami Vivekananda, is also reported to have fallen under the influence of Ghose after defecting from Vivekananda's mission, as illustrated by a report in *The Indian Nation* (Calcutta) of 26 May 1902:

> Certain phases of Hinduism seem to possess a peculiar fascination for some American women. One of these was for some time a Vedantist and a follower of Swami Vivekananda, who for a time made a name in New York or Chicago as a preacher of Vedantic Hinduism, but she has gone over to another Hindu sect, the sect of English-educated Vaishnavas of Bengal, who own the leadership of Babu Shishir Kumar Ghose. This lady is reported to be coming out shortly to India to work as a missionary of Neo-Vaishnavism.[75]

Though many in Vivekananda's circle, including Vivekananda himself, doubted the sincerity of Abhayananda's 'conversion' (on hearing of her final arrival in India, "as a follower of Chaitanya", he wrote: "Some rich men, I hear, have taken her up. ... She wanted money. May the Lord give her a lot!")[76], it appears that Baba Bharati did not share their scepticism as to her motives. While he did not mention it in his own recollection of the vision, Premananda's fateful dream of Chaitanya also included a cameo from Abhayananda, according to the account of the Baba's younger brother, Satyendra Nath Mukherjee. Writing to the eldest Mukherjee sibling, Kirendra Nath, Satyendra Nath claimed that 'Nadada' (Surendra Nath/Premananda) "got a command from Sree Chaitanya in dream [sic] to proceed to America to help Swami Abhayananda in her mission to spread Vaishnavism in the world"[77]—raising the possibility that it was a European Hindu who inspired his journey west in the first place.

If Sri Krishna Prem was not, then, the first Western Vaiṣṇava, he was "certainly the first to have any official affiliation with the Gaudiya Vaishnavism of Braj,"[78] as well as the first to become a guru in his own right—including, significantly, a guru to those who had been born Hindus. As the Australian academic Joshua Nash observes in the *Journal of Vaishnava Studies*: "Krishnaprem is most likely the first *videshi* (foreigner) who attracted *deshis* (Indians) to his feet."[79] "When the Beatles went to India [in 1968] to sit at the feet of the Maharishi Mahesh Yogi they were following an oft-trod path," adds his countryman, the religious studies professor Harry Oldmeadow. On the contrary, "Indians sitting at the feet of a Western guru preaching orthodox Hinduism was a much rarer event."[80]

Though his "Western education gave him a unique ability to interpret Indian mysticism for the Western mind,"[81] one of Krishna Prem's great achievements was to cut across cultural, national, racial and caste lines, as Gertrude Emerson Sen explains:

> His Western devotees and admirers were one thing, but more extraordinary has been the even greater number of Indians who have gone to Sri Krishnaprem, to remain loyal followers ever since. There are well-known ashrams in India where foreigners are to be found sitting at the feet of an Indian guru, but I know of no other person like Krishnaprem, himself "foreign" to begin with, who has drawn so many Indians to himself. They include government officials, well-to-do business-men, lawyers, a maharajah, professors, members of

the police force or army, many with no special label, and also many Indian women. It has been his unique privilege to break down the barriers of race and caste.[82]

Notes

[1]Roy, *Yogi Sri Krishnaprem*, 97.

[2]Brooks, *The Hare Krishnas in India*, 99.

[3]The 'divine play' associated with Krishna's latest incarnation in India, particularly those activities involving his playful interactions with the beautiful milkmaids, the *gopīs*, of Vraja.

[4]Kapoor, 'Śrī Kṛṣṇaprema,' 306.

[5]Pandey, *Guru by Your Bedside*, 195–196.

[6]Patlolla Niroop, email to the author, 9 July 2021.

[7]Madhava Ashish, letter to Andrew Rawlinson, 22 June 1988.

[8]Brooks, *The Hare Krishnas in India*, 99.

[9]*Ibid.*

[10]Haberman, 'A Cross-cultural Adventure,' 219.

[11]The Six Goswamis of Vrindavan, the chief followers and disciples of Chaitanya, whose writings form the theological basis of the Gaudiya-Vaishnava tradition. They are the brothers Rūpa and Sanātana, their nephew Jīva, Raghunātha Bhaṭṭa, Raghunātha Dāsa, and Gopala Bhaṭṭa Goswamis. Gopala Bhaṭṭa founded the Radha-Raman Temple in 1542.

[12]Haberman, 'A Cross-cultural Adventure', 219.

[13]Brooks, 'Gauḍīya Vaiṣṇavism in the Modern World', 164.

[14]*Ibid.*

[15]Brooks, *The Hare Krishnas in India*, 99–100.

[16]Haberman, 'A Cross-cultural Adventure', 220.

[17]Haberman, 'A Cross-cultural Adventure', 219.

[18]Haberman, 'A Cross-cultural Adventure', 220.

[19]The Gayatri *mantra* mentioned by Haberman is presumably the Kama Gayatri—given, along with the Gopal *mantra*, in Sanatana Goswami's *Hari Bhakti Vilāsa* as a Gauḍīya Vaiṣṇava *dīkṣā mantra*—rather than the better-known Savitri/Brahma Gayatri (a solar *mantra* originally associated with the Brahminical *upanayana* sacred thread ceremony).

[20]Brooks, 'Gauḍīya Vaiṣṇavism in the Modern World', 165.

[21]Haberman, 'A Cross-cultural Adventure', 219–220.

[22]Haberman, 'A Cross-cultural Adventure', 219.

[23]Though the *mahā-mantra* is the *mantra* most associated with *harināma-saṅkīrtan* today, the degree to which this was the case in Chaitanya's time is debated, and there are those who argue it was previously only ever chanted quietly (or even silently) on prayer beads (a practice known as *japa* meditation).

[24]Michael Sudduth, 'Gaudiya Vaishnavism', *Cup of Nirvāṇa*, (San Francisco: Michael Sudduth, 2012), http://michaelsudduth.com/gaudiya-vaishnavism (accessed 15 May 2022).

[25]Haberman, 'A Cross-cultural Adventure', 220.

[26]Kapoor, 'Śrī Kṛṣṇaprema', 307.

[27]Jagadananda Das, 'Women Saints in Gaudiya Vaishnavism', *Vaishnavi Ministry*, (Sacramento: ISKCON, 2020), https://vaishnaviministry.org/women-saints-in-gaudiya-vaishnavism (accessed 9 January 2023).

[28]Vaishnavi Heath, *Writing from the Gaudiya Tradition*: exegesis, PhD diss., University of Adelaide, (2014), 20.

[29]Aitken, email to the author, 24 June 2021.

[30]Haberman, 'A Cross-cultural Adventure', 220.

[31]*Ibid.*

[32]Brooks, *The Hare Krishnas in India*, 100.

[33]*Ibid.*

[34]Haberman, 'A Cross-cultural Adventure',p220.

[35]*Ibid.*

[36]*Ibid.*

[37]Kapoor, 'Śrī Kṛṣṇaprema', 306–307. Note that Madhava Ashish (103) spells the title 'Gauraprem Nidhanak.'

[38]Brooks, *The Hare Krishnas in India*, 100.

[39]*Ibid.*

[40]Swami BV Parivrajak, 'The First Western Vaishnava', *Vaishnava News Network*, 1999, http://www.-vnn.org/editorials/ET99107ET17-4959.html, archived at Radha.name, 2015, https://www.radha.-name/news/general-news/the-first-western-vaishnava (accessed 31 March 2023).

[41]*Ibid,*

[42]Deepanjan Ghosh, 'Charles Stuart: More "Hindoo" than British,' *Live History India*, (Mumbai: Live History India, 2020), https://www.peepultree.world/livehistoryindia/story/eras/charles-stuart-more-hindoo-than-british (accessed 2 August 2023).

[43]Julian Strube, *Global Tantra: Religion, Science, and Nationalism in Colonial Modernity*, (Oxford: Oxford University Press, 2022), 226.

[44]Brooks, *The Hare Krishnas in India*, 100.

[45]Gerald T. Carney, 'Baba Premananda Bharati (1857–1914), an Early Twentieth-Century Encounter of Vaishnava Devotion with American Culture', *Journal of Vaishnava Studies* 6.2, (1998), 161–88, cited in Gopal Stavig, 'Baba Premananda Bharati and the Vedanta Society' (part one), *Vedanta Kesari*, 103.2, (2016), 35.

[46]Gerald T. Carney, 'Baba Premananda Bharati: His Trajectory into and through Bengal Vaiṣṇavism to the West,' in Ferdinando Sardella and Lucian Wong (eds), *The Legacy of Vaiṣṇavism in Colonial Bengal*, (Abingdon: Routledge, 2020), 85.

[47]Also published as *Srimad-Gourangalila-Smaranamangal Stotram, Sri Sri Gourangalila-Smaranamangal Stotram* and *Srigouranga Smaranamangala or Chaitanya Mahaprabhu, His Life and Precepts.*

[48]Ferdinando Sardella, *Modern Hindu Personalism: The History, Life, and Thought of Bhaktisiddhānta Sarasvatī*, (Oxford: Oxford University Press, 2013), 96.

[49]Varuni Bhatia, 'Sisir's Tears: *Bhakti* and Belonging in Colonial Bengal,' *International Journal of Hindu Studies*, 21.1, (2017), 18.

[50]ABN Sinha, 'Sri Rupkala the Virakt,' *The Hindustan Review*, 37, (1918), 427.

[51]'Lord Gauranga by Shishir Kumar Ghose' (review), *Bhavan's Journal*, 14, (1967), 57.

[52]'Lord Gauranga or Salvation for All, Vol. II' (review), *The Theosophist*, 20.9, (1899), 567–568.

[53]Carney, 'Baba Premananda Bharati', 84.

[54]Premānanda Bhāratī, "The White Peril," in *The New York Herald* cited in "Appendix: Bābā Bhāratī's Newspaper Articles," in Neal Delmonico (ed.), *Śrī Kṛṣṇa: The Lord of Love*, (Kirksville: Blazing Sapphire Press, 2007), 341.

[55]Stavig, 'Baba Premananda Bharati and the Vedanta Society' (part one), 34.

[56]RA Rowan & Co. and Robt Marsh & Co., 'Venice a Center of Education' (advertisement), *The Los Angeles Times*, 26 March 1905, 24.

[57]Carney, 'Baba Premananda Bharati,' 90.

[58]Carney, 'Baba Premananda Bharati,' 92.

[59]Gopal Stavig, 'Baba Premananda Bharati and the Vedanta Society' (part two), *Vedanta Kesari*, 103.3, (2016), 28.

[60]Carney, 'Baba Premananda Bharati,' 92.

[61]'Bharati, Baba Premanand,' in Constance A. Jones and James D. Ryan, *Encyclopedia of Hinduism*, (New York: Facts on File, 2007), 80.

[62]Carney, 'Baba Premananda Bharati,' 94.

[63]Gerald Carney, 'Introductory Essay' in Premananda Bhāratī *Śrī Kṛṣṇa: The Lord of Love*, ed. Neal Delmonico (Kirksville MO: Blazing Sapphire Press, 2017), lxviii.

[64]*Ibid.*

[65]"In the years after his death, Premananda was condemned by American nativists such as Elizabeth Reed, who were mobilizing public support for the Asian Exclusion Act [sic], which passed in 1917." Jones and Ryan, *Encyclopedia of Hinduism*, 80.

[66]Elizabeth A. Reed, *Hinduism in Europe and America*, (New York: GP Putnam's Sons,1914), 127.

[67]Delmar DeForest Bryant (1858–1939), an Ohio-based alchemist and would-be 'sex mage' whose Adiramled School of Hermetic Science offered a form of occult 'healing' dubbed "Thought-sexation."

[68]Pat Deveney, 'Light of India,' *IAPSOP*, (Forest Grove, International Association for the Preservation of Spiritualist and Occult Periodicals, 2020), http://iapsop.com/archive/materials/light-of-india (accessed 17 May 2022).

[69]Dassee (more commonly *Dāsī*) means "servant (of);" this suffix (or its male equivalent, *Dāsa*), though not used in the Mirtola tradition, is typically added to the names of initiated Gauḍīya Vaiṣṇavas.

[70]Ghose, the founder of the Calcutta-based Gauranga Samaj, is credited (somewhat unconvincingly) in the same magazine (6.2, 126) with being "instrumental in popularising Vaishnavism in America."

[71]Shishir Kumar Ghose (ed.), 'Notes,' *The Hindu Spiritual Magazine*, 3.9, (1908), 235.

[72]Shishir K. Ghose, 'The Religious Convention and its Work,' *The Hindu Spiritual Magazine*, 4.3, (1909), 182.

[73]Haripada Adhikary, *Unifying Force of Hinduism: The Harekrsna Movement*, (Bloomington: AuthorHouse, 2012), 205.

[74]Adhikary, *Unifying Force of Hinduism*, 206.

[75]Rajagopal Chattopadhyaya, *Swami Vivekananda in India: A Corrective Biography*, (Delhi: Motilal Banarsidass, 1999), 282.

[76]*Ibid.*

[77]Carney, 'Introductory Essay', xxxii.

[78]Haberman, 'A Cross-cultural Adventure,' 223.

[79]Joshua Nash, 'A Note on Sri Krishnaprem: A Little Known Vaishnava Luminary,' *Journal of Vaishnava Studies*, 28.2, (2020), 73.

[80]Oldmeadow, *Journeys East*, 70.

[81]Falconar, *Sufi Literature and the Journey to Immortality*, 150.

[82]Sen, 'Sri Krishnaprem,' xxi.

9: The Whole Hog

"[W]ithout ... understanding of the cultural pattern of India ... there is no possibility of understanding the vast complex tissue of the Mystic Consciousness."[1]
— KC Varadachari

Having returned to Mirtola, Krishna Prem continued his training, under Yashoda Mai's guidance, in the "strict discipline of Hindu tradition: service of the Guru, personal austerity, meditation, ritual worship and study."[2] Yashoda Mai also emphasised the learning of the Bengali devotional songs (*kīrtans* or *bhajans*) of the Vaiṣṇava tradition, the heartfelt performance of which earned Krishna Prem renown across spiritual India and invitations to *kīrtan* festivals known as *kīrtan utsavas* (Ashish, 103). "He had a good singing voice, albeit in the European mode of voice production, though the feeling he poured into his singing was so stirring to his audiences that one never heard of any criticism on this score," writes Sri Madhava Ashish (Ashish, 103). Ethel Merston, one of George Gurdjieff's first English pupils, who visited Uttar Brindaban under Yashoda Mai and later introduced Madhava Ashish to Krishna Prem, regarded the latter as an "accomplished musician [who] was the only Westerner she ever heard who could play and sing like a Hindu."[3]

One such *kīrtan utsava* took place in the city of Monghyr (Munger), then in the province of Bihar and Orissa, in 1932–1933. Swami Sivananda Saraswati of Rishikesh—a *kīrtan* enthusiast who also sang at the event, as well as a similar *utsava* also attended by Krishna Prem in Etawah,[4] on the banks of the Yamuna—records his favourable impression of Krishna Prem's *kīrtan*:

> Sri Krishna Premi [sic] also known as Mr. Nixon, M. A. [sic] of Uttara Vrindavan, Almora, is a great Bhakta and a fine Sankirtanist. He evinces very keen interest in the movement. He sings and dances in divine ecstasy forgetting himself in Krishna Prem [pure love for

> Krishna]. He delivers lectures in Hindi and has now become a Sanskrit scholar. When an Englishman takes so much interest in Sankirtan, our Hindu brothers are lethargic and spend their time in sleeping only. What a shame![5]

A similar sentiment is expressed by Vimala Thakar, who lamented: "So many of the English have come to India and undergone a total transformation, whereas the Indians who live here don't have that inquiring spirit, don't have the commitment and determination to do it. They're still tied up in the words. But the foreigners came ... and they recognized what was here."[6] Sivananda, the founder of the Divine Life Society, later profiled Krishna Prem in his book *Satsanga and Svadhyaya* as one of 15 living *mahātmas* (realised souls) from whom "thirsty aspirants after the Truth" should seek "holy *darshan*;"[7] similarly, the Tamil poet and yogi Shuddhananda Bharati included "Sri Krishna Prem and Mrs. Chakravarti of Almora, the rapturous devotees of Krishna" in his list of Indian "Centres of Spiritual Dynamism."[8]

Another attendee at the Monghyr *utsava*, which began on 29 December 1932,[9] was the famed Gauḍīya Vaiṣṇava ascetic Ramdas Babaji. Ramdas also saw Krishna Prem passing into a trance during *kīrtan*, as well as his delivering two lectures, including one on the *Śikṣāṣṭaka*, an eight-verse Sanskrit prayer which is the only work known to have been composed personally by Chaitanya:

> About noontime on the first day of the conference, Sri Krishnaprem delivered a lecture on Sri Siksastakam in the presence of about 10,000 devotees. ...
>
> The same evening Sri Krishnaprem delivered a lecture on Bhakti Dharma in the Garrett Club in the presence of 10–12,000 devotees. [Ramdas] Babaji Maharaj was also present and was much satisfied to hear his lecture.
>
> On December 31, 1932, the last day of the conference, Babaji Maharaj came to know that Sri Krishnaprem was deeply engrossed in Nam Kirtan. Babaji Maharaj opened the window of his room and saw him chanting Mahamantra while playing karatal [hand cymbals]. Tears were flowing down the cheeks of Sri Krishnaprem and his body was trembling. ...
>
> Babaji Maharaj then said, 'Seeing him one enjoys the all encompassing mercy of Sri Nitaichand [Nityananda] and one is reminded of [Chaitanya] Mahaprabhu's saying—
>
> *pṛthivīte jato āche nagarādi grām*
sarbatra pracār hoibe mora nām

> "My name will be preached in every
> town and village of this Earth."[10]

Krishna Prem was also present, along with Bal Krishna and two other Radha-Raman Temple *Goswamis*, Krishna Chaitanya and Vijay Krishna, at a "nonstop festival of *harināma-saṅkīrtan*" that took place in Aligarh, near Vrindavan, in May 1933,[11] as well as an "ecstatic kirtan that went on till midnight," attended by Guha Roy Kalipada (the yogi and friend of Dilip Kumar Roy immortalised in the Allen Ginsberg poem 'Wichita Vortex Sutra'), held at the offices of Himadri Publications in Calcutta in the early 1940s.[12]

Madhava Ashish writes that, at the time, Krishna Prem was "thrilled" by the ecstatic symptoms (known in Sanskrit as the *sāttvika-bhāvas*) which overtook him during *saṅkīrtan*, which further increased his fame and garnered invitations to more *kīrtan* events. In allowing himself to "get carried away and ... leap up and dance, arms raised and singing, until he went into trance and collapsed" (Ashish, 103), Krishna Prem seemed to have left Professor Nixon behind for good, the joy of *kīrtan* "cut[ting] right across the intellectual arrogance of the man who thinks that the academic mind can achieve spiritual enlightenment" (Ashish, 103). He also notes that Krishna Prem may also have felt like he was emulating Chaitanya, the originator of the Gauḍīya Vaiṣṇnava tradition, "who also sang and danced and fell unconscious" (Ashish, 103) when leading *harināma-saṅkīrtan*, and who, in the words of Yashoda Mai, taught "that men should give up the pride of learning that keeps men separate and allow the tide of love for Krishna to sweep them clean of selfishness."[13]

Krishna Prem is clear, however, that such "emotional rapture," while a natural byproduct of the practice of devotional yoga, is commonly confused for the goal itself, and he criticised the "frothing emotionalism" that he felt too often passed for genuine *bhakti*.[14] Writing to Dilip Kumar Roy in 1935, he elaborated:

> About bhakti—the word is ambiguously used. Some people mean by it an emotional rapture *as such*. (Don't ignore these two small words.) In that case bhakti is not the highest thing. Others, including myself, mean by it self-giving to Krishna which is of course accompanied by emotional rapture but is not performed for the sake of the rapture. In that case it is the "highest" or something like highest. Loud applause from you at this point I suppose but be sure you don't misunderstand me. Before you can offer the "ghee" in the fire you have to know where the fire is and Krishna is in the Light, in the Light, in the Light![15]

Recalling his first visit to Mirtola, nearly 15 years after Monghyr, Madhava Ashish contrasts Krishna Prem's emotionally charged call-and-response temple *kīrtan* with the guarded intellectualism he says then otherwise characterised the man who would become his guru:

> After the evening service [he] sang in the temple ante-room, Krishna Prem leading and accompanying himself on a small harmonium, and Moti repeating each line of the song as is the custom in such communal singing. This was a different man; the intellectual barriers were down and emotion flooded him and throbbed through the temple. It was not the cheap, hysterical, auto-excitation one finds in many hymn-singing communities. It was the outpouring of an individual soul in longing for union with the divine beloved.[16]

The Indian mountaineer and anthropologist Navnit Parekh was impressed by both men's renditions of Hindu devotional songs when he visited Uttar Brindaban the following summer. Parekh describes the scene one evening after *ārati*[17] when Krishna Prem and Madhava Ashish performed Mira Bai's Hindi *bhajan* '*Mane Chakar Rakho Ji*' ('O Lord, Keep Me as Your Servant'):

> Now it was time for *bhajans* and *kīrtans*. Krishna-Premji brought out a harmonium while Madhav-Aashish brought a *mridangam* [two-headed drum]. ...
>
> Both, Krishna-Premji and Aashish-da, had very sweet and melodious voices. It was difficult to believe that two British-born *sanyasins* could recite and sing Sanskrit verses and Hindi *bhajans* with such purity of accent and chaste Hindi pronunciations. I was in ecstasy listening to these *bhajans* sung, in the silent fastness of [the] remote Himalayas. I felt I was being transported from this planet to a high Vaikuntha where Lord Shri Krishna lived.[18]

Balarama Reddy, a former resident of Sri Aurobindo Ashram and Sri Ramana Ashram who visited Mirtola in 1938, says Krishna Prem's musicianship was characterised by a "deep, genuine devotion" by which "all were impressed and moved." Writing about his stay at Ramana Ashram a decade later, when he sung *bhajans* for Ramana Maharshi, Reddy compares Krishna Prem's performance favourably to that of the professional musician and poet Harindranath Chattopadhyay:

> Harinath Chattopadyaya was eager to display his singing talent and harmonium playing. No one really asked him to do so, but that did not stop him. He began playing and singing, exhibiting copious skills, but all his talent fell flat in comparison to the natural talent that sprung from the devotion of Krishnaprem.[19]

In addition to *kīrtan*, Krishna Prem's *sādhana* included the quiet or silent chanting of *mantras* as a form of meditation, known as *japa*, though he was considerably less enthusiastic about it than would typically be expected of a follower of Chaitanya. Like *saṅkīrtan*, *japa* of the names of Radha and Krishna, typically in the form of the *mahā-mantra*, on a string of prayer beads (*mālā*) is a central pillar of Gauḍīya Vaiṣṇava practice: Iskcon devotees, for example, commit to chanting at least 16 'rounds' of 108 recitations of the Hare Krishna *mantra*—1,728 in total—every day, while ascetics such as Durlabh Das Babaji (who "did Nama-japa all day and night and never left it even for a moment except for a short while when he slept"[20]) and Ramakrishna Das Babaji (whose finger became "so straight and stiff that it could not be bent and used [for] eating"[21]) from his constant chanting[22] are portrayed as ideal Vaiṣṇavas in hagiographies such as those in *The Saints of Vraja*. At Uttar Brindaban, however, *japa yoga* was conceived as a warm-up exercise to the 'main' meditation session, rather than the highest form of communion with the divine: Madhava Ashish explained to one of his disciples that the purpose of *mantra* meditation is to quieten the mind, as a prelude to the kind of silent self-enquiry popularly associated with the practice of meditation.

Responding to his disciple Donald Eichert, who had asked for instruction on meditation, in 1962, Krishna Prem recommends a form of meditation that resembles the 'Who am I?'/'I am' practice favoured by *Advaitins* such as Ramana Maharshi:

> 1. *[Meditate o]n an actual problem.* Make it *clear* in your mind & then hold it steady till you get an answer coming up in your mind. Test the latter with your intelligence.
> 2. *Who am I?* Push *in* with it.
> 3. If there are intruding thoughts or images follow them back to their source so as to understand *why* they persist.
> 4. Just watch your thoughts as you would passers-by from a window-noting but not trying to stop them. Thus you learn that you are not the thoughts.
>
> All may be preceded by trying to feel the presence of Christ—Krishna—Guru *within you* and self offering thereto.[23]

The Mirtola ashramites also differed from conventional Gauḍīya Vaiṣṇavas in the *mantra* chanted: *japa* at Uttar Brindaban was of the *mantra* given to Yashoda Mai by the goddess Devi (see chapter six), rather than the typical 16-word Hare Krishna *mahā-mantra*.

Where he did agree with mainstream Vaiṣṇava authorities is on the poor efficacy of "mechanical," *bhakti*-less chanting as a means of achieving union with God. The *sādhaka* who does include *japa* in their "doing" should have already begun to cultivate a loving relationship with their object of their devotion, who must be kept at the front of their mind for the duration of the *japa* session, he informed his friend, the Sanskritist Govindagopal Mukherji, in 1941:

> *Nama-japa* can be done by anyone but it is only very effective in practice (whatever books may say) when the name is one which is so loved that its repetition calls up the image of its Bearer. Mere mechanical or loveless repetition is—I won't say useless—but of very limited use.
>
> Remember that nothing mechanical is of any use since that which is mechanical is dead and this path is the path of life.[24]

Elsewhere, Krishna Prem explained that *japa* is but one tool in a multi-faceted metaphysical arsenal that might also include "*pūjā*, writing, cooking, gardening or *prāṇāyama* [breathing exercises]"[25] (breath control being useful in making sure the *sādhaka* is not "disturbed should he experience a degree of ecstasy or trance with temporary cessation of the use of the faculties" during meditation[26]). This idea—as well as that of *japa* as a means of preparing the mind for silent meditation—seems to have been inherited from Yashoda Mai, who goes as far as to write that the "essence of the whole Path" is contained in the ability to suppress one's "senses and ego." "For this reason," she explains,

> all religions according to their own special methods teach the suppression of egoism. For instance, Vaishnavas, by prolonged repetition of mantras or of the Name of God or by singing kirtans together, put the senses to sleep by tiring them out. [Jñāna-y]ogis do the same by the exercise of pranayama, followers of the path of love by fires of separation that burn in their heart, devotees by the emotion of surrender and Buddhists by giving up the hope of gaining anything in a world which they realise to be empty like a dream. All of them achieve the same result by some means or other.[27]

Whichever of these spiritual practices one is drawn to, the most important thing, Krishna Prem told Dilip Kumar Roy, for yogis on the spiritual path is simply to "do:"

> Say what you will about 'pure' contemplation or 'pure' *bhakti*, the question we ordinary people always ask is: what are we to do to attain the Goal? *Do*; ... By 'doing' we light the Fire which is to burn up

> all doings. Without friction that Fire cannot be lit: without tending it cannot be maintained. We must handle in order to 'realise.' On no account should we despise what the alchemists called 'the manual work.'[28]

This conception of 'manual work'—which he advised should include a daily period dedicated to "strengthening the realisation of His [Krishna's] presence," and which may include the repetition of *mantras* ("uttering only the Sound of His form, that is His Mantra, watch for Him to appear," he guided Narendra Nath Kaul[29])—was, for Krishna Prem, epitomised by the famous verse from the *Kaṭha Upaniṣad*, as paraphrased by Swami Vivekananda, "Arise, awake, and stop not till the goal is reached,"[30] or by Krishna's instructions to Arjuna in the *Bhagavad Gītā*: "Remember me and fight."[31] As he explained to his *praśiṣya* Karan Singh, "all energies must be harnessed for the quest if it is really to be seriously pursued. If one wants to cross to the other bank of a lake one has to embark on the crossing. Merely standing on the shore and arguing or speculating about how deep the lake is or how long it will take to cross will not bring us an inch nearer the goal."[32]

In addition to learning Sanskrit *mantras* and Bengali *bhajans*, Krishna Prem continued his instruction in the Bengali language, and spoke either Bengali or Hindi, which he had also learnt from Yashoda Mai, to his guru.[33] He had also learnt to read Sanskrit, the sacred language of Hinduism, in Benares,[34] and used this knowledge to study in the original Hindu texts such as the *Bhagavad Gītā* (which, recounts the Kumaoni teacher Anuradha Joshi, he could recite "beautifully" with "perfect" pronunciation[35]), the *Bhāgavata Purāṇa* and the Upanishads.[36]

From contemporary correspondence it seems Krishna Prem, in stark contrast to the modern teachers seeking to detach Krishna *bhakti* from its Indian roots,[37] regarded this progressive Indianisation of his manners and person—in addition to speaking only Indian languages, he had long dressed like an Indian Vaiṣṇava, "with shaven head, *Chutily* (a tuft of hair at the crown), Vaiṣṇava Tilaka (sacred mark on the forehead) and wooden sandals with a peg, on his feet,"[38] and, after independence, encouraged his European disciples to apply for Indian citizenship[39]—as a natural consequence of his religious conversion. (Madhava Ashish claimed he and Krishna Prem were the second and third foreigners to be granted Indian citizenship; the first, he believed, was the British-born Gandhian activist and Hindu convert Verrier Elwin.[40]) In a December 1929 letter to Dilip Kumar Roy, Krishna Prem rails against those urban Westerners ('Megalopolitans') who sought to pick and choose which aspects of Indian culture they would adopt: "I would rather the Megalopolitan were confronted once and for all with the necessity of a choice," he writes, "so that if he chose India he should have to renounce his cultural pride for good and all and bow his head in the dust that Sri Krishna trod."[41]

In the same letter, sent from Almora, he criticises the hypocrisy of Europeans who looked down on those who had fully immersed themselves in India:

> I have often noticed that many European scholars will discourse eloquently about the beauty and healthiness and convenience of Indian dress, say, or Indian ways, but let any European take them at their word and go and put on a *dhoti* [a sarong or loincloth worn by Indian men] and he is damned at once. It is so with Western thought. It will talk eloquently but will never "put on the *dhoti*," and will regard you as vulgar if you attempt to do so.[42]

A famous anecdote from *Yogi Sri Krishnaprem* illustrates Krishna Prem's similar disregard for the bigoted ruling class of late imperial India and their rejection of all things Indian. Jashoda Ghosh, a mutual friend of Krishna Prem's and Roy's, describes the former's response to a British woman who had taken issue with his Indian dress:

> "Sri Krishnaprem carried with him a little Image of Lord Krishna, the one he worshipped daily. When we entered his compartment we found, on the opposite berth, an English lady, probably an Anglo-Indian. As we talked in English she must have inferred from his accent (as well as complexion) that he was an Englishman turned Hindu, that impossible anachronism in the twentieth century, with his beads, ochre-coloured robe and so on. She could not contain herself.
>
> "'Aren't you ashamed, you renegade,' she exploded, 'to hobnob with these natives, to flaunt these badges of superstition, to disown Christianity, to let down your kith and kin...?' So she went on ranting, a picture of the jingo gone mad. We got restive, but Sri Krishnaprem looked on, an amused smile flickering on his lips which only added fuel to the fire of her wrath and she shouted: 'What have you gained, may I ask, after throwing away everything: your culture, religion and country?' Sri Krishnaprem calmly produced his beloved Image of the Lord and answered, with his radiant smile: 'I have got Him, madam: my Krishna.'"[43]

Indians were equally surprised to see a white man in saffron robes, recalls Madhava Ashish, who joined the ashram in 1946: "[W]herever we went we attracted a crowd of curious bystanders. It was before the age of Hippies when people got used to seeing white skins in Indian dress. When a train stopped at a station, within a minute the windows would be filled with staring faces" (Ashish, 187).

Nixon had regarded himself as Indian since at least January 1927, before the move to Almora, as is clear from another letter to Roy in which he declares that, "though I can be tolerant to all countries, I have only one, and that, strange to say, is not England but India."[44] From then on, as Khushwant Singh observed in *The Times of India*, "[t]he only thing English that remained with him was his pipe."[45]

This complete embrace of India and its customs at the expense of his pre-existing Britishness was evident to Krishna Prem's university friend, the painter Roland Penrose, who visited with his then wife, Valentine, in early 1933. In March, the Penroses met Krishna Prem in Benares, where, as Roland noted approvingly in a letter to his brother Alec, it became clear the former Ronald Nixon had undergone a total transformation:

> At Benares (Varanasi), Roland found Nixon 'with his friends camping on the bank of the Ganges. Nixon has certainly gone the whole hog and accepted the Hindou [sic] religion with all it has, superficial and profound. Perhaps he's right ... I have the greatest esteem for his courage in doing the thing properly. The English people who hear of it throw their hands in horror and ask if he really wanted to go in for religion, why didn't he do it decently and become a padre? Nixon, in his own way, is offering some slight atonement for the sins of his compatriots and he is loved and respected by everyone. He has no small courage.'[46]

Roland was less impressed by George Poole, a former Christian minister, who, he felt, had merely exchanged his dog collar for a *dhoti* without undergoing any meaningful inner makeover. "[Poole] lives here [Mirtola] permanently and officiates in the temple. He is an ex-parson and has changed, again with great thoroughness, his former religion and rites for the worship of Krishna," he writes, "though unfortunately one still sees the same ritualistic Anglican underneath the eastern costume. He has all his reasons for what he is doing clearly tabulated but in these questions it is not reasons that can convince me."[47]

Madhava Ashish is more forgiving in his assessment of Poole (whom he never met), noting that for all his "sophistication," there was a "delightfully simple side" to the scholarly ex-vicar, illustrated by the following anecdote:

> He had built his house, a semi-two-storey bungalow, on the same level as the temple, but one hundred yards or so distant. I say 'semi' because it was built against the hillside, so the top floor at the back was again level with the land. It was built largely out of materials quarried from the bungalow in which Yashoda Mai and Krishna Prem had stayed up the hill while the temple was being built.
>
> When the house was complete, Yashoda Mai told George that he should perform a puja in which he would make an offering of the house to Sri Krishna as established in the temple. George took this quite seriously and did all that should be done. Then he came to Yashoda Mai and asked, rather nervously, now that he had offered the house to the Lord, where should he himself stay? (Ashish, 131–132)

While in Benares, the Penroses stayed at Radha Vilas as guests of Gyanendra Nath Chakravarti. Yashoda Mai, paying a visit to her husband and family at her former home, was present at the same time, though she did not go indoors and insisted on sleeping in a boat moored on the bank of the nearby Ganges. ("She does not come into the house as she has abandoned everything and taken the orange robe of a Sannyasini," writes Roland;[48] Hindu tradition holds that monks are forbidden from living in a house.[49]) Roland also recorded his favourable impression of the erstwhile Mrs Chakravarti, whom, he noted, was as at home discussing "the merits of café au lait and her memories of London & Paris"[50] as she was questions of philosophy with the crowds of "students and others [who would] come and squat round on the river bank"[51] every evening. (Similarly, on her first visit to Mirtola, Gertrude Emerson Sen observed how Yashoda Mai, though a "small figure in ochre dress, head shaven, a string of tulsi beads around her neck," could easily slip back into being "the gracious hostess of the old Lucknow days."[52])

While Yashoda Mai held court at the house, her disciple entertained the pilgrims of Benares, who were eager to pay their respects to the European *sannyāsī*, Penrose continues:

> You should see the scuffles that go on around Nixon as he runs backwards laughing and trying to protect his feet with his orange robe, at first sight it looks more like the opening manoeuvres of wrestlers than a competition in respectfulness. Some experts have a lightning

> method of getting at the feet of the master before he knows where he is and apparently feel much better for having succeeded. As soon as this is over normal conversation may begin but Nixon certainly has no easy job to answer questions in philosophy all day long from a crowd of people a great many of whom come more to show off their own knowledge or curry favour with a white man who has done so much to win their esteem.[53]

The couple also visited Uttar Brindaban (though with Krishna Prem and Yashoda Mai still in Benares, it was, in Roland's words, "a little like the box without the chocolates"[54]), which at that time consisted of just three buildings: the temple, the post office and Poole's house, in which the Penroses stayed.[55] Roland's impressions of Uttar Brindaban, given in another letter to Alec Penrose, provide a valuable account of the ashram's early years, as well as a description of the flora and fauna of the Kumaon Himalayas, including 'cat-like' martens. Life at the ashram, he writes,

> is completely à la Hindou and after two days of it one begins to wish for a few simple western devices such as a spoon to eat rice and sour milk with, a bath and a chair. One's legs and back get a little tired of doing everything frog fashion. However that is a minor point. The food is very good though strictly vegetarian and rather spicey and the air up here after the heat on the plains gives one new life. The forest except down in the valleys is very dry and sparse, the trees vary in kind according to the altitude, here they consist almost entirely of evergreen oaks and rhododendrons which are now covered with crimson flowers, otherwise there is a good deal of monotony and we consider that the Pyrenees have a charm of variety on a small scale which does not exist here. While I sit on a small summit writing with the line of snow peaks to the north and the hills spreading out as far as one can see on all sides I am continually distracted by the variety of strange birds and just now three large cat like animals ran past within twenty yards without seeing me. They were black on their heads, backs and tails and shaded off into a redish [sic] brown under. They had a beautiful serpent like motion as they leapt after each other snarling and chasing after their long tails.[56]

At this time the ashram employed a *pūjārī*, or temple priest, who would have also been responsible for the food enjoyed by the visiting Penroses. Though Yashoda Mai was a "wonderful cook" (Ashish, 129) she had become too ill to prepare the *bhoga* and the task was delegated to a Brahmin from one of the local villages. Employing outsiders, however, came with its own set of challenges, and it wasn't long before Krishna Prem could both speak and cook like a Bengali, as Madhava Ashish explains:

> From the beginning a pujari had been employed to cook and perform the worship. Krishna Prem would do any special puja, but the routine was done by the priest. As newcomers, they knew very little about the local villages and their affairs, so they would mostly employ whoever was willing and of the right caste. On one occasion they ran into trouble, finding that Yashoda Mai just could not eat the food produced by the new priest, so Krishna Prem began cooking her meals separately. Then they discovered the trouble. The new pujari came from a village where there had recently been a murder and no arrest had been made. Hill customs ruled that under such circumstances no one outside the village would take food from the hand of anyone belonging to that village. It seemed that Yashoda Mai's psyche would not allow her to take food from a man who might be a murderer. As soon as he went, she recovered.
>
> Other pujaris came and went. Then it was found that the current one was stealing to an unacceptable degree, and they were tired of pujaris and the constant stream of complaints against them. Krishna Prem announced that he would tell the man to go. But who would then do the cooking? ... Krishna Prem announced that he would cook. Yashoda Mai would tell him what to do. He would do it to the best of his ability. Yashoda Mai would then comment, criticise and tell him what he did wrong. Thus Krishna Prem became an expert cook in the Bengali style. So the pujari was got rid of and the temple became a quiet place again with Krishna Prem in the kitchen. (Ashish, 128—129)

From then on, he shared cooking duties with Moti Rani, taking charge of the kitchen full time after her death in 1951.[57] Even when others would help prepare the *bhoga*, it was always obvious when meals had been cooked by Krishna Prem, recalls Bill Aitken. "Without fail I could tell on which day Krishna Prem had been cooking by the taste of the food," he writes. "He used the same ingredients as the others but cooked with so much feeling you could taste the difference."[58]

'Ma', however, continued to keep a close eye on the kitchen. In spite of her failing health, she was capable of extraordinary bursts of activity, particularly after being made aware that an errant ashramite had violated one of Mirtola's many rules relating to ritual cleanliness. Madhava Ashish continues:

> Krishna Prem told me how she might be lying in bed with fever and pain, but if an emergency arose, such as a breach of discipline in the

kitchen which meant that the food could not be offered in the temple, she would go downstairs, take over the kitchen and cook again from the start as if there was nothing wrong with her at all.

Then she would go up to her room, lie down, and the fever would come back. Krishna Prem once asked her about this. Why could she not just get rid of the illnesses? She said she could, but if she did so the illness would have to go elsewhere, probably onto her dogs, and this she was not prepared to do. (Ashish, 136)

Notes

[1]Singh, *New Light on Sri Krishna & Gita*, 15.

[2]Madhava Ashish, 'Sri Sri Krishnaprem Vairagi', 89.

[3]Mary Ellen Korman, *A Woman's Work, with Gurdjieff, Ramana Maharshi, Krishnamurti, Anandamayi Ma & Pak Subuh: The Spiritual Life Journey of Ethel Merston*, (Fairfax: Arte Communications, 2009), 162.

[4]"I met Swamiji Maharaj twice, once at Monghyr Sankirtan Utsava, and once at a similar festival in Etawah." DN Jhingan, *Sage of Ananda Kutir*, (Rishikesh: Sivananda Publication League, 1944), 196.

[5]Swami Sivananda, *Practice of Bhakti Yoga*, (Amritsar: Em. Airi, 1937), 129.

[6]Townend, *The Hidden Master*, 264.

[7]Sri Swami Sivananda, 'Darshan Yoga or Holy Darshan of Living Mahatmas,' *Satsanga and Svadhyaya*, WWW edn, (Tehri Garhwal: Divine Life Society, 2000), https://www.dlshq.org/download/satsanga-and-svadhyaya/ (accessed 9 November 2022).

[8]Kavi Yogi Mahrshi Dr Shuddhananda Bharathi, *Experiences of a Pilgrim Soul*, (Chennai: BY Shuddhananda Library), ch. 92: 'Land of Ashrams,' para. 11.

[9]Subrata Dutta, 'Brief Biography of Sidhdha Sripad 108 Ram Das Babaji Maharaja (Contd),' NitaiSundar.com, Kolkata, 2007, https://web.archive.org/web/20090102123541/http://www.nitaisundar.com/site/Main.html?pagename=BabajiMahasaya-Bio3.html (accessed 16 April 2023).

[10]*His Divine Grace – A Brief Life History of Sripad Ramdas Babaji Mahasay*, (Birchandrapur: Sri Nityananda Janmasthan), cited in Sakhicharan Das, 'Babaji Maharaj and Sri Krishnaprem at Munger,' *Living in Sri Radhakund* [blog], 4 May 2009, https://sriradhakund.wordpress.com/2009/05/04/babaji-maharaj-and-sri-krishnaprem-at-munger (accessed 27 May 2022).

[11]Swami Sanatandev and Govindadas Vaishnav (eds), श्री उड़िया बाबाजी के संस्मरण (Śrī Udiyā Bābā Jī Ke Saṃsmaraṇa), vol. 1, (Mathura: Sadhan Press, 1952), 361.

[12]Joy Roy Choudhury, '"Don't Miss the Last Bus to Cross the Frontier:" Maha-Kriya Samadhi and the Countdown to the Coming Time', *Joy Roy Choudhury's Web Log* [blog], 21 October 2015, https://artcritique.wordpress.com/2015/10/21/dont-miss-the-last-bus (accessed 17 April 2023).

[13]Tandan, 'Metaphors and Quotes of Yashoda Mai', 1.

[14]Krishna Prem, 'The Yoga of the Gita,' para. 23.

[15]Sujata Nahar and Shankar Bandyopadhyay (eds), *Sri Aurobindo to Dilip, Vol 2 (1934–1935)*, (Pune: The Mother & Sri Aurobindo, 2005), 305, https://web.archive.org/web/20160321131726/http://aurobindo.ru/workings/sa/to-dilip/vol-2-e.htm (accessed 10 April 2023).

[16]Madhava Ashish, 'Sri Krishna Prem Through the Eyes of a Disciple', 12.

[17]A ceremony in which the *vigrahas* of Radha–Krishna are offered various items, particularly light in the form of a sacred flame, in an act of worship.

[18]Navnit Parekh, *Himalayan Memoirs*, (Bombay: Popular Prakashan, 1986), 48–49.

[19]N. Balarama Reddy, 'The Recollections of N. Balarama Reddy—Part VII', *The Maharshi*, 6.2, (1996), sec. 2, para. 5, https://archive.arunachala.org/newsletters/1996/mar-apr (accessed 4 December 2022).

[20]OBL Kapoor, 'Durlabh Das Baba Ji, in *The Saints of Vraja*, 4th edn, (New Delhi: Aravali Books International, 2015), 188.

[21]OBL Kapoor, 'Paṇḍita Śrī Rāmakṛṣṇa Dāsa Bābā Jī,' in *The Saints of Vraja*, 4th edn, (New Delhi: Aravali Books International, 2015), 188.

[22]The index finger remains outside the bag used to hold one's *japa* beads.

[23]Sri Krishna Prem, letter to Donald Eichert, 1962.

[24]Roy, *Yogi Sri Krishnaprem*, 203.

[25]Roy, *Yogi Sri Krishnaprem*, 252.

[26]Rutledge, *In Search of a Yogi*, 250.

[27]Tandan, 'Metaphors and Quotes of Yashoda Mai,' 7.

[28]Roy, *Yogi Sri Krishnaprem*, 252–253.

[29]Kaul, *Writings of Sri Krishna Prem*, 102.

[30]Karan Singh, *The Mountain of Shiva*, ebook edn, (New Delhi: Palimpsest, 2016), ch. 5, para. 113.

[31]Kaul, *Writings of Sri Krishna Prem*, 106.

[32]*Ibid.*

[33]Madhava Ashish, 'Sri Sri Krishnaprem Vairagi,' 89.

[34]*Ibid.*

[35]Anuradha Joshi, 'My Memories of Mussoorie,' *In Our Days* [blog], 24 November 2020, https://www.inourdays.org/women/my-memories-mussoorie (accessed 7 November 2022).

[36]Kapoor, 'Śrī Kṛṣṇaprema,' 295.

[37]Hridayananda Das Goswami's Iskcon offshoot, Krishna West, for example, as well as secular, new-age '*bhakti*' musicians.

[38]Madhava Ashish, 'Sri Sri Krishnaprem Vairagi,' 88.

[39]Aitken, *Footloose in the Himalaya*, 93.

[40]Ramachandra Guha, *Savaging the Civilized: Verrier Elwin, His Tribals, & India*, (Chicago: University of Chicago Press, 1999), 278.

[41]Roy, *Yogi Sri Krishnaprem*, 142.

[42]Roy, *Yogi Sri Krishnaprem*, 141.

[43]Roy, *Yogi Sri Krishnaprem*, 127.

[44]Roy, *Yogi Sri Krishnaprem*, 134.

[45]Khushwant Singh, 'Scholar-Turned-Swami' (review of *Initiation Into Yoga: An Introduction to the Spiritual Life*), *The Times of India*, 8 August 1976.

[46]King, *Roland Penrose*, 116.

[47]King, *Roland Penrose*, 115.

[48]Penrose, letter to Alec Penrose, 18 March 1933.

[49]Swami Nikhilananda, *Ramakrishna: Prophet of New India*, (New York: Harper & Brothers, 1948), 166.

[50]Penrose, letter to Alec Penrose, 18 March 1933.

[51]*Ibid,*

[52]Mehra, *Nearer Heaven than Earth*, 486.

[53]Roland Penrose, letter to Alec Penrose, 22 March 1933, Roland Penrose Collection, Scottish National Gallery of Modern Art Archive, Edinburgh, RPA370.

[54]Roland Penrose, letter to Alec Penrose, 20 March 1933, Roland Penrose Collection, Scottish National Gallery of Modern Art Archive, Edinburgh, RPA370.

[55]*Ibid.*

[56]*Ibid.*

[57]Madhava Ashish, 'Sri Sri Krishnaprem Vairagi,' 90.

[58]Aitken, *Footloose in the Himalaya*, 86.

10: Pūjāri

"[T]he Truth itself is beyond form, even though, initially, we have to seek it through concrete symbols and defined shapes."[1]
— 'Aropa' (Sri Madhava Ashish), *Faith & Fire*

Yashoda Mai's tenure as head of the Mirtola ashram saw all residents following the strict ritual purity laws observed by the highest Hindu caste, the Brahmins, of which she was a member and into which Krishna Prem—who, as a non-Indian, had no birth caste—had been inducted by GN Chakravarti. (Chakravarti, a member of one of the highest Brahminical *gotras*, or sub-castes, the Shandilyas,[2] had in Benares given the Brahminical sacred thread, the *upavīta*, to Krishna Prem, who later gave Brahmin initiation to disciples including Bob Alexander/Sri Haridas [Ashish, 82] and Sri Madhava Ashish [Ashish, 239].) These rules compelled ashramites to bathe multiple times a day, whatever the weather, since even the most mundane acts—defecating, touching a dog, eating 'unclean' food, or coming into contact with 'impure' people, such as on public transport—would result in the Brahmin becoming ritually contaminated:

> When the brahmachari performs any impure act, he pulls up the loop of the thread which hangs at his right hand and winds it round his ear, thus keeping it well away from pollution. There it stays until he has a bath—or makes use of one of the purificatory by-laws. When performing the major excretory function, the brahmachari may also divest himself of his regular clothing and put on a set specifically kept for this purpose, a set that is often of wool which has the peculiar ritualistic property of being purified by exposure to sunlight, so does not have to be washed.
>
> Particularly because of the cold climate in Mirtola, we were all given a set of clothes to be worn on our excursions to the pit latrine in the forest. On our return these permanently impure clothes were hung

> on a separate peg; we bathed, and resumed our normal still ritually pure clothing. (Ashish, 82-83)

As a "traditional Vaishnav ashram," confirms Satish Datt Pandey, Uttar Brindaban "followed an austere lifestyle with many dos and don'ts and elaborate rituals associated with cooking, eating, meditating and worshipping in the temple. Throughout the year, they bathed with cold water, fuel for heating in winters was strictly rationed, there was no tea and the rather spartan vegetarian food was cooked and eaten ritually. There were no 'mod cons', no 'attached bathrooms. Instead of shoes, there were the traditional wooden sandals known as kharaon, and there were no newspapers, radio or any other means of entertainment."[3] Anuradha Joshi, whose grandfather was a friend of Sri Haridas (Bob Alexander), remembers that Alexander was especially strict about his diet, consuming just five food items, two of which were salt and water;[4] Donald Eichert writes that the "authentic Bengali cuisine" favoured by Yashoda Mai and served at the ashram was "often eaten stone-cold."[5]

Those following these rules developed "a remarkable degree of self-awareness," writes Madhava Ashish, "for one had to know at any moment whether, for instance, one was in a fit state to enter the temple or the temple kitchen. This also involved being aware of what others were doing and whether they were observing the rules" (Ashish, 121). His elder sister, Penelope Phipps (1916–2013[6]), who made four visits to Mirtola in the 1950s and '60s and took initiation from Krishna Prem, recalls: "If one transgressed, breaking a rule, a method, a custom, a look or word reprimanded one. One thought, 'But why does it matter?' but came to see one was being taught to be more conscious—aware—and cease trying to impose my own opinions so often."[7]

Bill Aitken, who first visited Mirtola in autumn 1960, describes the interpersonal "dramas" that arose as a result of such a self-aware, close-knit way of living: "Such Brahmanical rituals and laws: this hand to be used for this, that one for that ... don't let your shadow fall on this, total awareness of how you eat, ritual bathing in freezing water. There were all sorts of tantrums, explosions and emotional heart-burn, feeling sorry for oneself and wanting to stab the guru and run away. Life in an Ashram brings out every gamut of human experience and emotion."[8]

The ashram, as is common within Vaiṣṇavism, also observed *ekādaśī* (literally "eleventh day"), when devotees of Krishna/Vishnu abstain from eating beans and grains such as rice and bread for a 24-hour period. These regular fasts, observed roughly twice a month, were borne with typical austerity at Mirtola—particularly when compared with the Goswamis of Vrindavan, as Madhava Ashish discovered when staying at the home of Krishna Chaitanya Goswami, one of the Radha-Raman Temple priests:

> Ekadashi is the eleventh day of the lunar cycle when one is supposed to restrain the senses. No grain may be eaten on that day. I had been introduced to this at the ashram and found it a miserable procedure. One had tea with nothing else in the morning, two or three boiled potatoes with ghee and salt and some curd at midday, and tea in the evening or milk if there was any, which was seldom. I could hardly imagine anything more austere, but assumed that these great Goswamis, whose personal discipline was frighteningly strict, must observe this fast more strictly than we did. If so, then what was the point of the invitation? I discovered, of course, that we were served a sumptuous meal with every sort of delicacy made from the flour of plants which were not grains, or did not count as grain, like the seeds of buckwheat. (Ashish, 163)

The strict regime at Uttar Brindaban did not, however, include the usual Brahminical–Vaiṣṇavite prohibition on intoxicants, which for some Vaiṣṇavas extends even to caffeine. (AC Bhaktivedanta Swami, the founder of Iskcon, claimed to have left his wife over her refusal to give up tea.) Tea and coffee were consumed by all at Mirtola, and some ashramites also indulged in nicotine and, in moderation, alcohol, including brandy (Ashish, 209) and sherry.[9] Krishna Prem continued to smoke the meerschaum of which Ronald Nixon had been fond (his one un-sadhu-like luxury, according to Madhava Ashish[10]), while Yashoda Mai, Moti Rani and Madhava Ashish all smoked cigarettes. According to the British writer Paul Brunton, Yashoda Mai was even responsible for encouraging other people to take up smoking. He recalls: "Her Holiness [Yashoda Mai] told a North Indian prince that it was not bad to smoke and offered him a cigarette herself. So naturally he smoked it, having received it from such holy hands. 'I could not refuse it,' the prince told me."[11] Brunton, who is credited with introducing the South Indian saint Ramana Maharshi to Western audiences, notes that both HP Blavatsky and GI Gurdjieff—spiritual personalities who would have a significant impact on the Mirtola philosophy—also smoked: "Blavatsky, the Theosophical seer, too often kept her fingers busy rolling long Russian cigarettes. Gurdjieff, the Armenian occultist and one-time teacher of Ouspensky, usually produced packets of cigarettes for his disciples to smoke, whilst himself indulging in oversized cigarettes."[12]

These small luxuries aside, all would-be yogis were expected to live the kind of "austere and orthodox life" (Ashish, 158) favoured by Yashoda Mai and Krishna Prem. Madhava Ashish recalls the cold baths, infrequent meals and rigid temple schedule that were still a feature of Mirtola life when he joined the ashram in the '40s, shortly after Yashoda Mai's passing:

> Krishna Prem was ... rising early to perform the temple *pūjā*, which

> lasted up to three hours, and then doing his morning *sandhyā* [meditation], which might go on till ten am. After a short break for tea, he would then have to the start the temple cooking which went on till twelve when *bhoga* [food] was offered in the temple and then taken down to the newly built *Samādhi* temple [tomb] of Yashoda Ma....
>
> One of the many hardships we had to get used to was the cold water bath which continued right up into December. When it was thought cold enough for us to start having a wood fire in our rooms at night, we were issued a large brass or copper water jar (*ghara*) which one stood in the fireplace and, if one managed things properly, got enough hot water for a really good bath. (Ashish, 158)

No one, including the elderly Yashoda Mai, the erstwhile grande dame of Lucknow high society, was spared the full Mirtola experience, adds Pandey:

> According to one account, a visitor to Mirtola during a rainy season saw that Ma was sleeping in her room with a badly leaking roof, on a bed covered with a sagging tarpaulin, resting on four bamboo poles. These had been fixed to the bed by Gopal Da, who himself slept under the bed! The generous visitor decided to make a contribution for the purchase of some tin sheets.[13]

The "strict orthodox ritual"[14] observed at the ashram greatly impressed the local villagers, according to Bill Aitken, though the spartan conditions could be challenging for the residents. In a letter included in his 1964 book *Himalayani Patra-Yatra* (*Correspondence from the Himalayas*), the celebrated Gujarati writer Kishansinh Chavda describes the harsh autumn nights at the ashram: "We have lots of warm clothes, many blankets and a fireplace in the room, but it always feels cold. In the morning, as soon as the sun rises, we go and sit in the heat."[15] Aitken, meanwhile, remembers how "one's heels developed wide cracks into which we stuffed a thick ointment made by Ashishda, which gave relief when seated. To avoid the exquisite pain when walking one minced along on the balls of one's feet."[16]

Locals were especially appreciative to see Hindu purification rituals "performed by sahibs [Europeans] when the British Raj was contemptuous of Hinduism,"[17] continues Aiken, as well as by the fact that "Gopalda was a man of learning" and Alexander "the top doctor of Lucknow" before he retired to run the ashram's clinic. "Mirtola also discreetly dispensed small cash loans to villagers in distress, and never insisted on repayment," he adds.[18] Madhava Ashish's disciple Jagdish Nautiyal, who worked for the Almora forest department, recalls that, on hearing that "there were three English sadhus [Krishna Prem, Madhava

Ashish and Haridas (Bob Alexander)] in the neighbourhood who lived in a temple," he initially "scoffed and said, 'spies;'"[19] he was, however, soon won over by the learned trio, who "were more Indian than most Indians I knew."[20]

Krishna Prem was similarly recognised as a genuine *sādhu* by the local religious authorities, as Gabriel Monod-Herzen recalls: "Sri Krishna Prem took me one day to the bottom of the neighbouring valley where, among the fragrant cedars, stands the old temple of Dandeshwar. While I was kindly requested to stay at the door, he entered the sanctuary to meditate there for a few minutes. While his blue eyes, his very British face, left no doubt about his European race, the *sannyāsī*'s dress guaranteed his right."[21]

Uttar Brindaban also attracted the attention of contemporary Bengali writers, who reported with approval on how their native tradition had been adopted by a handful of Britons over 1,000km away in the Kumaon hills.

Connecting Krishna Prem's religious conversion with Chaitanya's prediction that Krishna's names would one day echo out in "every town and village" on Earth, Jatindranath Roy, a writer for the Bengali periodical *Sri Sri Shyamsundar Barsha*, records how the "well-known English professor, R. H. Nixon M.A. [sic]" has taken the name Sri Krishna Prem Vairagi and is practising Vaiṣṇava *bhakti* in an ashram in the Himalayas. "Who can tell how many foreign devotees are hiding" from view, "silently practising the religion of love?" asks Roy, writing in 1932.[22] The story of the transformation of Ronald Nixon (here erroneously called 'Nicholson') into Sri Krishna Prem also gets nearly 10,000 words in Shankarnath Roy's *Bhārater Sādhak* (*Saints of India*).[23] Other *sādhakas* profiled in the 11-part series include Lāhirī Mahāśaya, disciple of the legendary Himalayan yoga master Mahāvatār Bābājī, the Vaiṣṇava saint Rāmdās Kathiabābā, and Trailaṅga Swāmī of Benares, who is said to have lived for 280 years.

Even Mahāvatār Bābājī—the 'deathless' yogi who is said to have lived in a cave in the remote Himalayas for millennia—apparently recognised Krishna Prem as a "messenger" of God, mentioning him by name during one his famous late-night 'visitations' to the Madras-based journalist VT Neelakantan in the 1950s:

> The ways of the Lord are, indeed, very mysterious. He sends His messengers to different parts of the world to elevate the people, according to the need of the hour. The messengers are born in one place, but they work in another distant clime. Saint Xavier was born in Spain, but he worked in India, Swami Rama Tirtha was born in Punjab, but he did most of his preaching in America. Sri Aurobindo was a child in Bengal, East India. He was educated in England, was a professor in Baroda, but he was practicing [sic] Yoga, preaching

> silently from Pondicherry, in South India. Sri Krishna Pram [sic] is an Englishman. He was a professor in Lucknow, U.P., but confined his spiritual activities in Uttara Brindavan, Almora. ... What a great mystery![24]

Word of Mirtola also made its way to Jawaharlal Nehru, whose father, Motilal, was a friend of GN Chakravarti.[25] Motilal wrote approvingly about a "young Englishman, who used to be a professor, [who] has gained the reputation of being a great yogi".[26] As his ashram grew in stature, however, Krishna Prem became the subject of the kind of outlandish stories which had sprung up around his wartime service. The American author Ken Winkler, who has written biographies of Almora stalwarts Lama Govinda and Walter Evans-Wentz, recalls that Krishna Prem "was rumoured to carry a Krishna statue on his head,"[27] while Aitken first visited Mirtola at the suggestion of the University of Durham's Dr Aravindu Basu, his thesis examiner, who told him about "a retired English colonel [sic] who lived in an ice cave in the Himalayas".[28]

Then, as now, the temple schedule revolved around the thrice-daily *āratis*—in the morning, noon and evening—as well as *darshan*, the 'divine sight' of the temple's Radha–Krishna deities, at select fixed hours.[29] The ashram's "whole life revolved round the temple services which were held at regular times during the day, primarily dawn, midday and sunset, and everything led up more or less directly to this temple worship and existed for it,"[30] confirms Denys Rutledge, who documented life at Mirtola for his travelogue *In Search of a Yogi: Himalayan Pilgrimage*. *Bhoga*, cooked by Krishna Prem, would also be offered to Radhikamohanji during the midday service.[31] Anne Marshall describes the ritual by which the *bhoga* would be consecrated as *prasādam*, the sacred remnants of food which has first been enjoyed by God:

> A bell started to ring from the temple and we went over to watch the *puja*. The shrine had been restored and was beautifully kept. Inside were two elaborately clad effigies, one of Krishna as the flute playing Govinda and the other of Radha, the chief of the Gopis....
>
> Before we could eat, an offering of the food had first to be made to the deities, and the food became *prashad*, blessed food. While a servant stood outside beating a gong, Sri Krishna Prem and Sri Madhava Ashish entered the shrine and prostrated. In accordance

> with the cult of personification, the gods must be tended like one's *guru* or one's kind, and this has particularly shocked some zealous missionaries. But, of course, the idols and the rituals are not to be taken literally; they are but symbols of devotion.[32]

Navnit Parekh details the significance of the *ārati* ritual, in which lamps, incense (*dhūpa*), water, cloth (usually in the form of a handkerchief) and a ringing bell are offered by the *pūjārī*, as explained by Krishna Prem:

> According to Hindu belief, there are five basic elements in the Universe. They are: earth, water, light or fire, air and ether. The devotee offers all these elements of the Universe to the Lord. The cloth signifies the earth; the water represents the element of water; the light is a symbol of light or fire; the incense signifies air; and the sound of the bell is the symbol of ether (space). Thus the ritual of the aarti is, in fact, a dedication of the entire Universe to the Lord. Similarly, all the five senses of the human-being are also offered to the Lord. The light represents the eye; the sound of the bell signifies the ear; the incense is the symbol of nose; the water denotes the tongue; while the cloth signifies the touch or the body.[33]

Tubu Chakravarti, a visiting devotee of Ramana Maharshi, notes that performing the ceremony deeply affected Krishna Prem. "[A]fter the *ārati* in the temple, when Gopalda would bring the *pancha-pradeep* [oil lamp] to us, I noticed a change in him," he writes. "His eyes would be half closed, turned to narrow slits. His hand holding the *pancha-pradeep* would be trembling a little. His steps would be a little unsteady. ... Superficially he would appear to be a little inebriated."[34]

Krishna Prem's attitude towards such *bāhya pūjā*, formal worship, is the subject of much of chapter 12 of *Yogi Sri Krishnaprem*, wherein he debates Moti Rani after she asks if they could not dispense with what she terms the "ritualism"[35] of so-called external worship. "No worship," he explains, "can be 'external' if done properly:"[36]

> Motirani still persisted: "But we do follow rites, arrange the flowers, ring the bell, offer water, burn incense and so on."
>
> "But why shouldn't we?" challenged Krishnaprem. "Love is expressed not only through words and looks and touch but symbols also. These are beautiful symbolic acts of worship offered to Him when He becomes a living reality to the sincere worshipper. Those

> who are not sincere, of course, don't count. At least when you are out to assess the total value of worship you can't say: I will only pick out formal worship and lip-service etcetera, and leave out the living adoration. My point is that in all true adoration, symbols and rites become living, when ensouled by the flame of love." …
>
> "[T]he prescribed rites, followed sincerely, do lead to something real and living and so just can't be scotched out of hand as dead formalism or ritualism pure and simple."[37]

These *āratis* were cacophonous affairs which could prove overwhelming for visitors or newcomers to the ashram; Aitken recalls the "visit of a famous British Catholic monk"—Denys Rutledge—"whose first impressions of the temple *ārati* ceremony convinced him he was in Hell, listening to (and recognizing) the rites of Satan."[38] (Rutledge remembers the incident slightly differently, saying that in the ritual he felt the presence of both Christ and the Devil.[39] As "the great brazen gong in the dome above boomed, throbbed and vibrated, its waves spreading out, engulfing and embracing all within its orbit,"[40] he writes, "I experienced a momentary approach of that panic that seems always to accompany contact with the Holy—and with the diabolic. … I saw clearly the point at which the true and the false so nearly coincide as to be almost indistinguishable; and I saw which was the true and which the false."[41]) Penelope Phipps remembers that when she first saw her brother "doing the arati I stood repeating the Lord's Prayer over and over as if to ward off the devil!"[42]

Timothy Leary, the Harvard psychologist turned psychedelic evangelist, who visited Mirtola shortly before the death of Krishna Prem (whom he called the "wisest man in India"[43]), was similarly taken aback by the noise of the ceremony, which he compared approvingly to the music of Jimi Hendrix:

> We went to the temple and I sat down and I was prepared to be very solemn, and suddenly, right next to me (there were only four or five lovers in this ashram, they didn't have a lot of people) an incredible noise started going—BA-BOOM! BA-BOOM! BA-BOOM! One man beating two drums: BA-BOOM! BA-BOOM! BA-BOOM! And there was another cat on a big triangle—CLANG! CLANG!
>
> BA-BOOM, BA-BOOM, BA-BOOM! CLANG, CLANG, CLANG! They really did blow your mind. In fact, it was like a more advanced Jimi Hendrix, right? Then, when you got dizzy, you just had to flip out on that sound trip. The vibrations in this small temple were overpowering. Suddenly, Sri Krishna Prem bounced in. He was about six-foot-two. And he began lighting incense, swishing the bullock's tail[44] to dust up the scene, doing his chant. BOOM, BOOM, BOOM,

> BOOM, CLANG, CLANG, CLANG—and the chant, and the incense going, and he's sailing around doing things and chanting, grinning and smiling. And this whole thing took about five minutes, and he took the candy for [Krishna] and said, "Here, take some." And that was all.[45]

Those better acquainted with the *ārati* ritual, however, recall the grace and sincerity with which Krishna Prem and his disciples performed the sacred ceremony. The Gujarati poet and scholar Umashankar Joshi, who visited in 1959, writes that he and his family were witness to "a real vision of how high a man can rise. As we left the ashram after arati, my eldest daughter said: 'We saw the peaks of the Himalayas and saw people who were like the peaks.'"[46]

For Krishna Prem, *bāhya pūjā* was symbolic of divine beauty, as exemplified by the mountains surrounding Mirtola, according to KM Munshi. "Once I asked Krishna Prem ... how he likes the daily worship of Sri Krishna in the wilderness a few miles away from Almora. He answered that the ceremonials of bathing the image, preparing food and offering it, chanting the praises—these brought him happiness," writes Munshi. "And what more can one wish for? These have become the symbol of beauty, the experience of which has become a settled frame of mind with him. He is right. Beauty is the living testimony of God. That is why when on mountain-tops or in vast spaces the presence of God is felt, transfiguring one's whole existence."[47]

In addition to Bal Krishna Goswami (who, as discussed in chapter seven, had been responsible for establishing the form of worship followed at Uttar Brindaban), early visitors to Mirtola included Sarala Behn (Ashish, 260), the English-born Gandhian activist; Sunyata and his guru, Anandamayi Ma[48] (who called Krishna Prem a "very advanced swami"[49]); and Bob Alexander and Moti Rani, both of whom used the visits to build themselves cottages in readiness for their eventual relocation to the ashram (Ashish, 128).

Alexander, now professor of medicine at King George's Medical College in Lucknow[50] (who had given up aa previous post at Madras Medical College in order to be closer to Krishna Prem[51]), "made good use of the proximity of Lucknow to the hills," writes Madhava Ashish, "travelling up to Almora whenever he could get leave. The overnight train from Lucknow to Kathgodam, and the bus from there via Ranikhet, would get him to Almora by around three o'clock in the afternoon. With long legs and a spare, athletic body, he would then cover the eighteen miles to Mirtola before dark" (Ashish, 82). Alexander would ultimately become a full-time *brahmachārī* in 1938, at the age of 38, taking early retirement and forgoing his pension (Ashish, 81) from the IMS, though he had achieved the rank of major[52] in the quasi-military structure of the service.

Moti Rani, meanwhile, joined her mother at the ashram around 1935, following the breakdown of her marriage (Ashish, 78), an ill-advised union which had been arranged only to satisfy her father's wish to see her wed before he died (Ashish, 77). Yashoda Mai, to the contrary, "appears not to have fussed over marriages"[53] and largely declined to intervene in the romantic lives of her children. The strictness of her *sādhana*, however, seems to have been a contributing factor in Moti Rani's originally leaving the family home and seeking out a husband; Brahmacharini Atmananda, a devotee of Anandamayi Ma, recalls Moti Rani (whose married name was Arpita Chatterji [Ashish, 11]) telling her "how hard her mother's rules had become after she became a *sādhu* and thus she felt compelled to leave her."[54] At that time, explains Madhava Ashish, she was "not yet ready for the detachment of sanyas and the restrictions of ashram life" (Ashish, 128)

Alexander's arrival coincided with the departure of George Poole, whose guru, finding him "even more strained and neurotic than usual" (Ashish, 131), had, for his own good, suggested he go back to England and get married. He obeyed Sri Yashoda Mai "without a word of complaint" (Ashish, 131), leaving behind his books and his house and enrolling in an art school near London.

Poole's most visible legacy at Mirtola was a piece of furniture designed to help with his meditation, as Aitken explains:

> There remained in my time a striking souvenir George had left of his practical dedication to the inner path. His English bones being unmalleable for padmasana (the yogic posture in which the Buddha achieved enlightenment) George had built for his meditation a commodious wooden chair, high, wide and sturdy, reminiscent of an abbot's raised seat in a Tibetan monastery. Its generous proportions allowed him while meditating to fold up his legs.... George showed no signs of returning [from London], [and] during the Mirtola spring cleaning that marked its theological revamp, the trappings of tradition along with library books were forsworn and even George's high chair found a taker. This came in the stout frame of the local Godfather, Dilip Singh, who gave George's high seat pride of place on the paved apron in front of his shop in Panuanaula. Before the coming of the motor road in the late 1950s the bridle path passed right in front of the shop, which apart from the dak bungalow above was the sole building that declared Panuanaula. For any visitor who climbed

> up the steep bridle path, the first glimpse of Mirtola and its resident mysteries would be of George's upraised throne, with or without [Singh].[55]

In London, Poole "met a woman of his own age who had just been freed from years of nursing her sick mother and was ready to marry," continues Madhava Ashish. "From the letters it seems to have worked out rather well."[56]

Yashoda Mai was not so gentle with all her students. "She did not encourage the many applicants who thought that an ashram was a convenient escape from the harsher realities of life or that it should provide a home for aged pensioners,"[57] explains Madhava Ashish, and those who were invited to stay could find themselves victims of a capriciousness that bordered on cruelty:

> With warm-hearted motherliness Yashoda Mai would agree to some man settling at the ashram under her guidance and make all necessary arrangements for his well-being. But then she would, as Krishna Prem put it, turn the pressure on. Non-observance of the ashram rules, personal habits such as nose-picking, laziness, failure to show respect to the guru, or even mistakes in ordinary speech might call forth sharp criticism spiced with crude analogies. She hit below the belt, saying the things other people only think, as if the polite pretences of social custom did not exist. If anyone answered back, it was a signal for a detailed listing of his shortcomings which might culminate with his being told how distasteful it was for the deity to have such a loathsome creature about the place. Almost invariably the poor fellow would take his loathsomeness away. Krishna Prem never quite understood why she did it.[58]

Though Madhava Ashish did not meet his *param guru*, having joined the ashram two years after her death, he saw much of her in her daughter, Moti Rani, who would become his *śikṣā*, or instructing, guru. (Krishna Prem was the *dīkṣā*, initiating, guru of both; Hindu tradition holds that while the disciple should have a single initiator, it is legitimate to take *śikṣā* from multiple gurus.) Yashoda Mai, writes Ashish, "was not an easy taskmaster. She admitted to having had trouble with her temper when young, and even as a mature and elderly woman she could make a scene. Having seen the daughter blowing the roof off, I can imagine what the mother was like."[59]

Like her mother, a mystic to whom Krishna would appear in the state of yogic trance known as *samādhi*, and like Madame Blavatsky, who claimed to have channelled messages from enlightened 'adepts' guiding humanity from remote ashrams in the distant Himalayas, Moti Rani was, according to the teachings of her *śikṣā* disciple, a vessel for a higher power, and "freely used her gift of occult powers to help deserving seekers."[60] In the hands of Moti Rani, he writes, Yashoda Mai's famous temper became a spiritual tool to produce rapid positive change in those subjected to her verbal attacks, though at the expense of her own physical and mental wellbeing:

> Moti's dedication to the Spirit was so total that she allowed herself to be used by the powers behind her to achieve effects quickly that might otherwise have taken lifetimes. Although there was that astounding detachment one finds in rare people of this sort, which allows a raging fury to turn to utter calm in an instant when the occasion demands, this did not mean that it was all a pretence and that she did not suffer. She suffered both in her feelings and in the effects these outbursts had on her sick body. And this real suffering was again used, because one could not but feel responsible for what she was undergoing. (Ashish, 167)

If Yashoda Mai's interpersonal interactions could be difficult to understand, even for her closest disciple, her relationships with the non-human residents of Uttar Brindaban were more straightforward. Her "compassion for animals was quite extraordinary" (Ashish, 136), and a menagerie of creatures inhabited the ashram—comprising a series of dogs (including Yashoda Mai's own spaniel, Sonny; Moti Rani's Lhasa Apso, Jolly; and Alu, the sole surviving puppy of a favourite village dog, Ram Pyari [Ashish, 137–138]), plus two parrots (Ashish, 139) and, briefly, a baby monkey (Ashish, 130). The animals were doted on, with the dogs even allowed to join the dinner table:

> In spite of all the orthodoxy, dogs were admitted to the verandah floor, which also served as the tea table, so one could have people humorously offering a biscuit to the wrong end of Jolly, the Apso terrier, because both ends looked the same and, since the floor space was narrow, he would retreat by walking backwards. At the same 'table' Alu ['Potato'] would sit beside one as if she were one of the guests. With her head at the level of one's shoulder, she would lean forward and delicately take from one's hand the biscuit that had paused on the way to one's mouth. (Ashish, 138)

This compassion extended even to troublesome creepie-crawlies: Krishna Prem claimed to have witnessed his guru carrying bed bugs by candlelight from her room to her bathroom, "because it was a cold night and she did not like to put them out" (Ashish, 137), and Madhava Ashish recalls that he became an "expert in catching flies in my hand, and releasing them out of the window," as "the rules were so strict that we were not allowed to kill so much as a fly" (Ashish, 172).

Yashoda Mai's unorthodox leniency with her dogs—an animal considered ritually unclean by most Brahmins—may be explained in connection with her *vātsalya* relationship with Bal Gopal, the infant Krishna, as she explained to Dilip Kumar Roy:

> "I used to abhor dogs," she went on. "I simply couldn't stand them. Now, one day, I had just offered Balgopal the bhoga I had cooked myself, when I found this street-dog, which had stolen in from behind, lapping up the milk-pudding. Shocked to the soul, I gave it a blow with my stick. The dog howled in pain ... when, lo, I saw my Lord ... my heart's Beloved ... the little Balgopal, lying prone inside the dog ... and ... and He was crying." She wiped her eyes and added: "Since that day I have adopted it and made it my constant companion."[61]

Roy's *Yogi Sri Krishnaprem* also provides a first-hand account of Yashoda Mai's celebrated psychic powers, including the talent for theophany which had originally attracted Krishna Prem back in Lucknow. After an emotional rendition of Roy's song 'Brindabaner lila' ('Krishna, the Evergreen'), performed for an audience of Krishna Prem, Moti Rani and "Alec" (Alexander), it emerged that Yashoda Mai, too, had been listening in. When the foursome found her, she was in her room, "sitting on her bed with folded hands, as though petrified, just two streaks of tears glistened on her cheeks in the candle-light:"[62]

> After a few minutes she opened her eyes, now swimming in tears, and gave a beatific smile. Then she asked me to draw near and sit close to her.
>
> I complied hesitantly, as so far I had never sat on her bed; the others sat on the floor on a mat.
>
> Ma placed a loving hand on my shoulder.
>
> "You didn't see anything, Baba?" she asked, tenderly.
>
> I caught my breath.
>
> "See? No! What should I have seen?"
>
> "Thakur!" she said simply. "He had come, and was standing beside you!"
>
> A shiver passed through my spine.
>
> "You mean Krishna?" I gasped.

> She smiled. "Whom else could I mean, Baba? When ..." she spoke now in staccato, through her tears ... "you were improvising on the last verse. He ... came first and stood for a second in my room and then ... then stepped across the threshold.... I ... could not follow Him that way. So I took the ... the other way ... till I got to the verandah ... and saw Him ... standing beside you, listening.... Yes, Baba ... I ... I did see Him, with open eyes ... as I often do.... You didn't see?"
>
> "No, Ma, But I did feel--"
>
> But she went on as though she had not heard: "And He was standing ... beside you ... in person ... looking so ... so tenderly ... at you! ... And ... I ... I appealed to Him: 'O Thakur, give him the ... the blessed boon of vision... so ... so he may see that you ... you yourself have come down to hear his song ... blessed, blessed, boy!'"
>
> I bowed down and kissed her feet and--wept.[63]

Yashoda Mai later told Roy that while this wasn't the first time Krishna had appeared to her in *samādhi*, he refrained from showing himself too often due to the deleterious effect it had on his devotee's physical health:

> "Do you see Him, all the time, Ma?" I asked, emboldened by her confidences.
>
> "I can see Him in my heart all the time," she answered. "But not outside—I mean, not always."
>
> "But why can't you, Ma?"
>
> She answered, after a brief pause: "I once asked Him. He said: 'If I appear before you too often your body will not last long.'"[64]

A slightly different version of the story, which references the craving Krishna is said to feel for the love of his devotees, is related by Roy's disciple, Indira Devi, in her book *Fragrant Memories*:

> "I asked Yashoda Ma—Krishnaprem's Guru—after my music at Mirtola, at their ashram: 'Mother, I sang to Him with every fibre of my being and saw nothing—except that I felt his presence. Yet, feeling is not seeing, Mother! You say you saw Him standing and listening intently to the music.'
>
> "Yashoda Ma: 'Not only did I see Him, I spoke to Him.'

"Dadaji [Roy]: 'Why did you not plead with Him to let me see Him too? I feel the presence but see nothing—not even His top knot if He has one.'

"Yoshada [sic] Ma: 'I asked Him just that.'

"Dadaji: 'What did He say?'

"Yashoda Ma: 'He said: "If my thirst is appeased, he will not sing like this again!"'"[65]

In addition to Krishna, Yashoda Mai reported dreams, visions and mystical experiences involving Radha, Ganesh,[66] and Koot Hoomi (Ashish, 153), one of the Theosophical 'Masters' whose pictures adorned her room at Uttar Brindaban.[67] Madhava Ashish describes one such encounter with Radha, Krishna's beloved:

> [H]er ... walls were covered with pictures of many divine forms of the Hindu pantheon, of no artistic merit but there because of some special association which pleased her. There were large pictures of her husband, Blavatsky, Blavatsky's Masters, a large oil painting of Durga and another of Krishna she had commissioned. And there were photographs of her favourite disciples. Right beside her bed, close to the head, in a narrow frame that fitted a particular bit of wall, was a bazaar print of Radha and Krishna on a swing, typical of the Krishna Lila. Half dazed by the pain, she felt little hands massaging her legs, as Indians love to do and have done to them when they are unwell—or indeed at any time. Looking up she saw that Radha was missing from the picture. (Ashish, 67)

Notes

[1]Tandan, *Faith & Fire*, 245.

[2]'Faces of Friends,' 204.

[3]Pandey, *Guru by Your Bedside*, 45.

[4]Joshi, 'My Memories of Mussoorie.'

[5]Donald Eichert, 'The Last English Saint,' *Mirtola Reflections*, (Mirtola, 2018), 3, https://mirtolareflections.com/pdf/The-Last-English-Saint.pdf (accessed 14 November 2022).

[6]'Penelope Phipps 1916–2013', *Ancestry*, Provo, Ancestry.com Operations, 2023, https://www.ancestry.co.uk/genealogy/records/penelope-phipps-24-xfxmtb (accessed 17 September 2023).

[7]Penelope Phipps, 'Sri Krishna Prem Remembered,' in Sri Madhava Ashish, *Where'er Love's Camels Lead: Sri Krishna Prem Remembered* (unpublished), (Mirtola: Sri Dev Ashish manuscript, 2015), 274.

[8]Tillis, 'Bill Aitken, Landour, Mussoorie, 20th December 1980'

[9]Timothy Leary, *Flashbacks – A Personal and Cultural History of an Era: An Autobiography*, (New York: GP Putnam's Sons, 1990), 219.

[10]Madhava Ashish, 'Sri Krishna Prem Through the Eyes of a Disciple,' 10.

[11]Paul Brunton, *Notebooks of Paul Brunton*, 5.3, para. 7,064, https://paulbrunton.org/notebooks/para/7064 (accessed 27 June 2022).

[12]*Ibid.*

[13]Pandey, *Guru by Your Bedside*, 48.

[14]Aitken, email to the author, 24 June 2021.

[15]Kishansinh Chavda, હિમાલયની પત્રયાત્રા, (Ahmedabad: Ravani Prakashan Gruh, 1964), ch. 12, para. 3, https://ekatra.pressbooks.pub/gujaratinibandhsampada/chapter/ (accessed June 2022).

[16]Aitken, email to the author, 2 July 2023.

[17]Aitken, email to the author, 24 June 2021.

[18]*Ibid.*

[19]"That was an involuntary reaction as I had been raised in an atmosphere where the English were detested and [in 1954] it was a mere 7 years since they had left India." Jagdish Nautiyal, 'How I came to know Gopalda' (email to the author), 16 October 2021, 1.

[20]*Ibid.*

[21]Monod-Herzen, 'Sri Krishna Prem, Yogi et Théosophe.'

[22]Jatindranath Roy, 'An Incident from Sri Gauranga's Temple of Scripture,' *Sri Sri Shyamsundar Barsha*, 2, (1932), 148.

[23]Roy, *Bhārater Sādhak*, 282–331.

[24]VT Neelakantan, SAA Ramaiah and Babaji Nagaraj, *The Voice of Babaji: A Trilogy on Kriya Yoga*, (Bangalore: Babaji's Kriya Yoga Order of Acharyas, 2003), cited in Edward Baldo, *Play of Life: A True Story of Compassion, Solidarity and Spiritual Development*, (Lincoln: iUniverse, 2007), 97.

[25]Herman AO de Tollenaere, *The Politics of Divine Wisdom: Theosophy and Labour, National, and Women's Movements in Indonesia and South Asia 1875–1947*, (Nijmegen: Catholic University of Nijmegen, 1996), 271.

[26]Parthasarathi, *Letters to Chief Ministers*, 560–561.

[27]Ken Winkler, *The Winter Line: A Memoir and Observations of Asia*, (Bloomington: AuthorHouse, 2010), 109.

[28]Aitken, *Footloose in the Himalaya*, 5.

[29]Sen, 'Sri Krishnaprem,' xiii.

[30]Rutledge, *In Search of a Yogi*, 243.

[31] *Ibid.*

[32] Marshall, *Hunting the Guru in India*, 151.

[33] Parekh, *Himalayan Memoirs*, 48.

[34] S. Chakravarti, 'Sri Krishnaprem's Visit to Sri Ramana Maharshi, Part II,' *The Maharshi*, 29.4, (2019), 1.

[35] Roy, *Yogi Sri Krishnaprem*, 84.

[36] Roy, *Yogi Sri Krishnaprem*, 83.

[37] Roy, *Yogi Sri Krishnaprem*, 85.

[38] Bill Aitken, *Sri Sathya Sai Baba: A Life*, Penguin UK edn, (London: Penguin Books, 2006), 192.

[39] Rutledge, *In Search of a Yogi*, 240.

[40] Rutledge, *In Search of a Yogi*, 239.

[41] Rutledge, *In Search of a Yogi*, 240.

[42] Phipps, 'Sri Krishna Prem Remembered,' 273.

[43] Dr Timothy Leary, *Starseed: Transmitted from Folsom Prison*, (San Francisco: Level Press, 1973), 6.

[44] During *ārati*, a *cāmara*, a yak's-tail fly whisk, is used to cool the deities.

[45] Timothy Leary, *The Delicious Grace of Moving One's Hand: The Collected Sex Writings*, (New York: Thunder's Mouth Press, 1998), 219.

[46] Umashankar Joshi, 'Self-examination and review' (સ્વાદ્યાય અને સમીક્ષા), *Sanskriti*, 2.7, (1968), 280.

[47] KM Munshi, 'Kulapati's Letter on Life, Literature & Culture, No. 77: The Himalayas, The Spirit of Beauty, The Magic Symbols,' *Bhavan's Journal*, 1.23, (1955), 13.

[48] Rai, 'A Short Biography,' xxx.

[49] Devi Mukherjee, *Shaped by Saints*, (Ananda India, 2020), ch. 12, para. 2, https://anandaindia.org/shaped-by-saints-a-pilgrims-journey-through-india/no-tibet-this-time/ (accessed 30 November 2022).

[50] Cuthbert Allan Sprawson CIE and Robert Dudley Alexander, *Moore's Manual of Family Medicine & Hygiene for India*, 10th edn, (Delhi: Manager of Publications, Government of India, 1936), 1.

[51] 'Robert Dudley Alexander (Sri Haridas),' 18.

[52] Supplement to the *British Medical Journal*, 1.787, (25 February 1939), 90.

[53] Abha Sah, 'The Guiding Hand,' *Mirtola Reflections*, (Mirtola: Mirtola Reflections, 2019), 5, https://www.mirtolareflections.com/admin/artical-images/The-Guiding-Hand.pdf (accessed 30 March 2023)

[54] Ram Alexander (ed.), *Death Must Die: A Western Woman's Life-Long Spiritual Quest in India and Its Fulfilment Through Her Guru, Shree Anandamayee Ma (The Diaries of Atmananda)*, (Varanasi: Indica Books, 2000), 266.

[55]Aitken, email to the author, 2 July 2023.

[56]*Ibid.*

[57]Madhava Ashish, 'Sri Sri Krishnaprem Vairagi,' 90.

[58]Madhava Ashish, 'Sri Krishna Prem Through the Eyes of a Disciple,' 24.

[59]Madhava Ashish, 'Sri Krishna Prem Through the Eyes of a Disciple,' 23–24.

[60]Seymour B. Ginsburg and Satish Datt Pandey, 'Introduction,' in Sri Madhava Ashish, *An Open Window: Dream as Everyman's Guide to the Spirit*, (New Delhi: Penguin Books, 2007), x.

[61]Roy, *Yogi Sri Krishnaprem*, 95.

[62]Roy, *Yogi Sri Krishnaprem*, 100.

[63]Roy, *Yogi Sri Krishnaprem*, 100–101.

[64]Roy, *Yogi Sri Krishnaprem*, 103.

[65]Indira Devi, *Fragrant Memories*, (Bombay: Bharatiya Vidya Bhavan, 1993), 7.

[66]Roy, *Yogi Sri Krishnaprem*, 103–104.

[67]These pictures of the 'Masters,' removed in the Madhava Ashish era, still adorned Krishna Prem's room at the time of Jagdish Shah's first visit, in December 1959.

11: Yogī

"We write to our Self—and then we have to clear up the mess."[1]
— Sri Krishna Prem (c. 1938)

In 1936, news came from Benares that Gyanendra Nath Chakravarti, 21 years his wife's senior, was dying. Yashoda Mai, in poor health, could not leave the ashram, but Krishna Prem went to be with Chakravarti, whose support and counsel had been instrumental in the early years of Uttar Brindaban, as well as encouraging his own leap of faith in Lucknow.

At Radha Vilas, Krishna Prem found Moti Rani attending her father amid an "unpleasant psychic atmosphere" produced by the other women of the household, who were already conspiring to deprive the Chakravartis' many adoptive children of their inheritance (Ashish, 125). To counter the "down-dragging effects of the household atmosphere," Madhava Ashish writes, Krishna Prem generated a psychic "screen," which allowed Chakravarti to die in peace and protected Moti Rani from the "spirits of the dead" (Ashish, 125). The pair then took their leave, boarding the first train for Almora without waiting for the cremation (Ashish, 125). With the exception of an uncharacteristic trip abroad, to Burma, it would be nine years before Krishna Prem left Mirtola again (Ashish, 127-126).

The Burma adventure came at the suggestion of Moti Rani, who had visited the neighbouring country, then still part of British India, with Bertram Keightley shortly after her father's death (Ashish, 120). The return journey was made in the company of Yashoda Mai, Krishna Prem and "a young boy referred to as Khoka" (Ashish, 120), presumably a Bengali follower of one or all of the Mirtola trio. Being in a non-Hindu country made it nearly impossible for the party to stick to the ashram's strict Brahminical regimen, so the rules were relaxed temporarily: "They would observe vegetarianism, but while away from the shores of India they would not concern themselves unduly with the questions of who cooked the food and under what conditions" (Ashish, 122).

The trip also led to the writing of Krishna Prem's fourth published book, *The Yoga of the Kaṭhopanishad* (1940)[2], a translation and exposition of the Upanishad of the same name that Moti Rani had suggested, somewhat over-optimistically, could be a bestseller that would pay for their journey to Burma (Ashish, 120). Dedicated to "M. R., best of pupils, for whom this book was written,"[3] *The Yoga of the Kaṭhopanishad* was Krishna Prem's first original work written as a book, 1938's *The Search for Truth* and *The Yoga of the Bhagavat Gita* having their roots in magazine articles published in the *Kalyan*, *Sanātan Dharma* (Benares), *Sankirtan* (Meerut) and *Shreya* (Vrindavan),[4] and *The Aryan Path*,[5] respectively. Another earlier work, *Initiation into Yoga*,[6] was a small booklet whose contents had originally appeared as two editorials in the *Review of Philosophy and Religion* of Allahabad. It was published in 1939[7] and reportedly proved popular with American soldiers during the Second World War (Ashish, 119).

Though he drew on the established Indian tradition of written commentaries on sacred texts, which in many cases "form traditions in their own right and are valued as 'original' works,"[8] Krishna Prem's approach to interpreting the *Bhagavad Gītā* and *Kaṭha Upaniṣad* was complex and unorthodox, reflecting both his myriad literary and religious influences and his ambivalence about the spiritual value of scripture.

The Yoga of the Bhagavat Gita opens with a striking repudiation of the traditional view (held by, for example, by Paramahansa Yogananda,[9] Sri Aurobindo[10] and AC Bhaktivedanta Swami[11]) that the *Bhagavad Gītā* (literally the "Song of Bhagavan [God]") refers to literal, historical events. Taking the position that "we can scarcely adopt the orthodox view that it was, as we have it, spoken by the historical Krishna on the battlefield of Kurukshetra,"[12] Krishna Prem interprets the text as purely allegorical, taking the famous dialogue between the warrior prince Arjuna and his charioteer, Krishna, "the inseparable friends,"[13] as symbolic of the eternal relationship between "Nara and Nārāyaṇa, the human soul and the Divine Soul, the *jīva* and *Ātman*"[14] described in the *Bhāgavata Purāṇa.* In Krishna Prem's reading, the *Mahābhārata*—the Sanskrit epic of which the *Gītā* is part—is, like most great works of art, "filled with symbolism,"[15] from the warring Pandavas and Kauravas, who represent light and darkness respectively,[16] to Krishna's role as charioteer, a symbol "that occurs in the Upanishads and also in the Dialogues of Plato"[17] and which in the Gita represents Krishna as the "manifested Ātman,"[18] Kaurava commanders Bhishma and Drona, meanwhile, are symbols "of blind faith and of established Law and Order and ancient Tradition"[19] and the Gita's narrator, Sañjaya, of conscience;[20] the attributed author of the text, the sage Vyasa, is also symbolic—of "the power of inspiration, the power which diffuses and extends downwards the higher knowledge."[21]

Krishna Prem's approach to the text, as well as his view that it is fundamentally a "textbook of Yoga, a guide to the treading of the Path,"[22] may have been influenced by Annie Besant, later the president of the Theosophical Society, whose 1905 translation focuses on the text's symbolic significance (whereby "Arjuna represented the aspiring soul, Kurukṣetra the soul's battlefield, Dhṛtarāṣṭra's sons [the Kauravas] the soul's enemies and Kṛṣṇa the divine word within"[23]) while similarly emphasising the "oneness of the spiritual path, 'though it has many names'"[24]. (Compare this with Krishna Prem's "The Path is not the special property of Hinduism, nor indeed of any religion. It is something which is to be found, more or less deeply buried, in all religions..."[25]). He also recommended Besant's translation to his own disciples.[26] This purely symbolic treatment, which disregards the historical context in which the *Gītā* was written, is described as a central weakness of an otherwise "exceptional work" by the German Indologist Georg Feuerstein, for whom *The Yoga of the Bhagavat Gita* (a "spiritual/hortatory" treatment, as opposed to the "philological/antiquarian" and "poetic" approaches) is notable for its "distinct disinterest in philological/historical matters."[27]

In turn, Besant likely drew her inspiration from her one-time guru, Gyanendra Nath Chakravarti, who urged readers to "take Krishna as the symbol of the immanent God, the inner Godhead."[28]

By arguing that the Krishna of the *Bhagavad Gītā* reveals "a single, coherent Path, a [single] Yoga, which must be progressively trod,"[29] Krishna Prem breaks with Gauḍīya Vaiṣṇava commentators, for whom the *Gītā* is primarily a *bhakti* text which establishes the primacy of devotional service over the yogas of action/work (*karma*) and knowledge (*jñāna*)[30]. He breaks as well with the scholarly view of the text as a "meaningful synthesis" which combines "the Upanisadic speculations about Brahman-ātman relation, the theism of the *Bhāgavata* [Krishna] cult, and the [eightfold] *Yoga* systems."[31] Though he "attached great importance to [the yoga] of devotion"[32] (*bhakti*), Krishna Prem subsumes the three classical yogas identified by Krishna under one unified yogic path:

> By Yoga is here meant not any special system called by that name, not *jñāna yoga*, nor *karma yoga*, nor *bhakti yoga*, nor the eightfold *yoga* of Patañjali, but just the Path by which man unites his finite self with Infinite Being. It is the inner Path of which all these separate yogas are so many one-sided aspects. It is not so much a synthesis of these separate teachings as that prior and undivided whole of which they represent partial formulations.[33]

He explained elsewhere that the *Gītā*, "if we free our minds from the influence of one-sided commentators, clearly sets forth ... a harmonious blending of head, heart and hands"—ie *jñāna, bhakti* and *karma*—"in which all shall be transformed into an instrument of the Divine Līlā."[34]

In support of this theory—that "the Yoga as originally taught by the eternal Krishna ... was a single, unitary and all-comprehensive Yoga" which was later "split up into parts" as it passed down the *paramparā* (succession of gurus and disciples)—Krishna Prem cites verse two of chapter four of the *Gītā*,[35] which in Besant's translation has Krishna telling Arjuna ('Parantapa'):

> "This yoga by great efflux of time decayed in the world, O Parantapa."[36]

In his personality and example, Krishna Prem embodied the same balance between yogic disciplines, according to Narendra Nath Kaul. "Some time one felt that the *bhakta* in him was predominant, but he maintained an exquisite balance between the two [*bhakta* and *jñānī*]," Kaul explains.[37] Similarly, the anthropologist Michael D. Jackson, who visited Mirtola in 1948 and 1951, remembers Sri Krishna Prem as "a scholar and a religious devotee [*bhakta*] rolled into one."[38]

Krishna Prem is also critical of those commentators—including "enthusiasts for ... devotion to a personal God"[39]—who are more concerned with propounding the views of their own philosophical school than with "straight-forward inquiry into the real meaning of the text."[40] Krishna Prem's audience, as he sees it, are spiritual aspirants of every stripe—"the Race that never dies"—whether *bhakta* or *jñānī*, Indian or European, Hindu or *mleccha*:

> To anyone who has eyes to see, the Gita is based on direct knowledge of Reality, and of the Path that leads to that Reality, and it is of little moment who wrote it or to what school he was outwardly affiliated. Those who know Reality belong to a Race apart, the Race that never dies, as Hermes Trismegistus puts it, and neither they nor 'those who seek to be born into that Race concern themselves with the flummeries of sects and schools.[41]

Indeed, for the author of *The Yoga of Bhagavat Gita*, "Hinduism did not seem to be much of an issue," observes the academic Catherine Robinson. "In his view, all religions rested on the same truth."[42]

He expounds upon this idea—which resembles the Theosophical teaching that all religious traditions contain a common inner 'great Truth'—in the essay 'Initiation into Yoga,' writing that "there does actually exist a Path the treading of which leads to full knowledge of the Truth. It is a Path that has existed in all ages and in all countries, though the names by which it was known have differed widely. The Quest of the Holy Grail, the Search for the Elixir of Life or the

Philosopher's Stone, the Devayāna or Pathway of the Gods are all terms for the same Path, the knowledge of which has always existed."[43] A striking example of Krishna Prem's famous non-denominationalism, apparent even at this early stage of his spiritual 'career,' *Initiation into Yoga* references the ideas of a plethora of thinkers, including Shankara, the Buddha, Christ, the Western philosophers Kant, Bergson and William James, the psychologists Freud and Jung, Socrates, the Christian mystics Meister Eckhart and William Blake, and the Theosophical 'Master' St Germain, as well as Buddhist scriptures including the *Dhammapada* and *Dīgha Nikāya* and non-Vaiṣṇavite Hindu texts such as the *Kaṭha* and *Maitrī* Upaniṣads—yet not a single Vaiṣṇava *ācārya* makes the cut.

Krishna Prem's *Gītā* also appears to reject the notion that Krishna, as the supreme person, is the ultimate form of the divine and the source of all *avatārs* and incarnations—a fundamental tenet of Gauḍīya Vaiṣṇava belief. Instead, Krishna Prem describes an impersonal "One Eternal, the Parabrahman, Rootless Root of all" that lies beyond even the spiritual world: "Beyond all Gods, beyond all time and space, beyond all being even, flames Its dark transcendent Light.[44]" From that "unthinkable abyss," a footnote explains incredulously, "some have tried to make a personal God!"[45]

An appendix to the book elaborates on Krishna Prem's dissenting conception of Krishna's ontological position vis-à-vis his *avatārs*, repudiating what he calls the "orthodox" view—"that Viṣṇu [or Krishna], conceived as a personal God, from time to time takes birth among men"[46]—in favour of a novel theory that effectively makes Krishna (along with the other *avatārs*, of whom Rāma, the Buddha and, for "the more liberal-minded, Christ," are listed[47]) into a Bodhisattva: a perfected man who has chosen to stay in the material creation in order to assist others on their journey towards enlightenment.

While acknowledging that this theory is likely to "repel ... the emotions of the devotee"[48] (*bhakta*), Krishna Prem holds, in an appendix dedicated to the topic of the *avatārs*, that "the real Krishna, Buddha, or Christ is not the outer form which, *like all other forms*, is illusory, but the birthless and invisible *Ātman* within, known to Buddhist tradition as the *Dharmakāya*." He elaborates:

> The best way of stating the position seems to be as follows. When after countless lives of suffering followed by the mystical seven lives of effort[49] a man has climbed the ladder and stands upon the edge of the Goal, two possibilities exist. If his past struggles have been motivated only by the wish for his personal salvation then he may, and in all probability will, merge himself within the white eternal Light and vanish for ever from the world of men. If on the other hand his efforts have been dominated by love and compassion for his fellows, instead of merging in the Light he may manifest that Light

> through his perfected but still existing lower vehicles of mind and body, thus bringing about a "descent" of that Light into the world of men. Thereafter "he" is no more a man as we understand the term but a mere vehicle for the manifestation of the Eternal. This is the true meaning of the *avataraṇa*, or descent.[50]

However, despite its stated universalism, Gabriel Monod-Herzen found *The Yoga of the Bhagavat Gita* "strictly Hindu in its arrangement and inspiration," writing that its real unorthodoxy lay in Krishna Prem's idiosyncratic scholarship. "[I]ts literary form, its style, its flashes of English humour salted with good-natured irreverence for academic scholarship—these traits place the author in the best tradition of writers from across the [English] Channel," the Frenchman says.[51]

The decision to translate the *Kaṭha Upaniṣad*—the story of a Brahmin boy, Nachiketas, who enquires from Yama, the Lord of Death, as to the nature of the Brahman, the ultimate reality, and of the Self, or universal soul[52]—rather than a Vaiṣṇavite text such as the *Bhāgavata Purāṇa* or one of the Vaiṣṇava Upaniṣads—may be attributed to Krishna Prem's belief that the book has real-world use as a guide to the same yogic path described in the *Gītā*. "The point of view from which this book has been written is that the *Kaṭhopaniṣad* is a practical treatise written to help us achieve a very real end. It is not in the least a compendium of Brahmanical speculations, something to be studied from a purely intellectual viewpoint," he writes in the preface. "On the contrary, it is an exposition of the ancient Road that leads from death to immortality, a Road which is as open to-day as it was when our text was written."[53]

A "more technical treatise"[54] than *The Yoga of the Bhagavat Gita*, *The Yoga of the Kaṭhopanishad* was considered by Dilip Kumar Roy to be Krishna Prem's masterpiece,[55] while Timothy Leary wrote that the author considered the "thin deep book" a labour of love when compared to the *Bhagavad Gītā*, a commentary on which "every student of the path must write."[56]

For Gerald Carney, Krishna Prem's treatment of the *Bhagavad Gītā* was shaped both by his own experience of the Great War and the spectre of another war in Europe. He writes:

> While he makes no explicit references to his own experience in war, the compassion directed toward suffering humanity by the disciple who serves the "All in all" would be a response to the varied sufferings of modern society. He draws extensively from the Upanishads, Plato and Plotinus, the Hermetic literature and Theosophical works, and the teachings of the Buddha from both Theravada and

> Mahayana; and also from Christian scripture, the British Romantics, Jung's studies of Chinese classics, and modern psychology.
>
> On every level, Krishna Prem's commentary on the *Bhagavad Gita* offers his personal teaching of a practical devotional path to Krishna against the tragic background of modern life. Written by one who fled the wasteland of post-World War I Europe to an audience facing the terrors of the Second World War, this text reprises the battlefield scene of Kurukshetra and Krishna's teaching there against the background of a world of suffering. Led by the *buddhi*, the enlightened mind, beyond the self to a vision of Krishna as the All in each and all, the disciple joins with Krishna in the selfless battle on behalf of his suffering brothers and sisters.[57]

The Yoga of the Kaṭhopanishad similarly draws on the work of a heterogeneous group of authors from both East and West to trace the strand of a common yogic path which, Krishna Prem writes, has always been "known to a few all around the world".[58] Reviewing the book for *Prabuddha Bharata*, Swami Jagadiswarananda of the Ramakrishna Math describes how, in a "beautiful English rendering of the whole Upanishad with a novel explanation," Krishna Prem "shows that this Upanishadic way is described in the sacred writings of the ancient races, the Sumerians, Egyptians, ancient Aryans, as well as in the teachings of the great world-teachers Pythagoras, Platinus [sic], Hermes, Plato, Laotze, Buddha, and others."[59]

A contemporary reviewer for *The Theosophical Movement* argues that *The Yoga of the Kaṭhopanishad* represents a Theosophist's reading of the *Kaṭha Upaniṣad*, noting that Krishna Prem makes "copious and apt use" of Madame Blavatsky's *The Voice of the Silence* and Mabel Collins's *Light on the Path*, "and more than once quotes the 'Stanzas of Dzyan' from *The Secret Doctrine*." Krishna Prem, like the Sanskrit scholar and Theosophist Charles Johnston, they write, "has drunk deep at the fount of Theosophy and a comparative study of their interpretations of this great Upanishad proves most interesting. The present volume offers not only a more exhaustive interpretation but also carries marks of deep meditation on the esoteric teachings of the Upanishad."[60] The author also notes that Krishna Prem uses his part of his commentary on chapter one, verse nine, to defend Blavatsky—whose 'manifestations' of letters from her Tibetan 'Masters' and other objects made her the target of criticism from scientific sceptics—from charges of being a charlatan. Krishna Prem writes:

> The attitude of all such towards those sons of their bosom who venture forth along the mystic paths and return thence with new wisdom has always been a somewhat doubtful one.... [I]t is always an anxious moment for the mystic when, returning with his hands laden

> with gifts, he wonders what sort of a welcome he is to receive.... In recent times we have seen how one of the greatest of such Initiates, H. P. Blavatsky, was received on her return. Slander and vilification met her everywhere and it was only with the most superhuman exertions, coupled with the 'boon of Yama,' that she was able to prevent her richly laded vessel from being overturned and its contents all spilled in the stormy turmoil that her coming raised.[61]

The extent to which *The Yoga of the Bhagavat Gita* diverges from what would be normally be expected of a Vaiṣṇava commentary is illustrated by a contemporary review of the book in *The Bombay Chronicle.* While the author praises Krishna Prem, an "earnest European lover of Eastern culture and student of Eastern lore," for "expound[ing] the message of the Gita in language which breathes earnestness and eloquence"[62], they are unable to detect allegiance to any philosophical school; by contrast, a translation by Swami Bhakti Hridaya Bon of the Gaudiya Math is clearly identified as "an exposition of the Gita from the standpoint of the Bhakti school founded by the great Bengali Vaishnavite saint of the fifteenth century, Sri Krishna Chaitanya".[63] Krishna Prem's commentary, with its relativisation of the path of *bhakti*, might instead be compared to Buddhist thought–which holds that "pure *bhakti* without knowledge (*dharma*) and work (*karma*) will simply bring attachment which will not bring joy and salvation but will bring pain at separation"–and might also be compared with the Vaiṣṇavism of the state of Assam, which "prescribes ... three *vastus* (jewels) together: *Guru* (*bhakti*), *Nam* (*knowledge*) and *bhakat* (*karma*)."[64]

Both of Krishna Prem's *Yoga* books served as effective, if unintentional, recruiting tools for Uttar Brindaban. The Indian historian Shripad Rama Sharma writes that his "pilgrimage" to Almora in the 1950s was inspired by *The Yoga of the Bhagavat Gita*, "which reinforced the lure of the Himalayas,"[65] while Karan Singh, who would go on to accept *dīkṣā* from Sri Madhava Ashish, read *The Yoga of the Kaṭhopanishad, Initiation into Yoga* and the "luminous commentary" of *The Yoga of the Bhagavat Gita* before his first visit to Mirtola.[66] "What was particularly impressive about his writings was the manner in which he drew on the Western mystical tradition—Plotinus, Hermes Trismegistus, Meister Ekhart [sic]—to show that the spiritual quest was a universal one and not confined to any particular religious tradition," Singh recalls.[67] Frank Baines, a British ex-serviceman who joined the ashram in 1946, just before Madhava Ashish, developed an interest in Krishna Prem and Mirtola after buying *The Yoga of the Kaṭhopanishad* from a bookstall in Lucknow; the book, he explains, "was full of tantalising glimpses and seductive insights, some thwarting and some titillating, about spiritual life. It contained some really fascinating comparisons between the ancient Greek, Christian and Hindu traditions. It became virtually my *vade mecum* and bible."[68] Baines later also read *The Yoga of the Bhagavat Gita.*[69]

Even the Tamil sage Ramana Maharshi—"perhaps the one man in India at the time whose spiritual attainment could not be doubted,"[70] in the words of Donald Eichert—was known to have directed his students to study *The Yoga of the Kaṭhopanishad,*[71] a favourite text of Ramana's.

The Yoga of the Bhagavat Gita also influenced a younger generation of spiritual seekers. The American *kīrtan* singer Krishna Das (Jeffrey Kagel) recalls that his godbrother, the hippie-era "spiritual celebrity"[72] Ram Dass (Richard Alpert)—a former Harvard psychology professor who had studied the religious use of psychedelics with Timothy Leary before becoming a disciple of Neem Karoli Baba—"read that out every day, out loud, [when] we were up in the mountains on a long retreat in the winter of '68–69, or '69–70 maybe. And every day we'd read out from that book. It was life changing."[73] Alpert also quotes from chapter two ("The Soul flees just at the very moment when we seem to hold its gleaming splendour in our hands and all we are left with is one more dead butterfly to add to our mouldering collection") in his 1971 countercultural bible *Be Here Now,*[74] and the commentary is said to have been a favourite among the "Neem Karoli *satsang*"[75] (community of disciples), which also included the American-born yogis Bhagavan Das (Kermit Michael Riggs) and Ram Rani (Yvette Rosser) and the *kīirtan* performer Jai (Douglas) Uttal. (Kagel, a *Yoga of the Bhagavat Gita* collector, revealed in 2022 that he owns "about eight" hardcover copies of the book, including a first edition.[76])

Despite his rejection of a literalist reading of the *Gītā*, it is clear that Krishna Prem did believe Krishna was a historical figure. Writing to Roy in 1936, he explained that "although all the accounts we have, even the *Mahābhārata* account, are shot through with symbolism and in the *Bhāgavat[a]* Krishna is symbolic from beginning to end,"[77] Krishna did descend to Earth in Braj some 7,000 years ago. Another letter to his disciple Narendra Nath Kaul asks, rhetorically: "Do you think that He isn't pulling all the strings of the world just as efficiently as He did long ago at the time of *Mahābhārata*?"[78] Moreover, 'The Birth of Sri Krishna,' from *The Search for Truth,* announces that it is "now more than five thousand years since the Supreme Lord manifested Himself with all His powers in the prison of Kansa in Muttra [Mathura]."[79]

At this time, as Haberman notes, the way in which Krishna Prem presented Hindu philosophy depended on his intended audience. In his books, Krishna Prem "tends to present Hinduism either in terms of a Vedantic discourse or in a symbolic fashion" suitable for Westerners more "attracted to an intellectualized form of Vedantic Hinduism" than to the "culturally specific mythology and the worship and service of concrete images" central to Krishna *bhakti.*[80] This is confirmed by the same letter to Roy, in which he reveals he does "not think it at all feasible to present Krishna's life to modern educated people otherwise than as a symbol."[81] By contrast, in private he would write lovingly of the "curves of [Krishna's] body, [which] are worth more than all the Infinites and Eternals and Absolutes. All the worlds are within the pores of His skin, and yet there He remains, no shadowy cosmic figure, but the eternal cowherd, in yellow dhoti, peacock feathers, maddening the soul with the melody from a bamboo flute."[82]

Ultimately, though, for Krishna Prem the search for the historical Krishna is an unimportant one: Whether or not the butter-eating infant in Gokul, the amorous youth in Vrindavan, the friendly charioteer in Kurukshetra, or the divine protector in Dwarka described in scripture reflect a historical personage (or personages) should be of little interest to the sincere seeker. This is because, as he explains to Roy, "What Krishna as a man may have done thousands of years ago is not what will give us 'the thing:' what He is doing in our hearts now is what we must know and that will not be found by concentrating entirely on His human aspect ages ago. If He wasn't in our hearts now the *līlās* of ages ago would be quite insignificant."[83] He sees this focus on a historical figure at the expense of the inner message as the reason Christianity is "tottering so—at least among the educated.... The Christians have pinned their faith on historical events and a historical Person. Modern knowledge has shown that we cannot be certain of those events or that Person ... and therefore the bottom is falling out of the whole thing."[84]

Nor is the 'thing,' called the "'*mṛtasañjīvanī vidyā*' (the knowlege that brings the dead back to life)"[85] to be found in books, Krishna Prem's or otherwise. In his review of Sri Aurobindo's *The Riddle of the World*, originally published in *The Aryan Path* in 1934, Krishna Prem explains that the method by which one realises the nature of God and the soul may only be learnt from a qualified teacher, and cautions against those who would set out on the 'path' alone, armed only with book learning:

> It is characteristic of this age of popular education that many people suppose that anything can be learnt by a patient study of books. But there are some things which can never be learnt in this manner and *yoga* (in any form) is one of them. *Yoga* is the art of the soul and it can never be learnt without the living contact with a master. All attempts to practise *yoga* without a guru, and a real guru at that, end either in disappointed failure, trivial psychism, ill-health or madness. The present writer has seen cases of all of the above occurring to uninstructed or ill-instructed would-be *yogīs*.[86]

This view, on the desirability of a human teacher, was one shared by Krishna Prem's disciple, Moti Rani. Shortly after Madhava Ashish (then Alexander Phipps) joined the ashram, one of his first jobs was to help transfer Krishna Prem's library from one room to another. It was, he said, "a remarkable collection of everything that could be connected with the spiritual path," including "Hastings' *Encyclopaedia of Religion and Ethics*, Frazer's *The Golden Bough*, alchemical texts, Buddhist and Hindu texts in Sanskrit and Pali, psychology, Theosophy, and a whole range of lesser books, from poetry to almost every Rider Haggard novel—from one room to another" (Ashish, 119). At the time, he remarked to Moti Rani that he "really must read Krishna Prem's books. 'When you have the man, what do you want his books for,' she said. And she went on to distinguish between the people who came for the books and the ones who came for the man himself, who was so much more than his writing" (Ashish, 119).

Krishna Prem's fidelity to his own guru, Sri Yashoda Mai, whom he considered a "*jīvanmukta*"[87] (a liberated, perfected sage), was total. Roy remembers the pair's "beautiful mother-and-son-cum-guru-and-disciple relationship." Krishna Prem, he writes, followed his guru "everywhere like a shadow" and "was at her beck and call at all hours," including at night-time, when he "slept on the floor, like a servant, on a bare blanket."[88] Narendra Nath Kaul, who visited Mirtola in April 1944, around seven months before Yashoda Mai's death, writes that Krishna Prem's devotion "had to be seen to be believed. Ma was frail and not too well.... He carried her in his arms to the small chabutra [dais] in the ashram compound in the morning. Whenever she called him he would leave everything and rush to her."[89] Valentine Penrose, in what she understood as the "brother–sister relationship" of disciple and guru, "witnessed exactly what she hoped she and her husband would achieve in their marriage."[90]

But while his love for Yashoda Mai the person was genuine, he was also, in these extraordinary acts of devotion, serving Krishna as the *paramātman*, or the "guru within."[91] Writing to Roy in 1946, he explained:

> [W]hen it is said that Guru and Krishna are the same it must be taken in a mystical, not literal, sense. It is not His body, nor yet His mind that is Krishna but the Divine Consciousness within Him. Krishna means the Divine consciousness and surely it is clear that the Guru manifests that consciousness and that, to his *chela* [disciple], that consciousness is more manifest, more apparent, in the Guru than anywhere else. It is that consciousness (and *shakti* of course) which is the true Guru—not the outer form in which it manifests. The outer form is human, and is limited and may even make mistakes. But the Divine consciousness within him is flawless and free from all error. ... It is just this that is the reason why we say that all Gurus are the one Guru because by Guru we mean the Divine consciousness and Grace manifesting in any particular personal vehicle with which we first (or most vividly) contact it.[92]

This is an idea found in Gauḍīya Vaiṣṇavism: The best-known biography of

Chaitanya, the *Caitanya-caritāmṛta*, relates that Krishna, as guru, "appears in the form of the teacher and initiator, but he is also present in the heart:"

> It is Krishna in the heart who says "yay" or "nay" to his presence externally. When the truth comes as a blinding light accompanied by the imperative to act in the service of Krishna, that is Guru.[93]

The idea of the inner, or *caitya*, guru, which "dwell[s] in the heart of every living being ... and speaks ... with the voice of conscience,"[94] underlies Krishna Prem's complementary belief in the importance of personal revelation (sometimes described, by other writers, as *sahaja-samādhi*), or 'listening to the heart.' There is, he writes, "a Light within us which knows the Truth, a Voice which commands the right with absolute certainty;" however, it is because "we usually do not listen ... that an outer Guru is a help upon the Path."[95] In *The Yoga of the Kaṭhopaniṣad*, he explains that there are some extraordinary *sādhakas* who "appear sometimes to have scaled the Peaks with the aid of the inner Guru alone," although "the ordinary aspirant needs an embodied Teacher, one who, though seeming 'other' than the disciple himself, can make manifest on this plane the voice of that Self which is in truth the Self of all."[96] This same divine spark is also emphasised in gnosticism, as well as the writings of Madame Blavatsky, an early influence, who urged individuals to "turn inwards to discover God: 'there being but ONE Truth, man requires but one church, the Temple of God within us; walled in by matter, but penetrable by any who can find the way; the pure in heart see God.'"[97]

It also explains his "readiness to pranam [kneel before, or touch the feet of] anyone in the position of Guru, no matter what he thought of him privately," as Madhava Ashish recalls. "What Krishna Prem was actually doing," he explains, "was to pranam the Guru within, never the personality" (Ashish, 191). Bill Aitken adds that Krishna Prem was also "dead against 'guru ninda'—the running down of anyone's guru to their face."[98]

"Although he had himself surrendered completely to his external guru," summarises Kaul, "he nevertheless had firm faith in Inner Guru, and wanted every seeker to light his own lamp."[99]

The Burma trip seems to have been a happy one, providing the Mirtola trio with "much cultural stimulus" (Ashish, 124) and the ashram with plenty of Buddhist bric-a-brac. Yashoda Mai brought back to India a large brass sculpture of the Buddha, and Moti Rani some decorative bells, which adorned a Burmese-style *stūpa*, modelled on a photograph, that she had built near her house at Uttar Brindaban (Ashish, 124). The Burmese Buddha found a home inside the temple, as Navnit Parekh describes:

> There was a wooden sculpture of a Gopi on either side of the temple-door and a huge brass-bell was suspended in front. We entered the temple respectfully and stood silently in the antechamber. On one side was a large but elegant image of Lord Buddha inside a niche. I was told that this brass-image was brought by Yashoda-Mai from Burma. On the other side was an image of Hanuman traditionally painted with vermilion.[100]

Parekh also provides a rare description of Radhikamohanji, the temple deities, and the altar (photography of which is forbidden to this day):

> In the sanctum-sanctorum were the exquisite images of Lord Krishna and Radha cast in *ashta-dhatu*. They were seated on a throne installed on a plastered platform. A brass discus (*sudharshan-chakra*) surmounted the throne. A Kadamba-tree was painted behind the deities to form a back-drop. Lord Krishna was clad in a saffron-coloured dhoti (*pitambar*) and He was sporting a peacock-feather on His head. He was holding a golden flute in His hands, while silver-anklets adorned His Lotus Feet. Radha Rani was clad in a beautiful pink saree.[101]

Ṭhākur's anklets are central to one of the many stories about supernatural phenomena involving the Mirtola *mūrtis* that have since passed into legend. Govindagopal Mukherji recalled that on a number of occasions, on opening the temple doors in the morning, Krishna Prem would find "His anklets on Her [Radha's] feet and Her necklace around His neck," as though the deities "had been playing at their human-divine love with great eclat throughout the night."[102] A similar story, told in *The Saints of Vraja* (a book in which, incidentally, Krishna Prem is the only non-Indian profiled), concerns two of Krishna Prem's disciples in Allahabad, Sunil and Arati, who sold the latter's gold bangles to pay for the train fare to Mirtola. On arriving for their visit, they were greeted by Krishna Prem, who explained: "I know everything. Rādhārāṇī has told me that in your eagerness to come here you sold them, because you were short of money. She has given Her own gold bangles to me and said, 'Give them to Āratī to wear. I do not like her hands without bangles.'"[103] (Sunil and Arati later moved to Mirtola but left after clashing with Madhava Ashish's hot-headed disciple David Beresford [Sri Dev Ashish].[104])

The divine couple were also said to have enjoyed partaking in human food, such as when Krishna Prem discovered that a portion of the halva pudding which had been offered to them as *bhoga* had been physically scooped out of the dish, a tale related to Dilip Kumar Roy by Moti Rani.[105] Another story, resembling Yashoda Mai's dream involving Ganesh, has Krishna Prem being woken up by a cold *Ṭhākur* (a phenomenon OBL Kapoor explains as being an example of *mādhurya-rasa*—devotee and God as lover and beloved—in which Krishna "actually feels hungry and thirsty, cold and warmth, and craves for all those things which his devotees offer Him"[106]):

> One night, while Kṛṣṇaprema was asleep, he heard someone calling, "Dādā, dādā!" With a start he looked all around, but could not see anyone. Thinking that it was an illusion he closed his eyes. But again he heard that sweet call "Dādā!" This time it was quite clear that the call came from inside the temple.
>
> But there was no one inside the temple except Ṭhākura (the deity). Could it, therefore, be the call of the Ṭhākura? He went near the temple. Again he heard – "Dādā, I am feeling cold. The window is open."
>
> A current shook his body. Hurriedly he opened the door of the temple, went in and closed the window. He covered Ṭhākura's body carefully with the quilt. While doing so, he said, "Ṭhākura, you also feel cold?"
>
> A streak of tears flowed down the cheeks of Ṭhākura!
>
> Kṛṣṇaprema was petrified. He gasped out, "Hā Ṭhākura!" and wept. But controlling himself somehow he wiped the tears of Ṭhākura with his *bahirvāsa* (outer garment).
>
> Ṭhākura slept.[107]

As the new brass Buddha settled into this spiritually potent environment, Krishna Prem for his part commemorated the trip to Burma by adopting the clothing worn by Buddhist monks of Rangoon—home of the spectacular Shwedagon Pagoda temple complex—a city in which, as Madhava Ashish notes, he had "found all his old enthusiasm for Buddhism returning" (Ashish, 123).

This renewed interest in Buddhism is evident from contemporary correspondence with Bal Krishna Goswami, in which Krishna Prem is warned by his *param guru* against trying to syncretise Buddhist and Vaiṣṇava beliefs,[108] as well as his writing throughout the 1930s: *The Yoga of the Bhagavat Gita*, *The Yoga of the Kaṭhopanishad* and *Initiation into Yoga: An Introduction to the Spiritual Life* all contain numerous references to Buddhist thought, while standalone articles such as

'Love in Buddhism' (originally published in *Sankirtan* and included in *The Search for Truth*) and 'The Kinsman of the Sun' (published in *Buddhism in England*[109]) build on the earlier essays which pre-date his initiation into Vaiṣṇavism.

Krishna Prem's attraction to Theosophy, and particularly the writings of Helena Petrovna Blavatsky, also continued unabated. In the latter part of the decade, with the encouragement of Bertram Keightley, he wrote a commentary on *The Secret Doctrine*, a massive two-volume tome in which Blavatsky, purporting to be working from a lost Tibetan text called the 'Stanzas of Dzyan' (part of a larger *Book of Dzyan*), charts the development of the *kosmos* and of human life on earth. As Gabriel Monod-Herzen notes, the project was something of a first: whereas texts such as the *Bhagavad Gītā* and *Brahma Sūtras* are the subjects of "innumerable commentaries", to his knowledge "not a single Theosophist, Asian or European" had then written a commentary on the 'Stanzas of Dzyan.'[110] Krishna Prem, however, was dissatisfied with the result, and put it aside, "to be read only occasionally by friends,"[111] until the mid-1950s.

Krishna Prem's enduring fascination with Buddhism and Theosophy, both of which reject the concept of a personal creator, is incongruous in view of his then-recent initiation into a tradition which holds dear the concept of a supreme person. (Blavatsky scoffed at what she called "the absurd idea of a personal God."[112]) Regarding *The Secret Doctrine*, Andrew Rawlinson observes: "It is surely very odd that a committed Gaudiya Vaishnava should make use of such an unorthodox source."[113] Robinson contrasts Krishna Prem with AC Bhaktivedanta Swami, noting that while the latter's "association with this tradition [Gauḍīya Vaiṣṇavism] was generally orthodox, Krishna Prem's was not."[114] Swami was a fierce critic of those who denied or minimised God's personhood. In his essay 'Theosophy Ends in Vaishnavism,' he attacked the Theosophical view of "Sree Krishna [as only] in His Impersonal Aspect Brahman" rather than as "the Personality of Godhead 'Bhagwan.'"[115]

According to Madhava Ashish, Krishna Prem even wore his new Buddhist garb (which comprised "a sort of vest which, according to the monastic rule, is supposed to be made of a patchwork of bits of waste cloth, but is actually whole cloth with seams put in by sewing machine [to] make it look as if patched" [Ashish, 123]) to Vrindavan—the holiest city of Chaitanya Vaiṣṇavism, considered the external manifestation of the 'hidden' (*gupta*) spiritual Vrindavan described in scripture—where he offended many of the *Goswamis* with his tactlessness (Ashish, 123).

Krishna Prem and Yashoda Mai were regular visitors to Braj while GN Chakravarti was alive (Ashish, 100), tying in their visits to the family home at Benares with tours of holy sites such as Barsana and Nandagram, believed to be Radha and Krishna's childhood villages, respectively, and Govardhan Hill, which Krishna is said to have lifted to protect the *brajavāsīs* from the ire of the rain god Indra. The pair also seem to have continued to visit the Chakravartis' disciples in Bareilly en route to Vrindavan; one letter, dated 29 January 1934, relates how the following month they planned to stay at the house of one Shyam Kumar Dikshit and attend a *Sarva Dharma Sammelan* ('Meeting of All Faiths') taking place from 10–12 February.[116]

These visits to Vrindavan in the company of his guru seem to have been formative experiences for Krishna Prem, who relished the holy atmosphere of the pilgrimage town and the piety of its residents. On one occasion, recalled Moti Rani, he had been so excited to be there that he "leaped from the tonga" (horse-drawn carriage) that brought them into Vrindavan "and dashed off to the Jamuna river to bathe" (Ashish, 162).

Satish Datt Pandey relates a conversation in Vrindavan between Krishna Prem and "one of the curious idlers who had surrounded him," attracted to the strange white *sādhu* with "glowing face and sparkling blue eyes." The local "asked what his *janmabhūmi* (place of birth) was. Picking up a handful of dust (of which there was no dearth in the streets of Vrindaban), Gopal Da replied in his clear Hindi, 'My real *janmabhūmi* is this.' Taken aback, but only for a moment, his questioner asked, 'And the unreal?' Gopal Da's response was, 'Having known the real, why should one bother about the unreal?'"[117]

Krishna Prem's joy at being in his "real *janmabhūmi*" was infectious: Moti Rani, who on visiting with her guru had been "overwhelmed by the magic of the place" was apparently disappointed when she returned alone: "[T]his time there was no magic; the place was flat and empty. She realised that she had, in some sense, seen it through his eyes or with his feelings. Now she could not bear to leave without seeing what she knew was there, but could not see without him. So she sent him a telegram to come at once. He came, and she saw" (Ashish, 152).

This enthusiasm was, however, tempered by what he saw as a lack of compassion among some Vaiṣṇavas for their fellow man, particularly given the importance of compassion (*karuṇā*) on the Bodhisattva Path adhered to by many Buddhists and Theosophists.[118]

Those spiritual seekers who are unable or unwilling to recognise Krishna in his material creation, writes Krishna Prem, are guilty of "mere selfish seeking of one's own salvation" to the detriment of others. He gives a striking example of the kind of the cruel caricature of *bhajana* (spiritual practice) he believes can develop as result:

> In Brindaban I once saw a Vaishnava dying of typhoid. All round, coming and going, were "Vaishnavas" with their *mālās* [rosaries] in

> their hands but there was no one to give him even a glass of water! What can be the value of such '*bhajan*' as that?[119]

Writing about the Buddhist practice of *Brahma-vihara* meditation, by which "the heart of the *sādhaka* is expanded till it dwells in the whole universe," Krishna Prem likewise criticises those Vaiṣṇavas who "stress the love of God as something different from this love of men.... Perhaps there will be some who will say that this love ... is very fine, but it is a love of humanity and not a love of God. Such an objection, however, reveals utter ignorance both of the nature of love and of the nature of God," he writes.[120]

Similarly, Pandey recalls Krishna Prem once chastising a male disciple who was rumoured to have been mistreating his wife. He is said to have pointed out to the wayward *chela* the "futility of worshipping the image of Radha Rani made of stone while maltreating the living Radha Rani of flesh and blood."[121]

Notes

[1]Sunyata, *Dancing with the Void: The Innerstandings of a Rare-born Mystic*, 1st Indian edn, (Delhi: New Age Books, 2004), 256

[2]James S. Helfer, 'The Initiatory Structure of the Kaṭhopaniṣad,' *History of Religions*, 7.4, (1968), 348.

[3]Krishna Prem, *The Yoga of the Kaṭhopanishad*, 1.

[4]Sri Krishna Prem, 'Preface,' in Krishna Prem, *The Search for Truth*.

[5]The first of the articles that comprise the majority of *The Yoga of Bhagavat Gita* was published as 'The Song of the Higher Life: I. The General Setting' in *The Aryan Path* of September 1935 (6.9, 534–539)

[6]Not to be confused with *Initiation into Yoga: An Introduction to the Spiritual Life*, a longer collection published by Quest Books in 1976.

[7]'Initiation into Yoga' (review), *Vedanta Kesari*, 26, (1939–1940), 274–275.

[8]Yamuna Kachru, 'Speaking and Writing in World Englishes,' 2009 edn, in Braj B. Kachru, Yamuna Kachru and Cecil L. Nelson (eds), *The Handbook of World Englishes, 2009*, (Chichester: Wiley-Blackwell, 2009), 377.

[9]Sri Sri Paramahansa Yogananda, *God Talks with Arjuna: The Bhagavad Gita*, 1st Indian paperback edn, 3rd impression, (Kolkata: Yogoda Satsanga Society of India, 2005), 863.

[10]Robert McDermott, 'Introduction,' in Rudolf Steiner, *The Bhagavad Gita and the West: The Esoteric Significance of the Bhagavad Gita and Its Relation to the Epistles of Paul*, (Great Barrington: Steiner Books, 2009), 54–55.

[11]Robert D. Baird, 'Swami Bhaktivedanta and the Bhagavadgita "As It Is,"' in Robert Minor (ed), *Modern Indian Interpreters of the Bhagavad Gita*, (New York: State University of New York Press, 1986), 215.

[12]Krishna Prem, *The Yoga of the Bhagavat Gita*, xiii.

[13]Krishna Prem, *The Yoga of the Bhagavat Gita*, xxii.

[14]*Ibid.*

[15]Krishna Prem, *The Yoga of the Bhagavat Gita*, xx.

[16]Krishna Prem, *The Yoga of the Bhagavat Gita*, xxii.

[17]Krishna Prem, *The Yoga of the Bhagavat Gita*, xxiii.

[18]Krishna Prem, *The Yoga of the Bhagavat Gita*, xxiv.

[19]Krishna Prem, *The Yoga of the Bhagavat Gita*, xxvii-xxix.

[20]Krishna Prem, *The Yoga of the Bhagavat Gita*, xxix.

[21]Krishna Prem, *The Yoga of the Bhagavat Gita*, 219.

[22]Krishna Prem, *The Yoga of the Bhagavat Gita*, xiv

[23]Catherine A. Robinson, *Interpretations of the Bhagavad-Gītā and Images of the Hindu Tradition: The Song of the Lord*, paperback edn, (Abingdon: Routledge, 2013), 108.

[24]*Ibid.*

[25]Krishna Prem, *The Yoga of the Bhagavat Gita*, xv.

[26]Kaul, *Writings of Sri Krishna Prem*, x.

[27]Georg Feuerstein with Brenda Feuerstein, *The Bhagavad-Gītā: A New Translation*, (Boston: Shambhala, 2011), 72

[28]Van Vrekhem, *The Mother*, part 2, ch. 4.

[29]Gerald T. Carney, 'Sri Krishna Prem and the *Gita*'s Yoga,' *Journal of Vaishnava Studies*, 16.1, (2007), 91.

[30]The influential Chaitanyaite commentators Krishnadas Kaviraj (c. 1520 – c. 1616) and Viśvanāth Cakravartī (c. 1638 – c. 1708) both consider "work and knowledge to be effective at all only when mixed with some devotion." In the Gauḍīya tradition, "[d]evotion receives the central position in the *Gītā* because it is the most secret, the most respected (since it gives vitality to the other two disciplines), and because it is the most rare." See Joseph T. O'Connell, 'Caitanya's Followers and the *Bhagavad-gītā*: A Study in Bhakti and the Secular, in Bradwell L. Smith (ed), *Hinduism: New Essays in the History of Religions*, photomechanical reprint, (Leiden: Brill, 1982), 43.

[31]Dr Rajen Barua, 'Buddhism and Bhakti,' *Boloji*, Houston (8 August, 2018), https://www.boloji.com/articles/50353/buddhism-and-bhakti (accessed 6 May 2023).

[32]Robinson, *Interpretations of the Bhagavad-Gītā and Images of the Hindu Tradition*, 128.

[33]Krishna Prem, *The Yoga of the Bhagavat Gita*, xiv.

[34]Sri Krishna Prem, 'Letters from Sri Aurobindo' (review of *Lights on Yoga*), *The Aryan Path*, 6, (1935), 521.

[35]Krishna Prem, 'The Yoga of the Gita,' para. 11.

[36]Annie Besant and Bhagavân Dâs, *The Bhagavad-Gîtâ*, (London: Theosophical Publishing Society, 1905), 77.

[37]Kaul, *Writings of Sri Krishna Prem*, v.

[38]Michael Jackson, *Between One and Another*, (Berkeley: University of California Press, 2012), 42.

[39]Krishna Prem, *The Yoga of the Bhagavat Gita*, xiii.

[40]*Ibid,*

[41]Krishna Prem, *The Yoga of the Bhagavat Gita*, xiv.

[42]Robinson, *Interpretations of the Bhagavad-Gītā and Images of the Hindu Tradition*, 127.

[43]Krishna Prem, *Initiation into Yoga*, 40.

[44]Krishna Prem, *The Yoga of the Bhagavat Gita*, 100.

[45]Krishna Prem, *The Yoga of the Bhagavat Gita*, 101.

[46]Krishna Prem, *The Yoga of the Bhagavat Gita*, 199.

[47]*Ibid.*

[48]Krishna Prem, *The Yoga of the Bhagavat Gita*, 199–200.

[49]Probably a reference to the Buddhist idea that the one who has achieved the first stage of enlightenment, known as a *sotapanna* ("stream-winner"), will attain *Nirvāṇa* after no more than seven rebirths.

[50]Krishna Prem, *The Yoga of the Bhagavat Gita*, 200.

[51]Monod-Herzen, Appendix C: 'On Sri Krishnaprem,' 310.

[52]Jones and Ryan, *Encyclopedia of Hinduism*, 299.

[53]Krishna Prem, *The Yoga of the Kaṭhopanishad*, 5.

[54]Monod-Herzen, 'On Sri Krishnaprem,' 310.

[55]Roy, *Yogi Sri Krishnaprem*, 48.

[56]Timothy Leary, *Jail Notes*, (New York: Grove Press, 1974), 29.

[57]Carney, 'Sri Krishna Prem and the *Gita*'s Yoga,' 118.

[58]Krishna Prem, *The Yoga of the Kaṭhopanishad*, 5.

[59]Swami Jagadiswarananda, 'The Upanishads Abroad,' *Prabuddha Bharata*, 51.12, (1946), 474.

[60]'In the Light of Theosophy,' *The Theosophical Movement*, 13.4, (1943), 62.

[61]Krishna Prem, *The Yoga of the Kaṭhopanishad*, 30.

[62]'The Riddle of the Gita,' *The Bombay Chronicle*, 30 October 1938, 44.

[63]*Ibid.*

[64]Barua, 'Buddhism and Bhakti.'

[65]SR Sharma, *Wisdom Beyond Reason,* (Agra: Lakshmi Narain Agarwal, 1957), 27.

[66]Verma (ed.), *Essays and Reflections by Karan Singh,* part 4 ('Essays'), ch. 2, para. 20.

[67]Karan Singh, *Autobiography,* (New Delhi: Oxford University Press, 1995), 206.

[68]Brian Mooney, *Frank Baines: A Life Beyond the Sea,* (London: Thorogood Publishing, 2011), 155.

[69]Mooney, *Frank Baines,* 158.

[70]Donald Eichert, Introduction: 'Sri Madhava Ashish,' in Sri Madhava Ashish, *Relating to Reality: Relating the Metaphysical Roots of Value to Their Applications in Every Field of Human Activity,* (New Delhi: Banyan Books, 1998), https://www.mirtolareflections.com/reflections-content.php?a-id=7 (accessed 6 November 2022).

[71]A. Devaraja Mudaliar, *Day by Day with Bhagavan,* 5th reprint, (Tiruvannamalai: Sri Ramanasramam, 2002), 185.

[72]Gary Scott Smith, 'Das, Bhagavan (1945 –),' in Gary Scott Smith (ed), *American Religious History: Belief and Society through Time,* (Santa Barbara: ABC-CLIO, 2020), 143.

[73]'Call and Response special edition: Conversations with KD July 18 2020,' *Call and Response with Krishna Das* [podcast], Q&A with Krishna Das, (New York: Kirtan Wallah Foundation, 18 July 2020), https://www.krishnadas.com/podcasts/call-response/call-and-response-special-edition-conversations-with-kd-july-18-2020 (accessed 4 October 2022).

[74]Ram Dass, *Be Here Now,* (Anselmo: Hanuman Foundation, 1978), 498.

[75]Sharon Gannon and David Life, *Jivamukti Yoga: Practices for Liberating Body and Soul,* (New York: Ballantine Books, 2002), 280.

[76]*Krishna Das Workshop and Chanting—Recorded live at Garrison Institute, NY April 2022* [online video], presenter Krishna Das, (New York: Krishna Das Music, 2022), https://www.youtube.com/watch?v=LtIZHQxYdLg (accessed 17 October 2023).

[77]Roy, *Yogi Sri Krishnaprem,* 178.

[78]Kaul, *Writings of Sri Krishna Prem,* 104.

[79]Krishna Prem, *The Search for Truth,* 14.

[80]Haberman, 'A Cross-cultural Adventure,' 223.

[81]Roy, *Yogi Sri Krishnaprem,* 178.

[82]Roy, *Yogi Sri Krishnaprem,* 166.

[83]Roy, *Yogi Sri Krishnaprem,* 178.

[84]Roy, *Yogi Sri Krishnaprem,* 179.

[85]Krishna Prem, 'The Birth of Sri Krishna,' in *The Search for Truth,* 14.

[86]Sri Krishna Prem, 'A Modern Yoga' (review of *The Riddle of the World*), in Dilip Kumar Roy, *Yogi Sri Krishnaprem,* 3rd edn, (Bombay: Bharatiya Vidya Bhavan, 1992), 300.

[87]Shankar Bandyopadhyay (ed.), *Sri Aurobindo to Dilip, Vol. 4 (1938–1950),* (Pune: The Mother & Sri Aurobindo, 2011), 148, https://web.archive.org/web/20160321132124/http://aurobindo.ru/workings/sa/to-dilip/vol-4-e.htm (accessed 10 April 2023).

[88]Roy, *Yogi Sri Krishnaprem*, 65.

[89]Kaul, *Writings of Sri Krishna Prem*, viii.

[90]King, *Roland Penrose*, 118.

[91]John Chambers, *The Secret Life of Genius: How 24 Great Men and Women Were Touched by Spiritual Worlds*, (Rochester, Vermont: Destiny Books, 2009), 196.

[92]Roy, *Yogi Sri Krishnaprem*, 245–246.

[93]Jagadananda Das, 'Bhaktivinoda Thakur's Meat Eating and Lalita Prasad Thakur,' Jagat [blog], 1 August 2007, https://jagadanandadas.blogspot.com/2007/08/rocanas-comments.html (accessed 22 January 2023).

[94]Krishna Prem, *The Search for Truth*, 7.

[95]Krishna Prem, *The Search for Truth*, 8.

[96]Krishna Prem, *The Yoga of the Kaṭhopanishad*, 72.

[97]Mark Bevir, 'The West Turns Eastward: Madame Blavatsky and the Transformation of the Occult Tradition,' *Journal of the American Academy of Religion*, 62.3, (1994), 755.

[98]Aitken, email to the author, 24 June 2021.

[99]Kaul, *Writings of Sri Krishna Prem*, vii.

[100]Parekh, *Himalayan Memoirs*, 46–47.

[101]Parekh, *Himalayan Memoirs*, 47.

[102]Roy, *Yogi Sri Krishnaprem*, 293.

[103]Kapoor, 'Śrī Kṛṣṇaprema,' 306.

[104]Aitken, email to the author, 2 July 2023.

[105]Roy, *Yogi Sri Krishnaprem*, 78.

[106]Kapoor, 'Śrī Kṛṣṇaprema,', 304.

[107]Kapoor, 'Śrī Kṛṣṇaprema,' 302.

[108]Niroop, email to the author, 9 July 2021.

[109]Sri Krishna Prem, 'The Kinsman of the Sun,' *Buddhism in England*, 13, (1939), 72.

[110]Gabriel Monod-Herzen, '"L'homme comme mesure de toutes choses" par Sri Krishna Prem & Sri Madhava Ashish', *Le Lotus Bleu*, 85, (1980), https://www.revue3emillenaire.com/blog/vie-et-oeuvre-de-sri-krishna-prem-par-gabriel-monod-herzen.

[111]Madhava Ashish, 'Preface,' in Krishna Prem and Madhava Ashish, *Man, the Measure of All Things*, 6.

[112]AT Barker (ed.), *The Letters of HP Blavatsky to AP Sinnett and Other Miscellaneous Letters*, (London: T. Fisher Unwin, 1925), 80.

[113]Rawlinson, *The Book of Enlightened Masters*, 381.

[114]Robinson, *Interpretations of the Bhagavad-Gītā and Images of the Hindu Tradition*, 127.

[115]AC Bhaktivedanta Swami, 'Theosophy Concluded,' *Back to Godhead*, 1.9,(1952?), https://www.backtogodhead.in/theosophy-concluded-2 (accessed 24 April 2023).

[116]'Letter from Shri Krishna Prem (Bhikhariji), (29 January 1934)', *Bhakt Ram Sharan Das* [Facebook page], 26 September 2023, https://www.facebook.com/ BhaktRamSharanDas/posts/787429920060928 (accessed 30 May 2024).

[117]Pandey, *Guru by Your Bedside*, 195.

[118]In Mahayana Buddhism, a Bodhisattva is an enlightened being who has chosen to help others reach enlightenment instead of ascending to *Nirvāṇa.* The Theosophical view, as explained by Mark Bevir, is similar, though it adds to the Buddhist concept Blavatskian ideas of evolution: Bodhisattvas are considered to be "highly spiritual beings near the end of their evolutionary cycle who have chosen to stay around and to help the less advanced." See Mark Bevir, 'Annie Besant's Quest for Truth: Christianity, Secularism, and New Age Thought,' *The Journal of Ecclesiastical History*, 50.1, (1999), 21, cited in Per-Olof Fjällsby, *Idealizing India: A Transformative Perspective on Theosophists [sic] Contribution to Education and Politics (1879–1930)*, (Karlstad: Karlstad University, 2016), 54.

[119]Krishna Prem, *The Search for Truth*, 26.

[120]Krishna Prem, *The Search for Truth*, 46–47.

[121]Pandey, *Guru by Your Bedside*, 130.

12: "Mirtola Teaching"

"[O]ne's thoughts were often 'heard,' and answered directly, or later."[1]
— Penelope Phipps

On joining Uttar Brindaban in 1938, Bob Alexander—given the name Ananda Priya, meaning one who loves *ānanda* (transcendental bliss, also used as a name of Vishnu/Krishna)—took over the running of the ashram's clinic full time, as well as the bee hives and one of its gardens, where he grew flowers for the daily rituals.[2] As a celebrated doctor of modern, evidence-based medicine, Alexander (Madhava Ashish recalls that the name Ananda Priya "never really stuck. He remained Bob to all of us" [Ashish, 19]) dispensed conventional "allopathic" treatments to local villagers, though Sri Yashoda Mai and Sri Krishna Prem were both advocates of homoeopathy, the alternative medicine system that uses preparations of primarily herbal ingredients diluted in water or alcohol. Alexander's dispensary was located in a one-room cottage originally built by Krishna Prem for his astrological practice. Under Alexander, it housed hundreds of bottles of flower solutions based on the system devised by homoeopath Edward Bach (Ashish, 84–85). In contrast, Yashoda Mai once treated her family with homoeopathy and possessed a store of *totkas*, traditional household remedies, which Madhava Ashish notes were "apt to be violent: An excessively fat *mahārāṇi* was given a glassful of warm ghee to drink every morning, with the result that she lost her appetite and lost her weight. A hysterical girl had chilli paste smeared into her eyelids—and became normal" (Ashish, 65).

Krishna Prem had taken up astrology—observing the stars using astronomical instruments he had made himself (Ashish, 108)—"firstly because he wanted to familiarise himself with a system of symbols that could be applied to anything and everything, and secondly because he wanted to find out just how much could actually be done by a study of the star charts themselves," explains Madhava Ashish. He continues:

> In talking to me about it, he said that the stars themselves are no

> more the powers which are ascribed to them than the hands of the clock are time. Indeed, he talked of the planets as being the hands of a very complicated clock with nine hands, which showed the pattern of the moment.
>
> By the time I came to know him [1946], he had become famous in the surrounding villages, and men frequently came to see him, asking those heart-wrenching questions: 'My son has run away. Where is he?,' or 'My wife is missing. Is she alive?' And Krishna Prem would set up a figure for the moment the question was asked—[practicing what is called h]orary astrology. (Ashish, 129–130)

By the 1940s, Krishna Prem's reputation had grown to the point that a significant amount of his time was spent dealing with astrological queries. One notable case involved Sarala Behn, whose participation in the Quit India movement had attracted the attention of the authorities. Sarala asked Krishna Prem whether she was going to be imprisoned; his reading indicated that unless she stayed at home, in which case she would be left alone, she would go to jail. She chose to continue her pro-independence activities in the open and was arrested (Ashish, 261–262).

According to Madhava Ashish, Krishna Prem gave up astrology after the latter's arrival in 1946, seeing in the stars themselves a message that he should discontinue the practice. "Shortly after I arrived, Krishna Prem had three consecutive cases within a week or two, in each of which the degree of the house on the ascendent was such that, according to the rules, no answer can be given," he explains. "He took this as an indication that he should stop this activity" (Ashish, 131). He was later critical of both astrologers—disparaging those who are "preoccupied with the *aṣṭagraha* [eight-planet] *yoga*", as well as those Brahmins whose "business [consists] of cashing in on the superstition with *yajñas* [fire sacrifices] etc. to allay the planetary malice"[3]—and of the practice itself. In another conversation, with his disciple Jagdish Shah, Krishna Prem outlined "the only true lesson that astrology teaches:" "If you are facing the Raas-mandal (the constellations) then your back is towards the ever-fixed Dhruva (pole star) but if you are facing the ever-fixed Dhruva then your back is towards the ever-changing Raas-mandal."[4]

However, belief in other esoteric and occultist concepts and practices—including telepathy, telekinesis, divination with tarot cards, curses, magic, ghosts and evil spirits, the astral plane, and the aforementioned homoeopathy—remained common among Mirtola ashramites.

As a believer in a "plenitude of other worlds and dimensions," Krishna Prem believed that the channelling of spirits "could, and did, take place, and could represent contact with other, discarnate, entities."[5] The ashram women, Yashoda

Mai and Moti Rani, were blessed with the gift of "accessing the astral worlds with astonishing matter-of-factness," according to Madhava Ashish (Ashish, 108), with the former in particular blessed with a "rare ability to see spirits and to talk to them" (Ashish, 110). While such unsolicited incursions from the other side did not seem to faze Yashoda Mai, who "quite happily talked to spirits and handled their demands" (Ashish, 79), they "did bother Moti ... [particularly those who] seemed to be aware that here was a person who might be able to see them and to whom they could tell their problems or could at least get attention from" (Ashish, 79). Moti Rani did, however, enjoy her other purported psychic abilities. "Reading thoughts, moving objects at a distance, and so inhibiting one's senses that she seemed to disappear [were] the fun part of it" (Ashish, 79).

Using intermediaries, 'Ma' was also said to be able to communicate over long distances by 'rapping' on solid objects, like the spirits of the dead in spiritualist seances:

> [One] story concerns a day when Ronald went off to a tea party with his Indian colleagues. They were sitting around a table in the garden, enjoying a discussion which had got onto the question of psychical phenomena. Suddenly there was a loud rap in the middle of the table. Ronald jokingly said that at a seance this would be taken as a psychic phenomenon. Everyone laughed and the party broke up. It did not strike him till later that the party had ended much earlier than expected. On reaching home he found Mrs Chakravarti there, and he told her the joke about the rap on the table. 'Yes,' she said, 'I was wanting you, and there were two babajis hanging about, wanting to get into birth through me,[6] so I sent them to call you.' (Ashish, 43—44)

Both Penelope Phipps and Jagdish Shah also attribute certain occult powers—known in Hinduism as *siddhis* and associated with "seers and highly evolved souls"[7]—to their spiritual master. According to Phipps, she and Krishna Prem were both proficient in the art of telepathy (thought transference), which she describes as feeling like an "electric current [which ran] between us."[8] She relates a telepathic conversation between the pair on her second visit to Uttar Brindaban:

> When we left in 1953 Gopalda told us, 'And if you have anything special to communicate, put it very clearly in your minds.' After a bit, as I resumed my life in England, I forgot this. On my next visit, I remembered it. Every morning Gopalda came down the path from the temple building to the garden beyond the cottage (where I was

> staying), to collect flowers for the morning arati. He never spoke before breakfast. I sat up in bed and said silently and clearly in my head, 'Good morning, Gopalda.' For the first time ever, he spoke aloud, 'Good morning, Penelope.' I 'jumped' inwardly. This I did with the same response for three mornings. We never discussed it, but later, on the third day, he said, 'If you can do that over twenty yards, Penelope, you can do it over thousands of miles. Distance doesn't make any difference.'
>
> When I had to leave for England, climbing the steps to the plane in Delhi, I said in my head, loudly and clearly, 'I AM NOW CLIMBING THE STEPS TO THE PLANE!' I heard, 'ALL RIGHT, DON'T SHOUT!'[9]

Tony Foster, a British disciple of Phipps, remembers that she used photos of Krishna Prem to continue to 'communicate' with her late guru even after his death.[10]

Shah, meanwhile, remembers once witnessing Krishna Prem ringing the temple bell telekinetically on his way up from the kitchen with the *Ṭhākurs' bhoga*: "One day I was standing near the stone stairs leading up to the mandir [temple], when Gopal Da, making his hurried way to the mandir, playfully clasped my hands with his wet hands and amazed me by simultaneously ringing the bell about a distance of at least 100 feet."[11]

While some visitors were put off by what they saw as the importance the "'Mirtola teaching' seemed to give to ghosts and psychic phenomena,"[12] the capacity to see ghosts was one of the "rather strange and unorthodox attributes" which Krishna Prem considered to be helpful to a spiritual seeker, according to Satish Datt Pandey.[13] Other desirable qualities included acceptance of the "androgynous nature of one's psyche" and a strong attachment to one parent.[14] Ashramites were, however, encouraged to minimise contact with the life they'd left behind, including their families. "Both Sri Krishna Prem, my param guru, and Ashishda were against maintaining family contacts," explains Bill Aitken, "arguing the Larkin viewpoint that 'They fuck you up, your mum and dad.'[15] Ashishda in particular was vehement on this issue."[16]

In a letter to Abha Shah, daughter of Jagdish and his wife Rambha, Madhava Ashish said identification with the family unit is one of the many impediments to self-realisation. "People find it difficult to 'go it alone,'" he writes. "They want the support of the company of others; they want the 'togetherness' of group activity. They don't feel strong enough to go their own way. But the inner work is essentially lonely, in the same sense that death is lonely—no matter how many people there may be sitting on the bed holding one's hand. ... [T]o find one's True Self, a whole lot of self-identification with family and culture, and all the things that tie one into a group, like shared customs, how you eat, what you wear, etc., have to be dropped."[17]

Madhava Ashish's own attitude appears to have been influenced by his god-sister, Moti Rani, who in the years following Yashoda Mai's death railed against the newcomer for what he calls his then "attachment to my mother [and] my sister" (Ashish, 184). The effect of this, he writes, was that he came to see that his mother's "doting and possessive care had sucked the marrow from my spine and turned me into a rather feeble young man. Disgust with myself and anger at what she had done to me, albeit with the best of conscious intentions, were helping to break the mother fixation and to open a road along which I might one day become something resembling a man—an event I owe entirely to Moti" (Ashish, 232).

Sri Krishna Prem was so opposed to mixing with "worldly" family and friends that even Dilip Kumar Roy—himself a *sannyāsī* in the ashram of his guru, Sri Aurobindo—admits to feeling "fairly disconcerted" when his friend of over 20 years declined to attend his 50th birthday celebrations in January 1947. "The more I pressed him the more determinedly he shook his head," Roy writes. "'Forgive me, Dilip,' he said. 'I just can't attend public meetings, still less sit on decorated platforms to be made much of and wheedled into making a "splendid" speech. You know how I love to hear you sing. But sing here, before the Lord, and I would bless your voice and, still more, your *bhakti*.'"[18] (Ultimately, after being "hectored and beseeched, berated and cajoled ... for full one hour" by Moti Rani,[19] he did attend the event, held at a pavilion on the Maidan in Calcutta, although only on three conditions: that his name would not appear in the newspapers, that he would not be made to sit on the dais with Roy, and that Roy would sing his devotional song 'Brindabaner Lila.'[20])

Krishna Prem's dismissive attitude towards the "friends and cousins, uncles and aunts"[21] of non-renounced life can be attributed to the seriousness with which he took his vow of *vairāgya*. For this reason, he disapproved of the extent to which his celebrated friend continued to participate in civic life after having supposedly forsworn the world. "Apropos" the proper conduct for a renunciate, "he gave me once a valuable advice so forcefully that I could nevermore forget it," Roy recalls:

> "Whenever you come out of your Guru's Ashram, Dilip," he admonished, "do not, for mercy's sake, go down to your worldly friends' level to oblige or gratify them. That would be sheer waste of time, to put it mildly. If they really want your company, let them remember that they will have to come up to your level to profit by your devotional songs or talks on things that matter. Let them not be allowed to forget, when they come to court your society, that one who

has left the worldly life cannot afford to behave like a worldling. In other words your die is cast and you can nevermore resume the role of the Prince Charming you once were to all who flocked to your durbar for small talk. For believe me, Dilip, do what we would, we could never again recapture what is gone any more than we could make a spent wave flow backwards. You can never revert to what you were in your pre-yogic days. I will say nothing against your collecting funds for your Guru's Ashram since he approves of it. But, surely, he can't approve of your accepting dinner engagements and speaking in public assemblies to be garlanded and applauded and lionized. Sing His Name by all means, but keep yourself to yourself. For what have you in common with these your friends and cousins, uncles and aunts who besiege you with their affection and keep overwhelming you with their presents and hospitality, compliments and sweet attention? *They* are not your kin. If mix you must with people, mix with those who can understand your *vairāgya*, loyalty and, above all, love of Guru and Krishna. Remind yourself constantly that they alone can be your true friends, the rest you have got to fend off as best you can with polite disclaimers. To sum up, don't come to Calcutta if you can't steer clear of these human leeches. I had rather they should sigh that you have changed beyond recognition than chuckle: 'He's the same old jolly good fellow, thank God!'"[22]

As her health worsened, Yashoda Mai was forced to hire an external teacher for the ashram's school, where she had formerly taught village boys literacy, arithmetic and basic English personally. Though some parents refused to allow their children to attend, "fearing that this strange Mataji would turn them all into sadhus" (Ashish, 116), some 14 boys passed through the school before its closure in 1940, their education gaining them white-collar jobs as *chaprasis* (junior messengers) in banks and government offices (Ashish, 117). The ashram's school was replaced by a new school in the nearby village of Panuanaula, built by the local council after being inspired by Yashoda Mai's example.[23]

The old school building was converted into accommodation for visitors, who at that time included pilgrims on their way to Tibet[24] and Jageshwar, the occasional local official, and travellers bound for the city of Pithoragarh, as well as a constant stream of local people seeking medical advice from 'Doctor Sahib,' Bob Alexander (Ashish, 249).

Yashoda Mai and Krishna Prem both valued quiet and privacy (Ashish, 251), to the extent that the latter became known as a "hater of visitors"[25] and the ashram gained a "reputation for standoffishness."[26] (Krishna Prem is said to have remarked once: "We pay a price for wearing this [the *sannyāsī*'s] cloth. Wherever we go we're surrounded by fools."[27]) Dilip Kumar Roy, however, notes that Krishna Prem refused to see those visitors "who came only to pose, one after another, pointless questions prompted by useless curiosity, as he was wont to put it,"[28] and Madhava Ashish said that he objected only to "contrived questions" which, he felt, treated him "like a model engine in a show-case where people put a coin in the slot to see the wheels go round."[29] Anne Marshall wrote that Krishna Prem "does not encourage ... the ignorant kind [of visitor] who admire the images of Radha and Krishna in the main shrine, and exclaim, 'Oh what pretty dolls! What do you do with them?'"[30] To this end, guests' needs were looked after by villagers hired specifically for that purpose (Ashish, 168), and Western visitors were vetted in advance by Boshi and Gertrude Emerson Sen, who provided an "affable but business-like screening"[31] service at Kundan House in Almora.

Those visitors who did make the cut, however, were welcomed into the inner sanctum and invited to join the semi-legendary fireside talks, held first in Yashoda Mai's and later in her successors' rooms, which remained a fixture of ashram life well into the Sri Madhava Ashish era. These intimate evening sessions—which may be seen as an evolution of the talks hosted by the then Professor Nixon back in Lucknow, when select students were invited to pass the evenings at the vice-chancellor's lodge—followed the final *ārati*, when the day's work and worship was done, and found the gurus in relaxed mood, with Krishna Prem reading aloud while Yashoda Mai knitted, embroidered or made carpets.[32] Gabriel Monod-Herzen, on his first visit in 1942, remembers:

> Every evening we foregathered in Yasoda Ma's room, her faithful dog included. Sri Krishnaprem would read aloud from H.P. Blavatsky's *The Voice of the Silence*. It was in the Indian style: long pauses between the sentences to allow the listener to savour the echo awakened in his consciousness. Occasionally, someone would tender a comment or ask a question. Sri Yasoda Ma's contributions were always brief, utterly impersonal but fraught nonetheless with mystic passion.[33]

Though Krishna Prem had, on becoming a disciple of Sri Yashoda Mai, turned over to his guru all his worldly possessions, she had chosen to preserve in its entirety his collection of books, which was housed separately from the main ashram building.[34] Sunyata, visiting from Cranks' Ridge, describes the ashram library in July 1940: "At Uttara Brindaban we sink into books into the rhythm of 'translation into rapport' through printed words. Marco pollis [sic] 'peaks and Lamas,' 'Alice in Wonderland,' Gerald Heard, 'Pain, Sex and Time,' Meister Eckhart, D.H. Lawrence's Last Poems, Whitman, Blake and Mahatma Gandhi."[35] The works of these great intellectuals and mystics were sometimes modified to fit the ashram's philosophy: an Indian disciple, Bhuvaneshwar Nath Mishra Madhav, recalls how, in Krishna Prem's hands, the narrator of Keats's 'Ode on a Grecian Urn' became a Vaiṣṇava *bhakta*: "Krishna is God, God is Krishna,—that is all Ye know on earth, and all ye need to know."[36]

Drawing on this vast library, as well as his own knowledge about "symbols and correspondences, planets and medicinal herbs, consciousness and form, the levels of the universe, ghosts, dreams, *mahātmās*, ritual gestures and their magical effects, and psychic phenomena,"[37] a typical session would see Krishna Prem—as Madhava Ashish explains—

> pile up conceptual images and set them glowing, lighten philosophy with laughter, lead his audience to high seriousness, then drop to trivial gossip and, catching at a thread, draw them up again. One cannot reproduce such talk, and little purpose would be served if one could. On these occasions his purpose was not to teach but to inspire. Many men can talk on a wide range of subjects and hold an audience with a show of learning and wit; university professors make a living out of it, as Krishna Prem once said, living like yogis on air ... hot air. Krishna Prem's own impassioned dedication to the spirit infused everything he said. Visitors would leave him charged, not merely with this play of original and interesting ideas but with some spark drawn from Krishna Prem's own unshakable certainty. When, as sometimes happened, a departed visitor would write, asking him to repeat his talk on paper, Krishna Prem would smile ruefully; the point had been missed. It was not what was said that matters, but what came through the words. If anyone grasped the certainty, nursing the spark of inspiration, then, when occasion permitted, Krishna Prem would turn to shorter and more practical instruction.[38]

"Krishna Prem captivated his visitors ... by quoting from the poets and the mystics to illustrate the point he was making," recalls Bill Aitken. "After supper he would throw another log on the fire ... pull out his pipe and have a contented puff. The atmosphere in these supper sessions was charged. The bare room where we sat on the planked floor on woollen mats turned into a magical chamber: mysteries were made clear and the deepest longings of the human soul answered. Krishna Prem became the vehicle for the wisdom of the enlightened."[39] Karan Singh, meanwhile, remembers Krishna Prem, "sat in one corner next to fire, cooking delicious potatoes and laddus [sugar sweets], while Sri Madhava Ashish sat opposite him" as the three "talked deep into the night."[40]

For an audience of primarily Western residents and visitors, the contrast between Krishna Prem's external Englishness—"six foot, big-boned but soft-fibred, blue-eyed, a high-domed shaven head with a stubble of white hair, and a lot of that pinko-white Anglo-Saxon skin that goes red in the sun"[41]—and his dedication to a thoroughly Indian mode of spiritual inquiry was striking. Gertrude Emerson Sen recalls her surprise at first setting eyes on this strange creature, at the Ramakrishna ashram near the Sens' house in Almora, in the early 1930s:

> I was startled to see a fair-skinned, blue-eyed stranger sitting among the monks on the floor. To judge from his physical appearance, he was obviously a foreigner, and English so it seemed, but he was wholly Indian in his *gerua* [saffron] dress, and the deep absorption with which he joined in the devotional chanting. ...
>
> Not long after this, Sri Krishnaprem unexpectedly came in to see us. His directness, his complete absence of self-consciousness and of even the slightest trace of pretence, and above all the deep respect and love he showed for India and Indian religious thought and feeling, at once attracted us to him.[42]

Frank Baines, who moved into the ashram in 1946, taking initiation at the same time as Alexander Phipps (later Sri Madhava Ashish), was less complimentary about his first impressions of Krishna Prem, which, he admitted, defied his own preconceptions of how an Indian *sādhu* should look. A "tall man, with the cultivated professional stoop (half-cringe) of the specialist expert in holiness and humility," he also "had huge ... red, but in addition positively disfigured by calluses, feet," recalls Baines. "He was a long-head, very definitely brachycephalic, bald, with cropped grey hair at back and sides, [and] a reddish complexion[.] ... He was about 43 and no beauty!"[43] Baines contrasts the apparent ordinariness of the man who stood before him with his own fantastical image of the author of *The Yoga of the Kaṭhopanishad*:

> God knows what I expected! My febrile imagination had led me to anticipate something really arresting. But Sri Krishna Prem ... proved to be remarkable unremarkable. I was deeply disappointed. He was an ordinary-looking man from whom my objectifying fantasy had required an impossible ideality.[44]

However, it was precisely because Krishna Prem "never pretended to be anything more than an ordinary man," neither giving "himself the airs of a conventional guru nor assum[ing] a false humility,"[45] that his counsel made such an impact. Madhava Ashish explains: "He never lectured in a monologue. The talks were conversational meetings in which visitors were expected to participate.... [I]f anyone produced a written list of questions or, worse still, paper and pencil to record the answers, he might refuse to talk at all. But when people came with personal questions and problems, he might give of himself until he was drained of energy."[46]

Singh, who first visited Mirtola in December 1958 (having secured the ashram address from KM Munshi),[47] confirms that Sri Krishna Prem placed "special emphasis on the emotional realms,"[48] in effect rejecting the traditional Hindu distinction between mundane love and its transcendental counterpart, called *kāma* and *preman* respectively in Sanskrit. Krishna Prem (*Kṛṣṇa-prema*), says Singh, embodied his name, writing of his *prema* for Krishna which was visible in the "strange radiance" in his blue eyes and the "inner joy" in his body whenever he spoke of his *Ṭhākur.*[49] However, earthly problems had to be "squarely faced and not brushed under the carpet, as it were, to fester and surface later as neurotic manifestations." Singh continues:

> He felt that while my intellectual development had proceeded rapidly, there had not been a corresponding emotional growth. He made it his business to correct this, and when an occasion arose of what he called 'a brush with the wings of Eros,' his sympathetic but firm handling of the situation was of tremendous value.... It is one of our troubles that we are so seldom able to integrate our love into what we conceive to be our spiritual life. We are too apt to think of the latter of as an affair of *japa* [meditation] or other such practices on a background of 'lofty' philosophy.... The spiritual life is essentially a *real* life concerned with *real* things, not with the substitutes of ritual and even most of what is called 'meditation.' First among these real things is love; when a man has it, he wants *nothing* else. It is the one-without-a-second. Many people will agree to this, but with the proviso that it is what they call 'divine' or 'spiritual' love, as if that power which has called forth the universe ... could ever be undivine or that which is essentially spirit could become unspiritual![50]

Krishna Prem gave similar relationship advice to Kaul, suggesting in a July 1946 letter that *kāma* can be a powerful spiritual tool when seen in its proper position as an 'earthly' reflection of one's inherent love for Krishna.

> "[T]here is no reason at all why the 'human companionship' should be incompatible with the higher life—provided you always remember that all love is ultimately love of Sri Krishna and it is because

He is seated in the heart of the wife (or husband) that the wife [or husband] is dear. If that is kept in mind then it is easy ... to walk the path hand in hand—perhaps easier than trudging on alone."[51]

Notes

[1]Phipps, 'Sri Krishna Prem Remembered,' 273.

[2]'Robert Dudley Alexander (Sri Haridas),' 19.

[3]Singh, *Letters from Mirtola*, 33.

[4]Shah, 'Memoirs,' 6.

[5]Seymour B. Ginsburg, *In Search of the Unitive Vision: Letters of Sri Madhava Ashish to an American Businessman 1978–1997*, (Boca Raton: New Paradigm, 2001), 188.

[6]Madhava Ashish here implies that, by conspiring only to be re-born to ("get into birth through") a great *jīvanmukta*, the troublesome 'holy men' are not serious about the spiritual quest. A genuine seeker would instead ask Yashoda Mai for *dīkṣā* in this life—a life they would then (like her adopted son, 'Gopal') dedicate to her and devote to her service.

[7]TN Ganapathy, 'The Way of the Siddhas,' in KR Sundararajan and Bithika Mukerji (eds), *Hindu Spirituality: Postclassical and Modern*, 1st Indian edn, (Delhi: Motilal Banarsidass, 2003), 234.

[8]Phipps, 'Sri Krishna Prem Remembered,' 276.

[9]Phipps, 'Sri Krishna Prem Remembered,' 275–276.

[10]Tony Foster, conversation with the author, 25 September 2023.

[11]Shah, 'Memoirs,' 7.

[12]Pandey, *Guru by Your Bedside*, 99.

[13]Pandey, *Guru by Your Bedside*, 98.

[14]Pandey, *Guru by Your Bedside*, 98–99.

[15]A reference to the Philip Larkin poem 'This be the Verse,' which begins, "They fuck you up, your mum and dad./ They may not mean to, but they do./ They fill you with the faults they had/ And add some extra, just for you."

[16]Bill Aitken, *Branch Line to Eternity*, (New Delhi: Penguin Books, 2001), 67.

[17]Shah, 'The Guiding Hand,' 7.

[18]Roy, *Yogi Sri Krishnaprem*, 116.

[19]Roy, *Yogi Sri Krishnaprem*, 117.

[20]*Ibid.*

[21]Roy, *Yogi Sri Krishnaprem*, 115.

[22]*Ibid.*

[23]'Ashram,' *Mirtola Reflections*, Mirtola, Mirtola Reflections, 2018, https://mirtolareflections.com/the-ashramm.html (accessed 9 January 2023).

[24]Monod-Herzen, 'On Sri Krishnaprem,' 309.

[25]Madhava Ashish, 'Sri Krishna Prem Through the Eyes of a Disciple,' 16.

[26]Aitken, *Sri Sathya Sai Baba*, 66.

[27]Eichert, 'The Last English Saint,' 4.

[28]Roy, *Yogi Sri Krishnaprem*, 115.

[29]Madhava Ashish, 'Sri Krishna Prem Through the Eyes of a Disciple,' 26–27.

[30]Marshall, *Hunting the Guru in India*, 149.

[31]Monod-Herzen, 'On Sri Krishnaprem,' 309.

[32]Madhava Ashish, 'Sri Krishna Prem through the eyes of a disciple,' 24.

[33]Monod-Herzen, 'On Sri Krishnaprem,' 309.

[34]Monod-Herzen, 'Sri Krishna Prem, Yogi et Théosophe,'

[35]Arwind Vasavada—His Life and Teachings, 'Sunyata's Letters: The Gardener and the Garden: 13-7-40,' 2009, https://arwindvasavada.webs.com/sunyatasletters.htm (accessed 9 November 2022).

[36]Bhuvaneshwar Nath Mishra 'Madhav,' (मीरा की प्रेम साधना) *Meera Ke Prem Sadhana*, (Delhi: Rajkamal Prakashan, 1965), 5.

[37]Madhava Ashish, 'Sri Krishna Prem Through the Eyes of a Disciple,' 26.

[38]*Ibid.*

[39]Aitken, *Footloose in the Himalaya*, 87.

[40]Verma (ed.), *Essays and Reflections by Karan Singh*, part 4 ('Essays'), ch. 2, para. 25.

[41]Madhava Ashish, 'Sri Krishna Prem Through the Eyes of a Disciple,' 4.

[42]Sen, 'Sri Krishnaprem,' xi.

[43]Mooney, *Frank Baines*, 103.

[44]Mooney, *Frank Baines*, 102.

[45]Madhava Ashish, 'Sri Krishna Prem Through the Eyes of a Disciple,' 29.

[46]Madhava Ashish, 'Sri Krishna Prem Through the Eyes of a Disciple,' 26–27.

[47]Verma (ed.), *Essays and Reflections by Karan Singh*, part 4 ('Essays'), ch. 2, para. 19.

[48]Singh, *Autobiography*, 250.

[49]Singh, *Autobiography*, 209.

[50]Singh, *Autobiography*, 250.

[51]Kaul, *Writings of Sri Krishna Prem*, 104.

13: War

"'Political, social and economic chaos' is no concern of yours. Pay attention rather to the chaos in your own soul and get on with your work."[1]

— Sri Krishna Prem (1946)

The outbreak of another world war, the second in Sri Krishna Prem's lifetime, appears to have made little impact on his philosophy or personal *sādhana*. Correspondence from this period makes scant reference to the hostilities, except when asked about them directly, and it appears from contemporary accounts that life at Mirtola carried on largely as normal even as hundreds of thousands of Indian volunteers (including Kumaoni troops, who were deployed in the Middle East, North America, Malaya and Burma) were sent to fight overseas. In a summer 1941 letter, as war raged in the Indian Ocean, Sunyata writes to a friend: "At Uttara Brindaban one feels good in sunshine and silence and untrying Peace...."[2]

Unmoved by Allied propaganda which sought to portray Hitler and the Axis Powers as uniquely dangerous to all humanity, Krishna Prem considered World War Two to be 'just' another war between competing powers, little different from the countless tragic conflicts preceding it—as is clear from a letter dated 21 July 1940, in which he responds to a query from Dilip Kumar Roy about his thoughts on the "present state of the world."[3] Contrary to what "the films say," Krishna Prem tells his friend, Hitler did not cause the war, or the "bitter waves of overt suffering that are sweeping over huge areas of our world." Rather, it is "we [humanity] who have been piling up that sorrow," having given over "lodging space in our hearts" to the hatred and fear made concrete by the Nazis: "These Hitlers and what nots are mere puppets worked by strings which neither they nor others see, great waves that dash upon our breakwaters to overwhelm them or to recoil in baffled fury. The force of Hitler is the force we have given him, we who project on others the devil that lurks within ourselves."[4]

The idea of Hitler as the embodiment of a collective will to violence resembles the thinking of the Swiss psychiatrist Carl Gustav Jung, whose wartime analysis famously compared the dictator to "the mirror of every German's unconscious."[5] "His Voice is nothing other than his own unconscious, into which the German people have projected their own selves; that is, the unconscious of seventy-eight million Germans," Jung explained. "That is what makes him powerful. Without the German people he would be nothing."[6] Jungian psychology was later studied in detail in Mirtola,[7] part of the wider reorientation of the ashram's teachings that began in the 1950s, alongside a range of ideas drawn from Theosophy, GI Gurdjieff's 'Fourth Way,'[8] and Freudian–Jungian psychoanalysis.

A similar view was held by Paul Brunton, who seemed to go as far as to attribute the Holocaust to the Jews' own bad *karma*, despite being Jewish himself, as his one-time disciple Jeffrey Masson explains:

> [P.B.] believed (along with Jung) that Hitler was a mystic, a medium, though an evil one. P.B. was convinced that the Holocaust was a result of mankind's karma and that Hitler was just a punitive instrument in its hand. "The suffering the Holocaust brings to people," he said, "is really the reactions of their own near or remote deeds. They are visited by the consequences of their own making."[9]

This same force, according to Krishna Prem, is, however, equally capable of lifting the collective unconscious, as he explains in a letter to Narendra Nath Kaul: "How far can individual *sādhana* affect the general public? All individual effort affects the whole cosmos. (A liner crossing the Atlantic raises its temperature slightly.) How much? That depends on the individual. Buddha for instance affected general consciousness quite considerably."[10]

Though having admitted elsewhere that he makes "no great very effort" to keep abreast of the conflict ("Since the war started we have even stopped taking any newspaper at all," he told the academic Abani Nath Roy in September 1943[11]) Krishna Prem expands indirectly on his thoughts about the Second World War in the article 'The Violence of War,' later collected in *Initiation into Yoga: An Introduction to the Spiritual Life* and reproduced in various Theosophical journals. According to this essay, war is inevitable so long as humans fail to tame this devil, here described as a "caged beast," which lives in all of us and desires only violence and cruelty:

> Thus do the periods of war and peace succeed one another through the weary centuries of history. ... [N]ever will violence bring violence to an end. As long as we nourish the brutes within our hearts with the desire-laden thoughts that are their life-blood, so long will they break out from time to time, and so long will periodical wars be inevitable.

> The only way to real peace is the taming of those inner beasts. We who have created them, bone of our bone and flesh of our flesh, must weaken them by giving them no food, must re-absorb them into our conscious selves from which in horror we have banished them, and finally must transmute their very substance by the alchemy of spirit. And this is yoga: Only yoga is peace.[12]

This view (on the 'brute within') was apparently shared by both by his predecessor and successor as head of Uttar Brindaban. Writing over 40 years later, in the wake of deadly communal violence in Gujarat, Sri Madhava Ashish laments "the worse than animal brutality that lurks beneath the civilised facade of every human being," while recalling how "Ma—Yashoda Mai—said that women's capacity for violence was the reason for keeping them away from sights of brutality, which might bring it to the surface. As for boys, remember *The Lord of the Flies*."[13]

Another letter from Krishna Prem to Roy, written in August 1943, nearly four years into the war, concedes that his point that "violence never pays" is a "subtle one,"[14] but emphasises that in times of war the spiritual seeker should focus on his own *sādhana* and trust in the divine will of "only the One whom I can see.... Perhaps you feel that it is our duty to take a side even if only in thought. Well, if you feel so by all means do so," he writes, "but, for myself, I feel that if one can keep one's gaze fixed on Krishna, however feeble our powers, we shall be doing something, however little, towards removing the fog of illusion, the *Rākṣasī māyā* [the deceptions (*māyā*) of the *Rākṣasas*, or demons], that envelopes the whole field and so will be doing what little we can towards helping others to see more clearly."[15]

While Krishna Prem is clear, in his second letter to Roy, that he does not have "any sort of sympathy for [Hitler]," he is confident that the Führer, "if all that we have heard is an adequate selection of the facts about him," is destined to be destroyed by the dark forces then sustaining him: "he seems to be one who has given himself to the service of evil forces and who is fated to be torn to pieces by the powers he serves."[16] This is because the war—like all events, past and future—"is part of the Divine Lila," and so the "victory of Krishna is certain."[17]

This religiously influenced pacifism (which might nowadays be criticised as 'spiritual bypassing') was in Krishna Prem combined with the deep secular aversion to war which had developed after the First World War, as described in chapter two, in which he and millions of other men of his age had seen first hand the horrors of modern industrialised warfare. It is, he suggests in 'The Violence of War,' an attitude common in fighting men, who, "after a few months of experience have been gained, are often to a surprising degree free from hatred, while those who sit in comfortable isolation only too frequently indulge their own baser excitements and passions by ... fanning the flames of hatred and violence."[18]

Those who would criticise this pacifism from a Hindu perspective, meanwhile, are urged to remember that the war described in the *Gītā* "was an affair for a professional order of knights who met in equal battle and lived for fighting. It has nothing whatever to do with the hideous attacks upon defenceless women and children that are the essence of modern war."[19] To ask, then, in the 20th century, 'Is war right?'

> we must substitute the question 'is it right to blind, poison, mutilate and disembowel innocent women and children,' for that is what modern war means when stripped of archaic rhetoric.[20]

Ironically, if Krishna Prem, by birth a Briton, could charitably be said to be only weakly in favour of the Allied cause, his spiritual contemporary, fellow Kingsman and guru to Dilip Kumar Roy, Sri Aurobindo—formerly a militant Indian nationalist who had settled in French-owned Pondicherry to escape the British-Indian authorities—was clear that he considered the war a titanic struggle between the forces of the divine, represented by the British Empire and its allies, and the demonic, working through Hitler and the Axis. Writing to Roy—who had taken issue with a godbrother, Nolini Kanta Gupta's, comparison of the war to Kurukshetra—Aurobindo explained:

> What we say is not that the Allies have not done wrong things, but that they stand on the side of the evolutionary forces. ...
>
> [W]e [do] not consider the war as a fight between nations and governments (still less between good people and bad people) but between two forces, the Divine and the *Asuric*.[21] What we have to see is on which side men and nations put themselves; if they put themselves on the right side, they at once make themselves instruments of the Divine purpose in spite of all defects, errors, wrong movements and actions which are common to human nature and all human collectivities. The victory of one side (the Allies) would keep the path open for the evolutionary forces: the victory of the other side would drag back humanity, degrade it horribly and might lead even, at the worst, to its eventual failure as a race, as others in the past evolution failed and perished.[22]

Responding to criticism of the equating of Britain and America with the Pāṇḍavas, the divinely assisted protagonists of the *Mahābhārata/Bhagavad Gītā*, Aurobindo further points out that these heroes were also flawed human beings, but that their moral faults are eclipsed by the just nature of the war:

> [W]ere not the Pandavas fighting to establish their own claims and interest—just and right, no doubt, but still personal claims and self-interest? Theirs was a righteous battle, *dharmya yuddha*, but it was for right and justice in their own case. The Allies have as good or even a better case and reason to call theirs a righteous quarrel, for they are fighting not only for themselves, for their freedom and very existence, but for the existence, freedom, maintenance of natural rights of other nations ... they too claim to be fighting for a *Dharma*, for civilised values, for the preservation of great ideals and in view of what Hitler represents and openly professes and what he wishes to destroy, their claim has strong foundations....
>
> The Divine takes men as they are and uses them as his instruments even if they are not flawless in character, without stain or sin or fault, exemplary in virtue, or angelic, holy and pure. If they are of good will, if, to use the Biblical phrase, they are on the Lord's side, that is enough for the work to be done. Even if I knew that the Allies (I am speaking of the "big" nations, America, Britain, China) would misuse their victory or bungle the peace or partially at least spoil the opportunities opened to the human world by that victory, I would still put my force behind them. At any rate, things could not be one hundredth part as bad as they would be under Hitler. The ways of the Lord would still be open—to keep them open is what matters.[23]

The Sri Aurobindo Ashram also contributed financially to the war effort. One typical donation, a 500-rupee contribution to the war fund of the then governor of Madras, Sir Arthur Hope, was accompanied by a note expressing "our entire support for the British people and the Empire in their struggle against the aggressions of the Nazi Reich and our complete sympathy with the cause for which they are fighting."[24]

Some Vaiṣṇavas of the former Gauḍīya Maṭh similarly supported India's colonial rulers in their struggle against Nazi Germany. The *sannyāsī* Bhakti Hridaya Bon (whose translation of the *Gītā* is referenced in chapter 11) notably made contact with Sir Vivian Gabriel of the British Library of Information to volunteer his services as a Hindu 'chaplain' to British-Indian troops. In an October 1940 letter to Gabriel, Bon also alludes to Kurukshetra, quoting Krishna in support of his view that Vaiṣṇavas are duty-bound to take up arms against the forces of evil:

> We hate to kill men and women, but we are also equally ready to combat evil doers. We do not incite war, but when it is forced upon us, it becomes the duty of every Hindu to face his enemies. Hindu philosophy teaches that the soul was not created and never will be destroyed; after death we pass on to a new life. So we are not afraid of death. In the *Gītā* Sri Krishna told Arjuna 'If thou be killed in battle thou shalt enter heaven; if thou emerge victorious thou shalt enjoy the world. Rise up, Arjuna, with a firm determination now to fight. Sin will not touch thee if thou fightest with the aim of final liberation, steadfast in weal and woe, for profit or loss, defeat or victory.' So I am glad to know that the Hindus of India are rising to the occasion. I am particularly proud to know that there is a Bengali squadron leader now on duty on the N.W. Frontier.[25]

Swami Bon's proposal was motivated in part by his desire that Hindu troops should have equality with their Muslim and Christian compatriots, who already had access to military chaplains. "The Christian and Moslem soldiers do receive such spiritual help from their respective Chaplains and *Moulavis*; there is no reason why thousands of Hindu soldiers of His Majesty should not be given similar facilities," he explained in a follow-up letter. "If His Majesty's Government will consider the proposal, you will please let me know the conditions. My humble services will be at the disposal of my co-religionists in the War-field," he added.[26]

The idea of World War Two as a modern Kurukshetra was not one, however, shared by anyone in Mirtola, with the newly arrived Ananda Priya (formerly airman RD Alexander of the RFC/RAF[27]) also viewing the war as an earthly conflict between rival powers rather than a spiritual battle between the forces of light and darkness. Madhava Ashish describes how Yashoda Mai and Krishna Prem conspired to help the 38-year-old doctor, who "by now had no sympathy for the British government" (Ashish, 84), avoid being called out of retirement by military recruiters:

> Having joined the ashram, [Alexander] was now a Brahmachari with the name Ananda Priya. His head had been shaven, he dressed in a white dhoti and chadar [shawl], and he wore the marks on the forehead which identified him as a disciple of the Brahma [Gaudiya] sampradaya. To this thoroughly un-British get-up, Yashoda Mai and Krishna Prem added a kamandalu, the hourglass-shaped water pot with a handle carried by many sadhus, and a long staff. He was sent off on his first venture into the world as a Brahmachari with their blessings.

> It must be appreciated that he was by now a senior and very well-known man in the medical world of British India, and that the British strongly disapproved of anyone 'going native,' as they called it. So when Bob appeared for the interview in his recently adopted dress, his reception was frigid. The interviewers, having assured themselves that it really was Major Robert Dudley Alexander, I.M.S. plus a string of degrees, humphed and said they would get in touch with him. He never heard from them again. (Ashish, 84)

Far from losing members to the fighting, Uttar Brindaban actually gained a new resident in the war years. Alice Beatrice Webb (b. 1870), known as 'Webbia,' was the widow of John William March Webb,[28] an Irish Royal Navy commander; both husband and wife were Theosophist disciples of the Chakravartis, and Mrs Webb, recently diagnosed with cancer, sailed from England in 1942 to die in the company of her guru (Ashish, 132). Though her time at Mirtola was short—she passed away in March 1943,[29] spending her last days in the old school building—Webbia left an outsized psychic legacy. Both Moti Rani[30] and Krishna Prem (Ashish, 136) reported visitations from the spirit of the departed woman in days after her death.

Despite her apparent attachment to the physical world, Sunyata wrote approvingly of Webb's calmness in the face of death, particularly in comparison to Achsah Brewster, who was also then terminally ill. Though suffering with "cancer in chest and shoulder and with spine partly gone," she, like Yashoda Mai, has "no complaints, grievance complex or ego-pity. But calm acceptance and enduring patience in inner central joyousness."[31] In contrast, Brewster "'accepts' but not really—only wordily—ego-deceivingly. She is really afraid to die—afraid of loneliness—and so she flutters and stirs up fuss in order to live."[32]

Four months earlier, Narendra Nath Kaul had written to ask his guru why Krishna did not intervene to "stop Ma's bodily suffering." In reply, Krishna Prem confessed his ignorance: "If I could answer that I should know many things. Perhaps neither she nor he think it worth while."[33]

Notes

[1]Kaul, *Writings of Sri Krishna Prem*, 104.

[2]Alfred Sorensen (Sunyata), letter to Barbara Hartland, 25 July 1941, Papers of Barbara Bruce, University of Bradford, Bradford, Cwl BBR/1/452.

[3]Roy, *Yogi Sri Krishnaprem*, 193.

[4]Roy, *Yogi Sri Krishnaprem*, 194.

[5]HR Knickerbocker, 'Is Tomorrow Hitler's?', *Omnibook Magazine*, February 1942, 134, http://www.oldmagazinearticles.com/carl-jung-studied-hitler (accessed 13 November 2022).

[6]*Ibid.*

[7]Bill Aitken, 'Sri Krishna Prem in the Last Years,' in Sri Madhava Ashish, *Where'er Love's Camels Lead: Sri Krishna Prem Remembered* (unpublished), (Mirtola: Sri Dev Ashish, 2015), 268.

[8]Eichert, 'The Last English Saint,' 4.

[9]Jeffrey Moussaieff Masson, *My Father's Guru*, ebook edn, (San Francisco: Untreed Reads, 2013), 212.

[10]Kaul, *Writings of Sri Krishna Prem*, 94.

[11]Roy, *Yogi Sri Krishnaprem*, 230.

[12]Krishna Prem, *Initiation into Yoga: An Introduction to the Spiritual Life*, 105–106.

[13]Sri Madhav Ashish, 'Violence,' *Seminar*, 309, (1985), 42.

[14]Roy, *Yogi Sri Krishnaprem*, 219.

[15]Roy, *Yogi Sri Krishnaprem*, 221.

[16]*Ibid.*

[17]Roy, *Yogi Sri Krishnaprem*, 194.

[18]Krishna Prem, *Initiation into Yoga: An Introduction to the Spiritual Life*, 104.

[19]Krishna Prem, *The Search for Truth*, 129.

[20]*Ibid.*

[21]A reference to the Hindu *asuras*, the demonic enemies of the *devas*, or gods.

[22]Roy, *Yogi Sri Krishnaprem*, 225–227.

[23]Roy, *Yogi Sri Krishnaprem*, 228–229.

[24]Sachidananda Mohanty (ed), *Sri Aurobindo: A Contemporary Reader*, (New Delhi: Routledge, 2008), 181.

[25]Måns Broo, 'Noblemen, Spies, and a Hindu Monk Going to War: Notes on Swami B.H. Bon in New York, 1940–41,' *Journal of Hindu Studies*, 13.1, (2020), 83.

[26]Broo, 'Noblemen, Spies, and a Hindu Monk Going to War,' 83–84.

[27]'UK, Royal Air Force Airmen Records, 1918–1940', *Ancestry*, Lehi, Ancestry.com Operations, 2017, https://www.ancestry.co.uk/search/collections/61400/ (accessed 13 November 2022). Original data: AIR 79 Royal Air Force Airmen Records, 1918-1940. The National Archives of the UK, Kew, Surrey, England.

[28]'1939 England and Wales Register', *Ancestry*, Lehi, Ancestry.com Operations, 2018, https://www.ancestry.co.uk/search/collections/61596/ (accessed 14 November 2022). Original data: Crown copyright images reproduced by courtesy of TNA, London England. 1939 Register (Series RG101), The National Archives, Kew, London, England.

[29]'India, Select Deaths and Burials, 1719–1948', *Ancestry*, Lehi, Ancestry.com Operations, 2014, https://www.ancestry.co.uk/search/collections/9898/ (accessed 14 November 2022). Original data: India Deaths and Burials, 1719-1948. Ancestry.com Operations, Inc.: FamilySearch, 2013.

[30]Roy, *Yogi Sri Krishnaprem*, 110.

[31]Sorensen, letter to Barbara Hartland, 25 July 1941.

[32]*Ibid.*

[33]Kaul, *Writings of Sri Krishna Prem*, 98.

14: Flying Solo

"He reasons ill who tells that Vaishnavs die
When thou art living still in sound!"[1]
— Kedarnath Datta Bhaktivinoda (1871)

In November 1944, Yashoda Mai asked Krishna Prem when Uttarayan, the celebration of the winter solstice, would fall that year. The 14 January 1945, he said. "Too late," she replied (Ashish, 140).

It had now been 14 years since Bob Alexander had given 'Ma' six months to live. In "almost constant physical pain" from her numerous ailments (Sunyata writes of "cramps, gallstones—tumour, 'heart' etc."[2]), Yashoda Mai, now in her 63rd year, was ready to leave, and Krishna Prem understood she had chosen the auspicious date of Uttarayan, the beginning of the sun's six-month northern orbit, for her departure. Though he understood, he urged his guru to wait, arguing that the longer she stayed, the better it would be for her disciples. Her answer was definitive: "No. You don't understand. It would all be very difficult" (Ashish, 140).

Present near the end was Sunyata, who saw in the ailing Krishna *bhakta* a shining example of non-dual awareness. "I remember a Himalayan silence—brief but eternal in the *Uttar* (north) Brindavan ashram," he writes. "I happened to be with my foster mother Sri Yashoda Ma. It was there that Anandamayee [Ma] and party stopped to greet the bodily invalid Sri Yashoda Ma, who was whole and free in the unitive life of *Advait* conscious awareness. It was marvelous to sense and [be] aware [of] the two Himalayan mothers together."[3]

Sri Yashoda Mai died early on 2 December 1944,[4] after refusing medical treatment for a sudden gallbladder attack. "The end," said Krishna Prem, "was utter peace, unspeakable, and the years seemed to fall way from her as, with her vision full of Sri Krishna, she dropped the body."[5]

Her body was taken for cremation at the small Shiva temple of Dandeshwar, at Jageshwar near Mirtola, the same morning. Krishna Prem, records Madhava Ashish, "noted wonderingly that the flames rose exceptionally high."[6]

The death of Yashoda Mai—the woman to whom he had devoted 20 years of his life—left Krishna Prem, now 46, in charge of the ashram the pair had co-founded 14 years earlier, and without a parental figure for the first time since he came to India. GN Chakravarti, into whose home Krishna Prem had been welcomed in the 1920s, had passed away eight years earlier, and even the man responsible for helping him get to India, Bertram Keightley, had died just over a month earlier. (Madhava Ashish relates Keightley's final moments on 31 October: "[W]ith his brain deteriorating from lack of blood, he suddenly came out of a coma, sat up and exclaimed 'Ma!' as he saw Yashoda Mai, and fell back dead [Ashish, 75].) Madhava Ashish writes:

> One has to imagine Krishna Prem's state of mind when he returned from the cremation of his Guru's body. At such a time the unbreakable routine of the temple keeps one going, and of course there are the duties such as sending telegrams to relations, but then night comes and one is alone with one's grief and uncertainties. (Ashish, 141)

The next three days did much to calm these anxieties. As Krishna Prem told Madhava Ashish later, for three consecutive nights he was awoken by a vision of his departed guru, who comforted her grieving disciple:

> 'I am at one with the Lord.
> I am at one with all beings.
> I shall be with you always.' (Ashish, 141)

Accordingly, by 5 December he could write to Dilip Kumar Roy: "I know she is ever with us and even nearer than before ... already I know why Sri Krishna told the wives of the sacrificing Brahmins in Brindaban that it is not by physical proximity that He is attained."[7]

Yashoda Mai's ashes were buried a few yards from the main entrance to the temple, in a small, initially enclosed *samādhi maṇḍir*. Satish Datt Pandey records that the door to the structure, and three of its walls, were later removed after Krishna Prem heard Yashoda Mai's voice tell him, "with a touch of annoyance, 'I don't live there!'"[8]

Swami Rama gives another anecdote illustrating Krishna Prem's belief that his spiritual master continued to provide *śikṣā* from the great beyond. In his autobiographical *Living with the Himalayan Masters*, Rama describes the marble statue of Krishna which had been placed in Yashoda Mai's *samādhi*, and which now appeared to be weeping:

> On one of my visits shortly after the statue was installed I noticed that Krishna Prem was wearing something on his arm. I asked him about it and he said, "You won't believe me." I said, "Please explain it to me."
>
> He replied, "... Fifteen days ago the statue of Krishna which was installed on the memorial started flowing tears. The tears dripped from the statue continuously. We dismantled the base of the statue to see if there was some source of the seeping water, but found nothing. There was no way that water could come up through the statue and flow from its eyes. When we put the statue back in place the tears began to flow once more. This made me very sad. I decided that I must be committing some mistake in my *sādhana* and that Ma was not happy with me. To keep myself ever reminded of this I took some cotton, soaked it in the tears, and put it in the locket which I am now wearing on my arm...."
>
> I said, "... Please explain to me why it occurs."
>
> He said, "The guru guides from the other side in many ways. This is an instruction to me. I have become lazy. Instead of doing my evening *sādhana* I have been retiring early. It was her habit to remind us whenever we fell into the grip of sloth and missed our practice. This has to be the right explanation." He became very serious and then started to sob. His love for his guru was immense, and this inspired me.[9]

Despite this reassurance of her continued presence, the physical loss of Yashoda Mai, who had been his "Guru, mother and everything,"[10] was hard to bear, and Krishna Prem only reluctantly assumed his new role as head of the ashram; he "accepted the responsibilities of both ashram and disciples, but he once told me he would have preferred the wandering life of the mendicant," Madhava Ashish recalled later.[11] With Uttar Brindaban now down to three full-time residents—"Two English '*sādhus*' and an unmarried Indian woman—an unusual ashram for India,"[12] in the words of Andrew Rawlinson—Krishna Prem increasingly turned for administrative support to Yashoda Mai's daughter, Arpita (known as Moti Rani), who returned to Mirtola several days later, having been away in Solan, in the Simla Hill States, visiting her elder sister at the time of her mother's death. (Her arrival preceded three weeks of heavy snow which, Madhava Ashish explains, would have made it impossible to take Yashoda Mai's body to the burning *ghāṭ* at Dandeshwar had she died any later; hence the cryptic remark that waiting until 14 January would make things "very difficult" [Ashish, 144].)

Born on 24 September 1916,[13] Moti Rani was five years old when she first met the man then known as RH Nixon; he called her 'Tuppence', from the English phrase "A penny plain or tuppence coloured" (a reference to the cost of picture postcards), on account of her colourful saris [Ashish, 159], while he was her *Chhotoba* [Ashish, 152], or simply 'Ba' (abbreviated from Baba, 'father').[14] "She was," recalls her godbrother and *śikṣā* disciple, Sri Madhava Ashish, "short and fat, with a typically round Bengali head, dark-skinned, poor features by the canons of Indian beauty, but magnificent eyes, fine skin, and hands that artists wanted to borrow. Her feet, deformed at birth, had been straightened out by treatment and looked normal enough, but she walked with a waddle and might fall over like a tin soldier at the slightest provocation."[15] Dilip Kumar Roy remembers her as a "delightful personality, as vivacious as she was single-minded and as devout as she was fond of laughter. She was always teasing everybody, not sparing even her own Guru, Krishnaprem..."[16]

Moti Rani became Krishna Prem's first disciple in 1933—he at first refused, telling her to ask her mother, but later relented (Ashish, 152)—and he came to rely on her as a "tower of strength"[17] in the years following Yashoda Mai's death:

> Though Krishna Prem was head of the ashram, expounded the teaching, and had won public acclaim as author, devotee, and man of considerable attainment, Moti, with her Hindu birthright, managed the day-to-day affairs. This was acceptable: the great man needed someone to look after worldly details while his mind roamed free in the infinite.[18]

"What was not so easily acceptable," adds Madhava Ashish, was her habit of intentionally provoking "emotionally charged situations" that "compelled one to practise the teachings ... Krishna Prem had articulated in relative calm"[19] amid what the former's manuscript describes as a "pressure cooker" atmosphere (Ashish, 91).

Madhava Ashish also writes about her similarities to Helena Blavatsky, who died 26 years before Moti Rani's birth and of whom she might "have qualified as a reincarnation":

> [S]he was uncannily like H.P.B. in many ways, sharing the same charm, wit, learning, violent temper which could cool in an instant, her range of psychic powers, and, unfortunately, the same illness [kidney disease] from which H.P.B. also died.[20] She, too, became totally dedicated to the service of those great persons whom H.P.B. called The Masters. (Ashish, 153)

Together, guru and disciple, as they appeared in the mid-1940s, gave the impression of an "oddly assorted pair," he adds: "Krishna Prem in his rough and ill-washed homespun cotton, shaving only on Mondays and Fridays, feet callused and cracked, imperturbably sitting like a sacred bull on a city pavement ... and Moti in Benares-embroidered silk saree, with bobbed hair and jewellery, delicate, dynamic, vivacious, and the centre of attention as by right."[21]

Krishna Prem's appearance by this time was the culmination of a sartorial evolution that reflected his 25-year spiritual journey. As Professor Nixon of the University of Lucknow, he would have worn suits acquired from a tailor in Duke Street, in London's West End, prior to setting off for India (Ashish, 37); these gradually gave way to Indian clothing, and contemporary photographs show the new *chela* of Monica Chakravarti in what looks today like proto-hippie attire, with robes, earrings and chunky neck beads complementing flowing, shoulder-length hair pushed back away from his face. He later adopted a *śikhā*, the tuft of hair (here called its Hindi name, *chutiya*) left by Vaiṣṇavas on the back of an otherwise shaven head, and the distinctive *tilak* of the Gauḍīya Vaiṣṇava *sampradāya*. Describing Nixon's appearance some time prior to his relocation to Chilkapita, Madhava Ashish writes:

> Ronald was by now wearing the Brahmachari's white dhoti and chadar, with shaven head, chutiya, the double strand of small Tulasi beads round the neck, and the 'caste mark' of the Gauriya[22] Sampradaya or Brahma Sampradaya. (Ashish, 94—95)

He also experimented briefly with facial hair, growing a "red, stiff beard that itched so much he could not bear it," but soon shaved it off (Ashish, 95).

Aside from the flirtation with Buddhist robes mentioned in chapter 11, Krishna Prem's appearance would remain consistent throughout the 1930s and '40s: clean shaven, including his head; barefoot, or rarely wearing wooden *pādukā* sandals; and clad in Vaiṣṇava neck beads, the saffron robes that symbolised his *vairāgya*, and *tilak* of Yashoda Mai's design. Such was the distinctiveness of this attire that when he visited Barsana again in the late 1940s, this time without his departed guru, and balding with white hair, the local priests still recognised him (Ashish, 101).

This uniform (albeit with the white cloth of the *brahmachārī* replacing the ochre of the *vairāgī*) also became that of Ananya Priya, as well as the three new initiates who settled at Uttar Brindaban after the war.

Notes

[1]Pandit Satkari Chattopadhyaya Siddhanta Bhushan, *A Glimpse into the Life of Thakur Bhakti-Vinode*, (Calcutta: Thakur Bhakti-Vinode Memorial Committee, 1916), 25.

[2]Sorensen, letter to Barbara Hartland, 25 July 1941.

[3]Rai, 'A Short Biography,' in Sunyata, *Dancing with the Void*, xxx.

[4]*Ibid.*

[5]Roy, *Yogi Sri Krishnaprem*, 234.

[6]*Ibid.*

[7]Roy, *Yogi Sri Krishnaprem*, 234–235.

[8]Pandey, *Guru by Your Bedside*, 47.

[9]Rama, *Living with the Himalayan Masters*, 366–367.

[10]*Ibid.*

[11]Madhava Ashish, 'Sri Krishna Prem Through the Eyes of a Disciple,' 26.

[12]Rawlinson, *The Book of Enlightened Masters*, 380.

[13]"Moti was ... one year younger than me, but actually born on the same day..." Mooney, *Frank Baines*, 104. Frank Baines was born on 24 September 1915 (Mooney, 11).

[14]Roy, *Yogi Sri Krishnaprem*, 74.

[15]Madhava Ashish, 'Sri Krishna Prem Through the Eyes of a Disciple,' 9–10.

[16]Roy, *Yogi Sri Krishnaprem*, 174.

[17]Roy, *Yogi Sri Krishnaprem*, 117.

[18]Madhava Ashish, 'Sri Krishna Prem Through the Eyes of a Disciple,' 15.

[19]*Ibid.*

[20]'HPB' actually died from influenza in the 1889–1890 pandemic, but suffered in her lifetime with Bright's disease, or inflammation of the kidneys.

[21]Madhava Ashish, 'Sri Krishna Prem Through the Eyes of a Disciple,' 10.

[22]Here Madhava Ashish uses an uncommon alternative rendering of 'Gauḍīya.' In this he may have been influenced by Krishna Prem, who seems to have preferred the spelling Gouriya (see his 1934 letter included in Kanupriya Goswami's জীবের স্বরূপ ও স্বধর্ম [*Jīvera Svarūpa O Svadharma*], 215).

15: New Faces

"'By magic, the mayik numbering of 'I am one: may I be many', was the universe created."[1]

— Sri Krishna Prem (c. 1942)

In 1946 a new era began at Mirtola, starting with the visit of Francis Trevean Baynes[2] (1915–1987), an English captain who had come to India during World War Two. Known as Frank Baines, he was the son of the celebrated architect of the same name (known for Thames House, now the headquarters of the Security Service, MI5, in London, and the restored roof of Westminster Hall, part of the Palace of Westminster). After a period in the merchant navy, Frank Jnr had enlisted in the military at the outbreak of hostilities and was transferred to India for officer training, where he saw action as a junior artillery officer on the North-West Frontier. He was then assigned to the Camouflage Training School at Kirkee, near Poona in the Bombay Presidency (modern Khadki, Pune, Maharashtra), and later led a Chindit unit in Japanese-occupied Burma. According to his biographer, Brian Mooney, Baines frequently "talked of his 'love affair with the Chindits,' and for rest of his life he was obsessed and traumatized by his experiences fighting in this unorthodox force behind enemy lines."[3]

Baines found his way to Mirtola after a chance meeting with Bob Alexander's sister, Constance, while recuperating in hospital in Shillong, in the Khasi Hills of north-eastern India. Eight years older than Bob, Constance was married to Sir Harold Dennehy,[4] chief secretary to the Assam government from 1936 to 1948 (Shillong then lying in Assam Province), and at the time of their meeting she was "engaged in one of those missions of mercy which such ladies were expected to undertake, of visiting the wounded," Baines recalls.[5] Having already read *The Yoga of the Kaṭhopanishad* and *The Yoga of the Bhagavat Gita*, and tried several times to reach Uttar Brindaban during the war, he procured a letter of introduction from Constance and arranged with her brother to visit the ashram. He writes about his first meeting with Krishna Prem, Moti Rani and Ananda Priya (Bob):

> [Krishna Prem] took me upstairs onto the upper verandah (glassed-in) where a cosy corner ... had been staked out with tables, chairs and cushions.
>
> Tea was served in decent, bell-metal glasses, and Dr Alexander joined us. I was conducted to the guest house, ... [where] supper was brought to me (two fat *parottas*—unleavened wheat cakes baked in a flat-iron with clarified butter—and a glass of hot, sweet milk), and I was provided with a small oil-lamp.
>
> My sleeping quarters were lined with a very catholic collection of books. I selected Jane Harrison's *Prologomena* [sic] *to the Greek Religion* and retired to bed. It was cold, lonely and utterly inhospitable.
>
> But evidently, I had made a good impression. Going up the steps that evening, I had even offered to take off my leather belt. I was so conscious to do the right thing that I would have discarded my trousers! My readiness to conform in this way seemed to have predisposed them in my favour.
>
> For there were *three*! At breakfast the following morning, much to my astonishment, a woman appeared. Moti was charming, charismatic, civilised, sophisticated, well educated, as well as fair, fat, and one year younger than me, but actually born on the same day, a circumstance which inevitably established a secret bond between us which continued more or less uninterruptedly right up to the day of my departure thence some four years later.
>
> It immediately became evident, of course, that I would never have been allowed to meet her had I not somehow passed a subtle test. The four us soon began to get on famously.
>
> The upshot was: that I was accepted, and after returning to England for demobilisation and paying my duty to my mother, I would come back to India, take an initiation in Hinduism, to be enrolled into their happy band.[6]

The second new arrival, Madhava Ashish (né Alexander Phipps), wrote later that Moti Rani was "attracted but not bowled over [by Baines]. However, she pushed Krishna Prem into accepting Frank as a new member of the ashram by saying that if he did not take on anyone because they did not measure up to his standards, then he would never get anyone at all. Krishna Prem reluctantly agreed, and Frank went off to England to get himself demobilised and then return" (Ashish, 157).

Alexander Phipps himself was of similarly distinguished parentage. His father, Lt Col Henry Ramsay (or Ramsey) Phipps,[7] was a First World War veteran and recipient of the Distinguished Service Order,[8] while his maternal great-grandfather, Alexander Campbell of Auchendarroch, was a Scottish laird.[9] Phipps was born in Edinburgh, Scotland, on 23 February 1920, and trained as an aeronautical engineer. He also came to India during the Second World War; originally assigned to work in a factory building gliders at RAF Dum Dum, near Calcutta, he instead found himself repairing Spitfire engines[10] until released from his wartime occupation in August 1946 (Ashish, 157). According to Bill Aitken, the death of Alexander's elder brother, Sqn Ldr Francis Constantine Phipps, in action in 1941[11]—and the unwanted "resultant transfer of affection" away from Francis to the younger son—was an important factor in his decision to leave Britain for India.[12]

Having visited Ramana Maharshi, "the radiance of whose attainment was almost visible,"[13] at her suggestion two years earlier, Phipps accepted an invitation from Ramana's student, Ethel Merston (1882–1967) to visit Krishna Prem at Mirtola. Soon after demobilisation, he returned to Almora, where she was renting a cottage. Merston's biographer, Mary Ellen Korman, writes:

> For the summer of 1946 Ethel rented a cottage in Almora. She got a pony to roam the countryside and visit the Viking [Sunyata] in his stone hut at Kalimat [Cranks' Ridge] where he lived in Silence, in his "Immortal Garden of Emptiness." ...
>
> During that summer in Almora, a young friend from Calcutta, Alec Phipps, came to stay with Ethel. Phipps, twenty-six years old and an aeronautical engineer from Edinburgh, Scotland, had visited Ramana Maharshi's ashram and the sage's presence had a transformative effect on him. He readily assented when Ethel proposed a visit to an ashram at Mirtola to stay a few days with Sri Krishna Prem, an English sannyasin.[14]

Though the "motley pair—the six-foot-two-inch Englishman [sic] and the angular spinster"[15]—had planned to hire a car and tour South India together, Phipps's "experience at Mirtola with Krishna Prem was such that on the way back to Almora, he told her he had decided to give up the world and would return to Mirtola to be with Krishna Prem as his *chela* (disciple) and take *sannyāsa* (renunciation of the world)." Korman continues: "He then settled his affairs and left for his new life."[16] Phipps himself remembers: "I had no idea at all of joining the ashram until I was leaving after my first visit. While my elderly friend for reasons best known to her was telling me that this was not my place and that I should go back to England and work there, I found myself striding on ahead to hide my tears from her. Never before in my life had I wept on leaving a place" (Ashish, 157).

Both Baines and Phipps (Madhava Ashish) admit to being unimpressed with their first glimpse of the ashram, and in particular the temple itself, which seemed drab and unappealing after the spectacular vistas presented by the walk from Almora. The former recalls his arrival at Uttar Brindaban:

> The path ... divided between high, grassy banks, skirted a little wooded ravine, and came out on a miniature platform. The plateau was neatly hemmed in by hills whose trees and shrubs all bent downwards towards it nicely. In the centre was a temple sporting a short, blunt *śikhara* (the nearest equivalent is spire), washed-over with cement and crowned by a gilded finial. It was encircled by a wooden-constructed corrugated-iron-roofed verandah on the first floor, supported from below on wooden posts, the woodwork painted the unflattering colour of red oxide, which had been turned into a sort of purply brown by the weather. The plateau was actually divided into two parts on different levels [and t]here was a small isolated shrine in the middle of the upper part, with a cement path which connected directly from it to the principal door of the temple—on account of the different levels, actually on the first floor—over a concrete bridge. Behind the shrine, and slightly elevated on the hillside, was another (this time in minimally more congruous harmony but still not right) quite agreeable house, bowered in trees, with a glazed in upper verandah which was reflecting the evening light....
>
> I was a bit taken aback. The aggregate presented an appearance of dereliction that was totally unaesthetic. I had imagined, in my innocence, that an inner devotion to the spiritual life would have transferred itself to the environment. This seemed not to be the case. A faint whiffle of anxiety surfaced within me, which I immediately suppressed. The word 'temple' implies, to a European psyche, visions of Dorian elegance and Lacedaemonian excellence. Perhaps I had been misled by my Hellenistic illusions.[17]

Phipps, similarly, writes that he was "repelled by the dead grey cement of the temple dome, the rusted iron roofing of an upper storey that leaned against it, and the brown-painted verandahs clad with iron sheet weather-proofing."[18] However, both men were encouraged by the eight-foot-high sea of marigolds that sprung up around Sri Krishna Vilas, which Baines compares to "exaggeratedly golden yellow and orange suns [shining] through misty cloud."[19]

Phipps was also "suspicious"[20] of the man who would become his guru. "I was not at first wholly sure that I liked him, though I had to admire his searching clarity of mind and to respect his intense devotion," he writes of his first impressions of Krishna Prem.[21] This initial hesitation dissipated at the end of his first week in the ashram, when, having "got through [Krishna Prem's] outer armour," Phipps caught a glimpse of "the man behind" the intellect, with whom he would become intimately acquainted in the years to come:

> It was the sort of man I had never seen before: simple, in the sense of uncomplicated, clean, soft and sun-like. I was torn between embarrassment at my intrusion and desire to feast my soul on such rare beauty. For the next few days I felt like the country bumpkin of legend who stumbled into fairyland.[22]

The final newcomer, a young Bengali who had also worked in the RAF during the war, arrived at the tail end of 1946. According to Madhava Ashish, Nilomani Dhole was "'related' to one of Krishna Prem's early disciples by virtue of living in the same little village some distance north of Calcutta. It emerged that what he really wanted was to win the reputation of having lived with a Mahatma in the Himalaya, possibly to be given sanyas, and then to return to his village and take over the job of managing a 300-year-old temple to Chaitanya Mahaprabhu which Krishna Prem's disciple was presently managing" (Ashish, 157—158).

Moti Rani took *sannyāsa* from Krishna Prem that November (Ashish, 158), receiving the name Sri Krishnarpita Mai—a reference to her birth name, Arpita, which signifies dedication to the divine. In time, the three new arrivals were also given initiation and Hindu names. Phipps, first up, was given the name Dev Ashish, meaning one who is blessed by God/the gods. (The name Sri Madhava Ashish was bestowed later, after his *vairāgya/sannyāsa* initiation.) Baines came next and was called Govinda Priya, denoting one who loves Govinda (a name of Krishna), and Dhole was renamed Keshab Priya (Keshab/Keshava being another name of Krishna). Phipps recalls: "Moti promptly called me Ashish, so the name stuck. Keshab's name also stuck. But Frank for most of us remained Frank" (Ashish, 158).

In Dev/Madhava Ashish's historiography, this period constitutes a distinct era in the life of Krishna Prem, and the ashram he had inherited, that continued until Moti Rani's death in August 1951. These five years were, he writes, characterised by the increasingly unpredictable behaviour of Yashoda Mai's daughter—whose frequent, seemingly "irrational outbursts of anger" (Ashish, 164) were, he explains, no ordinary barbs, but a targeted, deliberate, multi-year assault on what she referred to as the "elephantine ego" (Ashish, 235) of her guru, as well as those of her new godbrothers.

The first sign of trouble began that winter, when Moti Rani and Madhava Ashish were allowed to accompany Sri Krishna Prem on a trip to Vrindavan. The trip was, the latter writes, Moti Rani's first public appearance as the *vairāginī* Krishnarpita Mai, with shaven head and ochre robes, as well as his own first appearance in Indian dress.

In addition to dealing with jealously from other ashramites—"My favoured status in such matters did not endear me to the others," he recalls, "particularly to Bob who had been in the ashram for eight years but never taken out on a trip, and Frank whose position as blue-eyed boy I had usurped"—Madhava Ashish had difficulties fitting in with his new surroundings (Ashish, 159). He writes that he had "not yet learned how to behave as an Indian," and adds that "Krishna Prem ... was obviously unhappy at having to cater for such a dimwit" (Ashish, 161). Moreover, on the journey to Vrindavan, he was "given [his] first taste of Moti's often irrational anger" (Ashish, 161). "I think it had something to do with the food she wanted to eat and the restrictions which would now apply to her as a sanyasin," he remembers. "One had not catered for this sort of thing and it was upsetting. But since I had no preconceived notions of how she ought to behave, it did not shake my faith in either of them" (Ashish, 161).

Once there, the trio hired a car to take them on a tour of local pilgrimage sites. This trip, "like all journeys that one made with Moti ... was a mixture of heightened enjoyment punctuated by her often irrational outbursts of anger," continues Madhava Ashish. However, "those outbursts ... often only seemed irrational until one saw that she was reacting to one's unconscious motives" (Ashish, 164). Once a target for such anger, he explains, the important thing is to

> keep calm under attack. If one starts justifying and defending oneself one is, in the context of the inner work, fundamentally wrong, even if one's arguments are logically right. With few exceptions, all defensive arguments are in the service of the ego, and it always seemed that Moti's outbursts struck one's ego with deadly accuracy. It was as if even her failings were exploited by a daemon in the service of the Spirit. (Ashish, 164)

Such a method of 'teaching' was, it seems, reserved for those to whom Moti Rani was closest. For example, she apparently did not show this side of her personality to Dilip Kumar Roy (who notes only that, "after the passing of Ma, she had drawn much closer to [Krishna Prem]," and that the pair now spoke primarily in Bengali),[23] or to her family, with whom she would "switch into a different integration ... behaving as if they were the most adored people, as, indeed, for the moment they were, but when they left she was almost free of it" (Ashish, 166). Similarly, Bob Alexander was treated "very gently, for he was not malleable and could easily have cracked," according to Madhava (then Dev) Ashish (Ashish, 132).

Both men (Dev Ashish and Ananda Priya) were initiated as *vairāgīs* in early 1947, receiving the names Sri Madhava Ashish ("Blessed by Madhava") and Sri Haridas ("Servant of Hari")[24] in a rapid sequence of events that effectively settled who would succeed Krishna Prem as head of the ashram in the event of his death. (Moti Rani, with her health problems, was not expected to live past 35. [Ashish, 128]) Madhava Ashish continues the story:

> When the question of giving me sanyas in February of 1947 was being discussed, Krishna Prem and Moti were considering the seeming unfairness of giving sanyas to the newcomer, while Bob, who had been in the ashram for eight years and had effectively been Krishna Prem's disciple for some fifteen years before that, would be superseded. I was happily unaware of this weighing of seniority in years over the intangibles of inner potential, for in the event of Krishna Prem's demise, the senior sanyasi would normally be put in charge.
>
> We were all sitting together in Moti's glazed verandah late one afternoon, and Bob began to get up to attend to an evening chore. Moti brightly asked, 'Would you like sanyas, Bob?' And I saw Gopalda (as everyone affectionately called Krishna Prem) staring at her in astonishment.
>
> 'Don't tease me, Moti,' replied Bob as he headed for the ladder that served as a staircase to the verandah. There was dead silence in the room, and one got the feeling of all known processes stopping as the opportunity for a crucial life decision was given. The moment passed. Seconds later Bob climbed up the stairs again in a hurry. 'Moti! Are you serious?' And Moti regretfully said, 'Too late.' Had Bob been ready he would have seized the opportunity. Even had she been teasing, he could have held her to her offer.
>
> The result was that the succession was in an important sense settled in my favour ... and Bob was given sanyas in April the same year (with the name Sri Hari Das). But I was with Moti and Gopalda [the] next day as they watched Bob moving about in front of the temple. They shook their heads a little sadly. The gerua colour of the sadhu's dress had not struck through the surface to his soul. He had remained an English gentleman, now dressed in the ochre robes of the sadhu. (Ashish, 85–86)

The breakneck speed at which Madhava Ashish was given *sannyāsa* initiation—just six months after his first meeting with Krishna Prem—may be attributed to the latter's discomfort at the idea of running the ashram alone after Moti Rani's passing. His chosen successor, whose responsibilities at Mirtola grew into the 1950s, confirms: "It seems that his dislike of the idea of running the ashram as Pradhan Sevak ['chief servant', ie head] was so great that he was looking for a successor" as far back as the 1930s, "long before he had become the Trustee" following Yashoda Mai's death (Ashish, 178).

Notes

[1]'The magic of the Name and the Number,' *Vedanta Kesari*, 29.3 (1942), 93.

[2]Mooney, *Frank Baines*, 11.

[3]Brian Mooney, 'Introduction,' in *Frank Baines, Chindit Affair: A Memoir of the War in Burma*, (Barnsley: Pen & Sword, 2011), 10.

[4]'India, Select Marriages, 1792–1948', *Ancestry*, Provo, Ancestry.com Operations, 2014, https://www.ancestry.co.uk/search/collections/9901/ (accessed 23 November 2022). Original data: India, Marriages, 1792-1948. Salt Lake City, Utah: FamilySearch, 2013.

[5]Mooney, *Frank Baines*, 98.

[6]Mooney, *Frank Baines*, 103–104.

[7]'Ashish, Sri Madhava,' in Jones and Ryan, *Encyclopedia of Hinduism*, 49.

[8]'England & Wales, National Probate Calendar (Index of Wills and Administrations), 1858–1995', *Ancestry*, Provo, Ancestry.com Operations, 2010, https://www.ancestry.co.uk/search/collections/1904/ (accessed 23 November 2022). Original data: Principal Probate Registry. Calendar of the Grants of Probate and Letters of Administration made in the Probate Registries of the High Court of Justice in England. London, England ©Crown copyright.

[9]Eichert, 'Sri Madhava Ashish.'

[10]MRD Foot, 'Sri Madhava Ashish,' *The Independent*, 6 May 1997, 14.

[11]The elder Phipps, of the RAF's № 500 Squadron, was killed after his Blenheim IV bomber crashed off the coast of the Netherlands on 31 October 1941. He was 27.

[12]Aitken, email to the author, 2 July 2023.

[13]Madhava Ashish, 'Sri Krishna Prem Through the Eyes of a Disciple,' 14.

[14]Korman, *A Woman's Work*, 160–161.

[15]Eichert, 'The Last English Saint,' 2.

[16]Korman, *A Woman's Work*, 162.

[17]Mooney, *Frank Baines*, 101–102.

[18]Madhava Ashish, 'Sri Krishna Prem Through the Eyes of a Disciple,' 11.

[19]Mooney, *Frank Baines*, 102.

[20]Madhava Ashish, 'Sri Krishna Prem Through the Eyes of a Disciple,' 11.

[21]Madhava Ashish, 'Preface,' in Krishna Prem and Madhava Ashish, *Man, the Measure of All Things*, 8.

[22]Madhava Ashish, 'Sri Krishna Prem Through the Eyes of a Disciple,' 14.

[23]Roy, *Yogi Sri Krishnaprem*, 114.

[24]Both are names of Krishna.

16: Down South

"Journeying for a specific purpose gives one-pointedness to the purpose in view, which is helpful for awakening the psychic shaktis."[1]
— Sri Krishna Prem (1940s)

In India, expectations of the guru often go beyond that of purely religious counsel, with the spiritual master also expected to assist their followers in other aspects of their lives.[2] With numerous disciples, students and friends living outside Mirtola, Krishna Prem, regardless of his European origins, was no exception, and was frequently called upon to dispense more earthly advice (in writing and, less frequently, in person). One such request—from a couple in Calcutta suffering marital problems—was the catalyst for a 1948 pilgrimage to South Indian holy sites which became Krishna Prem's first extended journey outside the North (all "previous plans to come South [having] gone wrong for one reason or another"[3]) and, after the story of his escape in World War One, the second most written about and mythologised episode of his life.

Having agreed to go to Calcutta in person, Krishna Prem decided to also travel to Sri Aurobindo Ashram in Pondicherry, where Dilip Kumar Roy had been urging him to visit (Ashish, 178). Since he was now going so far south, he also planned to visit Tiruvannamalai, for the *darśan* of Ramana Maharshi, and Trichinopoly (Tiruchirappalli), Madurai and Rameswaram, homes respectively to famous temples to Vishnu, Meenakshi (Parvati) and Shiva. Notably, despite his repeated visits to Bengal (he had also travelled to Calcutta the previous year), at no time does Krishna Prem seem to have considered stopping off at Navadwip—the birthplace of Chaitanya and, for Gauḍīya Vaiṣṇavas, a major pilgrimage site second only in importance to Vrindavan—reflecting his ambivalent relationship with the originator of the *sampradāya* of which he was part.

The journey would be made alone, Moti Rani having declined to accompany her guru on health grounds. At Krishna Prem's request, she did, however, donate two small *mūrtis* of Radha and Krishna to take on the trip, "for then she would be with him all the time" (Ashish, 178). For these, he made a carry case which resembled the altar at Uttar Brindaban. "The little images were so fixed that on opening the doors they were ready for darshan as when one opens the doors of a temple," Madhava Ashish explains (Ashish, 178).

The year began with Krishna Prem in Allahabad, seeking legal clarification as to the nature of the charitable body, Thakurji Sri Sri Krishna Sri Sri Radhika Mohan Trust, under which the temple and ashram are run. There, he also attended the ceremony marking the ritual immersion of Mahatma Gandhi's ashes at the Triveni Sangam, the confluence of three sacred rivers, on 12 February 1948 (Ashish, 175). Yashoda Mai and Krishna Prem had first met Gandhi over 20 years earlier, when he stayed at the 'Castle' in Almora, in June 1926. The Kumaoni civil servant Pitambar Datt Pande (father-in-law of BD Pande, the one-time governor of West Bengal and Punjab) records that the trio talked about Krishna Prem's wartime service ("There must have been a lot of violence," Gandhi, then practising nonviolent resistance to the British-Indian government, is said to have remarked in jest....[and] Bapu [Gandhi] learned [Krishna Prem's] life story."[4]) Krishna Prem later criticised Gandhi for "blatant ignorance" for his claim that Krishna and the divine hero of the *Rāmāyaṇa*, Rama, are "creations of man's imagination."[5] "To believe that Rama [and] Krishna are imaginary is foolishness. This is all I know; nothing else," he wrote.[6] After Gandhi's assassination, Krishna Prem decried the "terrible" murder, but reflected that it "must be regarded as a willing sacrifice on [Gandhi's] part, and one which I felt had really succeeded in bringing about some change in man's fear-laden hearts."[7]

Much had changed in the last year, both at Uttar Brindaban, where "the three newcomers [were doing] a lot of adjusting" (Ashish, 167), and in the wider world. Kumaon was now part of the independent India for which Gandhi had struggled (in Almora, Earl Brewster was chosen to raise the new national flag [Ashish, 161]) and Krishna Prem, along with Madhava Ashish, Haridas and Govinda Priya (Frank Baines), found themselves guests in a foreign country, no longer Britons in a British dependency nor yet citizens of the new nation. Four out of the five destinations on Krishna Prem's itinerary were in this new country (specifically Madras Province, modern Tamil Nadu), with only nearby Pondicherry still under colonial rule, being the capital of the French *Établissements dans l'Inde.*

Krishna Prem travelled to Tiruvannamalai via Madras and Pondicherry (where he met with Dilip Kumar Roy[8]), spending part of the journey in the company of a former student he had met again by chance after more than 10 years. Perhaps owing to the lack of troublesome travelling companions this time, Roy notes that Krishna Prem's mood was noticeably better than the last time he saw his friend, in January 1947 (Roy's infamous 50th birthday party), when he had observed: "He had changed a great deal and would retire into his shell oftener than before."[9] By contrast, Roy writes, in November 1948 he was practically overflowing with *bhakti* for Radha, the queen of the *gopīs*—"a new inspiration which had enriched his personality" and which would "plant a new seed in me which was to flower out subsequently in my heart: I mean the Name of Sri Radha. He enjoined me to invoke Her Grace, subject, of course, to my Gurudev's approval."[10] Roy continues:

> Even his salutation had changed: he now said "Jai Radhe" [victory to Radha] with an ecstasy which had to be seen to be believed. I asked him how he had achieved Her Grace. He laughed and said: "There is only one way for us, Dilip: acceptance of the Guru's lead. It's *Ma*, of course, who brought me to Radharani's feet, who else could have guided me home? She told me that to attain Radharani's Grace four things were necessary: loyalty to the Guru, central sincerity, true humility and spontaneous trust—by trust I mean trust in Divine Grace, Radharani's Love."[11]

Krishna Prem was collected in Madras by Tubu Chakravarti, a devotee of Ramana Maharshi unrelated to Gyanendra Nath, and the pilgrimage south continued, soon turning into a column resembling a "triumphal procession" (Ashish, 179), with the party joined by, among others, the postmaster general of Madras, Tapo Gopal Mukherjee, and "one Upadhyaya who was then attached to the Rice Research Centre in Orissa and had boarded the train at Cuttack."[12] Krishna Prem stayed a couple of days in Madras, taking the opportunity to visit the Theosophical Society headquarters at Adyar, before heading to Tiruvannamalai and the Sri Ramana Ashram.[13]

Located near Arunachala, a holy mountain identified with Shiva, the ashram had sprung up around Ramana Maharshi (1879–1950), who had run away from home as a teenager and spent ten years in silent contemplation at Arunachalesvara Temple, at the foot of the hill, and in various caves on the mountain itself.[14] His absorption in "higher consciousness" was said to be so deep that he "neglected care of his body and was at times famished and chewed by insects,"[15] after which disciples began to gather to take care of his physical needs. The ashram was later visited by *sādhus* and intellectuals including Swami Sivananda, UG Krishnamurti, Paramahansa Yogananda, Swami Abhishiktananda (Henri Le Saux), Sunyata (whom Ramana called a "rare-born mystic"[16]) and Somerset Maugham (who used the Maharshi as the model for Sri Ganesha in *The Razor's Edge*). A young Alexander Phipps (Sri Madhava Ashish) also visited, and later called it "an experience which confirmed [his] dedication to the spiritual quest" (Ashish, i).

The meeting of the Maharshi, called 'Bhagavān' (literally "Lord", as in God, but used in South India as a term of respect[17]) by his followers, and Krishna Prem, is given considerable prominence in histories of the Ramana Ashram, with accounts of the latter's stay featuring in ashram publications such as the *Mountain Path*, *The Maharshi*, and the biography *Arunachala's Ramana*, in addition to several books by Dilip Kumar Roy (who had also visited in 1945).

Ramana Maharshi was an *Advaitin*, a "living example of non-dual consciousness"[18] who thought about the divine in purely impersonal terms. "Iswara [the personal aspect of God] is immanent in every person and every material object throughout the universe," he once explained, and "[t]he totality of all things and beings constitutes God"[19]. In contrast, Krishna Prem in 1948 was, as he wrote to Roy earlier in the year, still "sufficiently under the spell of name and form to prefer the name and personality of Sri Krishna [and Radha] to an impersonal (as far as name goes) Divine. I can surrender to the former but not to the latter."[20] However, neither man, the Radha–Krishna *bhakta* and the "greatest *jñānī* of modern times,"[21] saw the other's chosen yogic path as being incompatible with their own, and Ramana's comments on the equal merits of the three classical yoga *mārgas*—*bhakti*, devotion to a personal God; *jñāna*, knowledge (of the oneness of the Atman and Brahman); and *karma*, unselfish action—are in keeping with Krishna Prem's own, as expressed in his books. "When for instance a follower of *bhakti mārga* declares that *bhakti* is the best, he really means by the word *bhakti* what the *jñāna mārga* man calls *jñāna*," the Maharshi had told Roy on his visit three years earlier. "There is no difference in the state.... Only different thinkers have used different words. All these different *mārgas*, or paths or *sādhanas*, lead to the same goal."[22]

Chakravarti describes Krishna Prem's first meeting with 'Bhagavan,' on the evening of his arrival:

> I should ... explain that the Maharshi hardly ever looked at those who gathered round him. Most often he would just be sitting there, merged in trance, or, alternatively, sat looking at—what? Space? The hill? The sky? Or nothing? But the moment Gopalda stepped into the alley, Ramana turned fully and kept staring with those sparkling eyes of his at Gopalda.
>
> We went up to his seat, and I bowed down with my forehead touching the ground. Then I looked up and started to tell him about Gopalda who was lying prostrate before his seat. But the Maharshi stopped

> me short by waving his anga vastra [or anga baran, a cloth commonly worn over the shoulder in south India] impatiently and invited Gopalda to sit near the stone couch on which he was sitting. Here I must explain that no one was allowed to sit so close to the Maharshi. I also got the impression from the Maharshi's behaviour that he already knew Gopalda, so that a formal introduction was not necessary.[23]

This uncharacteristic behaviour continued throughout his stay at Ramana Ashram, with Krishna Prem additionally "always given the first seat at meals, just in front of the Maharshi's seat, so that the Maharshi could see and give necesary [sic] instructions about the food prepared for and served to Gopalda."[24] Ramana also arranged for Krishna Prem to be taken to see the caves in the mountain where he had lived before the ashram was built, as well as the *pathala lingam*, an abstract form of Shiva, at Arunachalesvara Temple. "When Gopalda returned from the excursion to the temple," Chavravarti continues,

> we found a huge crowd of pilgrims sitting in the verandah, engrossed in listening to the Maharshi. This in itself was a strange event, for, as I have said, the Maharshi hardly ever spoke to or looked at anyone. Our surprise became boundless when we found everyone looking at Gopalda and smiling and bowing. Later we were told that, breaking from his usual habit, the Maharshi had been narrating at length the story of Sri Krishna's sojourn in Mathura. And when he came to relate the eventual return of Sri Krishna to Brindaban, it coincided with Gopalda's return from the outing. This prompted the Maharshi to say something like this: "Ah! There you are. Have I not been telling you about Sri Krishna's return from Mathura? See. Here returns our Sri Krishnaprem."[25]

According to Chakravarti, "this sort of loving and affectionate respect was bestowed on Gopalda by the Maharshi on each and every occasion."[26]

Despite this, Krishna Prem spent the first two days of his visit in a "grave and solemn" frame of mind,[27] and Chakravarti, "unhappy on account of his seeming taciturnity," worried "whether I had done something to bring it about."[28] "All this time," he writes, "Gopalda sat with his head bowed. His face appeared to me to be extraordinarily red or flushed.

> Then I witnessed a peculiar incident: Gopalda suddenly jerked his head up and looked at the Maharshi, who was seemingly unconcerned.[29]

Though externally of little consequence, the incident in question precipitated a complete about-turn in Krishna Prem's mood, and the next morning, for the first time since his arrival in Tiruvanamalai, "Gopalda's face lost that strained, stern look," Chakravarti continues. "It was beaming with a smile. In a choked voice he said: 'Indeed, the Maharshi is Bhagavan. He knew what my heart yearned for.'"[30]

Multiple accounts of what had happened in that moment—one of several mystical episodes experienced by Krishna Prem during his trip to the South—are in circulation, with at least three (Chakravarti's, Roy's and Sri Madhava Ashish's) purporting to come directly from the man himself. These chroniclers, however, generally agree on the main details, recounted below by Tubu Chakravarti:

> Gopalda said that the moment he set foot on the station platform at Tiruvanamalai he found the whole environment surcharged with one persistent 'enquiry-like' mantra, 'Who am I?' Gopalda said there was no getting away from this 'enquiry' which kept repeating itself with 'hammering blows' (these two last words were Gopalda's). He said he could find no relief from this terrible 'contretemps.' He tried several answers, but all in vain. For instance, when he said "I am Krishna Prem," the retort was "Who is Krishna Prem? Who is Krishna Prem?" Then Gopalda said, "I am Sri Krishna's das (servant)." The immediate reaction was the enquiry, "Who is Sri Krishna?" No matter what reply Gopalda gave, there was no escape or respite from that ever-sounding, agonising enquiry. Gopalda went on to say that when he came and sat before the Maharshi that this ever-persistent phenomenon kept on, and he felt desperate. Then Gopalda changed his tactics and asked the question, "Who are you?" And with this question he looked at the Maharshi. He said he was not prepared for what followed. The Maharshi, or the Maharshi's body, just vanished. He was startled, but he said he realised what the Maharshi wanted to convey: the real Maharshi was not that body, possessing mind, life force, etc. But the answer still evaded him.
>
> He told me that he spent the whole of that night walking restlessly; there was no peace for him. He confided to me that he asked Radharani who Sri Krishna was, but he did not tell me what answer Radharani gave him, though her answer eased the otherwise unbearable situation.[31]

Roy similarly relates that Krishna Prem, having left the Maharshi's presence, "deeply disturbed, to meditate" on the question, sought answers from Radha: "I had no peace: the Voice gave me no respite, till, in the end, I had to evoke

Radharani who asked me very simply what answers I had given. I told Her but She shook Her head and then, at last, revealed it to me."[32]

Though Krishna Prem also declined to tell Roy what Radha had said (surmising, probably correctly, that his friend would surely "tell everybody"[33]), he did share her conclusion with Madhava Ashish on his return to Mirtola. Madhava Ashish writes:

> He was given accommodation across the road from the ashram. In the morning he bathed and performed the morning puja of the images of Radha and Krishna he was carrying with him. Having finished the puja, he begged Krishna to tell him who he was and what answer to give to Ramana. But Krishna remained obstinately silent. In despair he turned to Radha: 'You know who he is!' Instantly the answer came into his mind: 'Prem Swarup,' the self-nature of love.
>
> He told me it was as if Ramana Maharshi knew he had found the answer, for the whole place was throbbing with ānanda and stayed like that while he walked over to the ashram to sit before Ramana Maharshi. (Ashish, 179–180)

Krishna Prem later told Shantananda Puri he had seen, "clearly with his eyes, the shining Supreme God in Bhagawan Ramana."[34]

According to the *Encyclopedia of Hinduism*, Ramana commonly directed those who came to the ashram seeking self-realisation to the question "'Who am I?'—a self-inquiry that he insisted be used tirelessly as each student discovered deeper and deeper levels of awareness. The aim of this inquiry was for each person to find an awareness of non-duality, in which the oneness of the Self and cosmos could be perceived."[35]

That evening, the Maharshi asked Krishna Prem to sing. Balarama Reddy recalls that Krishna Prem, after requesting a harmonium, sang for his host and around 75 devotees with "genuine devotion, even pronouncing the words of the song with an Indian accent.... Bhagavan later commented, 'Here is one Westerner who embodies the intensity and devotion of a true Indian *Bhakta*.'"[36] (In Chakravarti's considerably embellished telling of the same story, Krishna Prem had only started to play the Bengali song 'Kanu kahe Rai' before he collapsed over the harmonium. Later, says Chakravarti, he "told me that as soon as he started singing he lost consciousness," having gone "into a trance and, for the first time in his life, experienced ananda," transcendental bliss.[37] (It is unlikely Krishna Prem would have used these words given that participating in *sankīrtan* produced similar effects in him in the 1930s.)

It seems to have been a memorable few days for both men, with Krishna Prem impressed by Ramana's obvious spiritual attainment and Ramana by the strength of Krishna Prem's devotion. The conservationist and spiritual aspirant Marie Byles notes that the "Maharshi did not ask Krishnaprem to cease from worshipping Lord Krishna and surrendering all to him," having recognised that "there are different ways for different temperaments,"[38] and Ramana took a great interest in Krishna Prem's *Ṭhākurs*, the Radha–Krishna deities he had been lent by Moti Rani prior to setting off from Mirtola. "He told me that Ramana Maharshi had tears in his eyes when he saw them," recalls Madhava Ashish, adding:

> When he got up to leave, it seems that Ramana Maharshi got up and went outside with him. Hence we have the photograph of them together. I think he also wanted to look at the little ivory image of Krishna he was wearing round his neck on a tulasi mala. (Ashish, 180)

The same incident is recounted by A. Devaraja Mudaliar, a devotee of Ramana, who writes that Krishna Prem told him: "Many people had told me Bhagavan was a pure *Jnani*. But I consider him a very great *Bhakta*. When I showed him my image of Lord Krishna, which I worship and carry about with me, tears came into his eyes as he handled it and gave it back to me. If this is not *Bhakti*, what else is it?"[39]

Famously, Ramana is said to have subsequently described Krishna Prem in turn as "a *bhakta* and *jnani* in one, a rare combination."[40]

For Krishna Prem, the overwhelming impression of the famous *jñānī* was of "Love with a capital L."[41] "Go and see him," he told Madhava Ashish later. "If you have eyes to see, you will see the thing shining there" (Ashish, 162).

Notes

[1]Kaul, *Writings of Sri Krishna Prem*, 109.

[2]"On a practical level, a guru often acts as a village priest or godfather, assisting his followers in all aspects of their lives. Indian devotees often seek the guru's advice on practical matters such as career decisions or the marriage of a child." Anne Cushman and Jerry Jones, *From Here to Nirvana: The Yoga Journal Guide to Spiritual India*, (New York: Riverhead Books, 1998), 27.

[3]S. Chakravarti (Tubu), 'Sri Krishnaprem's 1948 Visit to Sri Ramana Maharshi,' *The Maharshi*, 29.3, (2019), 1.

[4]Pitambar Datt Pande, प्रिव्त्न् (*Parivartan*), (Jaipur: Panchsheel Prakashan, 1975), 1,212.

[5]RK Prabhu (compiler), *Truth is God: Gleanings from the Writings of Mahatma Gandhi (Bearing on God, God Realization and the Godly Way)*, (Ahmedabad: Navajivan Publishing House, 1957), 74.

[6]Bhakta Ramsharan Das Pilkhuva, 'अंग्रेज् मिं. रोनाल्ड् निक्स्न् ने हिन्दू ध्र्म् कैसे स्वीकार् किया?' ('How did the Englishman Ronald Nixon Adopt the Hindu Religion?'), हिन्दू विश्व् (*Hindu Vishva*), *Chaitra* 1890 (April 1968), 25–29.

[7]MP Pandit (ed.), 'Sri Krishnaprem's Letters,' *The Advent*, 53, (1996), 14.

[8]This is disputed by Tubu Chakravarti, who insists Krishna Prem only visited Pondicherry once, after his stay in Tiruvanamalai.

[9]Roy, *Yogi Sri Krishnaprem*, 114.

[10]Roy, *Yogi Sri Krishnaprem*, 119.

[11]*Ibid.*

[12]S. Chakravarti, 'Sri Krishnaprem's 1948 Visit to Sri Ramana Maharshi,' 1.

[13]S. Chakravarti, 'Sri Krishnaprem's 1948 Visit to Sri Ramana Maharshi,' 2.

[14]'Ramana Maharshi,' in Jones and Ryan, *Encyclopedia of Hinduism*, 351.

[15]*Ibid*

[16]'Sunyata (Alfred Julius Emanuel Sorensen),' in Jones and Ryan, *Encyclopedia of Hinduism*, 427.

[17]S. Chakravarti, 'Sri Krishnaprem's 1948 Visit to Sri Ramana Maharshi,' 4.

[18]'Ramana Maharshi,' in Jones and Ryan, *Encyclopedia of Hinduism*, 351.

[19]David Godman (ed.), *Be As You Are: The Teachings of Sri Ramana Maharshi*, ebook edn, (London: Penguin Arkana, 1985), 231.

[20]Roy, *Yogi Sri Krishnaprem*, 257.

[21]Sara Grant, 'Hindu Religious Experience,' *The Way*, 18.1, (1978), 24.

[22]Mudaliar, *Day by Day with Bhagavan*, 36.

[23]S. Chakravarti, 'Sri Krishnaprem's 1948 Visit to Sri Ramana Maharshi,' 3.

[24]*Ibid.*

[25]S. Chakravarti, 'Sri Krishnaprem's 1948 Visit to Sri Ramana Maharshi,' 4.

[26]*Ibid.*

[27]S. Chakravarti, 'Sri Krishnaprem's 1948 Visit to Sri Ramana Maharshi,' 2.

[28]S. Chakravarti, 'Sri Krishnaprem's 1948 Visit to Sri Ramana Maharshi,' 3.

[29]*Ibid.*

[30]S. Chakravarti, 'Sri Krishnaprem's 1948 Visit to Sri Ramana Maharshi,' 4.

[31]S. Chakravarti, 'Sri Krishnaprem's Visit to Sri Ramana Maharshi, Part II,' 2–3.

[32]Roy, *Yogi Sri Krishnaprem*, 123.

[33]*Ibid.*

[34]Swami Shantananda Puri, *Fragrant Flowers (Soul-elevated Reminiscences of a Himalayan Monk)*, 2nd edn, (Bangalore: Parvathamma CP Subbaraju Setty Charitable Trust, 2002), 74.

[35]'Ramana Maharshi,' in Jones and Ryan, *Encyclopedia of Hinduism*, 351.

[36]Reddy, 'The Recollections of N. Balarama Reddy—Part VII,' sec. 2, para. 5.

[37]S. Chakravarti, 'Sri Krishnaprem's Visit to Sri Ramana Maharshi, Part II,' 3.

[38]Marie B. Byles, 'Krishnaprem and Maharshi,' in VS Ramanan (ed.), *The Silent Power: Selections from The Mountain Path and The Call Divine*, (Tiruvannamalai: Sri Ramanasramam, 2002), 26–27.

[39]A. Devaraja Mudaliar, 'My Recollections of Bhagavan Sri Ramana,' *Arunachala Ashrama Archives*, (New York: Arunachala Ashrama, 2018), https://archive.arunachala.org/docs/my-robsr (accessed 24 January 2024).

[40]Roy, *Yogi Sri Krishnaprem*, 126.

[41]S. Chakravarti, 'Sri Krishnaprem's Visit to Sri Ramana Maharshi, Part III,' *The Maharshi*, 29.5, (2019), 5.

17: All That Glitters

"[H]e saw Raṅganātha; making obeisance and praising him, he honored him fully.

...

All the people saw his absorption in prema ..."[1]
— Krishnadas Kaviraj, *Chaitanya Charitamrita*

From Tiruvannamalai the party, consisting of Krishna Prem, Chakravarti and Upadhyaya, pressed onto Pondicherry, where they stayed with Dilip Kumar Roy in his "enormous flat"[2] in the city's French Quarter.

Madhava Ashish writes that "there was a lot of kirtan in Dilip Kumar Roy's rooms, both Dilip and Krishna Prem singing" (Ashish, 181), Roy, true to form, having organised a large gathering in honour of his esteemed guest. Chakravarti continues:

> This would be held in Dilip's old-fashioned, spacious flat whose carpeted hall could easily hold one hundred people. That evening, not only the hall, but also the upper landing and even the stairs were packed with people. Gopalda spoke just a few words saying that he knew nothing more than what the *Bhagavad Gītā* says in Chapter 9, verse 34:
>
> > Fix your mind on Me; give yourself in love to Me; sacrifice to Me; prostrate yourself before Me; having thus united your whole self (to Me), with Me as your Goal, to Me shall you come.
>
> Whenever Gopalda was called upon to speak, he usually quoted the first line of this verse.[3]

A similar verse, also from the *Bhagavad Gītā* (ch. 18, v. 66), emphasising total surrender to Krishna, is inscribed over the temple door at Sri Krishna Vilas:

सर्वधर्मान् परित्यज्य मामेकं शरणं व्रज ।
अहं त्वां सर्वपापेभ्यो मोक्षयिष्यामि मा शुचः ॥

"Abandoning all duties, come to me for asylum, I shall liberate Thee from all sins. Worry not."[4]

On his return to Uttar Brindaban, Krishna Prem told Madhava Ashish he had in Pondicherry particularly enjoyed listening (with her permission) to another singer, a Bengali woman who had given up singing in public and now treated it as her private *sādhana*, as Krishna Prem often urged Roy to do. "He told me he saw her dhyan image—the mental image held by the person who is singing if, and only if, the mind is being held steady and not entertaining images of how much an audience is appreciating the singer, etc.," Madhava Ashish writes (Ashish, 181).

Roy also arranged for Krishna Prem to have *darśan* of Sri Aurobindo and the Mother, Aurobindo's French-born spiritual collaborator and heir, on his visit to Sri Aurobindo Ashram. After meeting Aurobindo and responding "warmly to [his] spiritual touch and blessings," Krishna Prem had a few moments with the Mother, during which "he made a very characteristic gesture which I shall never forget, a gesture of simple sincerity with a charm all his own,"[5] writes Roy:

> I took him up to the Mother and introduced him to her. He said that he had come for her blessings that he might give himself without reserve to his Guru and Krishna. Mother held his eyes for nearly a minute, then said:
>
> "But you have given yourself."
>
> "Not enough," he answered.
>
> Mother told us subsequently that his words had made a deep impression on her: and yet he had spoken but a few words![6]

Later, Krishna Prem told Govindagopal Mukherji he appreciated that Aurobindo had given him a "very beautiful broad smile," though he chastised Roy for making such a request of his guru. Mukherji remembers:

> On the previous night before the darshan, Dilip sent a note to Sri Aurobindo to inform him that next day, Sri Krishnaprem will also be accompanying him for Sri Aurobindo's darshan and in the line of devotees assembled for the darshan, the man next to Dilip will be Sri Krishnaprem. "If possible, please give him a smile, when he approaches you, O Guru." "Just think," Sri Krishnaprem told me,

> "how he dares order or command the Guru to oblige him! And what could the ever-obliging Guru do? He could not refuse any request coming from Dilip! As soon as I stood before him, he gave me a very beautiful broad smile!"[7]

Aurobindo wrote to Roy shortly thereafter that his brief physical meeting with Krishna Prem "confirmed and deepened and made more living the impressions I had already formed about him from his letters to you and what came through them and from such psychical contact as I had already made from a distance, *for the contact itself is not distant.* You know very well the value I have always put upon his insight into spiritual things, the brilliance and accuracy of his thought and vision and his expression of them (I think I described it once as *pashyanti vak* ['seeing speech']) and on as much as I knew of his spiritual experience and constant acquisition and forward movement and many-sided largeness. A closer perception of the spiritual person behind that is something more than a mental impression."[8]

Though Krishna Prem would have sympathised with many aspects of Sri Aurobindo's 'Integral Yoga'—particularly those teachings dealing with the complementary roles played by the different yoga systems (as spelt out in the *Gītā*) and the belief that spiritual practice must nourish "the whole human being: [on] the physical, emotional, mental, psychic (soul), and spiritual levels"[9]—he described Aurobindo as a *mahāpuruṣa*, a great personality, rather than a *mahātmā*, a fully realised soul, as "he talked of bringing down the 'Supramental' on Earth, not of one becoming something," records Jagdish Nautiyal.[10] According to Nautiyal, Krishna Prem was sceptical of these efforts (which focused on "engendering what they called the 'Supramental manifestation,' which would transform not only all human beings [into 'supermen']... but all life and even all matter"[11]). That approach, he believed, meant "[t]he world will remain what it is ... and the progress of mankind as such will be slow. However, individuals could break out of the rat race and progress towards *mahātmā*-hood."[12] (Aurobindo in turn was critical of aspects of the Mirtola teaching, particularly its "indulgence in occultist theories," which he attributed to the influence of Theosophy on Yashoda Mai.[13])

That Aurobindo had also consistently encouraged Roy in his inclination towards Krishna *bhakti* was not common knowledge, and Madhava Ashish writes that "the Pondicherry ashram members, when they listened to what he had to say, found him old-fashioned and ritualistic" (Ashish, 181). "Perhaps they did not see that he was not dogmatic about it," he explains, "which [is] what ma[kes] the difference between the orthodox pundit and the man who is travelling the path and using a particular mode of expression that suits him" (Ashish, 181).

This last visit to Pondicherry is notable for being the final time Krishna Prem was photographed in the Vaiṣṇava dress—with neck beads, shaven head and Gauḍīya Vaiṣṇava *tilak*, as documented in photos included in *Yogi Sri Krishnaprem*—which had been his uniform for over 20 years, but with which he would largely dispense in the 1950s. Sri Chinmoy—who later found fame in the United States as guru to the likes of Carlos Santana, Roberta Flack and John McLaughlin, but who was then a teenage resident of Sri Aurobindo Ashram—additionally recalls seeing Krishna Prem with Roy: "Both of them had red tilaks on their foreheads and they were wearing japa beads. Dilip-da had a single, long, loose strand of small beads around his neck. Krishnaprem had dark, thick, round beads and he had wound them twice around his neck. I remember that Krishnaprem was very tall and thin."[14]

The next destination, Srirangam in Trichinopoly (the hometown of Gopal Bhatta Goswami, founder of Krishna Prem's Vaiṣṇava *paramparā*), found Krishna Prem over 100 miles south of Pondicherry and even further from home, where the atmosphere was growing increasingly strained.

At Uttar Brindaban, Govinda Priya had alienated his godbrothers, as well as the formerly sympathetic Moti Rani, after he was blamed for a mysterious bundle which had been "plainly placed ... with magical intentions" (Ashish, 168) under Madhava Ashish's pillow earlier in the year. This putative attempt at black magic against Madhava Ashish, of whom Baines was, according to Brian Mooney, growing "increasingly jealous,"[15] necessitated a psychic 'closing' on the part of Moti Rani and Krishna Prem in order to protect the victim's health. One effect of this magical shield (other than to improve Madhava Ashish's health) was to cause a painful illness in Baines, who was whisked off to Almora in a *dandi* to be operated on by a doctor friend of Bob Alexander (Ashish, 169).

Moti Rani, meanwhile, was incensed by letters Krishna Prem had been sending home which extolled the virtues of the ex-pupil with whom he had become reacquainted, whose initial association with the ashram had ended in ignominy. Madhava Ashish explains:

> The one who we were concerned with was a high-caste Brahmin whose father seems to have disapproved of what he was doing. He would not risk alienating his son's affections by a direct show of disapproval, but he did it indirectly by saying that the day chosen for initiation by Krishna Prem was a very bad day which no competent astrologer would have selected. (In fact the day was probably taken

> from the Bengali almanac or Panjika). However it was done, the result was that the young man did not appear for initiation on the appointed day. Yashoda Mai and Moti Rani considered this a gross insult to the Guru, and he became persona non grata in the ashram. In spite of this background, Krishna Prem obviously seemed to have forgiven the young man's mistake when they met more than ten years later.
>
> However, Moti began to get angry when letters started arriving from Krishna Prem telling of the meeting and praising the young man for his devoted service as he accompanied Krishna Prem on his journey. (Ashish, 178–179)

Oblivious to the trouble brewing at Mirtola, Krishna Prem, Chakravarti, Upadhyaya and Asher Bhai, a Gujarati visitor to Ramana Ashram who had requested to join the pilgrimage, proceeded to Trichinopoly, where they stayed with devotees of Ramana Maharshi. At the mediaeval Ranganathaswamy Temple in Srirangam, the largest temple complex in India and the largest functioning temple in the world (only the abandoned Angkor Wat is bigger),[16] Krishna Prem was overwhelmed as he *praṇāmed* before the presiding deity, Ranganatha, a local form of Vishnu. As he recounted to Roy on his return journey via Pondicherry:

> "As soon as I prostrated myself in the shrine before the Lord's Image, I lost my outer consciousness and saw—O Dilip, it was—it beggars description!"
>
> "I saw," he went on in moving terms, "a vast ocean made of liquid light—the *apah* (waters) before the cosmic creation, was it? I don't know. For Time had stood still till a breath of Love started a ripple in the hushed ocean of Light, when countless white lotuses erupted on the blue waves, one after another, and on each flower stood a lovely Krishna with Radha—She smiling and He playing His magic flute. But O Dilip, what beauty, what music and ... and what bliss! The music of the spheres ... from harmony to harmony ... the diapason ...!" He shook his head ruefully, "Pale, dead, frozen words ... how could they outflash the living Flame that is Krishna, the throbbing Love that is Radharani ...?" He shivered as his voice trailed off into silence.[17]

For Krishna Prem, this "extraordinary vision" was the "high point of the whole journey," he told Madhava Ashish (Ashish, 181).

Taken together with his experiences at Ramana Ashram, as well as the "*dhyān* image" of the singer in Pondicherry, it has been suggested that this vision of

Radha and Krishna forms part of what Madhava Ashish describes as his guru's *chamak* phase (literally "a sudden flash," Bengali *camaka*), characterised by the proliferation of wonder and astonishment at miraculous phenomena (*camatkāra*):

> A friend in Nainital who had met a lot of sadhus remarked of this trip that all mahatmas go through a stage of chamak, which implies the glitter of psychical phenomena, great visions and things of that sort. He suggested that this was Krishna Prem's chamak stage. (Ashish, 183)

From Srirangam, Krishna Prem proceeded to Madurai, where the party were joined by Balarama Reddy, and to Rameswaram, where they stayed with a friend of Asher Bhai. A stop at Madurai's Meenakshi Temple passed without incident. ("There was no crowd. Gopalda prostrated himself before the murti in the dusty hall. And that was all that happened," writes Chakravarti[18].) However, visiting Ramanathaswamy Temple in Rameswaram, which restricts entry to Indian Hindus, was less straightforward. Madhava Ashish continues the story:

> Without the slightest hindrance they went straight up to the inner sanctum, as close as anyone is permitted to go. Their South Indian friend [Reddy] arranged for a very long recitation to be made, and so long as that went on they had the right to stand there. Completely satisfied, they went back to the dharamshala [guesthouse for pilgrims] where they were staying, cooked their meal, ate, and were resting when the temple bullock-cart arrived with an invitation from the head of the temple committee to whom the Sarvadhikari [manager] at Raman Ashram had written. So they all went off again to the temple.
>
> The gentleman they met was polite and said how honoured they were to be visited by such a great saint, but of course they had their rules which did not permit anyone of foreign birth to enter the inner temple, though they would be happy if he had darshan from the fourth mandapam (gateway) and do the parikrama (circumambulation) from there. And they would be delighted to show him the temple jewellery. So without saying a word about the morning visit, they did what was permitted, said they were grateful but would not stop to see the jewels, and went home.
>
> Krishna Prem later heard that this story had been repeated to Ramana Maharshi. It was said that he laughed. 'That is just like the Lord,' he said. 'First he gives you his darshan and then he says you can't have it.' (Ashish, 181–182)

Krishna Prem returned via Madras and Calcutta, arriving back at Mirtola to a hostile reception from Moti Rani, still furious about his renewed acquaintance with the man who had failed to turn up for *dīkṣā* in the 1930s. "Thank God someone is pleased to see me," he said when Sonny, Yashoda Mai's dog, greeted him warmly (Ashish, 183).

His initial reaction to the tirade that followed was one of bemused surprise. "[T]otally unable to see that he had done any wrong, Krishna Prem "argued and justified all his actions, puzzled, but not angry," remembers Madhava Ashish. "He was sorry to have upset Moti, but did not see what there was to apologise for. A young man had cared for him selflessly. He had been ill and needed care. Krishna Prem had even stopped off to visit his house and do the naming ceremony for his son. The people in Madras had been wonderful. Tubu Chakravarti had been wonderful. Dilip Kumar Roy had been wonderful. What was wrong with it?" (Ashish, 183).

With Krishna Prem having failed spectacularly in his attempts to pacify his furious disciple,

> Moti's attack built up in a crescendo. The man's name became a mantra, repeated again and again with increasing volume. She sat up in bed and kept us awake for hours. It started again next morning with patches of quiet only when Krishna Prem had the temple cooking to attend to. The thing became a nightmare which neither Krishna Prem nor any of the rest of us could understand. (Ashish, 183–184)

Thus began a two-and-a-half-year ordeal in which Moti Rani used her remaining "beleaguered time to," in the words of Donald Eichert, "make life hell for the two Englishmen-turned-Hindu monks"[19]—to the extent that Krishna Prem, as well as the local people who "heard her railing at her Guru," began to suspect that she had gone insane (Ashish, 184–185). Madhava Ashish described verbal attacks, where she "might sit up all night raving at one's emotional entanglements" (Ashish, 175). He explains that they "alternated between Krishna Prem and myself. When one was in favour, the other was being bashed, Krishna Prem for allowing his judgement to be swayed by the flattery of having so many people admiring him on his journey [in South India] … and I for my attachment to my mother, my sister, and the substitute parents,[20] plus almost everything else I did because my motives were invariably wrong" (Ashish, 184).

Despite this, Madhava Ashish's literary output—including his manuscript, his letters and 'Sri Krishna Prem Through the Eyes of a Disciple,' the lengthy essay prefacing Krishna Prem's *Initiation into Yoga: An Introduction to the Spiritual Life* (1976)—is full of affection for and devotion to Moti Rani, who, in his retrospective view, was almost solely responsible for a profound transformation in both himself and his guru, who could no longer hide his human side behind an intellectual barrier of "polished armour."[21] Krishna Prem, too, was "as devoted to his guru's daughter as he had been to his guru."[22] In Madhava Ashish's telling, the pair's treatment at the hands of Moti Rani, though painful for everyone involved, represented her Bodhisattva-like dedication to helping others along the spiritual path:

> Moti's inner beauty might at times have been shrouded by storm clouds, but the longer I knew her, the more I became aware that her passionate nature was utterly dedicated to the spirit, regardless of what it cost her. If she undertook to help someone on this path, she would spare neither herself nor him in the effort to change his nature, 'shatter it to bits and then remould it nearer to the heart's desire.' Though the modes were different, it was the same aspiration that flamed in both Krishna Prem and Moti: a rapier in the hands of Krishna Prem, a scimitar in Moti's."[23]

At the time, such 'crazy wisdom' was difficult to recognise as such, and Madhava Ashish recalls being "often unhappy and filled with negativity at the charges levelled against me that I could not understand" (Ashish, 185). However, he adds, "my heart told me that she was utterly sane" (Ashish, 185). He gives an example of the kind of practical results that could be obtained following Moti Rani's 'teachings':

> When, for instance, I stopped writing to my mother as a token of my attempt to break the bond, Moti, through whose hands the mail came and went, noticed it and told me that I must write once a month. What had been a pleasure now became an agony and helped to free me more than any mere stopping of writing could have done. (Ashish, 185)

Achieving such tangible, visible results may have made it easier to stomach Moti Rani's uncompromising personality and spiritual instruction—as would the fact she was the only ashramite who claimed to "have seen and touched" the Theosophical 'Masters,' "and to be in constant communication with them" (Ashish, 153). This was an ability she had apparently inherited from her father,

Gyanendra Nath Chakravarti, who was thought by "prominent Theosophists ... to be 'if not a Mahātmā, at least an occultist of high rank and in direct communication with the Masters of H. P. B.'"[24], Koot Hoomi and Morya, who were said to live beyond the Himalayas in distant Tibet.

Such intense guru–disciple relationships, which might appear abnormal or even abusive to Western observers, are common in India—Madhava Ashish remembers that Boshi Sen "understood what Moti was doing to me, because his own Guru, Swami Sadananda of the Ramakrishna Mission, had treated him similarly" (Ashish, 167)—with the *śiṣya* (disciple) trusting that though the spiritual master "can be a strict disciplinarian, ... his or her actions are always guided by selfless love."[25] It is notable, however, that Moti Rani's ire was not directed towards anyone to whom she had given initiation (*dīkṣā*); Krishna Prem was her *dīkṣā* guru, making Madhava Ashish her godbrother, albeit a junior one to whom she could give instruction (*śikṣā*). "Moti Rani ... was nominally Krishna Prem's disciple," observes Eichert, "but in the sequel [to the Sri Yashoda Mai era] played the part of guru to both the expatriate Englishmen."[26]

Notes

[1]Edward C. Dimock Jnr (trans.) and Tony K. Stewart (ed.), *Caitanya Caritāmṛta of Kṛṣṇadāsa Kavirāja*, (Cambridge, MA: Harvard University Press, 2000), 465–466.

[2]S. Chakravarti, 'Sri Krishnaprem's Visit to Sri Ramana Maharshi, Part III,' 5.

[3]S. Chakravarti, 'Sri Krishnaprem's Visit to Sri Ramana Maharshi, Part III,' 6.

[4]Parekh, *Himalayan Memoirs*, 46.

[5]Roy, *Yogi Sri Krishnaprem*, 5.

[6]*Ibid.*

[7]Nahar, Danino and Bandyopadhyay, *Sri Aurobindo to Dilip*, Vol. 1 (1929–1933), 10.

[8]Roy, *Yogi Sri Krishnaprem*, 5–6.

[9]'Aurobindo (Sri)', in Jones and Ryan, *Encyclopedia of Hinduism*, 53.

[10]Nautiyal, 'How I Came to Know Gopalda,' 2.

[11]'Aurobindo (Sri),' in Jones and Ryan, *Encyclopedia of Hinduism*, 53.

[12]Nautiyal, 'How I Came to Know Gopalda,' 2.

[13]Bandyopadhyay, *Sri Aurobindo to Dilip*, Vol. 4 (1938–1950), 148.

[14]'Dilip-da and his friend Yogi Krishnaprem,' in Chinmoy, *My Dilip-Da-Adoration*, Sri Chinmoy Library, 2007, para. 4, https://www.srichinmoylibrary.com/dda-8 (accessed 9 December 2022).

[15]Mooney, *Frank Baines*, 114.

[16]J. Gordon Melton, *Faiths Across Time: 5,000 Years of Religious History*, (Santa Barbara: ABC-CLIO, 2014), 884.

[17]Roy, *Yogi Sri Krishnaprem*, 122.

[18]S. Chakravarti, 'Sri Krishnaprem's Visit to Sri Ramana Maharshi, Part IV,' *The Maharshi*, 29.6, (2019), 2.

[19]Eichert, 'The Last English Saint,' 3.(Although Madhava Ashish was born in Edinburgh, his cut-glass RP accent meant he was often mistaken for English.)

[20]Madhava Ashish had befriended an older English couple in Calcutta who, he recalls, Moti Rani regarded as "parental substitutes for my psyche and therefore dangerous."

[21]Madhava Ashish, 'Sri Krishna Prem Through the Eyes of a Disciple,' 8.

[22]Madhava Ashish, 'Sri Krishna Prem Through the Eyes of a Disciple,' 15.

[23]Madhava Ashish, 'Sri Krishna Prem Through the Eyes of a Disciple,' 16.

[24]West, *The Life of Annie Besant*, 183–184.

[25]Kali Om, 'The Guru-Disciple Relationship,' *Yoga Chicago*, 20.2, para. 9, https://yogachicago.com-/2014/01/the-guru-disciple-relationship (accessed 20 December 2022).

[26]Eichert, 'The Last English Saint,' 3.

18: Pilgrims

"This world is like a rest-house on the pilgrim road.
Travellers come and stay the night, converse with fellow travellers,
share their experiences of the difficulties on the road,
are friendly or hostile to one another, and then depart and meet again no more."[1]
— Sri Yashoda Mai (1937)

Though both men would survive this trial by fire—Krishna Prem emerging "from the ordeal a softer, kinder and very much wiser man" devoid of the layer of "intellectual indifference which [he had] habitually raised between himself and others"[2]—others were not so fortunate.

Frank Baines finally left the ashram in February 1951, unable to tolerate becoming the new object of Moti Rani's attention. According to Madhava Ashish, Baines had manipulated Bob Alexander (left in charge while Krishna Prem and Moti Rani took what would become an eventful trip down to the plains) into sacking a number of employees of the ashram farm and hiring his own cowherd 'favourite,' who delivered "what little milk there was ... to Frank's cottage for their enjoyment" (Ashish, 220). The resulting row led to Baines being ordered to leave, writes Madhava Ashish, who had already fallen out with Baines after the 'bundle' incident in 1948:

> But before he had time to leave Almora, Moti had second thoughts. By her reasoning, Frank had come for the inner work, and she had no right to drive him away. So she sent him a message that he could return if he wished. Krishna Prem laid out the Tarot pack and said it was absolutely clear that he would not return, and he said he would despair of me if I could not see the truth of this reading in his layout. After what he had done to me, I loathed Frank and feared him, and I was absolutely certain that he would return, Tarot or no Tarot. He returned, and I got no pleasure at all from being proved right (Ashish, 220).

On Baines's return to Uttar Brindaban, he became for the first time a target for Moti Rani's anger, and it "was not long before he was being lambasted in a manner I was all too familiar with," continues Madhava Ashish—a situation which led to a temporary armistice between the warring ashramites and imbued his own treatment with a spiritual significance hitherto lacking:

> After a particularly bad outburst from Moti in front of us all Frank left the room. I grabbed one of Moti's cigarettes and ran after him, sensing that this might be more than he could take. He was now a companion in misery and I wanted to help.
>
> We squatted together on the verandah, sharing the cigarette. He gave a mirthless laugh, and my intuition told me that he was seeing the grim humour in receiving sympathy from the very person he had tried to get rid of. 'I demand better treatment than this,' he said—a phrase that remained with me as representing a total rejection of all that the inner work is about.
>
> Nothing I could say made any difference. The next day he told Moti he was leaving. This time he was leaving by his own choice, and Moti had no second thoughts. 'There, but for the grace of God, go I,' was my unspoken feeling. Seeing Frank suffer under Moti's whiplash had somehow changed my feelings both for him and for the punishment. What had been unadulterated hell was now modified by a sense of meaning (Ashish, 220–221).

In Baines's own words, his commitment to the 'path' was ruined by doubts he had about life at Mirtola. "In spite of my enthusiasm I did indeed have a good many reservations," he wrote. "These were to accumulate and gain force over the years, and were eventually to wreck my commitment."[3] Brian Mooney, Baines's biographer, notes that he "never quite fitted in" at the ashram,[4] and "[i]n many respects Frank turned out to be a square peg in a round hole: he talked volubly, remained actively homosexual and seemed at times to get on better with the animals than with his fellow monks."[5] He also seems to have rejected at least part of the strict Brahminical regimen followed by other ashramites: unlike Krishna Prem, Haridas and Madhava Ashish, who insisted on cooking their own food according to the traditional rules, Baines happily took his meals in the family dining room when visiting the Shahs in Naini Tal, recalls Jagdish.[6] From Mirtola, Baines went to Calcutta, where he became a columnist for *The Statesman*, and later returned to England, becoming a successful author. He died in 1987.

It is unclear when Keshab Priya, who joined the ashram alongside Baines and Madhava Ashish in 1946, left Uttar Brindaban, though no mention of him is found in the Mirtola literature after Moti Rani's death in 1951. An acquaintance reports that he became disillusioned with the later Mirtola teaching, which he felt prioritised *jñāna* over *bhakti*, and ultimately "left Almora because he wanted to be with more traditional Vaiṣṇavas." ("Krishna Prema's successors were a little too not-Indian for him," the friend adds.) He did, however, realise his ambition of taking over the running of his village *mandir*, and outlived his one-time guru. Iskcon *sannyāsī* Jayapataka Swami explained in 1976 that one "Shri Keshav Priya Brahmacari ... a disciple of that Krishna Prem, that Mr. Nixtan [sic]," was then still managing a 400-year-old temple founded by Mahesh Pandit, a companion of Nityananda, in Palpara, West Bengal.[7]

Sri Krishnarpita Mai, Moti Rani—the vivacious, mercurial, maddening daughter of the first Mirtola guru and teacher to the second and third—died of heart failure on 31 August 1951, less than a month shy of her 35th birthday and the same day as her older brother Ratan. All four of Yashoda Mai's children passed away within a 12-month window: Bhalli, the eldest, in November 1950; Bulbul, the eldest daughter, in February 1951; and Ratan and Arpita (Moti Rani) in August 1951 (Ashish, 237). "You who knew and loved her can imagine the gap she leaves behind—at least to the senses," Krishna Prem wrote to Dilip Kumar Roy that October. "You know how much she was the life and soul of the place."[8]

Moti Rani's passing was preceded by two final trips out of the ashram. The first, a pilgrimage to the eighth-century Badrinarayana Temple at Badrinath—a difficult 125-mile walk from Mirtola to a destination 11,000 feet up in the Garhwal Himalayas—took place over a five-month period in spring–summer 1949. Part of the Chota Char Dham pilgrimage circuit, in what is now the Chamoli district of Uttarakhand, Badrinath is mentioned in several Hindu scriptures, including the *Mahābhārata* and the *Bhāgavata Purāṇa*, the latter of which tells of how God, "in his incarnation as the sages Nara and Nārāyaṇa, has been undergoing great penance [there] since time immemorial for the welfare of all amiable living entities."[9]

The party, consisting of Krishna Prem, Moti Rani and Madhava Ashish, were seen off from Almora by Earl Brewster, with whom they stayed, and Khazan Chand, a prominent local doctor, once patronised by the Nehru–Gandhi family,[10] who was "very fond of Moti." "He was weeping, for he never expected to see Moti again," remembers Madhava Ashish. "To his mind the trip"—which would see Moti Rani walk nearly every step of the way at an average speed of 1mph—"was madness" (Ashish, 193).

Given Moti Rani's failing health, there was no time to book in advance the forest bungalows which dot the pilgrimage route, meaning the trio would often find it difficult to secure lodgings for the night (Ashish, 192). They also found it a problem to purchase food that could be prepared in a way that would accommodate their strict Vaiṣṇavite demands.

In the event, Moti Rani averaged six miles a day, stopping frequently to use a folding commode to relieve her "perennially upset tummy" (Ashish, 196). Krishna Prem insisted on carrying it, meaning he "had to find answers for the people who wanted to know what holy picture of the Lord he had in the [carrying] bag" (Ashish, 192). Despite her obvious health problems, Moti Rani attracted almost as much attention from fellow pilgrims as the two "white-skinned, gerua-clad figure[s]" who accompanied her, writes Madhava Ashish, who recalls one occasion where a

> row of pilgrims were squatting beside the road taking a rest. Moti was holding onto Krishna Prem's arm, and I was pushing her from behind. As we passed the pilgrims, they leant forward to touch Moti's feet. On this journey this sort of thing was happening time and again. With us she might be behaving wildly, but it was as if a great light was shining through her and simple people responded to her directly. (Ashish, 211–212)

This 'wild' behaviour escalated as the party entered Chamoli, where "there was a violent outburst of Moti's anger against Krishna Prem," culminating in Moti Rani refusing to go a step farther towards Badrinath and Krishna Prem sent to book seats on a returning bus for next morning.

Madhava Ashish continues:

> When one is constantly subjected to such outbursts, one reaches a point where it washes over one like a wave. One is numbed by the assault, and the capacity for the ordinary sort of rational thinking goes into abeyance. I could not believe that Moti would really turn back, yet this is just what she was swearing she would do.
>
> When Krishna Prem had left, she turned to me. 'Don't tell him. When we leave in the morning I shall take your arm and we shall walk up the Badrinath road.' And that is what happened. Until the moment we walked away, Krishna Prem did not know we were not catching the bus.
>
> That was a terrible day. Moti attacked both of us with unrelenting fury. At one point I was literally set to crawling on the road, rubbing

> my nose in the dirt, while pilgrims passed us—quite possibly understanding with their unencumbered peasant intelligence that the Guru was teaching her disciple a lesson in humility. What I had said or done is of no importance, and I do not remember it. (Ashish, 204–205)

The three pilgrims reached Badrinaraya Temple just before Krishna Prem's 51st birthday on 10 May, only to be refused entry (presumably on the grounds of Krishna Prem and Madhava Ashish's visible non-Indianness) by the presiding *dharmādhyakṣa*, or master of ceremonies. However, "Moti, of course, took up the cudgels, so much so that the *dharmādhyakṣa* took to going to the temple by a route that did not pass the spot where Moti was sitting," Madhava Ashish explains.

> In the end, as we circled the temple just before leaving, the Secretary seized Krishna Prem and I by our hands and dragged us up to the inner doors beyond which only the Rawal [priest] may go. Moti had won her point, though it was nothing to be particularly happy about: a victory over hide-bound orthodoxy and a small-time pundit. What was important was something quite different, something that was as much in every step of the journey as it was in whatever one found at the end. (Ashish, 213)

On the return journey, the ashram took possession of a new dog, Dabbu, a *Bhotia* (Himalayan sheepdog) puppy purchased by Krishna Prem from a group of migrating hill people (Ashish, 213–214). By this point, both Krishna Prem and Moti Rani were beginning to suffer from vitamin C deficiency, characterised by sore tongues and throats, though the latter was apparently still able to bring her famous faith healing abilities to bear on other people. When one "unhappy man went past on a horse, groaning with back pain and begging Moti to help him," writes Madhava Ashish, "she had him off the horse and lying flat on his face with his back bare. I produced the bottle of lotion for sprains (which we had not had to use) and liberally applied it together with a lot of her psychic power, for the man got up cured and went on his way singing her praises" (Ashish, 217).

Back in Almora, the vitamin C-starved pilgrims "filled ourselves with vegetables and fruit" while their "old friend Dr Khazan Chand declared that Moti's survival was a triumph of mind over matter, [as] his wife disclosed that he had been up on the roof of his house at night, pouring out libations towards Badrinath with prayers for Moti's safe return" (Ashish, 218).

The second trip, from November 1950 to February 1951 (prior to Baines's leaving), was rather less strenuous, taking in Lucknow, where Moti Rani had a dentist's appointment; Calcutta, where Madhava Ashish, at the ailing Moti Rani's urging, bought the Ford estate car which would deliver them back to Mirtola; and Benares, where the party spent a fortnight with Krishna Prem's sister, Barbara Dobb (Ashish, 224—228). Madhava Ashish remembers Krishna Prem's reunion with Barbara after 30 years apart:

> It was a happy fortnight, with Moti putting herself out to make the visit pleasant for Barbara. I would fetch Barbara from Clarke's Hotel where she was staying to spend the day with us. There was a trip to Sarnath [where the Buddha is said to have delivered his 'sermon in the deer park' shortly after attaining enlightenment], a boat ride on the Ganga, and a trip to the maharaja's palace at Ramnagar. Finally, Barbara was put on the train to Lucknow where she would join [her husband] Maurice. (Ashish, 228)

In Lucknow, in November 1950, Krishna Prem also met for the last time with Roy, who describes this final meeting, also attended by Dilip Kumar Roy's new disciple Indira Devi:

> When [we learnt] that Motirani was very ill we were both greatly concerned—for Indira too had grown to admire and love her with all her heart, having heard from me all about her aspiration, purity, simplicity and courage which could laugh death to scorn. This time we both were deeply moved to see how she had flowered despite her protracted illness. She could hardly move without help. It was, indeed, a touching sight to see the tenderness with which Krishnaprem lifted her feet with his hands to deposit them in the motor car everytime she had to go out to the doctor's. We were no less impressed by her cheerfulness. Her face was wan and emaciated, but her laughter was still as refreshing and radiant as before, and last, though not least, she was sparring, joking and teasing everybody as vivaciously as ever! Krishnaprem once told me with some pride: "What courage!" I told him: "Yes, Krishnaprem, she is one in a million and has always reminded me of Hugh Walpole's saying: 'It is not life that matters but the courage you bring to it.'"[11]

After this "relatively calm interlude," the next six months—from the trio's return to the ashram in February to Moti Rani's death that August—were characterised by "the violence of her attacks on Gopalda and [Madhava Ashish, which] rose in a crescendo" (Ashish, 230). The hapless Britons, dismissed as "godless aliens" who might not even know how to cremate her body properly,[12] found the final stage of Moti Rani's onslaught particularly difficult to endure; at one point Krishna Prem was said to be on the brink of suicide.[13] This "unabated fury" (Ashish, 231)—which Madhava Ashish characterises as a "direct attack on the ego, for any display of the ego's self-defence mechanism in the form of excuses, self-justification, evasions and even apologies and pleas for forgiveness might give rise to raging fury in which she could throw [verbal] things at me which I must return so that she could throw them again" (Ashish, 230)—was, however, finally beginning to have the desired effect. He writes:

> I had been pulped into a jelly but now I was beginning to find something in the depths of my being that was firm and supportive.
>
> Moti's attacks continued ... but she had brought me to a point where new life had begun to grow. (Ashish, 231)

Notes

[1]Tandan, 'Metaphors and Quotes of Yashoda Mai,' 3.

[2]Madhava Ashish, 'Sri Krishna Prem Through the Eyes of a Disciple,' 27–28.

[3]Mooney, *Frank Baines*, 105.

[4]Mooney, *Frank Baines*, 114.

[5]Mooney, *Frank Baines*, 105.

[6]Shah, 'Memoirs,' 2.

[7]Prahlad Nrsimha das, 'Room Conversation About Māyāpur Construction', *Bhaktivedanta Vedabase*, Czech Republic, 2017, https://vedabase.io/en/library/transcripts/760819r1hyd (accessed 28 September 2022).

[8]Roy, *Yogi Sri Krishnaprem*, 262.

[9]His Divine Grace AC Bhaktivedanta Swami Prabhupāda (trans.), *Śrīmad Bhāgavatam*, Canto 3: 'The Status Quo,' ch. 4 ('Vidura Approaches Maitreya'), v. 22, *PrabhupadaBooks.com*, 2014, https://prabhupadabooks.com/sb/3/4/22 (accessed 21 December 2022).

[10]Sonia Gandhi (ed.), *Two Alone, Two Together: Letters Between Indira Gandhi and Jawaharlal Nehru, 1940–1964*, (London: Hodder & Stoughton, 1992), 438.

[11]Roy, *Yogi Sri Krishnaprem*, 127–128.

[12]Pandey, *Guru by Your Bedside*, 61–62.

[13]*Ibid.*

PART III

UNIVERSALIST

19: "Attainment"

"Ashish has now taken charge of the whole place—including me."[1]
— Sri Krishna Prem (1958)

Moti Rani was cremated in Benares at the Manikarnika *ghāṭ* (Ashish, 237), among the oldest and holiest of the cremation grounds that line the Ganges in that holiest of cities. Krishna Prem, Haridas and Madhava Ashish arrived in Benares in the early morning. There, with the assistance of a party of men from the local Anandamayi Ma ashram who "with great kindness stopped and took over all the arrangements that we were too exhausted to make" (Ashish, 237), and the help of the attendant at the *ghāṭ*, they committed her exhausted body to the eternal flame.

Moti Rani had requested a cremation in Benares,[2] and both Krishna Prem and Madhava Ashish felt a similar pull towards the city and the river that lies at its heart, which they interpreted as a symbol of the quest to reconnect with and return to one's true, divine nature, free of the 'contamination' of material life. Satish Datt Pandey describes a favourite analogy of the gurus, that of "the 'north-flowing Ganges:'"

> Symbolizing the flow of life, the manifested universe, her [the Ganges'] source was 'up there' in the pure, pristine glacier. During the course of the flow, however, the pure waters receive all kinds of contamination as they rush towards the ocean of death. But then at some stage of its course, the river makes a distinct about-turn and starts flowing north again—towards its source. At that site it is regarded as being at its sacred best. For those who care to take note of and learn from concrete symbols, this was a potent pointer that it is possible for us also to consciously reset our normal orientation towards our source. ... [I]t is possible to be free—free from whatever makes us forget our source, effectively delinks us from it, keeps us from standing in our

> true nature, and deludes us into believing ourselves to be what we are not.[3]

The story of the frenetic journey down from Ranikhet to Benares—with Madhava Ashish, kept awake with tea, cigarettes and glucose sweets, driving the trio, plus Moti Rani's body, overnight from Ranikhet in the rapidly disintegrating Ford they had purchased in Calcutta (Ashish, 236)—became the stuff of legend, and was recounted by Krishna Prem and Madhava Ashish for years after the event. (The latter compared it to the *Mahābhārata*'s account of Arjuna's chariot bursting into flames at the end of the Kurukshetra war.[4]) It also travelled well beyond the confines of Mirtola: the French philosopher Alain Daniélou, in his autobiography *The Way to the Labyrinth*, writes of hearing about the "series of fantastic adventures" involving "rented cars [sic] that kept breaking down."[5]

Penelope Phipps shares her recollection of one of "the stories we were told of [the gurus'] life" at Mirtola:

> I still have a vivid recollection of Gopalda's telling me that when Moti Rani was dying of kidney trouble, she had expressed a wish that her body be cremated at Benares. In their old car Ashish drove with Gopalda, on and on, for about two days, as the journey had to be done quickly in the heat, twice falling asleep, and the car twice going off the road. Ashish said, 'That car was held together by love. I am an engineer and I know!' Gopalda said, 'Your brother has been through a lot, Penelope. Not many people could have stood it.'[6]

Madhava Ashish recalls that it took him and Krishna Prem—who returned to the ashram via Bankura, where they visited Yashoda Mai's brother, and Vrindavan —"a fortnight to get back to some sort of [normality]" after Moti Rani's cremation. "Gopalda remarked that he felt the two of us were living in a single vast sphere which separated us from the world. 'I see you pushing against it sometimes, but it does not give way,' he said" (Ashish, 238).

As time went on, the transformative effects of Moti Rani's relentless, unconventional 'teaching,' particularly in the last six months of her life, on the two men started to become clear—especially in Sri Krishna Prem, who, writes Madhava Ashish, had finally begun to shed the "shining intellect[tual] ... armour" that formerly "kept one from entering the magic circle of his dedication to Sri Krishna and his Guru:"[7]

> It slowly appeared that, in smashing the two of us and then using the extreme intensity of the situation, Moti had left two broken and

> re-made people with nothing but each other to hold on to. Hence Gopalda's feeling of the glass sphere which contained us. I was no longer the inferior disciple of the great scholar and famous Krishna-bhakta, Sri Krishna Prem, with his smooth, impenetrable exterior and a barbed-wire fence around his heart. For a companion I had a warm-hearted, gentle, still very learned and utterly human friend. I fell as completely in love with him as I had with Moti. Indeed, as time went on, one saw that Moti's hammering had released his repressed feminine side. (Ashish, 239–240)

Key to this transformation was the fact that Krishna Prem, because of the "suffering [Moti Rani] imposed on him," had "come to accept emotional pain as an essential part of life," Madhava Ashish adds, "against which one must not erect barriers when one aspires to psychic wholeness."[8] Satish Datt Pandey and Sy Ginsburg suggest that while Krishna Prem, "endowed with a razor-sharp mind, phenomenal memory and a great flow of feelings[,] taught in his own way," Moti Rani "created conditions and opportunities for practising and integrating the teaching."[9]

Gabriel Monod-Herzen recounts his impressions of the 'new,' warmer Krishna Prem described by Madhava Ashish on his second visit to Mirtola in 1953, nine years after the first:

> Arriving at Uttar Brindaban, seeing my friend's tall figure appear at the top of the path, I had the distinct impression that I found him internally grown and transformed.
>
> The very life of the community had evolved. Its founder was no longer there; in front of the temple entrance, a small monument had been erected to contain her ashes. Her daughter, Moti Rani, had also left this world after receiving ordination [*sannyāsa*]. The lives of those who remained had been stripped of what was not essential. Mentally and materially, visitors were welcomed more easily; the human warmth was greater than before. It was all just outward forms, but I knew from experience that they could only be the faithful expression of an inner change ...[10]

Pandey, who "only saw the end product of what [Krishna Prem] had gone through," says it was obvious that their "sustained effort" to hold on in the face of Moti Rani's attacks "had gone a long way to helping [him] to hold on to that 'something' [in oneself] that is not shaken by any turmoil."[11]

These changes were also apparent to Gertrude Emerson Sen, to whose Kundan House, a "natural stopping-off place between Almora and Mirtola,"[12]

Yashoda Mai, Krishna Prem, Haridas and, later, Madhava Ashish were regular visitors. "If he had ever had any ego," Sen writes, "it seemed to have utterly vanished into thin air. One night after dinner, when he had already washed his mouth with cold water, a jug of hot water was belatedly brought. 'I have just rinsed my mouth,' he said. 'But this is hot water!' my husband insisted. 'All right,' he said sweetly, and proceeded meekly to rinse his mouth again."[13] Her husband, the scientist Boshi Sen, with whom Krishna Prem had enjoyed decades of good-natured intellectual jousting, now joked: "There is no longer any fun in talking to you. We agree about everything."[14]

Karan Singh, whose *Autobiography* relates Krishna Prem's influence on both his inner and outer life, including the decision to become involved in national politics, writes that by the time of his first visit to Mirtola in 1958, Krishna Prem and Madhava Ashish had become so alike that they gave the impression of being one person in two bodies:

> During the conversation Sri Madhava Ashish would join from time to time in such an effortless manner that it appeared almost as if I was talking to a single mind divided into two bodies. The relationship between the guru and his disciple—'Gopalda' and 'Ashishda,' as they were called—was unique. Sri Krishnaprem's words came from the depth of great spiritual achievement, the vision of a true seer. When he spoke of Krishna, his beloved, the eternal lover of all beings, his eyes would glow with a strange radiance and his whole body seemed vibrant with inner joy. Never will I forget the glory of his presence when, along with Ashishda, the three of us would sit by the glowing embers in that little room in Mirtola, talking deep into the long winter nights. We talked of everything—politics, people, relationships, books, dreams. To every topic they would bring a fresh approach, constantly linking outer activity with inner aspiration. They looked upon life as a series of concentric circles, each covering different areas of activity but all centred in the self. Here were the great teachings of the Upanishads brought alive by a pair of vibrant Englishmen born and raised ten thousand miles away from India. Keen intellectual perception combined with deep emotional empathy enabled them to analyse my life-situation in a manner no one else had ever done, and in the process gave me a deeper awareness of my inner being. And even more eloquent than their words were their silences, when their eyes would lock into a flow of power so tangible that I hardly dared breathe lest it be disturbed.[15]

Madhu Tandan also writes about "two men, one with clear blue eyes that seemed not to look at you but through you, and the other—much younger—who seemed to telepathically pick up a half-finished sentence from his companion."[16] "Those fortunate to encounter this unique pair at Mirtola," adds Donald Eichert, "or strolling by the lake in Nainital were magicked. A vision in *gerua* (ochre), they radiated a kind of cool fire. People gravitated to them.... "[17]

Where guru and disciple did diverge, their relationship was characterised by a parent–child dynamic (in contrast to what Valentine Penrose described as the brother–sister bond of Krishna Prem and Yashoda Mai), according to Singh, who considers himself a disciple of both.[18] In his semi-autobiographical novel *The Mountain of Shiva*,[19] Singh—who was himself hailed as a "rare example of a prominent politician, a great scholar, and a sincere spiritual practitioner, all rolled into one,"[20] by the yogi and educator Sri Madhukarnath (Sri M)—writes about his impressions of 'Madan,' the protege of the guru of 'Ananda Ashram':

> Calm, gentle, dedicated, he assisted Maharaj [Krishna Prem] in the daily prayers and arati in the temple, and took over when Maharaj was on tour. Apart from his outer beauty, he developed an inner dimension that was as rare as it was precious. He was totally devoted to Maharaj, who looked upon him as his spiritual son, rather like Ramakrishna did to Vivekananda.[21]

Singh also recalls the pair's propensity for laughter, connecting their sense of humour with Krishna Prem's statement in *The Yoga of the Kaṭhopanishad* that 'laughter was given by the Gods to man and it was one of their choicest gifts.' Singh says, "It was amazing how alert and nimble their minds were, and what a tremendous sense of humour they had.... Contrary to the popular conception that gurus are sombre, rather boring fanatics, here was a pair full of fun and laughter."[22] Similarly, Dilip Kumar Roy remembers:

> [O]nce it so happened that I just could not face the music; it seemed as though the odds were hundred to one against me and so, in sheer despair, I wrote to Krishnaprem that I had finally decided to call it a day, admitting defeat. In explanation, I added that I had made up my mind to retire into a complete seclusion where I must henceforward stay in sombre silence, bidding good-bye to laughter and the merry-go-round of social life.
>
> To that he wrote back with alacrity:
>
> "But what is this awful news about your giving up laughter? Give up anything else you like: arguing, visitors, reading, writing,—but if you give up laughing, I, for one, shall weep. I read it out to Moti and she, too, was quite horrified! If you don't at once forswear such

> an awful heresy I shall never dare to meet you again. It would really be too awful! You would come silently into the room, perhaps brushing away a tear from your eye, and say to me in a solemn tone: 'Brother! shall we meditate together a little?' Appalling! And then we should look at each other surreptitiously from downcast eyelids to see whose meditation was deepest! And then: 'Shall we have a little holy talk together, brother?' Ghastly! I don't really believe you can be contemplating anything so dreadful!"[23]

For Sri Madhava Ashish, who was at this time legally confirmed as Krishna Prem's successor, as well as given responsibility for initiating new disciples, one of his guru's "most outstanding qualities" was "the way he could divest himself of authority, handing over the trusteeship of the ashram, the uncompleted manuscript of a book, responsibility for the temple management, even his personal correspondence and the initiation and instruction of his followers to a disciple who was thereby forced to overcome his reluctance to face any such challenges."[24] This "handing over"—after which new disciples were considered jointly the *śiṣyas* of both men—was "a definite psychic act and not a mere outer formality," Krishna Prem explained to Singh, "so that I would not care to (even if I could) go back on it now though I am entirely associated with him in any *dīkṣā* that he gives."[25] Jagdish Shah remembers he and Rambha being given *dīkṣā* by "Ashish Da," who "whisper[ed] the mantra in our right ears [while] Gopal Da stood on our left side."[26]

The book described by Madhava Ashish was Krishna Prem's unfinished commentary on the 'Stanzas of Dzyan,' the volume of esoteric history (written in a supposedly lost language of Atlantis called Senzar) known only via HP Blavatsky's *The Secret Doctrine* (1888). Feeling unable to finish the book, originally started in the late 1930s (see chapter 11), Krishna Prem now tasked his disciple with completing the job:

> In the intervening years of spiritual discipline his nature had changed and developed so markedly that he told a friend who was pressing him to publish: 'I cannot finish it. The man who wrote it no longer exists. But,' he added, 'I might rewrite it.'[27]

The first volume, which correlates with volume one ('Cosmogenesis') of Blavatsky's *The Secret Doctrine*, detailing the origin of the universe, was first published in 1966 by the Theosophical Publishing House in Adyar as *Man, the Measure of All Things: In the Stanzas of Dzyan*, and attributed to Sri Krishna Prem and Sri Madhava Ashish. ("Although he insisted my name appear as co-author, the book is his," the latter writes in the preface to the first US edition, published in

1969. "If I have contributed anything of value, it is because he has guided me in all things since I first met him."[28]) A "transcendentally difficult book about the origin and purpose of the Universe,"[29] *Man, the Measure of All Things* was followed by *Man, Son of Man*, which deals with volume two ('Anthropogenesis') of Blavatsky's *The Secret Doctrine*, describing the Lemurian, Atlantean and other 'Root-Races' that preceded (and will succeed) man over millennia. *Man, Son of Man* is by Madhava Ashish alone, and was released in 1970.

Krishna Prem continued to work on the *Man* books well into 1965, the year of his death. "Extraordinarily," he and Madhava Ashish "turned to this abstruse text with relish at bedtime after a hard day's work on the temple and farm that began at 5 a.m.," recalls Bill Aitken, visiting in April of that year. "Pumping up a Petromax lamp to give brilliant light to replace the flickering flame of the kerosene lantern they sent away visitors at 10 p.m. and got down (on the floor) to some seriously introspective writing.... The source of their enthusiasm was both mystifying and electrifying."[30]

The other man who at one time might have been considered a potential successor to Krishna Prem, Sri Haridas, died of leukaemia aged 58 on 18 July 1957.[31] After his diagnosis in February he refused all medical treatment, continuing to work in his dispensary after telling the doctors at Lucknow—many of them his old students, who begged him to stay in hospital—"I know you can keep me alive on other people's blood. I am not prepared to live like that" (Ashish, 88).

Having largely escaped the attentions of Moti Rani, Haridas's "basic character," according to Madhava Ashish, "remained that of an English gentleman" (Ashish, 82). However, in facing his own mortality, Madhava Ashish says, the former Dr Alexander "handled himself better than many" *sādhus*:

> [O]ne day he came to Gopalda. "Today it took me half an hour to get up to the dispensary," he said, "I don't feel I can go on." "Then stop," replied Gopalda. From then to his death was exactly twelve days. It was like a man going downstairs. If one asked him what he would like for food the next day, by the next day he could not take it. We moved him from the temple room to Moti's old cottage, which had been fitted up for Moti with a flush commode, and so would be much more convenient for a sick person. Also, there was room for his

> Gopalda to stay and look after him, which would have been difficult in the tiny temple room.
>
> We also offered him the use of an interior-spring mattress, which had been left behind when Mrs Webb died. He refused it. "After all," he said, "when one is going to leave the body one can't expect to be comfortable." (Ashish, 88–89)

Haridas's King's College obituary describes both his skill as a physician and his dedication to the inner quest. In his lifetime, it notes, people would travel to Uttar Brindaban

> for twenty miles or more, on foot or carried in litters, to obtain his treatment, and he would see some fifty or sixty patients a day. He could work, if necessary, without any of the modern aids to which doctors are accustomed. Often it would seem beyond his powers to attend to all his patients personally, and yet somehow he always did. This, the thing that he knew best how to do, he thought of as his own personal offering to the Lord....
>
> He had a wiry intense nature which, even when his health had begun to fail, made him drive himself mercilessly; yet he often said that he regretted his choice of a profession, and that if he were born again he would not repeat it. Medicine was never more than his outer life. His real interest was the yoga for which he had come.[32]

Haridas's passing left Krishna Prem and Madhava Ashish as the only remaining full-time ashramites, and Krishna Prem as the sole resident disciple of the late Sri Yashoda Mai. The ashram dispensary, meanwhile, moved to Panuanaula, a larger village 3km from Mirtola, and was manned by Kishan Singh Negi, who had worked for Alexander since boyhood, when the late doctor had trained him as a compounder. The dispensary space at Uttar Brindaban, located in the temple basement, become a storeroom.[33]

The Canadian journalist Donald Eichert, Krishna Prem's disciple from 1957[34] and a resident of Mirtola in the Madhava Ashish years (an attempt to live in the ashram in Krishna Prem's time having been quickly abandoned because Eichert "missed his chocolates, nuts and city life," according to his Keble College obituary [35]) suggests that by the time of Monod-Herzen and Singh's visits, Sri Krishna

Prem had achieved the self-realisation, or spiritual attainment, towards which he had been working for the past three decades. According to Eichert, Krishna Prem "realized in the early 1950s,"[36] with Madhava Ashish following in 1956, during a four-month stay in Calcutta with his guru. (A Bengali disciple of Krishna Prem is said to have observed: "Maharaj, I am seeing a wonderful change in Ashishda." "Yes," replied Krishna Prem. "What it took me twenty years to do, Ashish did in ten."[37])

Eichert leaves the nature of such 'realisation,' which might also be called liberation or enlightenment, unclear, and the concept has different connotations in the various spiritual traditions with which the Mirtola gurus were associated. Whereas for an *Advaitin,* liberation (*mokṣa*) comes with the understanding that individual souls are nondifferent from the impersonal Brahman, this view is rejected by Vaiṣṇavas because it precludes the possibility of a loving relationship between Krishna and his devotees.[38] (The *Bhāgavata Purāṇa* even states that "devoid of the presence of the beloved Lord, *mokṣa* is, in fact, equal to hell."[39]). For Gauḍīya Vaiṣṇavas, *prem,* holy love for Krishna, is the final and highest objective of life. For Buddhists, meanwhile, *Nirvāṇa* is the extinguishing of the "triple fire of greed, hatred, and delusion" which leads to doubt, worry, anxiety and fear.[40]

While the esotericist Bruce Burger assesses that Krishna Prem had 'attained' in the *Vedantic* sense, having "personally realized the Self, the Himalayan Truth that all creation is the play of consciousness of the universe as one living being,"[41] Madhava Ashish is more ambiguous, writing that his guru achieved, or at least neared, a nonspecific form of *mūkti* (emancipation)—any form of liberation from *samsāra,* the cycle of death and rebirth—in the years following Yashoda Mai's death. Expressing his opinion that the *Yoga* books came from the pen of an inspired, but not yet realised, man, he writes: "Many people will feel that a disciple should not dare to question his Guru's status in this fashion. My personal feeling is that it damages our perceptions of the Spirit if we portray a man as a mahatma before he is one. I had the inestimable privilege of living with Krishna Prem for nineteen years while he changed from being an inspired, dedicated and very remarkable man to something approaching the complete or 'Perfected' man." (Ashish, 145–146)

This 'perfection,' Aitken remembers, manifested as an obvious "divinity which Gopalda's being radiated:"

> hard to define, impossible to put into words, yet utterly as real as love in the heart. Which, "when a man has it, he wants nothing more."[42]

Madhava Ashish highlights an incident which challenged his guru's belief in the Vaiṣṇava doctrine, drawn from the *Bhagavad Gītā,* that one's consciousness at the time of death determines the destination of the soul and which also helped him along to the "final stage" on his spiritual journey:

> [I]t was after the monsoon in [1945] that he fell ill in Brindaban and found his famous mind to be uncontrollable on account of the fever. And then he reasoned to himself: Since most people are ill when they die, and if illness disturbed the mind in this manner, what could be made of the teaching that the person's state of mind at death determines his after-death experience? If this were true, then the outlook for himself would be bad.
>
> It was only then that he fully understood that what has to be found is totally beyond the thinking mind. Thus he set foot upon the final stage of the inner path. (Ashish, 146)

Elsewhere, Madhava Ashish writes that this attainment—described, using Krishna Prem's own words, as "feeling and thought [being] fused into a unity"—was "complete" by the early '60s, ten years after Moti Rani's death.[43] In him, he explained, it was his mind that developed late, under Krishna Prem's tutelage; in Krishna Prem, it was the other way round: "It was his undeveloped, unexploited emotions that led to transformation."[44] Singh confirms that this fusion involved integrating the "two halves of the human psyche—the male and the female, [or] the emotional and intellectual." Without this integration," Krishna Prem taught, "man remains a partial being constantly at war with himself, unable to move onward across what the *Kaṭha Upaniṣad* calls the razor-edged path."[45]

Mirroring the shedding of his inner "armour," Sri Krishna Prem now began to dispense with the external baggage he had accumulated in the preceding decades, beginning with the most visible reminder of his diminished intellectualism: Uttar Brindaban's voluminous library.

Formerly occupying pride of place in the ashram, the library became the first victim of what Madhava Ashish calls the "great clear-out [of] 1956" (Ashish, 108), with its books given away and the library building itself transformed into residential quarters.[46] "There are no books in it now," observed Anne Marshall in the late 1950s. "Krishna Prem and Madhava Ashish have disposed of them all."[47] Similarly, Timothy Leary recalls being told: "We have given most of the library away. [We kept only] old alchemical texts [and a]ncient gnostic commentaries."[48] By Krishna Prem's estimation, the pair got rid of some three quarters of the ashram's books. ("Too many books aren't a good thing," he explained to his friend Rajen Ganguli.[49]) Yet he remained a voracious reader: Jagdish Shah remembers his guru "finishing five of Churchill's six volumes of *The Second World War*" ("He would have read all six but the first one had been lost by a friend," Shah adds).[50] Moti Rani's small "rose-covered cabin" was also turned into a guesthouse.[51]

Also included in the "great clear-out" were the bookcase Krishna Prem had made for Yashoda Mai at Chilkapita—burnt "as part of his effort to break from the images of what he had been in those days" (Ashish, 108)—as well as *vigrahas* of Krishna, Ganesh and the Buddha and several Shiva *liṅgams*.[52] Gertrude Emerson Sen remembers:

> We had, on former occasions, been gifted with a silver cup of Moti Rani's and a brass incense-burner of Haridas's. Now other things began to come down from Mirtola. A baby Krishna of brass and a stone Krishna in the flute posture arrived. They were followed by a little Burmese carving of a Buddhist monk and begging bowl. Next, a heavy box of books made its appearance, and we heard that several more boxes of books were on their way to the Ramakrishna Ashram and the local college. The bee-hives had already gone elsewhere. They were just cleaning up, we were told—throwing away, giving away, getting rid of superfluous things, generally simplifying life at Mirtola.[53]

The marble Krishna statue in Yashoda Mai's *samādhi*, as well as a small Buddha temple located nearby, were also found new owners.[54]

This process of simplification also extended to Krishna Prem's appearance, with both he and Madhava Ashish doing away with the *tilak* and wooden neck beads that had formerly identified them to the world as Vaiṣṇavas. Emerson Sen continues:

> The Vaishnava mark on the forehead, the yellow U with a thin black line drawn through the centre and running down to the bridge of the nose, had been wiped off. He no longer wore his *mālā* of *tulsi* beads, or if he did, it was hidden beneath the new style of dress he had adopted, for greater comfort—a straight cotton sheet, dyed *gerua*, sown [sic] up at the sides but with openings left for the arms to come through, and a hole cut in the middle for the head. This was tied round the waist with a folded twist of cloth, and in winter he added an old sweater. It was not a very becoming garment but, then, he cared nothing about his looks.[55]

Bill Aitken compares this new garment to the light robe worn by the famous Sultanganj Buddha sculpture, with Krishna Prem returning to the Buddhist-inspired dress with which he had briefly experimented in the 1930s. This "diaphanous ... white cotton sheet slit in the middle for the head to go through" was left open at the sides in the warmer plains but "stitched up in the cooler hills," Aitken explains. "He hand dyed it gerua (brick-red ochre), after the colour of the flames of the funeral pyre, to signify sannyas or Vaishnav vairagya—renunciation and death to worldly things."[56]

The decision to dispense with *tilaks*, meanwhile, may have been influenced by the increasing importance Krishna Prem placed on the 'integration' of all aspects of the human psyche: intellectual and emotional, masculine and feminine, active and meditative. Pandey writes:

> Talking about the well-known practice in many sects, including the Vaishnav, of putting a *tilak* (a caste mark, often in sandal paste) on various parts of one's body, he explained that the idea behind this was to declare that that particular area was being offered to the deity. Thus, *tilaks* were put not only on the forehead but also on the arms and chest. Never, however, anywhere below the waist—that part of the body being 'impure' and not fit to be offered. Thus, convention cuts our human integration into half, concluded Gopal Da, and offers only one half! (The other half remains unoffered, a mess left behind, which will bog one down.)[57]

Ralph Metzner, who studied with Lama Govinda in the 1960s,[58] recalls that Krishna Prem explained this concept in the context of the esoteric tantric tradition which emphasises the presence of the divine feminine (Devi) in material nature. He writes:

> [A]mong certain sects of the Hindu *tantra*, known as "followers of the left-hand path" (*vāmacārī*), the acceptance of the female took the form of yogic *sādhanā* by couples rather than the individuals, and the union of male with female was practiced on both the inner and the outer planes, preferably of course by the woman as well as the man. The left side of the body in *tantra* is the female side ... A deeper interpretation of the term was given to me in conversation with the late Srī Krishna Prem, an Englishman who had made a profound, lifelong study of the Hindu yogas and *tantras*. The left hand is our undeveloped hand, our more unconscious aspect; and so the *vāmacārī* represents the strategy of developing one's weakest function in order to bring about integration; a strategy we find especially influenced by the Sūfis and by Gurdjieff.[59]

Jagdish Nautiyal comments on the feminine qualities brought to the surface in Krishna Prem by Moti Rani's rough treatment, writing that "[a]ffection seemed to ooze out of him and he gave me the feeling of a mother (not father);"[60] as does Aitken, who was initiated by Madhava Ashish (who gave him the mantra) in the presence of Krishna Prem and the *Ṭhākurs*. "I love Gopalda more," he says, "because (if not too fanciful) the divinity in Ashishda still comes across as [one] that I associate with the stern male Abrahamic deity, whereas Gopalda's divine nature was that of alma mater—exposure to the broad bosom of the pre-Abrahamic Mother Goddess."[61] Elsewhere, Aitken writes about Krishna Prem's "strong maternal instinct" and his deploring of "the lack of it in others," such as Sarala Behn, whom he described as "a man without a penis."[62]

To followers of Ramakrishna Paramahamsa, the prominence, in the masculine figure of Krishna Prem, of perceived feminine qualities would be in accordance with Ramana Maharshi's earlier assessment of his visitor as a "*bhakta* and *jñānī* in one" (ie possessing both *bhakti* and *jñāna*). According to Ramakrishna—a one-time priest of the Kāli temple in Dakshineswar, Calcutta (modern Kolkata)—*jñāna*, "mere knowledge of God," is 'male,' while *bhakti* is 'female.' "*Jñāna*, being a male, is obliged to stand and wait in the outer court of Divine Mother [Kāli]'s home," he argued, "whereas *bhakti*, being female, goes direct to the inner apartments, to the very presence of the Mother."[63]

However, the Mirtola teaching—reflecting Jungian ideas about the *animus* and *anima*, the unconscious masculine and feminine aspects of a person[64]—primarily connected these masculine and feminine sides with, respectively, the rational and irrational halves of one's psyche, Krishna Prem explaining that "in every man there is a woman (and vice versa) who may come to the surface at appropriate moments."[65] To ensure the 'right' side of their personality surfaced in such moments, ashramites were encouraged to work on balancing their 'male' and 'female' sides and to recognise if one half had become dominant. Pandey gives a practical example of such work dating from the final years of Krishna Prem's life, when the "feminine aspect of his psyche was becoming more prominent and evident:"

> When he was seriously ill with an abdominal obstruction, a doctor was brought in during a visit to Nainital, who advised an exploratory opening up of the abdomen. As soon as the doctor left, Gopal Da flew into a temper and wanted to leave immediately. No amount of reasoning seemed to pacify him. Then it suddenly struck Ashish Da that the real reason for his anger was that many years ago the same doctor had treated and almost killed Moti Rani, for whom Gopal Da has immense love and regard. Once this was suggested to him, all his anger vanished. The seemingly impossible irrationality of the 'feminine' side of a person's psyche can often be dealt with and reconciled

by listening to appropriate rational ('masculine') advice, which may help in identifying the hidden reason behind it. In this case, Ashish Da had provided that advice and Gopal Da had listened to it [to his] advantage.[66]

Notes

[1]'Sri Krishnaprem's Letters,' 20.

[2]Phipps, 'Sri Krishna Prem Remembered,' 274.

[3]Pandey, *Guru by Your Bedside*, 14–15.

[4]Pandey, *Guru by Your Bedside*, 14–15.

[5]Alain Daniélou, *The Way to the Labyrinth: Memories of East and West*, (New York: New Directions, 1987), 168.

[6]Phipps, 'Sri Krishna Prem Remembered,' 274–275.

[7]Madhava Ashish, 'Preface,' in Krishna Prem and Madhava Ashish, *Man, the Measure of All Things*, 8.

[8]Madhava Ashish, 'Sri Krishna Prem Through the Eyes of a Disciple,' 28.

[9]Ginsburg and Pandey, 'Introduction,' in Madhava Ashish, *An Open Window*, x.

[10]Monod-Herzen, 'On Sri Krishnaprem,' 311.

[11]Pandey, *Guru by Your Bedside*, 62.

[12]Sen, 'Sri Krishnaprem,' xiv.

[13]Sen, 'Sri Krishnaprem,' xviii.

[14]Mehra, *Nearer Heaven than Earth*, 507.

[15]Singh, *Autobiography*, 209.

[16]Tandan, *Faith & Fire*, 25.

[17]Eichert, 'The Last English Saint,' 4.

[18]Karan Singh, conversation with the author, 13 June 2021.

[19]The book, which follows the spiritual journey of young 'Ashok' (Singh), recasts Krishna Prem as 'Ananda Maharaj,' a devotee of Shiva, and Madhava Ashish as 'Madan,' as well as relocating most of the action to an ashram near Srinagar, in Singh's homeland of Kashmir.

[20]Sri M, *Apprenticed to a Himalayan Master: A Yogi's Autobiography*, 4th imp., (Kodagu: Magenta Press, 2011), ch. 49, 'The Kailash-Manasarovar Yatra,' para. 1.

[21]Karan Singh, *The Mountain of Shiva*, ch. 10 (Epilogue), para. 19.

[22]Singh, *Autobiography*, 208.

[23]Roy, *Yogi Sri Krishnaprem*, 48–49.

[24]Madhava Ashish, 'Sri Krishna Prem Through the Eyes of a Disciple,' 29.

[25]Singh, *Letters from Mirtola*, 14–15.

[26]Shah, 'Memoirs,' 5.

[27]Madhava Ashish, 'Preface,' in Krishna Prem and Madhava Ashish, *Man, the Measure of All Things*, 6.

[28]*Ibid.*

[29]Eichert, 'The Last English Saint,' 5.

[30]Aitken, 'Sri Krishna Prem in the Last Years,' 266.

[31]'Robert Dudley Alexander (Sri Haridas),' 19.

[32]'Robert Dudley Alexander (Sri Haridas),' 19.

[33]Bill Aitken, email to the author, 7 January 2023.

[34]'Our Contributors,' *India International Centre Quarterly*, 26.4/27.1, (1999/2000), 192.

[35]'Donald Peter Eichert (1948),' *The Record*, (2011/2012), 41.

[36]Eichert, 'The Last English Saint,' 4.

[37]*Ibid.*

[38]Ravi M. Gupta, *The Caitanya Vaiṣṇava Vedānta of Jīva Gosvāmī: When Knowledge Meets Devotion*, (Abingdon: Routledge, 2007), 14.

[39]Edwin F. Bryant, *Bhakti Yoga: Tales and Teachings from the Bhāgavata Purāṇa*, ebook edn, (New York: Farrar, Straus and Giroux, 2017), 129.

[40]Damien Keown, 'The Meaning of Nirvana in Buddhism Explained,' *Tricycle*, (New York: the Tricycle Foundation, 2016), https://tricycle.org/magazine/nirvana (accessed 27 December 2022).

[41]Bruce Burger, *Esoteric Anatomy: The Body As Consciousness*, (Berkeley: North Atlantic Books, 1998), 179.

[42]Bill Aitken, email to the author, 24 June 2023.

[43]Madhava Ashish, 'Sri Krishna Prem Through the Eyes of a Disciple,' 28.

[44]Pandey, *Guru by Your Bedside*, 39.

[45]Singh, *Autobiography*, 208.

[46]Bill Aitken, email to the author, 2 September 2022.

[47]Marshall, *Hunting the Guru in India*, 150.

[48]Leary, *Jail Notes*, 30.

[49]Pandit, 'Sri Krishnaprem's Letters,' 23.

[50]Shah, 'Memoirs,' 3.

[51]Ginsburg, *The Masters Speak*, 14.

[52]Shah, 'Memoirs,' 2.

[53]Sen, 'Sri Krishnaprem,' xviii.

[54]Shah, 'Memoirs,' 2.

[55]Sen, 'Sri Krishnaprem,' xvii-xviii.

[56]Bill Aitken, email to the author, 21 June 2021.

[57]Pandey, *Guru by Your Bedside*, 193.

[58]Jay Stevens, *Storming Heaven: LSD and the American Dream*, (New York: Perennial Library, 1988), 204.

[59]Ralph Metzner, *Maps of Consciousness*, 2nd printing, (New York: Macmillan, 1972), 33.

[60]Nautiyal, 'How I Came to Know Gopalda,' 1.

[61]Aitken, email to the author, 24 June 2021.

[62]Aitken, *Footloose in the Himalaya*, 83.

[63]Narasingha P. Sil, 'Kali's Child and Krishna's Lover: An Anatomy of Ramakrishna's *Caritas Divina*,' *Religion*, 39.3, (2009), 291.

[64]In his writings, Jung equates the *animus* with the male concept of Logos (representing rationality) and the *anima* with its feminine counterpart, Eros (the desire for 'psychic relatedness').

[65]Pandey, *Guru by Your Bedside*, 100.

[66]Pandey, 217–218.

20: Opening Up

"I like manual labour. Whenever I've got waterlogged with study I've taken a spell of it and found it spiritually invigorating."[1]
— Larry Darrell, *The Razor's Edge*

As the 1950s gave way to the '60s, the gurus extended their "great clear-out" to Mirtola's philosophy, gradually de-emphasising Vaiṣṇava ritual and theism in favour of a universalist, non-sectarian doctrine, drawing from a range of influences, that Pandey describes as a "secular and dynamic spirituality … that cannot be covered by any known cult label."[2]

Having "worked out the teaching for themselves in the years following World War II," Krishna Prem and Madhava Ashish "saw that they could dispose of many of the unnecessary rituals of orthodox Vaiṣṇava Hinduism, and they did so," relates Sy Ginsburg, who writes that the teaching increasingly focused on exercises to enhance students' self-awareness, akin to the mindfulness practised by Buddhists, the *ātma-vicāra* (self-enquiry) of *Advaita Vedānta* or the 'self-remembering' of GI Gurdjieff. "Although they maintained the Hindu temple at the centre of the Mirtola ashram which is essentially a farm, the practices they continued were in terms of techniques to enhance self-awareness. Ashish liked to call it, 'being aware of being aware.'"[3]

Madhava Ashish explains that the pair's new philosophy was fundamentally an empirical one, based on direct experience: "Krishna Prem and I went through an intense period through the fifties when we abandoned a heavy burden of mental baggage and worked out a reformulation of the teaching as a strictly human enquiry based on first hand evidence only. In effect, this meant that one had only one's awareness of being aware as the starting point."[4] In his opinion, he adds, the validity of any metaphysical system "derives [only] from the truth of the mystical experience of the unity of being."[5]

The farm referenced by Ginsburg also expanded during this period, beginning its growth from "a small farm, which supplied many of the Ashram's simple needs,"[6] into the highly developed farmland cultivated in Madhava Ashish's time. Until his final illness, Krishna Prem personally tilled the fields—"He cooked, cleaned, and worked about the temple and garden as unaffectedly as the most ordinary of men," recalls Madhava Ashish[7]—the farm complementing the "beautifully maintained ashram garden," established in Sri Yashoda Mai's time, which "appeared to be better suited to the stately English home their upper-class accents evoked" than a Himalayan hermitage.[8] (Denys Rutledge found the trim garden with its "green lawn and flowering shrubs" reminded him of "an English country vicarage,"[9] while Donald Eichert writes of discovering in Mirtola an "improbable jewel in a rustic Kumaon setting."[10]) Writing to Rajen Ganguli in May 1959, Krishna Prem explained:

> "[W]e are here becoming an ashram of gardeners (if not actually farmers) in the effort to grow a little food and a few flowers for Thakur in the face of all the animals of the jungle to say nothing of our own neighbours' cows. It is not an easy task.[11]

Madhava Ashish also used his practical skills to introduce "basic amenities like latrines and water storage tanks."[12]

The farm programme would take off fully after Krishna Prem's death under the stewardship of Madhava Ashish, who upgraded the ashram's farmland "to become a test bed of new methods for the backward local cultivators,"[13] and his Australian protégé, David Beresford (later Sri Dev Ashish), who joined the ashram in December 1963.[14] Sy Ginsburg writes: "The improvement of the ashram's land had been undertaken by a young Australian disciple, Dev Ashish—who later became Mirtola's head. Dev, with the aid of Ashish's Western knowledge, raised high-yielding dairy cattle (in contrast to that area's norm, water buffalo and inferior breeds of cows) that produced superior milk, butter, and ghee much prized by the local inhabitants, thereby transforming the farm into an example of how improved management can make degraded land useful again."[15] Madhava Ashish was awarded the Padma Shri, India's fourth-highest civilian honour, in 1992 for his efforts in 'scientific farming.'[16]

Ken Winkler, visiting Mirtola in 1985,[17] was struck by the ashram's development compared to what he describes as the desolation of the surrounding countryside:

> The road to Miratola [sic] passes through a gnarled series of hills and hollows so broken and convulsed that even subsistence farming seems problematic. The forest tracts are strictly secondary growth, skinny and ragged in appearance and scarred with pitch channels. It has been logged, and the remaining trees that have escaped the

> axe are slowly being pruned to death. There is a sense of isolation here, almost an abandonment that nags at travelers as there is little encouraging activity. The few stone houses possessing any substance looked uninhabited, though some doorways sported a cow or two watching the passing traffic.
>
> Krishna Prem's ashram is an exception. Though originally conceived as a Hindu spiritual retreat, it has turned through hard work and planning into both a Himalayan garden and an experimental farm. Flowers explode along the paths, sunlight floods the open areas, and the silence—it's as if all sound from the surrounding mountains has vanished. Only a few birds, or out-of-sight footsteps, an occasional temple bell vibrates through the trees. The ashram has slowly worked to sustain itself through its own produce, and their woodlot provides enough fuel through the winter months. With such a graphic example, what happened to the neighborhood? Why couldn't anyone else replicate their efforts?[18]

Winkler compares the Mirtola farm project—whose growth the green-fingered Ashishes successfully balanced with the demands of running the temple and ashram—favourably with the efforts of Anagarika and Li Govinda at their house at Kasar Devi (Cranks' Ridge), which they rented from the American-born Tibetan Buddhist and Theosophist Walter Evans-Wentz (1878–1965):

> One afternoon, while my wife and I sat in [the Mirtola] garden, [Madhava Ashish] launched into a story of Lama Govinda having problems with his long-distance landlord, Dr. Walter Evans-Wentz. Shri Ashish was large, and when he straightened up to make a point, his robes waved, his arms gestured and he punctuated his main points with a hand-rolled cigarette. Dr. Evans-Wentz knew nothing about running a Himalayan farm or an ashram. He proved to be fussy, badgering the Govindas about trying this or that crop, doing this or that with local religious figures. The Lama, struggling to make the newly-created Buddhist center pay for itself, would [say] in exasperation that the good doctor had to make a decision, either a farm or a study center, but "not both." Shri Ashish managed the process much more successfully and his presence proved a galvanizing one.[19]

Joshua Nash observes that the "ecological enquiries undertaken in the Mirtola Uttar Vrindavan temple" by Krishna Prem, Madhava Ashish and Dev Ashish "link what are perennial environmental concerns with the status of then early modern Vaiṣṇavism. Hints of similar philosophical eclecticism and their association with natural principles are present in contemporary Vaiṣṇavism-inspired ecospirituality like that of the Vrindavan Ecological Concept,"[20] which encourages "ecologically aware pilgrimage" to a Vrindavan "undergoing environmental shocks and stresses of rapid 21st century development, urbanization and the consequent destruction of almost all natural habitats."[21]

In his preface to *Man, the Measure of All Things*, Sri Madhava Ashish suggests that Krishna Prem's rejection of many of the practices with which Uttar Brindaban had previously been associated was down to the realisation that the "orthodoxy of the Krishna cult had been a safe channel for his feelings, rather than a necessary adjunct to the truth"—upon which "he simplified the whole paraphernalia of the specifically Vaishnava religion with which he had been surrounded."[22]

> Guided from within, he deliberately broke away from the sacred structure of sectarian do's and don'ts; yet none of it was aggressive in the way that such structure breaking is apt to be. The more whole he became, the more simple and wholly loveable he was. His old attitude of 'I care for nobody. No, not I' was gone. Previously he had left one with one's admiration rather chilled by a suspicion that he really would not care what happened to the disciples he barely tolerated when he could at last turn his back on the world for ever. Now there could be no question of his not caring.[23]

However, this kind of change in one's *sādhana* over time also has a parallel in Gauḍīya Vaiṣṇavism, whose sacred texts draw a distinction between *vaidhi-bhakti* and *rāgānuga-bhakti*—devotional worship according to rules and regulations and to one's own inclination, respectively. As the Chaitanyaite saint Jiva Goswami explains, *vaidhi-bhakti*, guided by strict scriptural injunctions, is suitable for new practitioners who do not yet have a fondness (*ruci*) for *bhakti*;[24] advanced *sādhakas* experiencing spontaneous, natural devotion for Krishna have more freedom to dispense with what they consider unnecessary rules governing one's spiritual practice. Catherine Robinson alludes to this idea when she writes:

> One explanation for any possible divergence [between Krishna Prem's status as a Hindu guru and his later, non-Hindu ideas and actions] is chronological: perhaps his earlier insistence on strict observance of orthodoxy was inspired by his respect for his predecessors and his consequent readiness to follow the path they had followed to reach the goal; whereas later he had the confidence to change the norms established by his own guru, dispensing with many aspects of orthodoxy whether in his teachings or in his conduct.[25]

Moreover, the identification of the human self with the Absolute (an *Advaitin* doctrine, summarised by the mantra *Ahaṁ Brahmāsmi*, "I am Brahman" or "I am divine," which is often rejected or reinterpreted by Vaiṣṇavas[26]) and a belief in the inherent divinity of man were part of Krishna Prem's personal philosophy at least as early as the 1930s, as evidenced by a February 1936 letter to Dilip Kumar Roy. "As for Gurus as 'incarnate Gods' as Subhash [Chandra Bose, Roy's friend and later the leader of the collaborationist Indische Legion and 'Indian National Army' in World War Two] ridicules it, well, why not?" he asks. "All men are incarnate Gods for one thing—only they know it not; for another, if I can see the God in some man either because he has seen It in himself or because through him a Light has shone for me, why should any one get annoyed? Presumably because he has not seen God anywhere himself, is it not?"[27]

Despite these wide-ranging changes, the temple, once described by Krishna Prem as a "magical point of intersection between this world and the powers of divinity,"[28] continued to form the "complex, even paradoxical, heart of the ashram."[29] Though the temple worship was simplified, keeping "only those parts of the ceremonies that speak directly to the human soul,"[30] the *pūjā* and thrice-daily *aratis* of the Radha–Krishna deities remained and the ashram continued to be centred "around the divine love [*prem*] of Radha–Krishna as the symbol of the only real thing."[31] As Krishna Prem explained to Jagdish Shah: "We don't worship the two idols, but the force which binds them together. We are Prem-Pujaris."[32]

A later visitor, the travel writer Martin Buckley, remembers the evening *arati* in the mid-80s, attendance at which was still deemed essential 20 years after Krishna Prem's death: "[W]ith blown conches, waved fly whisks and the banging and rattling of a variety of instruments ... David [Dev Ashish] led the propitiation of the ashram's household god, Krishna, the God of Love. The ashram's founder, Krishna Prem, had believed love to be the key fact of the religious life. I gathered that Ashish Da had moved beyond ritual devotion; for the rest of us it was deemed necessary."[33]

Asked once why he had continued this ritual worship when "he had seen the Truth behind the symbol," recalls his disciple Madhu Tandan, Madhava Ashish replied: "It helped me at a particular stage. Why dismantle it? Why not leave it intact as it may help to ferry someone else across the river of life?"[34] In this sentiment, he echoed his own guru, who described all spiritual paths as the "shadows on the earth of the ones who have learned to fly."[35] Donald Eichert notes that the regime established by Yashoda Mai and Krishna Prem continued to exert an influence even after their passing, as the ashram, under Madhava Ashish, began its transformation from "an inward-turned establishment, supplying personal instruction about the spiritual path to people who found their way there," to one "participat[ing] more actively in public affairs" and practices "other than the strictly spiritual:"

> The foundation of the teaching had been laid by Krishna Prem's exposition of Vaishnava Seva—service of the Lord—in which every action, feeling and thought is dedicated to the deity established in the temple. In making one's whole life revolve around that outer centre, the centre comes to life in the devotee's heart.[36]

According to Aitken, Krishna Prem considered doing away with the temple worship—and even breaking his vow of *vairāgya*—after having a dream wherein he destroyed the temple *mūrtis* with a crowbar.[37] This dream was interpreted as a reminder that "the outer structure is not as enduring as the temple's symbolic meaning," Aitken explains.[38] He was discouraged from doing so only by the thought that the Mirtola villagers would not understand why the temple was abandoning the last vestiges of its Hindu character. "Ideally Gopalda, having outgrown the need for either temple or sannyas, would have jettisoned both, but having taken the bodhisattvic vow to help others on the way he felt any extreme reversal of behaviour might weaken the faith of the villagers devoted to the temple deities," adds Aitken.[39] While continuing with what Madhava Ashish characterises as an "undercurrent of Radha–Krishna devotional modes of expression"[40] alongside the new influences, Krishna Prem was, however, clear that the "finger that points to the moon"—in this instance, *bāhya pūjā* of Radhikamohanji—"should [not] be mistaken for the moon:" the Absolute, which is "beyond all dualities, beyond both spirit and matter."[41]

These changes to the Vaiṣṇava character of the ashram may be considered surprising both in light of Krishna Prem's unwavering fidelity to his own guru, Yashoda Mai, who had aligned Uttar Brindaban with Gauḍīya Vaiṣṇavism, and his emphasis on the need for a seeker to surrender themselves completely to a spiritual master in order to progress on the 'path.' As he wrote to Roy, "*Gurupādāśraya* (surrender to the Guru) is the first step in *bhajana* and *sādhana* [spiritual cultivation and practice], [and] without it nothing is possible."[42] "The true Guru," he added, "is appointed by the Lord Himself to lead you home."[43]

Indeed, as is clear from his correspondence with Roy, when Krishna Prem could be persuaded, reluctantly, to give spiritual counsel to people who were not his own students, it was with the caveat that his instructions must not conflict with those of the recipient's guru—said to be the one who, by opening the disciple's "eyes, which were blinded by the dark veil of ignorance," grants them a vision of the "self-effulgent Consciousness that pervades all three worlds and everything movable and immovable," to quote the 'Guru-Stotram,' a Sanskrit hymn in praise of the guru which was performed at Mirtola.[44] As he explained to Roy in 1948 (after more than 25 years as friends), one's guru must take precedence above all else: "I know how much you value our friendship and that you should be willing to break it off if I went in a direction contrary to what your Guru approves was quite the most heartening thing you have ever written to me."[45]

Krishna Prem summarises his thoughts on *gurupādāśraya* in one of his most famous letters, dated 29 September 1945 (some nine months after Yashoda Mai's death) and included in Roy's *Yogi Sri Krishnaprem*:

> Krishna and Guru are one: but, if I leave Him, Krishna may leave me—at least He may smile His "*Samo'haṃ sarva-bhūteṣu*"[46] smile and say: "Well, if you don't care for me then I don't care for you—at least not more than I care for the louse on a monkey's backside." But my Guru will never leave me whatever I do. I might leave Her but She would never leave me. I may fall from the Path, return to the flesh-pots and wallow in their filthy slops for five lives or fifty lives, I may blaspheme the Sacred Stone within my heart and die cursing God and man—all this and more I may do but She will never leave my side. Each separate folly of mine will be a stab of sorrow in the heart of Her who is sorrowless but She will never turn away Her face nor cease from trying to assuage the pains that I must suffer from my own foolish acts. Never, never will she leave my side nor cease to guide my steps until I stand in that eternal Braja where She stands now. God-forsaken and man-forsaken I may be, but Guru-forsaken, never.[47]

To deviate, then, from the guru's instructions—or, worse, to reject them altogether—would be an unthinkable act for any serious religious seeker, akin to spiritual suicide. Even Jiddu Krishnamurti—as a boy ill-advisedly elevated to the status of a messianic 'World Teacher' (Maitreya) by the post-Blavatsky Theosophical Society—is criticised by Krishna Prem as a *gurudrohī* (betrayer or hater of the guru) for cutting ties with his 'discoverers,' Annie Besant and her Theosophical collaborator, CW Leadbeater.[48] (By contrast, Krishna Prem's Cambridge friend Christmas Humphreys regarded the "courageous way in which ... Krishnamurti denounced these trappings of vicarious claim [as] one of the high-lights of modern religious history."[49])

However, such surrender to the guru (and by extension Krishna), as Krishna Prem explained to Narendra Nath Kaul, is "not the surrender of doubts and the 'right of private judgment'"—rather it is the natural process of letting go of one's ego that comes with progressing along the 'path': "the blissful surrender of self, and [it] comes in due time, bringing a peace and happiness before [the] unknown. It is the free and spontaneous act of the soul before its Master and neither can nor should be limited elsewhere."[50]

Moreover, while it is not recorded whether Yashoda Mai 'approved' of the changes at Mirtola, it is unlikely, given his devotion to his guru, that Krishna Prem would have forged ahead had he felt they did not have her support. As documented in chapter 13, her reassurances ("I shall be with you always") were key to encouraging Krishna Prem to assume the mantle of guru in the difficult months following her death, and both he and Madhava Ashish would continue to pray to 'Ma' for guidance in the years to come (the latter noting that he would "invariably get the reply, 'Go back to Moti'" [Ashish, 231]). "Some have criticized him ... because he changed the pattern of the Ashram established by his Guru," Ashish wrote shortly after Krishna Prem's passing. "[However, w]hether she spoke outwardly or within his heart, her voice determined all his actions, and he listened to none other."[51]

Indeed, Yashoda Mai herself was critical of those who she felt observed the externals of the Vaiṣṇava tradition at the expense of following its "essential teachings." She writes in *Punaravartin* (1937):

> We claim ... to be following the teachings of the *Gita* or the *Bhagawat* [*Purana*] but in fact our following is like that of a man who, ordered by the doctor to drink milk, first extracts all the butter and only drinks what is left. We leave aside the essence of the teachings and swallow only the silver paper in which they were wrapped.
>
> Instead of understanding and trying to follow the essential teachings we pride ourselves on our strict observance of a lot of outward rites and ceremonies, of rigid caste restrictions and superstitious practices.[52]

Krishna Prem, too, had long emphasised that *bāhya pūjā* such of the kind observed at Mirtola is secondary to the inner meaning symbolised by such external ritual. His interpretation of the *Kaṭha Upaniṣad,* for example, recasts Nachiketas and his father, Vājashravasa, as allegories for esoteric and exoteric religion respectively, with Nachiketas representing "the quickening Spirit that lies within all things" and Vājashravasa "orthodox traditional religion, devoted as always to outer forms."[53] One who follows the example of the son—"a symbol of the reborn Spirit which slumbers in the heart of all religions"[54] and "giveth life"[55]—will find themselves a "disciple of the Inner Path" to the ultimate truth.[56] In this, he writes, they are "opposed to Vājashravasa"—a stand-in for "the externalism ... inherent in all exoteric religion: ... the letter which killeth [life]."[57]

He may also have felt buoyed by the apparent enthusiasm of the 'Masters' of Theosophy, with whom Moti Rani and her father were said to be in communication, for the new regime emerging at Mirtola. Bill Aitken alludes to Krishna Prem also being in direct communion with these far-flung *Mahātmās*, first described by Madame Blavatsky. He writes that the "entire Mirtola makeover from orthodox to liberal I understood was at the promptings of the Theosophical Masters. The gurus saw themselves primarily as dedicated instruments of their Masters' timeless spiritual sovereignty."[58]

Other 'Masters' venerated at the ashram included the Buddha (whose birthday was celebrated as Buddha Jayanti[59]), Jesus and, of course, Krishna, who were recognised alongside Theosophy's Koot Hoomi, Morya and Djual Khool,[60] as well as the Mirtola gurus (including, after his death, Krishna Prem):

> One of the central tenets of the [Theosophical] Society was a belief in a hierarchy of discarnate 'ascended' Masters.... Given the importance of the early Society to Prem and Ashish, and the intense loyalty they felt toward it, it's perhaps not surprising that Ashish always took great care to pay homage to this hierarchy. [H]olidays were celebrated at Mirtola for the birthdays of all the Masters recognized there, including Buddha, Djwhal Khul, Gurdjieff, Jesus Christ, Koot Hoomi, Krishna, Maurya, the Mirtola gurus Sri Yashoda Mai and Sri Krishna Prem....[61]

Sri Madhava Ashish, having by now completely rejected the concept of Krishna as *Svayam Bhagavan,* wrote in 1969 that it is these 'Masters' who are responsible for the acts of grace often attributed to a personal God. "[T]o say that the divine power encompasses personality does not mean that there is a personal God, for the universally diffused awareness does not discriminate between the bliss of one individual and the suffering of another," he explained. "The undeniable fact of personal grace is to be attributed to the intervention of those Perfected Men at one with divinity whom HPB called the Masters."[62]

During what Aitken describes as the gradual transition "from the traditional to the ashram's modified ritual,"[63] dream analysis, inspired by the ideas of CG

Jung, "seemed almost to supersede temple worship, judging from the intensity of concentration put into the former," he recalls. Though "[i]nitially sceptical of the benefits of dream interpretation," Aitken—who first arrived on 10 October 1960 and made an annual visit to Mirtola each December[64] before settling for good in April 1965, having relocated from Sarala Behn's Gandhian ashram in Kausani—writes that he "was soon to learn of its astounding life-changing potential."[65] Similarly, Penelope Phipps, trained as a psychiatric social worker,[66] recalls that her first reaction to being exposed to dream analysis was that the gurus were "not psychologically trained" for such work, but ended her thinking "by realizing that dreams could be interpreted on levels that I had not known existed."[67]

Madhava Ashish considered the introduction of dream interpretation into ashram life as a continuation of "the work Moti had begun," with he and his guru engaging in what he called "a long-term psycho-analytical adventure, with a vivid dream life which led us from one point to the next" (Ashish, 240). In his book *An Open Window: Dream as Everyman's Guide to the Spirit,* he recalls that he and Krishna Prem

> went through a high period when a night without a dream was a wasted opportunity, a forgotten dream was a breach of trust. We hurried through our many chores to be free to pace up and down in the morning light, seeking meanings and their ramifications.[68]

Neither man was a *devotee* of Jung. (Madhava Ashish wrote that the pair despaired at "the way he could lead his readers up to a point where the next sentence should have affirmed the reality of the Spirit, but then back down.... He was an outstandingly remarkable man. But he had not approached that step into what lies beyond the ego-integration ... when the 'I' [is] annihilated before the transcendental identity can be found."[69]) However, Freudian–Jungian 'dream work' was one of a number of new, notably non-Indian disciplines allowed to take root at Uttar Brindaban as Vaiṣṇavite ritual receded. Sy Ginsburg recalls that his mentor, Sri Madhava Ashish, "would say very often, 'We need to use the tools that these men, [Sigmund] Freud, who called dreams the royal road to the unconscious or subconscious, and Jung, brought us. We need to use the tools that they discovered, but we don't need to accept their conclusions.'"[70] ("Read Jung, but don't become a Jungian," was Krishna Prem's instruction to Madhava Ashish.[71]) Krishna Prem—who had earlier been critical of Freud's psychoanalysis, as he believed it would "drive out or kill spirituality because it claims to explain away many spiritual things"[72]—now also put "considerable emphasis on dreams which he believed, along with Jung, carried important signals to us from our subconscious selves," confirms Karan Singh. "If properly interpreted, these could give valuable indications on our inner situation, particularly our emotional problems."[73]

Dream interpretation has been an important psychoanalytic technique since the time of Freud, as the journalist Oliver Burkeman explains:

> The basic premise of psychoanalysis ... is that our lives are ruled by unconscious forces, which speak to us only indirectly: through symbols in dreams, "accidental" slips of the tongue, or through what infuriates us about others, which is a clue to what we can't face in ourselves.[74]

The gurus also shared Jung's belief in the reality of occult phenomena, which was to be the cause of his break with Freud, his former mentor.[75]

Dreams, of course, were considered important even before the great mental and physical clear-out of the 1950s—for example, Yashoda Mai's dreams of her Ganesh deity and Chaitanya's appearance to Krishna Prem—but were given greater significance and analysed more deeply following the deaths of Moti Rani and Haridas. Madhava Ashish describes having dreams regarding the latter, which were interpreted to mean he was having trouble 'letting go' of physical items following his passing:

> We had not been in any particular hurry to dispose of Bob's personal belongings from his room except for clothes, bedding etc., which are always got rid of at once. But almost from the first day I started having dreams in which I would see a particular item in Bob's room which carried a peculiar sheen. We interpreted this to mean that perhaps Bob was being held back by his attachment to these articles. A particular example was a Japanese image of the Buddha in brass which Gopalda had given him. But the series of dreams continued until we had found homes for or destroyed almost every item in the little room. (Ashish, 89)

This increasingly detailed study of one's dream life could also help with deciphering the complex symbolism contained in esoteric texts such as *The Secret Doctrine*, explains Madhava Ashish, who writes about the "dreams which threw light on the Cosmogenesis and Anthropogenesis of the *Stanzas of Dzyan* on which we were writing a commentary."[76] Dreams could also, properly interpreted, apparently warn of impending danger: Madhava Ashish had a prophetic dream involving a high wall the night before he fell repairing the temple roof,[77] an accident which left him in Ramsay Hospital[78] in Naini Tal with a broken left thigh and right hand.[79]

Notes

[1]W. Somerset Maugham, *The Razor's Edge*, (London: Vintage Books, 2000), 306.

[2]Pandey, *Guru by Your Bedside*, 7.

[3]Gurdjieff Internet Guide, 'Sy Ginsburg, USA,' *Katinka Hesselink Web Developer*, (Leiden: Katinka Hesselink, 2002), http://www.katinkahesselink.net/sufi/ginterviewl.html (accessed 9 January 2023).

[4]Sri Madhava Ashish, letter to Jacob Needleman, 22 October 1996, *All & Everything '97: The Proceedings*, (Bognor Regis: International Humanities Conference, 1997), 217.

[5]Madhava Ashish, letter to Jacob Needleman, 22 October 1996, 219.

[6]Madhava Ashish, 'Sri Sri Krishnaprem Vairagi,' 89.

[7]Madhava Ashish, 'Sri Krishna Prem Through the Eyes of a Disciple,' 29.

[8]Aitken, *Footloose in the Himalaya*, 44.

[9]Rutledge, *In Search of a Yogi*, 243.

[10]Eichert, 'The Last English Saint,' 2.

[11]Pandit, 'Sri Krishnaprem's Letters,' 21.

[12]Ginsburg, *The Masters Speak*, 16.

[13]Eichert, 'The Last English Saint,' 5.

[14]Bill Aitken, email to the author, 7 January 2023.

[15]Ginsburg, *The Masters Speak*, 15.

[16]Eichert, 'The Last English Saint,' 6.

[17]Ken Winkler, email to the author, 23 July 2021.

[18]Winkler, *The Winter Line*, 95–96.

[19]Winkler, *The Winter Line*, 97–98.

[20]Nash, 'A Note on Sri Krishnaprem,' 74.

[21]Joshua Nash, 'The Vrindavan Ecological Concept and the Seven Levels of Human Ecology,' *Vrindavan Today*, (Vrindavan: Vrindavan Today, 2017), https://web.archive.org/web/20180405025306/http://news.vrindavantoday.org/2017/10/vrindavan-ecological-concept-seven-levels-human-ecology (accessed 22 February 2023).

[22]Madhava Ashish, 'Preface,' in Krishna Prem and Madhava Ashish, *Man, the Measure of All Things*, 9.

[23]*Ibid.*

[24]Rembert Lutjeharms, 'An Ocean of Emotion: Rasa and Religious Experience in Early Caitanya Vaiṣṇava Thought,' in Ravi M. Gupta (ed.), *Caitanya Vaiṣṇava Philosophy: Tradition, Reason and Devotion*, (Farnham: Ashgate, 2014), 198.

[25]Robinson, *Interpretations of the Bhagavad-Gītā and Images of the Hindu Tradition*, 168.

[26]"[AC Bhaktivedanta Swami] Prabhupada … interprets that the famous Vedic phrase 'Aham Brahmasmi' does not mean 'I am Brahma[n],' but [ex a realisation that 'I am not this body, I am spirit, soul, *part and parcel* of the supreme Brahman,'" (emphasis added). Uday Mehta, *Modern Godmen in India: A Sociological Appraisal*, (Bombay: Popular Prakashan, 1993), 49.

[27]'Krishnaprem's Letter to Dilip, February 9, 1936', Sujata Nahar and Shankar Bandyopadhyay (eds), *Sri Aurobindo to Dilip*, vol. 3 (1936–1937), The Mother & Sri Aurobindo, 2007, 43, https://motherandsriaurobindo.in/disciples/dilip-kumar-roy/books/sri-aurobindo-to-dilip-volume-iii/ (Accessed September 9, 2024).

[28]Pandey, *Guru by Your Bedside*, 123.

[29]Pandey, *Guru by Your Bedside*, 118.

[30]Madhava Ashish, 'Sri Krishna Prem Through the Eyes of a Disciple,' 28.

[31]Aitken, *Sri Sathya Sai Baba*, 14.

[32]Shah, 'Memoirs,' 5.

[33]Martin Buckley, *An Indian Odyssey*, (London: Hutchinson, 2008), 121.

[34]Madhu Tandan, *Faith & Fire* (Gurgaon: Harper Collins, 1997), 247.

[35]Gannon and Life, *Jivamukti Yoga*, 13.

[36]Eichert, 'Sri Madhava Ashish.'

[37]He is clear, however, that "there was never the possibility of breaking the images [in waking life]. If the temple was demolished they would have been re-housed."

[38]Aitken, email to the author, 2 July 2023.

[39]Aitken, email to the author, 24 June 2021.

[40]Madhava Ashish, 'Preface,' in Krishna Prem and Madhava Ashish, *Man, the Measure of All Things*, 9.

[41]Pandey, *Guru by Your Bedside*, 26.

[42]Roy, *Yogi Sri Krishnaprem*, 143,

[43]Roy, *Yogi Sri Krishnaprem*, 109.

[44]"[T]hey recited hymns in praise of the Guru: अखण्डमण्डलाकारं व्याप्तं येन चराचरम् ....||." Parekh, *Himalayan Memoirs*, 48.

[45]Roy, *Yogi Sri Krishnaprem*, 255.

[46]"I am equally disposed to all living things"—*Bhagavad Gītā 9.29.*

[47]Roy, *Yogi Sri Krishnaprem*, 241–242.

[48]Bandyopadhyay, *Sri Aurobindo to Dilip*, vol. 4 (1938–1950), 248.

[49]Humphreys, 'From Branches to the Root,' 118.

[50]Kaul, *Writings of Sri Krishna Prem*, 92.

[51]Madhava Ashish, 'Sri Sri Krishnaprem Vairagi,' 91.

[52]Tandan, 'Metaphors and Quotes of Yashoda Mai,' 4.

[53]Krishna Prem, *The Yoga of the Kaṭhopanishad*, 15.

[54]Krishna Prem, *The Yoga of the Kaṭhopanishad*, 16.

[55]Krishna Prem, *The Yoga of the Kaṭhopanishad*, 15.

[56]Krishna Prem, *The Yoga of the Kaṭhopanishad*, 16.

[57]Krishna Prem, *The Yoga of the Kaṭhopanishad*, 15.

[58]Aitken, 'Sri Krishna Prem in the Last Years,' 270.

[59]Shantananda Puri, *Fragrant Flowers*, 84.

[60]Koot Hoomi and Morya—described respectively as a Kashmiri Brahmin and an Indian Rajput—are said to have lived with the former's Tibetan student, Djual Khool, at Tashi Lhünpo monastery in southern Tibet during Blavatsky's lifetime. She claimed Morya first appeared to her in 1851 in London, where she was tasked with forming the Theosophical Society "to gradually prepare the way for others" to receive the Masters' wisdom.

[61]Ginsburg, *In Search of the Unitive Vision*, 127.

[62]Sri Madhava Ashish, '*The Secret Doctrine* as a Contribution to World Thought,' *The American Theosophist*, 57.5, (1969), 4, https://www.theosophical.org/files/resources/articles/Secret-Doctrine-as-a-Contribution-to-World-Thought-Madhava-Ashish.pdf (accessed 23 January 2023).

[63]Aitken, 'Sri Krishna Prem in the Last Years,' 269.

[64]Aitken, 'Sri Krishna Prem in the Last Years,' 263.

[65]*Ibid.*

[66]Penelope Phipps B.Sc. (H & SS), 'Adoption (A Study of the Problems involved in Child Guidance Cases, from the View-point of a Psychiatric Social Worker,' *Mental Health*, 12.3, (1953), 98.

[67]Phipps, 'Sri Krishna Prem Remembered,' 274.

[68]Madhava Ashish, *An Open Window*, xviii.

[69]Ginsburg, *The Masters Speak*, 236–237.

[70]'Sy Ginsburg Exchange March 2005,' *Gurdjieff Internet Guide*, (Amden: Gurdjieff Internet Guide, 2005), https://web.archive.org/web/20150611192047/http://www.gurdjieff-internet.com/article-details.php?ID = 223&W = 9 (accessed 31 March 2023).

[71]Madhava Ashish, *An Open Window*, xvi.

[72]Nirodbaran, *Talks with Sri Aurobindo*, (Calcutta: Sri Aurobindo Pathamandir, 1966), 239.

[73]Singh, *Autobiography*, 249.

[74]Oliver Burkeman, 'Therapy Wars: The Revenge of Freud,' *The Guardian*, (London: Guardian Media Group, 2016), https://www.theguardian.com/science/2016/jan/07/therapy-wars-revenge-of-freud-cognitive-behavioural-therapy (accessed 19 August 2023).

[75] David Elkin, 'Freud, Jung and the Collective Unconscious,' *The New York Times*, 4 October 1970, 218, https://www.nytimes.com/1970/10/04/archives/freud-jung-and-the-collective-unconscious-jungs-has-been-the-only.html (accessed 3 February 2023).

[76] Madhava Ashish, *An Open Window*, xviii.

[77] Tandan, *Faith & Fire*, 79.

[78] Shah, 'Memoirs,' 2.

[79] Singh, *Letters from Mirtola*, 31.

21: De-structuring

"An essential requirement of any real yoga is complete detachment from any personal prejudices or sectarian notions."[1]
— Sri Krishna Prem (1934)

From the late 1950s the steady trickle of visitors to Uttar Brindaban (known as *darśanārthīs*,[2] those who have come for *darśan*) became a flood—a phenomenon driven chiefly by the construction of a new motor road from Almora to Mirtola, built in 1956–57 (Ashish, 98), which allowed travellers and pilgrims to cut out the 18-mile bridle path from Almora which had previously been the only way of accessing the isolated ashram. Until then, those "who would brave the journey for the sake of the Mirtola ashram alone were relatively few and had good reasons for coming" (Ashish, 249); the new road, recalls Sri Madhava Ashish, "put an end to all that. Pilgrims now sit in roaring buses, many of them miserably car-sick, and are carried straight to their destination and straight back again" (Ashish, 251)

Some of these motorised travellers would test Krishna Prem's newfound tolerance for unannounced visits—he was, in the words of Madhava Ashish, "by no means a misanthropist, nor was he lacking in compassion, but he objected to being treated as an animal in a zoo" (Ashish, 252)—and he soon ceased singing *kīrtans* in the temple after visitors began demanding he "sing for them, and to sing immediately because they had to catch the return bus" (Ashish, 104). In general, however, the pilgrims who, "as if drawn by a magnet ... began to flood the little ashram"[3] were welcomed warmly by a "man who had previously resented the least invasion of his privacy [but] now opened his heart to these travellers on the dusty road of life, constantly giving of himself."[4] As Krishna Prem himself reflected: "Life is busier than it used to be—motor roads have reduced, if not destroyed, our 'splendid isolation,' but that, too, is more in other hands than ours and all is well."[5]

Denys Rutledge, who arrived at the ashram "unexpectedly without any introduction," was nevertheless welcomed by Krishna Prem and Madhava Ashish, who "invited me to share their meal and pressed me to stay the night, or even several nights, or to come again," he writes. "But this was because they knew that I had not come from mere curiosity; I had come to learn," he speculates. "Like them I was looking for the light...."[6]

Other visitors to Uttar Brindaban during this period report being startled by Krishna Prem's revelation that he 'knew' they were coming, even if they, like Rutledge, had turned up unannounced. In *The Mountain of Shiva*, 'Ashok' (Karan Singh) is bemused to be told that 'Ananda Maharaj' is expecting him;[7] similarly, Kapila Vatsyayan, the Indian classical dance scholar and one-time member of parliament, recalls how Krishna Prem, on her arrival, "stepped out of the [temple], walked up to her, and said, 'So, you've come.'"[8]

Rutledge also describes how Mirtola provided food and shelter for visiting holy men—albeit of a modest enough nature that it would not "encourage those whose primary hunger might be rather for earthly sustenance, illusory as that might be, than for the higher spiritual pastures":

> At a little distance from their own ashram there is a small open-fronted building for the use of visiting sadhus, where they may receive shelter and meals for three days. It seemed to be implied that after three days they should either move on or declare their intentions.[9]

For Madhava Ashish, the way Krishna Prem dealt with the end of Mirtola's seclusion signified a further evolution in his guru, who now taught increasingly by example rather than by instruction:

> He now embodied the truths he had previously so keenly perceived, so it was now the man and not simply the cogency and clarity of his thought that impressed people who met him. Previously he had given expression to the truth in a glittering parade of words, now it was as if the wordless truth shone through him, so that people often found as much teaching in his casual acts and gestures as they had done in his books.[10]

"There is an old saying that when the lotus blooms, one does not have to send an invitation to the bees. They come of their own accord," observes Gertrude Emerson Sen. "Krishnaprem never sought disciples, never permitted himself to be advertised.... Neither did he allow himself to become the centre of the ashram. No life-sized photographs of him were to be seen plastered about. Only a single painting of the guru, Sri Yashoda Mai, still hangs in the little room that once was hers.[11] Nevertheless, we watched with the years an ever-increasing stream of men and women, from many countries and from every part of India, going on pilgrimage to Mirtola."[12]

Among these visitors were several influential followers of George Gurdjieff, including the Sanskritist Philippe Lavastine,[13] Gurdjieff's secretary, Olga de Hartmann,[14] and Lizelle Reymond,[15] who later ran a Gurdjieff group in Geneva. (Madhava Ashish met Gurdjieff's closest disciple, Jeanne de Salzmann, later, in 1971 in New Delhi.[16]) Another one-time Gurdjieffian, a Cockney self-made businessman called Walter Wiers, visited the ashram each winter and was authorised by the gurus to include the "Mirtola teachings" in his Gurdjieff study group in London.[17]

By this time, however, the philosophy had been simplified to the extent that it could be hard to pin down exactly what these teachings were. Bill Aitken writes that in the early 1960s "[t]here was no Mirtola teaching as such," with Krishna Prem and Madhava Ashish, who referred to themselves as "pupil–teachers,"[18] each pursuing their own philosophical interests—the former Theosophy and the Sufi poems of Jalal ad-Din Rumi and the latter the Gurdjieff system—and encouraging their students to do the same. (At the time of his death, Krishna Prem was learning Persian in order to read Rumi in the original;[19] the Sufist scholar Krishna Khosla, who visited Mirtola and discussed Rumi's *Masnavi* with Krishna Prem, recalls: "He was a great initiate, the greatest I have ever met."[20])

> They explored, and urged pupils to explore, diverse spiritual teachings: Advaita, Buddhism, the Sufi masters, and mystics of all traditions, but the bedrock was the Way of the Bodhisattva—a commitment to compassion: 'having crossed over to the other shore he helps others to cross.'[21]

"The Theosophical understanding of the compassionate Bodhisattva concept was the backbone of their belief and teachings while I was there," adds Aitken.[22] Pervin Mahoney, a disciple of Madhava Ashish and former resident of Mirtola, confirms: "This is an essential aspect of the mature final guide he evolved into: that the man of attainment 'remains available' to help others."[23]

Though Krishna Prem did not use the term, preferring "universal,"[24] the latter-day Mirtola philosophy—with what Sy Ginsburg and Satish Datt Pandey affectionately call its "hotchpotch of Vaishnavism, Advaita, Buddhism, Sufi mysticism, Theosophy, Gurdjieffianism [and] 'this dream business'"[25]—may also be considered a proto-example of the kind of eclectic, syncretistic thinking, "distilled from ingredients collected from regions far and wide"[26] and influenced by the hippie counterculture, that later flowered into the New Age movement in the West.

What teaching there was "was adapted to [the] individual needs"[27] of the *sādhaka*, though not everyone appreciated the introduction of psychotherapeutic methods into the de-Hinduised Mirtola, which was beginning more to resemble a psychoanalytical retreat than a conventional ashram. One woman with "spiritual inclinations" left disappointed after Krishna Prem and Madhava Ashish analysed her dreams of Shiva *liṅgams* (an unavoidably phallic representation of the god of destruction) "along 'Freudian lines.'... She felt terribly let down and did not care to have anything to do with such uncharacteristic sadhus," Pandey recalls.[28]

For the gurus, modern psychological and psychoanalytic techniques were useful tools to "clear the ground and bring the mind under control" before entering a meditative state,[29] and Krishna Prem warned his students against "abandoning the psychological inquiry" in favour of meditation-only *sādhana*.[30]

Krishna Prem also came to view a person's spiritual progress in terms of their psychological 'wholeness'—a Jungian concept—emphasising the transformative power of love, meditation, courage and hard work in order to rid oneself of unwanted habits and hang-ups. Madhava Ashish explains:

> [H]e laid considerable stress on meditative practices, regarding them as the most essential part of the work, [but] he held that the work is not complete until the whole from which all things have come is reflected in the wholeness of the man. A man under the sway of inhibitions and compulsions he regarded as partial or incomplete. If through fear one attempted to avoid certain areas of worldly experience, then, when one turned to meditation, the inner or psychic causes of that fear would rise up and bar one's progress. He therefore saw the work as a dialectical process: the facing of outer challenges opening the way to inner perception, and self-surrendering to the spirit in meditation giving rise to a trans-personal courage with which the challenges of life can be met. That self-surrender, he said, is the surrender of love, and the courage is the courage of love.[31]

This idea also has parallels in Theosophy: the Mirtola favourite *Light on the Path* advises that the "whole nature of man must be used wisely by the one who desires to enter the way.... [N]ot till the whole personality of the man is dissolved and melted—not until it is held by the divine fragment which has created it, as a mere subject for grave experiment and experience—not until the whole nature has yielded and become subject unto its higher self ... [can one gain access to] the Hall of Learning."[32]

While "very much an Ashishda enthusiasm,"[33] the influence of Gurdjieffian thought in particular became such at Mirtola that, in the view of Ginsburg (who was introduced to Gurdjieff by Madhava Ashish), the two gurus practised "their own form of the [W]ork,"[34] the system of self-development taught by Gurdjieff also known as the 'Fourth Way' (so called because it combines elements of all of what are defined as the three traditional spiritual paths: the way of the *fakir*, or ascetic; the way of the monk; and the way of the yogi). Ralph Metzner found Krishna Prem "a remarkable figure who," he said, had "integrated Hindu and Buddhist teachings with the esoteric wisdom traditions of the West, including Gurdjieff."[35] ("Amusingly," remembers Aitken, Metzner had earlier visited the "Kausani ashram sniffing out if there were any LSD believers, but on finding Sarala [Behn], the formidable English lady in charge and a puritan Gandhian, he had to hastily backtrack and pretend he was a tourist."[36])

According to Aitken, Krishna Prem "did accept Gurdjieff as an enlightened being, but unlike Ashishda he neither pushed the Gurdjieffian work nor referred much to it. I suspect he found some of Gurdjieff's methods alien."[37] Pandey writes that "Gopal Da told a friend that he did not apply Gurdjieffian methods on his disciples because 'my hands are not as strong.'"[38]

Gurdjieff—who, like HP Blavatsky, claimed to have travelled in Asia, including Tibet, and the Middle East before arriving in the West as a teacher—taught that humans are 'unfinished' machines, born without souls[39] and spending most of their lives in a kind of waking sleep; a trance state towards which society at large contributes by "discouraging any sort of self-observation."[40] To help his students break out of this hypnotic state, Gurdjieff introduced the 'Work:' a "path of effort and struggle, conscious labor and voluntary suffering, ... blood, sweat, and tears"[41] which emphasises being present in the moment while struggling against one's unconscious automatism.

Given its stress on 'conscious labour'—"the effort to sense, remember, and observe oneself"[42] by being completely attentive to a particular task—some writers have connected the strenuous regimen observed at Mirtola, where everyone, including the gurus, were expected to work a full day in the temple or on the ashram farm, with Gurdjieffian thought. Aitken, who recalls "the frenetic pace and killing pressure a new arrival like me had to undergo,"[43] describes a scene which would be familiar to inmates of Gurdjieff's Institute for the Harmonious Development of Man in Paris (known as the *Prieuré*), where the 'Work' combined "hard physical labor [with] active meditations:"[44]

> Many of us *gurubhāis* [godbrothers/sisters] were from a sedentary intellectual background and complained of being in a rut. We were then set such rigorous physical demands that the rut would soon seem pleasurable in retrospect. Whatever else Mirtola was, it was

> a million miles from most people's idea of an ashram. If, as most of us did, you cherished the illusion you had nothing more to learn and hence could be easygoing on your own weaknesses (while being hard on others), you were made to work manually until either you dropped from exhaustion or got the message. You could not complain because the gurus performed the same schedule with a smile, setting the example of how to 'wash the feet in the blood of the heart.'[45]

Yet hard physical work had been a fact of life at Mirtola (whose earliest residents had built the ashram complex literally by hand) long before Madhava Ashish discovered the 'Work'—to the extent that when "Gopal Da and Ashish Da came to know the details of [Gurdjieff's] 'method' ... [t]hey would certainly have found nothing new or unfamiliar in it," writes Pandey,[46] who recalls how "Haridas, a high-ranking physician of British extraction, used to cut grass in the jungle in spite of many local people offering to do the job in his place," and Madhava Ashish, after a "full day of hard physical work," remarked: "I did not know whether I was standing on my feet or on my head."[47] Krishna Prem, writes Aitken, also "taught by example, and if [he or Madhava Ashish] saw a disciple shun the dirty jobs they would do them themselves;"[48] it was "quite common," he adds, "for visitors on their way to have darshan of the Mirtola gurus to assume that these scurrying figures doing all the ashram chores were hired hands."[49] On announcing that she wished to renounce her life and move into the ashram, Vatsyayan recalls being told by Krishna Prem: "How about first digging potatoes before thinking of coming to this ashram? Go out and soil your hands with cultivation."[50]

Writing to Narendra Nath Kaul in May 1943 (prior even to the arrival of Madhava Ashish at Mirtola) about his views on 'educational reform,' Krishna Prem is clear that, "[f]rom the point of view of this Path," everyone should be "trained to use their hands and their imaginations as well as their 'brains'"—the opposite of the "utterly one-sided merely 'mental' viewpoint" he felt was being imparted to students in schools and universities.[51] (This recommendation brings to mind the "harmonious blending of head, heart and hands" he recognised in the path set forth by the *Bhagavad Gītā*.)

Similarly, the practice of 'turning the pressure on'—using the tensions between ashramites as a learning experience to promote personal and spiritual growth—is "found in practically all ancient traditions," so it "would not be fair to regard it as solely a Gurdjieffian influence on this Vaishnav ashram," explains Pandey.[52] Even Madhava Ashish—"unlike Mr G"—did not create artificial "'work situations' for his followers," Pandey continues: "He tried to make the most of the situations that developed in the normal course of events. Perhaps, one could say that he preferred to leave it to Thakur...."[53]

For Denys Rutledge, the gurus' conception of work resembled less Gurdjieff's *Prieuré* than a Benedictine monastery, where the goal is to "re-establish through manual work a proper harmony between body and soul." Krishna Prem and Madhava Ashish "agreed that once a regular rhythm of life was established work involved no necessary break with prayer, but led to a state in which action was simply the material reflection of prayer, work was prayer," he writes.[54]

It may, however, have been a visiting Gurdjieffian, Walter Wiers, whose actions led to Krishna Prem breaking with the final, and most strictly observed, of the ashram's formerly labyrinthine system of rules and regulations. Aitken explains how the presence of Wiers, a disciple of René Daumal's widow, Vera, influenced the gradual abandonment of much of the complex ritual surrounding the preparation, offering and eating of food:

> [I]t was Walter's gross presence that made them break with Mirtola's past. One day Walter was being his usual ritually disgusting self and Ashishda and Gopalda, incensed and about to wreak their wrath upon him, looked at one another and instead burst out laughing. Here they were supposed to be dedicating their lives to total love and were placing the feelings of a dead image [the *vigraha*] above the living divine in Walter.[55]

Timothy Leary describes two other visitors—one wearing leather and another who washed up the ashram dishes in the 'wrong' way—whose behaviour may also have led to similar pressure to relax the strict "canned ritual" observed at Mirtola:

> [Krishna Prem] had been an orthodox Brahmin, and you know that really can get pretty uptight. He told us that once some sincere pilgrim came into the temple and was wearing leather shoes and it threw them into a big flap and they had to close the temple and purify everything for three or four days to undo that. Or another time, a well-meaning student came and washed the dishes when the monks were out for a walk. He didn't know that the dishes were supposed to be washed in a special way. This food was not supposed to touch that food.
>
> Sri Krishna Prem told me that they eventually realized that much of that canned ritual was a drag! It was just making us uptight, and it was making everyone else uptight. Gradually Sri Krishna Prem and his friends began to refine their living on this mountaintop in such a way that the ritual was all natural. It was just the best, easiest style to do anything that you have to do anyway.[56]

Pandey, meanwhile, remembers that "Gopal Da told us about a dream in which he saw a *shilpkar* [artisan] boy enter the temple kitchen and eat the food cooked for the deities. As a result, the kitchen orthodoxy was given up—perhaps from the next meal. However, the practice of cooking the food for Thakurs and offering it to them before starting one's meal was continued."[57]

In his final years, Krishna Prem even abandoned the wholly vegetarian diet he had observed strictly since at least the early 1920s—a far cry from the days when he had threatened to reject an initiated disciple because they started eating fish. (The "poor man," relates Pandey, "relented immediately and promised never to touch fish again."[58]) Though the ashram remained a meat-free zone, "in his last months Krishna Prem amazed his hosts on an Almora outing by once eating chicken—'to destroy structures,' as he said."[59] These Almora hosts were likely Boshi and Gertrude Sen, the latter of whom writes about witnessing what she calls the "old bonds" restricting Krishna Prem having "suddenly snapped."[60] In contrast to the days when Yashoda Mai and Krishna Prem would turn up at Kundan House with their own "shiny new pots, ... dry ingredient[s] and *masalas*, fresh vegetables [and] brass thalis,"[61] the latter was now entirely unconcerned about the ritual around preparing food. Nor did it "matter any more to him what anybody ate. Now, after forty-five years, he said, he himself would not mind eating anything!"[62]

Jagdish Shah remembers Krishna Prem indulging in a similar act of 'structure-destroying' culinary rebellion by purchasing a tin of corned (bully) beef from an Almora department store:

> Once, while returning from Nainital, Gopal Da stopped the taxi in front of M/s L.R. Shah, a department store which prided itself in selling everything from a gramophone needle to a piano. The owner, Sri Gopal Sah, seeing the revered customer enter the shop, rose from his chair and came to attend him. Gopal Da went straight to the Almirah [cupboard] which stocked imported foodstuffs and picked a tin of bully beef. Gopal Sah, without batting an eye, wrapped and gave it to him.
>
> This was amazing coming as it did from Gopal Da, a 'proud vegetarian' from birth, who did not take meat even when he was a fighter pilot during the First World War, and whose respect and reputation was well established in Almora from the days he and Ma lived in nearby Chilkaptia Bungalow and as a Vairagi collected Bhiksha [alms] for their daily vegetarian meals from some chosen houses in Almora—Gopal Sah's house being one of them.
>
> Perhaps this was one of his many acts to break deep structures he prided and identified himself with.[63]

Years later, Shah asked Madhava Ashish what he had done with the tin of (still uneaten) contraband. His response: "I buried it in the forest."[64]

Notes

[1]Sri Krishna Prem Vairagi, 'A Christian Sadhu' (review of CF Andrews, *Sadhu Sundar Singh: A Personal Memoir*), *The Aryan Path*, 5.12, (1934), 774.

[2]Shah, 'Memoirs,' 3.

[3]Madhava Ashish, 'Sri Krishna Prem Through the Eyes of a Disciple,' 28.

[4]*Ibid.*

[5]Pandit, 'Sri Krishnaprem's Letters,' 24.

[6]Rutledge, *In Search of a Yogi*, 234.

[7]Singh, *The Mountain of Shiva*, ch. 4, paras 22–23.

[8]Jyoti Sabharwal, *Afloat a Lotus Leaf: Kapila Vatsyayan (A Cognitive Biography)*, (New Delhi: Stellar, 2015), 277.

[9]Rutledge, *Ibid.*

[10]Madhava Ashish, 'Sri Krishna Prem Through the Eyes of a Disciple,' 28.

[11]This painting is still there.

[12]Sen, 'Sri Krishnaprem,' xix.

[13]"[I]n the early sixties all sorts of Gurdjieff people started visiting Krishna Prem, including Olga de Hartmann and Phillipe [sic] Lavastine, and we discovered that what had taken us years of agonising work to arrive at had been taught for more than 25 years in Paris by Gurdjieff." Madhava Ashish, letter to Jacob Needleman, 22 October 1996, 217.

[14]*Ibid.*

[15]Ginsburg, *In Search of the Unitive Vision*, 82.

[16]'Sy Ginsburg, USA', *Gurdjieff Internet Guide*, (Amden: Gurdjieff Internet Guide, 2002), https://web.archive.org/web/20180409171621/http://www.gurdjieff-internet.com/article-details.php?ID=24&W=9 (accessed 22 January 2023).

[17]Bill Aitken, email to the author, 25 June 2021.

[18]Aitken, *Sri Sathya Sai Baba*, 14.

[19]Madhava Ashish, 'Sri Krishna Prem Through the Eyes of a Disciple,' 29.

[20]Falconar, *Sufi Literature and the Journey to Immortality*, 150.

[21]Teachings, *Mirtola Reflections*, (Mirtola: Mirtola Reflections, 2018), https://www.mirtolareflections.com/the-teachings.html (accessed 23 January 2023).

[22]Bill Aitken, email to the author, 30 June 2021.

[23]Pervin Mahoney, email to the author, 23 June 2023.

[24]Eichert, 'The Last English Saint,' 4.

[25]Ginsbury and Pandey, 'Introduction,' xii.

[26]*Ibid.*

[27]Aitken, *Footloose in the Himalaya*, 86.

[28]Pandey, *Guru by Your Bedside*, 192.

[29]Madhava Ashish, *An Open Window*, 5.

[30]*Ibid.*

[31]Madhava Ashish, 'Sri Krishna Prem Through the Eyes of a Disciple,' 29–30.

[32]Collins, *Light on the Path*, 7–11.

[33]Aitken, email to the author, 30 June 2021.

[34]'Sy Ginsburg, USA,' *Gurdjieff Internet Guide.*

[35]Ralph Metzner, 'Introduction,' in Timothy Leary, *Psychedelic Prayers & Other Meditations*, (Berkeley: Ronin Publishing, 1997), 19.

[36]Bill Aitken, email to the author, 28 June 2021.

[37]Aitken, email to the author, 30 June 2021.

[38]Pandey, *Guru by Your Bedside*, 62.

[39]'The Way of the Sly One: Gurdjieff, Ouspensky, & Jung', *Jungianthology Podcast* [podcast], presented by Ken James, CG Jung Institute of Chicago, 21 January 2018, https://jungchicago.org/blog/the-way-of-the-sly-one-gurdjieff-ouspensky-jung (accessed 21 January 2023).

[40]PT Mistlberger, *The Three Dangerous Magi: Osho, Gurdjieff, Crowley*, (Ropley: O-Books, 2010), 486.

[41]Mistlberger, *The Three Dangerous Magi*, 267.

[42]Paul Beekman Taylor, *Gurdjieff's America: Mediating the Miraculous*, (Cambridge: Lighthouse Editions, 2004), 123.

[43]Aitken, email to the author, 24 June 2023.

[44]Mistlberger, *The Three Dangerous Magi*, 57.

[45]Aitken, 'Sri Krishna Prem in the Last Years,' 268.

[46]Pandey, *Guru by Your Bedside*, 61.

[47]Pandey, *Guru by Your Bedside*, 60.

[48]Aitken, *Footloose in the Himalaya*, 87.

[49]Aitken, *Footloose in the Himalaya*, 96.

[50]Sabharwal, *Afloat a Lotus Leaf*, 278.

[51]Kaul, *Writings of Sri Krishna Prem*, 91.

[52]Pandey, *Guru by Your Bedside*, 60.

[53]Pandey, *Guru by Your Bedside*, 96.

[54]Rutledge, *In Search of a Yogi*, 244–245.

[55]Aitken, email to the author, 24 June 2021.

[56]Leary, *The Delicious Grace of Moving One's Hand*, 218.

[57]Pandey, *Guru by Your Bedside*, 47.

[58]Pandey, *Guru by Your Bedside*, 108–109.

[59]Eichert, 'The Last English Saint,' 4.

[60]Sen, 'Sri Krishnaprem,' xviii.

[61]Sen, 'Sri Krishnaprem', xiv.

[62]Sen, 'Sri Krishnaprem,' xviii.

[63]Shah, 'Memoirs,' 6–7.

[64]Shah, 'Memoirs,' 7.

22: Legend of a Mind

"There is no short-cut to the Goal. The whole course has to be run by each disciple ... each chapter has to be lived through in its proper sequence."[1]
— Sri Krishna Prem, *The Yoga of the Bhagavat Gita*

It is not known what the 'mother' temple, Sri Radha-Raman Mandir in Vrindavan, or the wider Gauḍīya Vaiṣṇava community thought of the reforms at Mirtola, which diluted heavily the strict Vaiṣṇavite character for which the ashram was until then known.

Philosophically, Uttar Brindaban had always been something of a square peg in a round hole—from its myriad non-Hindu influences to its complex and evolving understanding of who, or what, Krishna is—and, had the Chakravartis not had a pre-existing relationship with Bal Krishna Goswami of the Radha-Raman Temple, it is easy to imagine that it might have aligned with one of the many other Krishnaite *sampradāyas* inhabiting Braj. Krishna Prem's monistic, Advaita-influenced Vaiṣṇavism, for instance, arguably had more in common with the teachings of Chaitanya's contemporary, Vallabha, and his Puṣṭimārg (the path of grace), than with Chaitanya himself, whose philosophy of *Achintya Bheda Abheda* (inconceivable oneness and difference) generally leans more towards a dualistic understanding of the relationship between God (Krishna) and his creation. However, while they do not address the post-1951 changes at the ashram, several of Bal Krishna's Chaitanyaite spiritual heirs have in recent years written approvingly about Uttar Brindaban: For example, a 2021 article in the *Sandarshan* newsletter of Radha-Raman Temple priest Chandan Goswami draws heavily on *Yogi Sri Krishnaprem* to tell the life story of Yashoda Mai, who, it notes, "entered [Krishna's] eternal *līlā*" in 1944,[2] while Shrivatsa Goswami—a regular visitor to Mirtola to this day—has written how, "[e]ven in the twent[y-first] century we find many manifestations of Vrindavan, whether it is the Uttar Vrindavan in the Himalayas near Almora, following the vision of Yogi Krishna Prem, or it is ISKCON's New Vrindavan in West Virginia."[3]

The name Uttar Brindaban had, in fact, fallen out of vogue in the 1960s, in favour of the 'Mirtola ashram' or simply Mirtola.[4] Ostensibly done for practical reasons—to avoid confusion with the 'main' Vrindavan, now in the state of Uttar Pradesh—the renaming was symbolic of what Satish Datt Pandey calls the "unobtrusive but major process of reorganization started by Gopal Da some years after Ma's passing away."[5] Krishna Prem had also stopped giving Vaiṣṇava names to new disciples—Donald Eichert, initiated in 1957, was the last to receive a spiritual name: Mrinal,[6] referring to the lotus flower.

In Sri Madhava Ashish's view, though "[t]echnically ... Yashoda Ma could be called a Gauriya [sic] Vaishnava" because of her initiation by Bal Krishna Goswami, in reality her choice of *vairāgya* guru "had nothing to do with the Chaitanya bit of it" and everything to do with Bal Krishna being "a remarkable man [who] could give the [Vaiṣṇava] mantra Ma wanted."[7] As a result, he explains,

> In her attitudes and in the dispositions she made, there is no sign of the peculiarities of the Chaitanya cult. (Ashish, 103)

Bill Aitken suggests that by the '60s the gurus were "embarrassed and sought to distance themselves from their earlier flaunting of the Vaiṣṇava lifestyle when faced by the Krishna Consciousness movement's brash popularisation."[8] While Iskcon (the International Society for Krishna Consciousness)—the primary exponent of the type of reformed Gauḍīya Vaiṣṇavism that would come to be called 'Krishna Consciousness,' or the 'Hare Krishna movement,' in the West—would not be incorporated until July 1966, eight months after Krishna Prem's death, its predecessor organisation, the Gauḍīya Maṭh, was formed in 1920, around the time he first came to India. Headquartered in Calcutta (and characterised by Madhava Ashish as a "contentious order"[9]), it claimed over 64 *maṭhs* (ashrams or monasteries) in India and had been making Western disciples since at least the 1930s, so it is very likely Krishna Prem was aware of that institution, whose missionary fervour stood in stark contrast to the attitudes of both the Mirtola gurus and traditional, non-evangelising Chaitanya Vaiṣṇavism.

"Proselytizing was abhorrent" to Krishna Prem, confirms Madhava Ashish: "He did not want anyone to follow him or to join the particular sect to which he was outwardly affiliated. If he wanted anything, it was that people should get a feeling for the essential and non-denominational truth and grope their way towards it by any means that suited their particular characters and idiosyncrasies."[10] He recalls a "warning Krishna Prem used to give: 'Anyone who cries 'Walk up. Walk up' has the same motive as the market shopkeeper. He wants your money.'"[11]

According to Denys Rutledge, the gurus were equally suspicious of large religious organisations like the Gauḍīya Maṭh, being of the opinion that "sadhus tend to deteriorate in proportion as they organize and form into large communities."[12]

Despite this, several prominent gurus in the proselytising Saraswata line, including Iskcon's AC Bhaktivedanta Swami Prabhupada (who claimed 10,000 initiated disciples[13]), have spoken positively about the form of Gauḍīya Vaiṣṇavism practised at Mirtola. For Prabhupada, the Krishna Prem (whom he erroneously calls 'Krishna Premi,' lover of Krishna) depicted in *Yogi Sri Krishnaprem* was emblematic of the appeal 'Krishna Consciousness' held for Westerners:

> Prabhupada said: ... "Yogi Krishna Premi ... was a great [V]aishnava and was recognised as the first foreign Krishna's [sic] devotee in India. He was one Krishna Premi, but we are now making many Krishna Premis."[14]

By the end of 1964, it was clear Krishna Prem was not well.[15] The ashram, though having made some concessions to the modern world (a pine cone-burning boiler now supplied Mirtola with hot water, for example[16]) remained a remote and spartan place to live, a world away from the "latrines, bathrooms, electric lights, taps, blankets ... and various other comforts like refrigerators and cars"[17] enjoyed by residents in the 1970s and '80s, and lacking in the modern sanitation and medical facilities available in larger towns. Krishna Prem had developed a hookworm infection,[18] which in turn led to a relapse in his ileitis (inflammation of the ileum in the small intestine)—an illness with which he had suffered for more than 25 years[19] but which, at the age of 67, would prove fatal.

Fortuitously, an influx of visitors—as well as two new residents, Australian David Beresford and Scot Bill Aitken—helped to relieve the pressure on the ailing guru during the period of his illness. These guests included Sri Madhava Ashish's mother, Lorna (known as 'Loopy'[20]), and sister, Penelope; Beresford's parents, Nelson and Flora;[21] Kishansinh Chavda and his Theosophist wife, Savitri Behn (the latter of whom took "over the kitchen without a word"[22]); Walter Wiers and his clique of Gurdjieffians, who brought thermal clothing from London;[23] and Timothy Leary, his then wife, the German–Mexican fashion model Nena (Nanette), and fellow psychologist and psychonaut Ralph Metzner. In particular, the addition of Beresford (who, as Sri Dev Ashish, would take over as head of the ashram after Madhava Ashish's death in 1997) and Aitken—two strong young men who could help with the physical demands of running a 60-acre ashram and farm—to the Mirtola ranks was greeted with relief by Krishna Prem. "What would we have done," he asked, "if Thakur had not sent Bill and David?"[24]

Though rarely referenced after the fact by Krishna Prem, nor mentioned by Madhava Ashish in the 'Visitors' chapter of his manuscript (Ashish, 242–262), Leary attached great significance to his visit to Mirtola in January–February 1965,[25] finding room for the story of his meeting with Krishna Prem—the "wisest man in India"—in four of his books (*Jail Notes*, *Starseed*, his autobiography *Flashbacks*, and the collection *The Delicious Grace of Moving One's Hand*) and finding inspiration in the guru's advice to continue his own spiritual journey in the West.

Leary, along with colleague Richard Alpert (later Ram Dass), had been dismissed from Harvard in 1963 amid controversy over his experiments with psychedelic drugs such as psylocibin and LSD, and was at the time of his visit living at a country estate in Millbrook, New York, donated by wealthy sympathisers, which was to be the headquarters of a new foundation for psychedelic research. According to his *New York Times* obituary, "[i]t turned out to be more like a hippie commune, suffused with Eastern religion. Guests meditated and took drugs. The neighbors were horrified."[26] He came to India on his honeymoon with Nanette, visiting Calcutta, Varanasi (Benares) and Delhi, where they met up with Metzner, who recommended Almora as the best place "from which to absorb the continent's message."[27] There they stayed with Lama Govinda, to whom Leary had dedicated 1964's *The Psychedelic Experience* (based on the *Bardo Thodol/Tibetan Book of the Dead*), and Li Gotama, before taking a jeep to Mirtola at the recommendation of "the mysterious Sufi alchemist Brahma Singh,"[28] who advised: "If you're looking for a guru to tell you what's going on in the universe, go see Sri Krishna Prem."[29]

Though the Mirtola gurus were unenthused by the prospect of uninvited visitors, the newlyweds were invited in for tea, Leary recalls, after Madhava Ashish recognised him as "that chap that got bounced from Harvard for giving [Aldous] Huxley's satori pills [LSD] to prisoners and Episcopalians."[30] Impressed by the couple's sincerity, as well as Leary's descriptions of the "Reckless Cerebral Courage" of America's emergent youth counterculture (Krishna Prem "especially enjoyed hearing about the Reluctance of Respectable Scientists, the Alarm of Administrators, the Fury of Parents,"[31] Leary writes), Krishna Prem and Madhava Ashish recounted how they had moved beyond the "ancient prescriptions laid down in the Vedas," the foundational texts of Hinduism, towards a 'purified' form of religion emphasising the living divine in the seeker:

> "We purified, really purified, the rituals," said Sri Krishna Prem. "We eliminated everything that was rote, repetitious, traditional but not

> relevant to the moment. And why, we asked ourselves, were we worshipping and taking care of a little Krishna doll and neglecting the Krishna in the living humans around us? We concluded that to contact the inner divinity we needed the day-to-day push and shove of living with a spiritual partner, the emotional elbowing, the close friction with the intimate beloved. That is our yoga now."[32]

Mirtola, Leary recalls, felt "more like a hunter's cabin than a rectory;"[33] he was immediately at home, and over sherry he and Krishna Prem "passed many hours in conversation"[34] discussing Harvard, Millbrook, *bhakti*, *tantra*, Gurdjieff, Maharishi Mahesh Yogi (whom Krishna Prem criticised as "seek[ing fame] and money"[35]), reincarnation and, inevitably, psychedelic drugs. Krishna Prem "knew all [about] LSD"[36] but disapproved of the use of drugs as a spiritual aid, warning Leary that entheogenic chemicals could ruin the discipline required to stay on the spiritual path:

> Over the centuries our Hindu philosophers have seen everything come and go. Empires, religions, famines, good times, invasions, reforms, liberations, repressions. And drugs.
>
> Drugs are among the most influential and dangerous powers available to humans. They open up glorious and pleasurable chambers in the mind. They give great power. Thus they can seduce the searcher away from the Path.[37]

Aitken describes the advocates of psychedelics in religious terms, noting that those urging others to turn in, tune in and drop out often behaved in a manner similar to the spiritual proselytisers so detested by Krishna Prem. "The poppers of LSD pills believed they had the key to the goal and behaved like missionaries," he says. "The Mirtola attitude to LSD—an artificial agent to enlightenment—[was that it] gave more of a mental sensation than provide[d] the experience of divine consciousness. Expanding our state of mind widens the sensations but does not deepen awareness of the Thing."[38] Aitken further observes: "It seems they liked Tim as a genuine seeker but found his enthusiasm for LSD a passing fad. They regarded LSD as a corner-cutting device. The way to the goal of love cannot avoid suffering and the seeker should embrace suffering rather than devise ways to get round it."[39]

Contemporary correspondence corroborates Aitken's view that Krishna Prem was unconvinced as to the merits of entheogens such as LSD. Writing to Jagdish Shah on 29 January 1965, before Leary's second and final visit to the ashram, Krishna Prem describes his impressions of his "latest visitors:" "three Americans [sic] (two professors of Harvard) interested very seriously in the use of new drugs (L.S.D.) for inducing ecstatic states:"

> They gave us some literature & are expected to come to spend Sunday & the night with us. Interesting stuff but, so far, I am not satisfied that it is satisfactory though one certainly mustn't be prejudiced. After all 'sadhu mahatmas' *have* used various drugs from time immemorial *but* there has always been a feeling that it wasn't altogether satisfactory.[40]

Leary also writes, more contentiously, that the now 67-year-old Krishna Prem, in contrast to what Gertrude Emerson Sen calls his once "open and flagrant identification of himself with India and Indians,"[41] no longer considered India to be the spiritual oasis he had as a younger man. According to Leary, Krishna Prem now believed it was unnecessary for him to have come to India, and viewed Hindu and Buddhist descriptions of reincarnation—a fundamental belief common to almost all Indian religious traditions—as a reflection of their writers' frustration at their inability to break from a predetermined course. Leary describes their conversation:

> Sitting on a small rug that Ashish threw on the grass Sri Krishna Prem smiled. "I am now going to present you with a mandala, a philosophic diagram, a key to illumination in the twentieth century." I leaned forward curiously as he unrolled a chart.
>
> It was a standard map of the world.
>
> "Meditate on this sacred diagram," he said. "Can you imagine what the Buddha would have said if he had had this map? Now let me show you a yogic trick to convert this into a map of time, not just space." He turned the map so that west was up and east was at the bottom. "Do you understand?"
>
> "East is past and west is future?"
>
> "Yes. I have recently lamented the navigational error we made many years ago. To come east in search of wisdom was a mistake. The eightfold path leads west. Consider this: the Hindu theory of reincarnation of souls dates back to 4,000 years ago, when everyone—maharajah, brahmin, peasant, everyone—lived all their lives in one place, in one family, in a fixed caste. There was no concept of change. There was not even the possibility of movement in status or lifestyle. Everything was predestined. Your job, your marriage, your friends, your enemies, your aging, your death—all fixed on one stone in the marsh.
>
> "The only opportunity for change came with death. Can you understand what these Hindus in the villages around us experience? There

> is no concept of change in their life. Transmigration of souls is the only way they can conceive of altering destiny.
>
> "To the westerner it is very different. We can move our bodies. We don't have to wait until death to change reality. We use cars, planes, radio, television to move from one reality to another.... Since the philosophers of the past couldn't migrate in their bodies, they invented a theory of migrating souls.
>
> "Today the searcher can reincarnate as many times as he or she can move from one stone to the next. The wisdom of our age is movement and change. Evolution is the key to illumination."[42]

Whether Leary is a reliable chronicler of the latter-day evolution of Krishna Prem's religious beliefs is up for debate. Leary's recollections of their conversations contain several factual errors (for example, Krishna Prem was not at university with Huxley, who went to Oxford, as he claims in *Flashbacks*, nor was he ever "a devotee of Ramana Maharishi"[43]), though his descriptions of other aspects of life at Mirtola in the mid-1960s—the temple *ārati*, the simplified ritual, the gurus having given away most of its library—are accurate, and his affection and admiration for Krishna Prem, whom, he writes, "spoke with wisdom"[44] and "radiat[ed] pure love,"[45] seems to have been genuine. According to Metzner, Krishna Prem was "probably as close as Tim has ever come to accepting a teacher."[46]

However, Krishna Prem's reported repudiation of transmigration is not found outside of Leary's writings, and *Man, the Measure of All Things*, published in 1966, contains commentary that appears to support the reality of reincarnation, describing the "cyclic ascents and descents which are the reincarnations of man."[47] Additionally, Sy Ginsburg writes that both Krishna Prem and Madhava Ashish "believed in the reality of reincarnation [holding]... with the Theosophists a belief in an obligatory pilgrimage for every soul or essence ... through countless cycles of reincarnation in accordance with cyclic and karmic laws. According to theosophical doctrine, during these incarnations the essence evolved from the lowest mineral form, through plant, animal, human and superhuman states, to a level of consciousness that knows its identity with Universal Oversoul or Absolute—one ultimate reality."[48]

For Aitken the conversation, though plausible in its content, lacks context, framed as it is by Leary as "an unedited recall of an academic exchange between two bright professors engaged in a duel of original and provocative ideas.... What is overlooked," he writes, "is that the reader is only privy to 50% of the conversation: to Gopalda's answers to Tim's queries. Hence the whole exercise being one-sided risks taking Gopalda's replies out of context. And context is everything."[49]

Aitken is even more sceptical as to the veracity of Krishna Prem's alleged confession about having made a "navigational error" more than 30 years earlier, explaining that that while, "philosophically speaking, the universality of the wisdom Gopalda imbibed from Yashoda Mai is found (theoretically) anywhere on Earth,

> Gopalda's flagrant identifying with India and Indians was why he and Ashishda chose to become Indian citizens and why he insisted Dev and I take Indian citizenship to reinforce Mirtola's indebtedness to Mother India and demonstrate thanksgiving for and loyalty to her unique ability to confirm (and in their case deliver) the reality of our soul's inner wisdom. Only She preserves the secret which the Hindu psyche understands but the western psyche has to painfully learn....
>
> To quote Gopalda as saying he believed it was unnecessary for him to have come to India is more likely to be a theoretical reply to the question, 'Is it necessary to come to India for enlightenment?' Correct in abstract philosophical terms, the answer is totally misleading in physical, psychological and spiritual terms.[50]

The journalist Mick Brown writes that although Leary self-identified as Hindu, "his Hinduism proved somewhat provisional," and that he seemed "less interested in exploring traditional paths to enlightenment than in seeking affirmation that psychedelics was [sic] the way, the truth and the life."[51] Some of Leary's students, including at least three Millbrook residents, later took Vaiṣṇava initiation (as Mohanananda Das,[52] Paramananda Das and Satyabhama Devi Dasi[53]) from Iskcon's Bhaktivedanta Swami.

The last word belongs to Krishna Prem, who, reflecting on the Leary party's visit, asked: "If they were satisfied" with the wisdom of the West, "why have [they] come to India?"[54]

Notes

[1]Krishna Prem, *The Yoga of the Bhagavat Gita*, xv.

[2]'Shri Yashoda Ma Vairagini,' *Sandarshan*, 1.37, (2021), 3.

[3]Shrivatsa Goswami, 'Journey as Creation: Vrindavan,' *India International Centre Quarterly*, 30.3-4, (2003–2004), 214.

[4]This change took place in 1963 or early 1964—see, for example, the published correspondence between Rajen Ganguli, a friend living at Sri Aurobindo Ashram, and Krishna Prem, whose letterheads dispense with "Uttar Brindaban" between 6 November 1963 and 15 May 1964.

[5]Pandey, *Guru by Your Bedside*, 45.

[6]Aitken, 'Sri Krishna Prem in the Last Years,' 267.

[7]Aitken, 'Sri Krishna Prem in the Last Years,' 267.

[8]Aitken, email to the author, 30 June 2021.

[9]Madhava Ashish, letter to Andrew Rawlinson, c. April 1988.

[10]Madhava Ashish, 'Sri Krishna Prem Through the Eyes of a Disciple,' 27.

[11]Madhava Ashish, letter to Andrew Rawlinson, 22 June 1988.

[12]Rutledge, *In Search of a Yogi*, 242.

[13]His Divine Grace AC Bhaktivedanta Swami Prabhupāda (trans.), *Śrīmad Bhāgavatam*, Canto 10: 'The Summum Bonum,' ch. 2 ('Prayers by the Demigods for Lord Kṛṣṇa in the Womb'), v. 26, *PrabhupadaBooks.com*, 2014, https://prabhupadabooks.com/sb/10/2/26 (accessed 30 January 2023).

[14]Ksirodak Sayee Vishnu Maharaj, *Sweet Memories of His Divine Grace (Srila AC Bhaktivedanta Swami Prabhupada: Founder–Acharya, International Society for Krishna Consciousness)*, (Vrindavan, Bhakti Vedanta Swami Ashram Trust, 1997), 20.

[15]Sen, 'Sri Krishnaprem,' xviii.

[16]Aitken, 'Sri Krishna Prem in the Last Years,' 267.

[17]Pandey, *Guru by Your Bedside*, 48.

[18]Roy, Yogi *Sri Krishnaprem*, 288.

[19]*Ibid.*

[20]Shah, 'Memoirs,' 4.

[21]Aitken, 'Sri Krishna Prem in the Last Years,' 268–269.

[22]Singh, *Letters from Mirtola*, 64.

[23]Aitken, 'Sri Krishna Prem in the Last Years,' 267.

[24]Phipps, 'Sri Krishna Prem Remembered,' 278.

[25]Leary's *Flashbacks* places the visit in March; this conflicts with a letter from Krishna Prem to Jagdish Shah, dated 29 January 1965, in which the former writes about his "latest visitors."

[26]Laura Mansnerus, 'Timothy Leary, Pied Piper Of Psychedelic 60's, Dies at 75,' *The New York Times*, 1 June 1996, 1, https://www.nytimes.com/1996/06/01/us/timothy-leary-pied-piper-ofpsychedelic-60-s-dies-at-75.html (accessed 3 February 2023).

[27]Leary, *Flashbacks*, 211.

[28]Leary, *Flashbacks*, 212.

[29]Leary, *Flashbacks*, 217.

[30]Leary, *Flashbacks*, 218.

[31]*Ibid.*

[32]Leary, *Flashbacks*, 219.

[33]*Ibid.*

[34]*Ibid.*

[35]Leary, *Jail Notes*, 30.

[36]*Ibid.*

[37]Leary, *Flashbacks*, 221.

[38]Aitken, email to the author, 28 June 2021.

[39]*Ibid.*

[40]Krishna Prem, letter to Shah, 29 January 1965, 2.

[41]Sen, 'Sri Krishnaprem,' xx.

[42]Leary, *Flashbacks*, 220–221.

[43]Leary, *Flashbacks*, 221.

[44]Leary, *Jail Notes*, 30.

[45]*Ibid.*

[46]Stevens, *Storming Heaven*, 205.

[47]Krishna Prem and Madhava Ashish, *Man, the Measure of All Things*, 357.

[48]Ginsburg, *In Search of the Unitive Vision*, 193–194.

[49]Bill Aitken, email of 9 February 2023.

[50]*Ibid.*

[51]Mick Brown, *The Nirvana Express: How the Search for Enlightenment Went West*, (London: Hurst, 2023), 369.

[52]'It is our duty,' *Srila Prabhupada Lila*, (Touchstone Foundation, 2015), https://srilaprabhupadalila.org-/read/8707 (accessed 11 September 2023).

[53]Hayagriva, *The Hare Krishna Explosion*, 178.

[54]Krishna Prem, letter to Shah, 29 January 1965, 2.

23: Freedom

"Of all the men I have ever met, he was the greatest."
— Karan Singh

Like Yashoda Mai and Haridas before him, Sri Krishna Prem initially rejected medical treatment for his illness, preferring to leave responsibility for his care solely in the hands of *Ṭhākur*.

In *Man, the Measure of All Things*, Krishna Prem and Madhava Ashish write critically of "the way we unquestioningly identify our own good with the good of the body," which they connect with the kind of materialistic "thinking that measures the standard of living by the number of flush closets or motor cars to the square mile, thus confusing technical progress with well-being. It confounds literacy with education, and pleasurable sensations with happiness, sees adherence to a code of moral behaviour as spirituality, substitutes a dry study of systems of thought for inner knowledge, and replaces sentiment by sentimentality."[1] Repeated offers by Dilip Kumar Roy—now living at an ashram of his own, Hari Krishna Mandir in Poona (modern Pune in Maharashtra), with his disciple Indira Devi—to fly Krishna Prem and Madhava Ashish to Poona and pay for the former's care, though "just what could be expected of [Roy's] loving heart,"[2] were therefore rejected. As Krishna Prem explained to Satish Datt Pandey, "My doctor is here (pointing to his heart) and in the temple."[3] (He was also fond of parodying Tennyson's 'The Revenge:' "Sink me the ship, Master Gunner—sink her, split her in twain / Fall into the hands of God, not into the hands of doctors."[4])

Both Bill Aitken and Gertrude Emerson Sen describe Krishna Prem in his final months in fructiferous terms: "He hung like a ripe fruit," writes Sen, "and I knew that a ripe fruit does not cling long to the branch."[5] "Like a ripe fruit," Aitken echoes, "Gopalda bore all the signs of having arrived."[6] This 'arrival,' for the latter, was best illustrated by the freedom with which Krishna Prem held forth on all manner of subjects, giving talks in which he fielded questions about *kāma*, for example, which might be rejected as inappropriate by less liberated souls:

> Puffing away at their pipes the Mirtola gurus' conversation was laid back, literary and utterly scintillating. It ranged over every subject under the sun and after the Gandhian taboos [at Kausani] it came as a liberating moment to hear Gopalda's airily dismissive opinions such as 'Sex is after all only a matter of holes,' This freedom of thought and affirmation of life's erotic juices I found intoxicating. People talk endlessly of freedom but Gopalda so far is the only person I have met who was worthy to represent that state.[7]

"Krishna Prem was the only holy man of any denomination I have ever met who treated every subject as fair: nothing was taboo," Aitken elaborates. "His mind was a mirror of nature: nothing is small, nothing is great, nothing is good, nothing is dirty.... [H]e had no hang-ups, [and] he understood everyone's deepest feelings."[8]

This openness about matters of the flesh did not, however, translate into an abandonment of Krishna Prem's vow of celibate *vairāgya*—even if, according to Aitken, both Mirtola gurus "made it clear they would not necessarily follow the path of *brahmacharya* if they were to do it all again."[9] Aitken continues:

> All the relationships I saw were of a guru–*śiṣya* nature and bore the mark of the traditional Hindu pride of a guru in having "made" or fashioned his disciple into guru material.... The line of gurus gave off the feeling of family, Yashoda Mai having motherly feelings for Gopalda, Gopalda having brotherly feelings for Ashishda and Ashishda having fatherly feeling towards his prodigal son, Dev [Ashish]. I found no hint of any lusting after the flesh.
>
> Sex was viewed as a grave mystery but nowhere near as alluring as the divine mystery of love.[10]

Satish Datt Pandey recalls similar "un-sadhu-like" comments from Krishna Prem, who was dismissive of what he called "sacroids:" those neuroses, particularly common in holier-than-thou *sādhakas*, which impede one's spiritual growth by rendering one unable or unwilling to "face the whole of oneself."[11] (As he chastised Dilip Kumar Roy in November 1964, "[p]lease don't call me *His Holiness*! My *Ṭhākur* isn't *holy* and my Guru isn't *holy* and I am certainly not *holy* myself nor intend to be."[12]) Pandey writes:

> It was certainly with a view to pointing out some such 'sacroid,' or the danger of one developing in the psyche of one of his earnest young disciples, that Gopal Da made a seemingly un-sadhu like remark once. 'We should do everything for the Lord,' he said to [my

> friend] Karti, 'we should even piddle for the Lord.' It would have been difficult for me to believe that Gopal Da would make such a statement if Karti had not told me this—Karti whose sacroids were as well known to some of us as they were little known to him.[13]

'Freedom,' Pandey adds, was defined by Krishna Prem in terms of breaking the cycle of *samsāra*: In response to the question, "What is it [life] all about?" Krishna Prem stated: "It is about freedom—freedom from compulsions, including compulsive births and deaths."[14]

If, as Donald Eichert suggests, Krishna Prem 'attained' in the early 1950s, the liberation described by Aitken came only after 30 years of the dedicated treading of a path characterised in *The Yoga of the Kaṭhopanishad* as being as unforgiving as the edge of a razor: "Sharp as a razor's edge is that Path hard to cross and difficult to tread: so say the Seers."[15] Both Yashoda Mai and Krishna Prem were open about the spiritual life not being for everyone—the former was known to remark that "one has to be a bit mad to go this way"[16]—and were not shy about telling those thought to be lacking the discipline and tenacity to stay the course that they might be better off doing something else instead. "If you can possibly do anything else, do it, don't attempt this," Krishna Prem advised;[17] another time, he warned: "[I]f you fear 'the unknown' then come not this way. This is the unknown path."[18]

Having dedicated his life to what Madhava Ashish calls the "essentially lonely"[19] inner work—"Others can help, as signposts help a traveller on his way, but the journey must be undertaken by each one of us alone,"[20] he explained to Karan Singh (whom he referred to by his nickname, 'Tiger')—Krishna Prem came to favour "the 'lonely heights' over the 'populous valleys,'" notes Andrew Rawlinson, quoting *The Yoga of the Kaṭhopanishad*, "and generally espoused what might be called the ideal of a spiritual elite."[21] As Krishna Prem writes in *The Yoga of the Bhagavat Gita*, the person committed to the spiritual quest, "[w]hether he lives in crowded cities or on lonely mountain peaks ... is a Homeless One, for he may fulfil all social duties, yet neither family, nor caste, nor race holds him in bondage."[22] Such 'homelessness,' he explains, is not to be feared, because it is better to

> 'be alone rather than with a fool.' And if you do find the person who is not a fool, one who really is worth giving all the rest for, then 'Grapple him/her to your heart with hoops of steel,' Don't 'else'—But, I warn you, such are rare—fools are common![23]

Pandey connects this solitary outlook with the "subtle truth" of the Biblical aphorism "'Many will be called but few chosen.'" "The 'calling' to the 'path,'" he explains, "is each person's birthright," though most "prefer to throw away our chances and opt for a 'mess of pottage,' which we try desperately to validate as the normal life of a well-adjusted individual in a well-adjusted society."[24] Membership of the 'spiritual elite,' suggests Aitken, is restricted to the chosen few who, by their determination and persistence, have been able to effect the inner transformation which is a prerequisite for admission:

> As a huge effort was required to make the seeker worthy of crossing that inner threshold, very few were favoured with access to the 'Hall of Learning' (Blavatsky's phrase in *Voice of the Silence*). That state of extraordinary grace which charged the gurus' frames and made possible their phenomenal daily routine had only been won after many lost battles.[25]

Writing to Sunil Kumar Dutta, a follower of Sri Aurobindo, on 17 October 1965, Krishna Prem advises that he is afraid he does not have "any spiritual way of healing [Dutta's] bodily illness." "If I did," he adds, "I would surely use it myself as I have been laid up with illness for the last six months or more."[26]

That the letter in question was sent less than a month before his death is remarkable, if not unusual for Krishna Prem, who continued to correspond with other disciples, friends and curious strangers to the very end. Another letter, dated 30 October 1965, concedes that he is not "frightfully well" but assures Singh he will "keep going, as well as updating his student about the movements of visitors and the important business of that year's wheat sowing.[27] Writing to Dilip Kumar Roy two weeks earlier, he admits that his "ileitis, [which] goes back in its origin some twenty-five years or more," is the "sort of thing [that] doesn't just clear up and vanish like a thunderstorm in a summer sky, though one may certainly hope for improvements and a build-up of some strength again." "In any case," he adds, "all is in the hands of our Friend [God] and all is well."[28]

Krishna Prem expresses a similar, if more direct, sentiment (referring to "Bhagavan," God/Krishna, rather than the more ambiguous "our Friend"), in his letters to Dutta, which also indicate that he was now accepting medical treatment after his earlier refusal. "One should take whatever medical help one can get," he writes. "[F]or the rest one must try to realise that we are in the hands of Sri Bhagavan, and that peace lies in His Will, not in ours."[29]

In addition to talk of health, dreams and matters of the spirit, Krishna Prem's final letters and conversations demonstrate a preoccupation with current events that would have been unthinkable 20 years earlier, when he had stopped reading the news altogether. Correspondence from late 1963 and early 1964, included in *Letters from Mirtola (Written by Sri Krishnaprem and Sri Madhava Ashish to Karan Singh)*, includes reflections on the recent deaths of John F. Kennedy[30] and Aldous Huxley[31] and the threat posed by the sectarian "communalism" in India,[32] while a letter to Roy, sent in the aftermath of the Indo–China War of late 1962, warns of the "peril to India" presented by "Chinese materialism."[33] Another letter about the "invasion emergency," to Jagdish and Rambha Shah, echoes Krishna Prem's World War Two rhetoric about trusting in the Absolute in times of conflict, advising: "For this defence [of India] there are divine forces available & active (that nature of which I need not remind you) but they also need the vehicle of dedicated and clear minds & hearts through which to work."[34] In addition to the increased popularity of LSD, Timothy Leary's 1965 conversations with Krishna Prem reveal in the latter a prior knowledge of the growing importance of mass media, such as television and films, in the West: "Sri Krishna Prem," Leary recounts, "was fascinated to know that I had been in a movie studio in Hollywood, asking me many questions about how films were made and distributed. He seemed to think that the mass media would replace the oral tradition of teaching."[35]

Letters to disciples were generally written in the early afternoon, with the evening reserved for work on the manuscript that became *Man, the Measure of All Things*, Aitken remembers. He describes Krishna Prem's typical daily routine in 1965:

> Gopalda's daily routine as I remember it began with Ashishda lighting the upstairs hamam [stove for hot water] then coming down to blow the shankh [conch shell used for *ārati*], while Gopalda, after doing jap[a], bathing and washing his own clothes, would go into the garden to pick flowers for morning *ārati*, which either he or Ashishda would perform till Gopalda fell ill shortly after my arrival in April 1965.
>
> After breakfast the two of them would walk to 'see-off point' in the jungle and discuss swapna vichar [dreams] for an hour or more, then return for coffee served on the baitak [seating area] outside the kitchen. Ashishda would hold interviews upstairs with gurubhais while Gopalda did the cooking according to Thakur's Bengali menu. He also baked two small loaves of brown bread in the embers of the chula [outdoor stove] for supper.
>
> After mid-day arati and bhog the gurus rested, read Rumi and the works of Dr Jung, and attended to their correspondence. Earlier Gopalda had made achar [pickle] including green walnuts from

Yashoda Mai's recipes, brought old gh[ee] back to life by a chonk of fresh lemon leaves, and made marmalade from the ashram gulguls [lemons].

Around 3pm Ashishda made tea and a snack for everyone, enjoyed with gup [chat] on the tea veranda, after which the gurus would go for a walk round the estate checking on the various jobs performed by Tillu and Lallu, the farm hands. They would then enter into dhyan [meditation] while [Kishansinh Chavda's wife] Savitri Behn would prepare the supper and I would blow the shankh for evening arati.

After supper in the kitchen (or upstairs in Gopalda's room when there was no crowd and he made roasted alu [potatoes] in the wood fire), the evening gathering would ask questions about the inner path. Gopalda's magical exposition would create an extraordinary mood of beatitude to elevate the soul to cloud nine.

At 10pm the meeting dispersed and, pumping up the petromax [lamp], the gurus sat on the floor, spread out their notes and worked late on their commentary on HPB's stanzas.[36]

What degree of importance was placed on Radha, Krishna and their Vraja *līlā*—personages and concepts to which Krishna Prem had once attached "immense significance"[37]—in the 'new' Mirtola of the mid-1960s is a complex topic.

As discussed in chapter six, Krishna Prem differentiated between Krishna the legendary *avatār* and Krishna the Absolute, though he referred to them interchangeably and by the same name. Writing to Karan Singh in 1964, he espouses the view that in speaking of 'Krishna' one refers not to the "One Divine Reality" as it/he is, but only to one possible "synthesis of our feelings towards" it/him.[38] Similarly, *Ṭhākur*—originally a Bengali name of Krishna—also became, in the Mirtola vocabulary, a designation for the "unmanifest source" of classical *Vedānta*, meaning Pandey can describe his guru, Madhava Ashish, as "above all, ... a Vaiṣṇav, which does not keep him from being, at the same time, a true Advaitist."[39] He explains:

> Calling, and regarding, the Source Thakur gives it a certain warmth and closeness in place of the coldness and aloofness of 'the unmanifest.' It makes 'that one thing' (a favourite expression of Gopal Da) somehow much more real than a mere philosophical concept, however sophisticated, can ever be expected to be.[40]

The post-Moti Rani changes to the ashram—which, tailored to "the challenges raised by a different generation," now taught "how to experience the immediacy and certainty of what the gurus called, simply, 'the Thing'"[41]—left little space for many of the received wisdoms of traditional Vaiṣṇava devotionalism. Krishna Prem was inspired by the universalist, secularist, humanist[42] poetry of Rumi. (Though usually identified as a Sufi Muslim, Rumi had a "non-religious, non-ethnic, and non-geographically bound philosophy[43] and is said famously to have declared: "I belong to no religion. My religion is love.") Like Rumi, Krishna Prem increasingly, in a practice continued by his successors, emphasised the importance of 'love' without reference to a specific person or deity who should be the destination. As Aitken puts it:

> If you put the question how they managed it [their daily routine], their reply was: 'Love is the guide.' (As a Sufi poet [Ibn Arabi] wrote: 'Love is the guide and love is the goal, Where'er love's camels lead the one true goal is there.')[44]

KM Munshi notes a change in Krishna Prem's *sādhana* that began as early as the mid-1950s:

> Today, this ex-professor of English, a profound student of the *Bhagavad Gita*, spends his days and nights in the service and contemplation of the Lord. A great love and with it a deep and mature understanding have descended upon him. Love is self-sufficient, he said. 'There is no why; no wherefore; it is its own law.'[45]

In his letters to Karan Singh, Krishna Prem stresses the importance of seeing beyond religious symbols to the truth beyond: that "there is nothing greater than Love in this or any world."[46](Singh had asked about the image of Shiva, though the same would be true of the divine couple, Radha–Krishna.) "[H]owever much the symbols glow for us, we have to pass through them to that which they symbolise," he comments, "and speaking for myself, I find nothing more full and nothing which gives more meaning to an otherwise meaningless universe than the state of actual love."[47]

Krishna Prem also clarifies that this "'divine' or 'spiritual' love"—"'the breath whose smile kindles the universe'"[48]—is of the same substance as the romantic or erotic love felt by humans for each other. Taking aim at those who would reject the physical aspect of such love, as well as praising the esoteric *Vaiṣṇava-sahajiyā* love poetry scorned by many conservative Gauḍīya Vaiṣṇavas, he explains: "[L]ove is one—there is no love but love, of course the thing that worries our 'spirituals' is that love has a physical component which, like all physical things is apt to claim more than its share of the attention. But 'so what?' as they say. So has meditation...."[49]

With this emphasis on the transformative power of love ("the key to the whole business," in the words of Madhava Ashish[50]), it might be considered ironic that at the ashram formerly known as Uttar Brindaban Krishna—paramour of the *gopīs*, whose unselfish devotion to their cowherding lothario is presented as the highest form of love—was now forced to share the space with other, less obviously 'loving,' teachers: Jung, Gurdjieff, Blavatsky. It is clear, however, that Krishna Prem considered his post-'attainment' orientation—nonconformist, nonaligned, and in opposition to what he considered the fossilised dogmas of organised religion—no less imbued with divine *prem* than his earlier, more exclusive devotion to the *Lord of Love*. This, recalls Madhava Ashish, was obvious from the many subtle changes to his personality, particularly the affectionate way in which he interacted with disciples and friends:

> It was not as a sometime ritualist and author of books that he won the love and respect of his many intimate friends and followers who sought the path he had trodden, for people drew strength more from his presence than from what he said. All treasure the memory of his radiant personality, his blue eyes that seemed to see right through one, his humour, his dis-concerting questions before which falsities crumbled to dust, the love he gave so freely, and, above all, the fire of spiritual certainty whose central flame gave significance to the many facets of his nature.[51]

He writes that it was a long time before he and Krishna Prem were able to fully reconcile the ashram's "'new,' almost secular approach to the truth" and love with what he calls "the real truths of the devotional approach."[52] The piecemeal pace of change is evident from a letter sent in August 1954—three years after Moti Rani's death—to Huta (Savita Devjibhai Hindocha), a disciple of the Mother of Sri Aurobindo Ashram, in which Krishna Prem sounds every bit the *bhakta* of old, writing that to be "a worshipper of Sri Krishna" is "the best thing that any of us can be, the one thing that, in the end, no one will have cause to regret. All else changes and passes away: He alone stands the same forever. May His blessings be with you and guide you to His feet." He also notes that he has enclosed a "charn-tulshi" (the *tulsi* necklace worn by Gauḍīya Vaiṣṇavas) with the letter.[53]

The sentiment resembles another comparatively late example of Krishna Prem's devotionalism, expressed in a 1950 letter to Narendra Nath Kaul:

> Constantly keep His feet in your heart—blindly if necessary—and refuse assent to any suggestions that it is 'useless' or 'superstitious'

> or 'merely a form'.... If you hold fast He will never desert you. His feet are the 'place to go to,' the 'direction from which to seek help.' There is no other for anyone.[54]

The abandonment of decades of Brahminical ritual and superstition was a similarly gradual process: Jagdish Shah describes Mirtola at the turn of the '60s as still being "very orthodox and ritualistic." "Harijans [untouchables] (and even Penelope [Phipps])," he writes, "were not allowed entrance even to the ante-chamber of the temple," and Krishna Prem—despite his earlier repudiation of astrology—would place *tulsi* leaves on food containers during lunar eclipses to "ward off [the] evil eye" of the mythical celestial body Rahu.[55]

Madhava Ashish's own lightbulb moment came, he explains, when he realised that "*Omnia vincit amor* (love conquers all), the Vaiṣṇava greeting *Jai Radhe* (victory to Radha) and Krishna as Prema Swarup (the self-nature of love) were all saying the same thing, and one did not need to get stuck with a particular image." Referencing the popular image of Govinda, the divine cowherd, he adds: "The love which glues the universe together is utterly real and needs no peacock feathers, flutes, necklaces and caste marks [tilaks] to make it visible."[56] As for Radhikamohanji, the temple's Radha–Krishna deities, "it was the love between them that mattered," says Aitken.[57]

According to Singh, however, "the idea that [Krishna Prem] drifted away from Krishna" in this period is "complete, absolute, utter nonsense." While his guru had "a lot of other influences," Singh says, he "remained devoted to *Ṭhākur* all his life. ... *Ṭhākur* was his love and *Ṭhākur* was his lover."[58] Devi Mukherjee, a disciple of Paramhansa Yogananda who visited Mirtola in 1963, also remembers "a great devotee" who "spoke only of Krishna." Mukherjee adds, "He was like butter: soft and lovable, yet with great strength of character—like Krishna himself!"[59]

For the philosopher and yogi Haridas Chaudhuri, Krishna Prem was neither an *Advaita Vedāntin* nor a pure Vaiṣṇava, but a *parabhakta*[60] who charted a middle course between the desire for *moksha* and desire for eternal but detached companionship with a personal God. "Total self-giving to Krishna places one above the disputes of the Vedantist and the Vaiṣṇava," Chaudhuri writes. "The Vedantist says: 'I want to be one with the Supreme.' The Vaiṣṇava says: 'The Supreme is Honey. I do not want to be one with Honey – I want to enjoy Honey.' Krishnaprem says: 'It is not a question of what I want or don't want. It is essentially the question of what Krishna wills.'" Chaudhuri concludes: "This is *parabhakti*."[61]

Indeed, despite incorporating belief in an "imageless Divine,"[62] Krishna Prem's mature philosophy ascribed to the cosmos a personality denied to it by 'pure' *Advaita*, which recognises only the existence of Nirguṇa Brahman, and whose adherents he had earlier dismissed as "rather dry"[63] and whose practice, in their contemporary form, he had dismissed as sterile.[64] As Madhava Ashish elucidates,

> Sri Krishna Prem['s] ... spiritual quest had as its bedrock a compassionate view of the universe, approximately corresponding to what is known as the Bodhisattva doctrine. In this view, the world is still an illusion, in the sense that it is not what it appears to be—solid lumps of matter floating in time and space. However, it is a meaningful illusion, pervaded by love, through which the undifferentiated source of all being becomes aware of the multifold qualities that inhere in it. These concealed qualities or potentialities become separated and objectifiable or knowable when differentiated in the creative outpouring. That source—'He', 'She', 'It', 'That', no pronoun is adequate to describe it—requires a vehicle through which the perception of its qualities in manifestation can take place. Without such a vehicle, the source would remain ignorant of its own name.
>
> That vehicle is Man—the aware and self-aware through whose eyes THAT sees everything: sees and joy[s] in being.
>
> Man discovers his identity with the Source of all things. Looking outwards through Man's eyes, the unmanifest Source knows itself in manifestation.[65]

This worldview is the origin of what Aitken describes as the main "Mirtola teaching" in Krishna Prem's final years: that "man is divine".[66] The title of the latter's final published work, *Man, the Measure of All Things*, is also a reference to this concept, as expressed in Protagorean terms (*homo mensura*).

This view bears the influence of Meister Eckhart, "perhaps the greatest of the Christian mystics," who wrote, according to Krishna Prem, that God "sees His own image in Man—and nowhere else,"[67] and may also have been inspired in part by his earlier Vaiṣṇavism, which holds that the ultimate reality—Krishna—feels the greatest *ānanda* (bliss) when he experiences himself through his devotees,[68] but finds its greatest exponent in the personage of Helena Petrovna Blavatsky. In their commentary on her masterwork, *The Secret Doctrine*, Krishna Prem and Madhava Ashish explain:

> It is only through him who is 'one with his Father,' him whose personal self is but a vehicle for his Father's will, that the Father's divine power can manifest freely with all its wondrous freedom. When that

> occurs, as it has now and then occurred, we gasp and idly prate of Gods, not knowing that beyond all Gods is Man, the heart of each of us, Ruler of all that is.[69]

Man, the Measure of All Things also contains the gurus' interpretation of the Blavatskian conception of the universe: the "manifested Cosmos" whose living "breath" is at "the Root of all being," and which is contrasted with that which is "dead and mechanical:"[70]

> The one Reality is not a static absolute as conceived by some philosophers. It is not a gigantic geometric figure laid up somewhere in the heavens, or rather in the void. It is living Being and the pulsation of its life continues ceaselessly even in, what might seem to us to be, the frozen sterility of the Cosmic Night.[71]

Elsewhere, Blavatsky wrote and spoke extensively on the Bodhisattva Path as described by Madhava Ashish and alluded to by Krishna Prem. ("If one tries to help someone else, the water flows through one like a pipe.... It comes, in fact, from beyond the self," Krishna Prem explained to Singh.)[72] Her *The Voice of Silence*—one of Krishna Prem's favourite, and most frequently quoted, books—was recognised by the 14th Dalai Lama as having "influenced many sincere seekers and aspirants to the wisdom and compassion of the Bodhisattva Path"[73] (a concept adapted from Mahāyāna Buddhism), while the *Light on the Path*[74] finds Hillarion, a Greek 'adept' of Blavatsky's 'Brotherhood of Masters' channelled by author Mabel Collins, reassuring spiritual seekers that such bodhisattvas, "those who have passed through the silence, and felt its peace and retained its strength, [...] long that you shall pass through it also."[75]

Notes

[1]Krishna Prem and Madhava Ashish, *Man, the Measure of All Things*, 198.

[2]Roy, *Yogi Sri Krishnaprem*, 288.

[3]Pandey, *Guru by Your Bedside*, 118.

[4]Sri Madhava Ashish, letter of 9 July 1982.

[5]Sen, 'Sri Krishnaprem,' xix.

[6]Aitken, 'Sri Krishna Prem in the Last Years,' 269.

[7]Aitken, 'Sri Krishna Prem in the Last Years,' 265.

[8]Tillis, 'Bill Aitken, Landour, Mussoorie, 20th December 1980'.

[9]Aitken, email to the author, 25 June 2021.

[10]Bill Aitken, email to the author, 4 July 2021.

[11]Pandey, *Guru by Your Bedside*, 193.

[12]Roy, *Yogi Sri Krishnaprem*, 281.

[13]Pandey, *Guru by Your Bedside*, 193–194.

[14]Pandey, *Guru by Your Bedside*, 12–13.

[15]Krishna Prem, *The Yoga of the Kaṭhopanishad*, 177.

[16]Ginsburg, *The Masters Speak*, 142.

[17]Pandey, *Guru by Your Bedside*, 255.

[18]Kaul, *Writings of Sri Krishna Prem*, 98.

[19]Sah, 'The Guiding Hand,' 7.

[20]Singh, *The Mountain of Shiva*, ch. 4, para. 63.

[21]Rawlinson, *The Book of Enlightened Masters*, 382.

[22]Krishna Prem, *The Yoga of the Bhagavat Gita*, 121–122.

[23]Krishna Prem, letter to Eichert, 1962.

[24]Pandey, *Guru by Your Bedside*, 21.

[25]Aitken, 'Sri Krishna Prem in the Last Years,' 269.

[26]KD Sethna (ed.), 'Two unpublished letters of Sri Krishna Prem to Sunil Kumar Dutta,' *Mother India*, 39.9, (1986), 546.

[27]Singh, *Letters from Mirtola*, 83.

[28]Roy, *Yogi Sri Krishnaprem*, 288.

[29]Sethna, 'Two unpublished letters,' 546.

[30]Bill Aitken remembers how Krishna Prem, "always concerned to demolish the religious mumbo jumbo most ashrams like to foster, ... put paid to the fantasy of a [Bombay] devotee who claimed the Mirtola gurus had foreknowledge of President Kennedy's assassination. It turned out the devotee's driver heard the news on a village radio early in the morning and conveyed it to Gopalda before his master had got out of bed."

[31]Singh, *Letters from Mirtola*, 56–57.

[32]Singh, *Letters from Mirtola*, 61.

[33]Roy, *Yogi Sri Krishnaprem*, 269.

[34]Sri Krishna Prem, letter to Jagdish and Rambha Shah, 13 November 1962.

[35]Leary, *Flashbacks*, 221.

[36]Bill Aitken, email to author, 17 December 2020.

[37]Pandey, *Guru by Your Bedside,* 195.

[38]Singh, *Letters from Mirtola,* 66.

[39]Pandey, *Guru by Your Bedside,* 128.

[40]*Ibid.*

[41]Aitken, 'Sri Krishna Prem in the Last Years,' 270.

[42]Mostafa Vaziri, *Liberation Philosophy: From the Buddha to Omar Khayyam (Human Evolution from Myth-Making to Rational Thinking)*, ebook edn, (Delaware: Vernon Press, 2019), 274.

[43]Mostafa Vaziri, *Rumi and Shams' Silent Rebellion: Parallels with Vedanta, Buddhism, and Shaivism*, (New York: Palgrave Macmillan, 2015), 9.

[44]This is likely Krishna Prem's translation from the Persian, which he had learnt in order to read Rumi in the original. So says Aitken, 'Sri Krishna Prem in the Last Years,' 269. Compare that with a contemporary rendering by William C. Chittick: "I practice the religion of love, wherever its camels turn their faces | This religion is my religion and my faith." See William Chittick, 'The Religion of Love Revisited,'*Journal of the Muhyidden Ibn Arabi Society* 54 (2013), 37.

[45]Munshi, *Janu's Death and Other Kulapati's Letters,* 55–56.

[46]Singh, *Letters from Mirtola,* 67.

[47]Singh, *Letters from Mirtola,* 60.

[48]From Percy Bysshe Shelley's 'Adonais'.

[49]Singh, *Letters from Mirtola,* 50–51.

[50]Sri Madhava Ashish, entry for July 2022, Mirtola Ashram Calendar 2022.

[51]Madhava Ashish, 'Preface,' in Krishna Prem and Madhava Ashish, *Man, the Measure of All Things,* 9–10.

[52]Madhava Ashish, *An Open Window,* xix.

[53]Huta, *The Story of a Soul,* vol. 1 (1954–1955), The Mother & Sri Aurobindo, 2021, ch. 1 ('Undated?'), paras 42–45, https://motherandsriaurobindo.in/disciples/huta/books/the-story-of-a-soul (accessed 25 May 2023).

[54]Kaul, *Writings of Sri Krishna Prem,* 106.

[55]Shah, 'Memoirs,' 2.

[56]Madhava Ashish, *An Open Window,* xix.

[57]Aitken, email to the author, 2 July 2023.

[58]Singh, conversation with the author, 13 June 2021.

[59]Mukherjee, *Shaped by Saints,* ch. 12, para. 2.

[60]As defined by Swami Sivananda, a *parabhakta* is one "who sees the Lord only everywhere, who sees the whole world as Lord Krishna (*vāsudevasarvam iti* [everything is Vāsudeva – *Bhagavad Gītā* 7.19])." See Swami Sivananda, 'Para Bhakti,' *Sivananda Online,* (Rishikesh: Divine Life Society,

2020), https://www.sivanandaonline.org/?cmd=displaysection&section-id=451 (accessed 31 January 2023).

[61]Haridas Chaudhuri, foreword, in Dilip Kumar Roy, *Yogi Sri Krishnaprem*, 3rd edn, (Bombay: Bharatiya Vidya Bhavan, 1992), vii.

[62]Singh, *Letters from Mirtola*, 56.

[63]Sen, 'Sri Krishnaprem,' xv.

[64]Krishna Prem, 'Letters from Sri Aurobindo,' 520.

[65]Madhava Ashish, *An Open Window*, 98–99.

[66]He contrasts this idea with the "Semitic" (Judaeo–Christian) teaching that "man is worthless." See 'Bill Aitken: Nature as the Footprint of the Divine,' *Heart of Conservation* [podcast], interview with Bill Aitken, Ranikhet, Lalitha Krishnan, 9 August 2020, https://earthymatters.blog/2020/08/09/bill-aitken-im-a-traveller-who-writes-not-a-writer-who-travels-heart-of-conservation-podcast-ep19-show-notes-coming-soon (accessed 31 March 2023).

[67]Singh, *Letters from Mirtola*, 56.

[68]The German convert Sadananda (Ernst Georg Schulze) explains: "[In his heavenly abode] Goloka Krishna experiences Himself through the *bhaktas* (gopis, parents, relatives, friends, animals, stones, plants, trees, sky, sun, stars, the cit [consciousness]-world) more intensely than He could experience Himself as a lonely Krishna." See Sadananda, 'The self-experience of God increases through the division into subject and object' (letter to Vamandas, 18 November 1960), Svami Sadananda Dasa (Ernst Georg Schulze) [Facebook page], 23 May 2020, https://www.facebook.com/Svami.Sadananda.Dasa/posts/3121263321230517 (accessed 14 July 2023).

[69]Krishna Prem and Madhava Ashish, *Man, the Measure of All Things*, 404.

[70]Krishna Prem and Madhava Ashish, *Man, the Measure of All Things*, 87.

[71]Krishna Prem and Madhava Ashish, *Man, the Measure of All Things*, 80.

[72]Singh, *Letters from Mirtola*, 69.

[73]'"The Voice of the Silence" by H. P. Blavatsky,' *The Theosophical Society*, (Pasadena, California: Theosophical Society (Pasadena), 2002), https://www.theosociety.org/pasadena/ts/silence.htm (accessed 17 July 2023).

[74]Like *The Secret Doctrine*, both *The Voice of Silence* and *Light on the Path* purport to be translations of a book of Eastern wisdom otherwise lost to history. Their source material—dubbed *The Book of Golden Precepts*—is, according to Blatavsky, a sister work to the *Book of Dzyan* on which *The Secret Doctrine* is supposedly based.

[75]Collins, *Light on the Path*, 23.

24: Setting Sail

"[H]e was not of the ordinary type. We have lost a great soul from earth."[1]
— Sarvepalli Radhakrishnan, president of India

Sri Krishna Prem died at Naini Tal, en route to Jaipur for emergency medical treatment, around 4am on 14 November 1965,[2] some six months shy of his 68th birthday. At Ramsay Hospital, he was allocated the same first-floor room formerly occupied by Madhava Ashish,[3] where he spoke his final words: "My ship is sailing."[4]

Throughout the "protracted and painful illness which led to his death," for which he sought treatment only when the pain became overwhelming, Krishna Prem had "continued guiding his disciples, constantly demonstrating in a manner more powerful than words the supremacy of the human spirit over the sufferings of the body," recalls Madhava Ashish,[5] who describes for Dilip Kumar Roy his guru's final moments:

> [J]ust when his condition was stable and the doctor who had come here was well pleased, there was a sudden deterioration. By the time we realised that this was not one of the usual mild upsets, it had become very serious. A Jaipur surgeon happened to come and advised immediate operation. It took another day to get a car and we left for Jaipur on the 13th. But he was too weak to stand the journey and collapsed at Kathgodam, so we went up to the little hospital at Nainital where, on the morning of the 14th, he slowly and quietly left his body.[6]

The atmosphere of this final journey, with Krishna Prem "carried down the mountain on a simple carrying-chair, a bath-towel strung across two small struts of wood nailed to the back of the chair, to rest his head on, a small skull-cap on his slightly bald head,... surpassed that of Pope Pius XII being carried into the audience hall of the Vatican,"[7] writes his disciple Penelope Phipps, who accompanied her guru as far as Almora.[8] Though he had by now accepted medical intervention to prolong his life, Krishna Prem, following the example set by Sri Yashoda Mai and Sri Haridas, was nevertheless prepared for the end, Phipps explains, recalling an earlier conversation between the pair:

> 'Some people who have had to fight all their lives,' he said, 'continue automatically. They cannot stop, they fight an illness when old, when it might be a chance to go. They survive, maybe to get something worse before long. When your time comes, fix your mind on whoever you want to meet you, and they will be there. At the end of an out-breath, open up your hands, and let yourself go.'[9]

In fact, at the time of his illness Krishna Prem was already, he believed, "on an extension" to his earthly life, which he had sought prior to the final visit of Penelope and 'Loopy' Phipps, according to Shah. He had already been warned that this "extension," granted by the *Ṭhākurs*, would be physically painful, adds Shah:

> [One] morning seeing the worry and concern on my face, he said, "Don't worry. When They gave me an extension, They had told me it will be painful."[10]

In *The Art of Dying While Living*, a collection of conversations with Vimala Thakar, she compares Krishna Prem's final months to those of Socrates, who faced his demise similarly fearlessly. "So had died another person called Krishna Prem in 1965 in Mirtola, the Uttar Vrindavana in [the] Himalayas. This is the way to welcome death," she said. "So was it welcomed by Socrates centuries ago, and when the poison was given to him, he started watching the effect of the poison in his body."[11]

Karan Singh writes about his final meeting with Krishna Prem, in the Naini Tal home of Jagdish Shah, in June 1965, recalling his *param* guru's warmth and strength of spirit, which shone through despite his failing body:

> I was shocked to see Gopalda. He looked dreadfully ill and had changed almost beyond recognition from the robust, vigorous man I had met a few years earlier. He was suffering from intestinal obstruction and was in great pain, but he greeted me with his usual warm affection and retained his spiritual presence, despite his serious illness. We spent the night at a hotel and took leave of him the next

> morning. When I bowed to touch his feet he embraced me warmly and held me to him for several moments. His flashing blue eyes were filled with love and power; I think we both knew then that we would never see each other again in this life. Of all the men I have ever met, he was the greatest.[12]

Krishna Prem's last letter to Singh, sent on 30 October 1965, testifies to the fortitude described by Thakar, with 'Gopalda,' labouring under the pain of advanced ileitis and a month from death, the model of the 'attained' man so admired by his pupils, ready to continue on but with no fear of the end:

> [A]ll goes on as usual and we have nearly completed our wheat sowing. Ashish's mother and sister are here and Kishan Singh and Savitri [Chavda] expect to leave in a day or so. I trust all goes well with you—macrocosmically as one might say, as well as microcosmically. I can't say am frightfully well but चल तो रहा [life goes on].[13]

Krishna Prem's body, like Sri Yashoda Mai's, was cremated at Dandeshwar, having been carried there from Panuanaula by a crowd of local villagers.[14] "Within an hour or two of his death more than a hundred Indian peasants from neighbouring villages gathered to meet the car which brought his body from the hospital, insisting with great love on their right to carry him on their shoulders along the last few miles of road," recalls Madhava Ashish. "For thirty-five years he had lived amongst them and they gave him reverence."[15] Bill Aitken remembers "the villagers with their axes... [hewing] branches for his bier" and a funeral procession that was "more triumphal than funereal."[16]

At his request, Krishna Prem's ashes were interred in Yashoda Mai's *samādhi mandir*,[17] with only a separate memorial stone marking the earthly reunion of teacher and disciple. Containing his *praṇām mantra*, in praise of the guru, it reads:

गोपालं मायशोदायाः श्रीराधार्पितमानसम् ।
कृष्णप्रेमाभिधं वन्दे गुरुमानन्दविग्रहम् ॥

"I worship guru Sri Krishna Prem, who is the embodiment of bliss, who is Yashoda Mai's Gopal, and whose consciousness and heart are devoted to Sri Radha."

Writing to Karan Singh, and likely still in shock, on 16 November, Madhava Ashish describes Krishna Prem's death in anticlimactic terms, noting that he has "never before seen anyone go with so little sense of loss, rather, a sense of continued presence." He adds: "Of course one feels grief, but love and grief go together. We have lost him yet not lost him. It is a paradox."[18] According to his sister, Penelope Phipps, there was, however, a comet in the sky—a sign of a "great rishi" (sage) leaving this world—at the time of their guru's passing;[19] Jagdish Shah remembers seeing what he describes as a "meteor arch across the sky" over Naini Tal's Ayarpatta hill as Krishna Prem took his final breaths.[20]

Sri Madhava Ashish's immediate sense that Krishna Prem was not really 'gone' may have been strengthened by the latter's experience of the death of Yashoda Mai. Govindagopal Mukherji elaborates on the posthumous 'visits,' described briefly in chapter thirteen, that provided relief from the sorrow he felt following his own guru's passing:

> "You can well imagine," [Krishna Prem] told me after her passing, "how derelict we felt directly after Ma had dropped her body. So I won't dwell on it.
>
> "We cremated her at Dandeshwar beside a little stream—a *jharna*—and returned to Mirtola around midnight. I was dog-tired and went off to sleep at once.
>
> "In the small hours of the morning her dear familiar voice awakened me. 'Wake up, Gopal!' it rebuked me. 'How can you go on sleeping? It's time for meditation. I am here!'
>
> "Galvanised, I started up and cried out in pain: 'If you are here Ma, how is it that I can't see you? Won't you reveal yourself to me?' 'No,' came the answer, 'you will have to come up to me by dint of your meditation.'
>
> "Next night she came again—a disembodied Voice; only to add: 'I abide with you—within you.' On the third night: 'I am with all of you, I tell you.'
>
> "And so it went on: she kept visiting us like this manifesting herself from one plane of consciousness to another to efface as it were the line of demarcation between the two worlds—of life and death."[21]

His successor was not, however, immune from grief, and as the impact of Krishna Prem's passing was felt, "Ashishda had a bad time," recalls Aitken, "and only the companionship of Dev [Ashish] helped him through it. His health failed [and] he smoked too much...."[22] In a letter to Abha Shah, Madhava Ashish confirms he was "ill after Gopalda's death," noting that it wasn't until the following year (after a restorative break in Kashmir[23]) that he "agreed to live and to face my reluctance to take on the responsibility of handling all the disciples Gopalda had left."[24] (Krishna Prem had nearly 100 initiated *śiṣyas* at the time of his death.[25])

In general, though, the succession from Sri Krishna Prem to Sri Madhava Ashish, which had largely been settled in the upheavals of the 1950s, was a smooth one. An attempt by the charismatic Walter Wiers and his London 'Mirtola' group to "stak[e] a claim" on some of Krishna Prem's Western disciples was seen off, and though some Bengali disciples were "reluctant to transfer their affections" (Madhava Ashish's Bengali being "rudimentary"), Delhi and Bombay soon replaced Calcutta as recruiting centres for the ashram, recounts Aitken.[26] (Wiers later became an adherent of the Faithism of Oahspe and published his own commentary on that spiritualist "*New Bible*."[27]) "After [Krishna Prem's] death, [Madhava Ashish] withdrew further into his privacy. Yet as the small but steady trickle of people came asking for help, seeking answers to their inner queries, [Madhava Ashish] extended himself, honouring the convictions and teachings of his late guru," explains Madhu Tandan.[28] Tandan describes the sense of continuity present in the guru's quarters at Mirtola, formerly occupied by Yashoda Mai and then Krishna Prem, and now by Madhava Ashish:

> I walked into a small mud-plastered room which had a single piece of furniture in it, an old chest of drawers. He [Madhava Ashish] was sitting cross-legged on an age-darkened wooden floor, facing the fireplace over which was a mantelpiece on which [Krishna Prem]'s photograph rested. Hanging above it was the portrait of the founder of the Ashram, a woman with gaunt cheeks, sitting in meditation. A harmonium and a rolled-up mattress lay in the corner of the room, which had been occupied by these three generations of gurus. The air of stillness made it seem as though their prayers had soaked into the walls.[29]

"When Krishna Prem passed on in 1965, there was no break in the parampara [succession]," adds Donald Eichert. "What Krishna Prem was, Madhava Ashish had become, and with as firm a hand he taught the way."[30]

Beyond his room, Krishna Prem bequeathed to his successor next to nothing in material terms, "he who seemed to possess most in eternal terms" having owned "worldly possessions that could fit easily into one tin box," in the words of Aitken.[31]

Though written about Yashoda Mai, it is striking that the following text by Gerald Carney could just as easily be describing Krishna Prem, illustrating the extent to which 'Gopal' and 'Ma' were united in their rejection of the material trappings often associated with 'renounced' spiritual teachers:

> Yashoda Ma did not fit the image of a *jagad-guru* [world-guru], with tours, texts, ashrams, and an image curated by followers for the media. Her life at Mirtola ... remained focused on her own *sādhana*, which she shared with others.[32]

For Aitken, his *param* guru resembled true ascetics such as the Buddha and Christ, "who owned nothing between them." True to his own vow of *vairāgya*, Aitken writes, Krishna Prem left behind little beyond a "spare set of sannyasi's robes."[33]

The 68-year period covering Krishna Prem's life was marked by huge changes in both India and the Western world, encompassing the end of colonial rule in the subcontinent, the diffusion of Hindu and Buddhist ideas beyond Asia, and the breaking down of the barriers between East and West—developments to which he, along with a handful of other spiritual pioneers, had a front-row seat.

Though he criticised the 'Megalopolitan' creators of this new, globalised world, lamenting that its nations, and in particular India, were in danger of "merg[ing] into a common hotch-potch from London to Yokohama,"[34] he in many ways personified it—his embrace of Hinduism heralding the dawn of an age when concepts such as yoga, karma, mantras and reincarnation are understood across the world and the Indian religions, like the Abrahamic faiths, are increasingly seen as belonging to humanity as a whole rather than a specific national group. When, in 1923, Roy introduced Ronald Nixon to his social circle as "an English Hindu or a Hindu Englishman, if you like," it was intended as a (good-natured) joke at Nixon's expense; however, his acceptance, in his later identity as Sri Krishna Prem, by Indian-born practitioners of Hinduism disproved the widely held belief "that a foreigner cannot really penetrate the social world of Hinduism as a convert," in the words of David Haberman.[35] "Krishnaprem's widespread admiration within India and his success in attracting faithful followers challenges such assumptions," Haberman adds.[36]

According to Charles Brooks, Krishna Prem's influence is most keenly felt in Vrindavan, where his initiation into the lineage of Bal Krishna Goswami represents an "important historical precedent" for the Western devotees whose *sankīrtan* parties are now a common sight in the streets of Braj.[37]

Ironically, given his well-known hostility to being written about[38] and ambivalence about the value of the written word (it being "quite impossible for us to understand in any real sense the meaning of what is written in any book"—a collection of "black marks on white paper" whose meaning "depends on the ideas in our own minds"—"no matter who the author may have been"[39]), it is books, both by and about Krishna Prem, which represent perhaps his greatest legacy today. In the same way that, in his lifetime, the *Yoga* books and the original *Initiation into Yoga* pamphlet served as advertisements for the ashram at Uttar Brindaban, the essays contained in the expanded *Initiation into Yoga: An Introduction to the Spiritual Life* and the biographical sketch and letters in *Yogi Sri Krishnaprem*, both published posthumously, continue to attract modern spiritual seekers to the personality behind them. Vijaysinh Chavda, son of Kishansinh, writes that the former text serves as a kind of "informal initiation ... into the strange Mirtola ways, where whatever one did or spoke counted."[40]

"He never wanted his letters to be published. He didn't want to be remembered. How could Gopalda, who did away with his personal will to serve the will of Thakur, have a will of his own in this matter?" asks a latter-day Mirtola convert, Promila Chitkara, who believes that his "Thakur's will prevailed through Dilip Roy['s *Yogi Sri Krishnaprem*]. Devotees of Krishna whose hands Gopalda's letters reached began looking for his books."[41] Similarly, the author of the present biography 'discovered' Sri Krishna Prem indirectly through Roy's writing. Chitkara observes:

> After half a century of his passing away, seekers from different geographical locations, of different backgrounds, and yet a common goal are coming to Mirtola to 'experience' the Uttar Brindaban that Gopalda and Ma created, to find more about him, to get more of his teachings, his life.[42]

She senses a divine hand in the recent flurry of interest in his life and philosophy, which led to the publication, in 2019, of Tubu Chakravarti's detailed account of Krishna Prem's 1948 visit to Sri Ramana Ashram and a new ebook edition of *Yogi Sri Krishnaprem*,[43] as well as the inauguration of a permanent memorial to 'Professor Nixon' at Lucknow University around the 55th anniversary of his death, in November 2020. (Speaking about the memorial, Ranu Uniyal, the university's current head of English, said: "We are happy and proud that the department of English was blessed by his presence, and it was in Lucknow that he found his spiritual guide and mentor, who opened the path of self-realisation for him through *bhakti* and selfless service to God."[44]) In 2023, the Theosophical Publishing House at Adyar announced new editions of *The Yoga of the Bhagavat Gita* and *The Yoga of the Kaṭhopanishad.*

While he would argue that he did not invent anything new—the path followed at Mirtola being the same as that trod previously by Madame Blavatsky and her Mahatmas, Chaitanya, Shankara, Mohammed, Jesus, the Buddha, and the incarnated Krishna: ubiquitous, indivisible and eternal[45]—the novelty of Krishna Prem's teachings, and their dissemination to a global audience over the internet, must also play a part in this curiosity; no Hindu leader before or since has so comprehensively melded Eastern thought with ideas adapted from Western psychology and esotericism.

Yet if books, articles and commemorative materials can serve, in Krishna Prem's words, as a useful reminder of the reality of the "path laid down by those who have gone before ... and reached the goal"[46]—it was, after all, a statue (of a *luohan* buddha) which cemented the young Ronald Nixon's commitment to the spiritual quest—the real truth, he taught consistently, is within, beyond teachers and ancient scriptures, and accessible to all. As Sri Krishna Prem and Sri Madhava Ashish remind us in the former's final published work, *Man, the Measure of All Things*:

> We have got so used to accepting it on external 'authority' of some sort, that it is not easy for us to adjust ourselves to the idea that no authority whatever, whether of sacred scripture or whether of men, can guarantee truth, but that it reveals itself in all its infallibility within the pure consciousness. Hence, if we would learn wisdom, we must seek it not primarily in books or teachers but in our hearts.... [47]

Having transcended the orthodoxies first of his English upbringing and then of the faith into which he'd been initiated, Krishna Prem exhorted us to follow no one; to open our minds, listen to our hearts, and find our own way home.

"Only in the heart of man is there anything to be gained or lost."[48]

— Sri Krishna Prem and Sri Madhava Ashish, *Man, the Measure of All Things* (1966)

Notes

[1]Roy, *Yogi Sri Krishnaprem*, 132.

[2]Singh, *Letters from Mirtola*, 83.

[3]Shah, 'Memoirs,' 5.

[4]Sen, 'Sri Krishnaprem,' x-xi.

[5]Madhava Ashish, 'Sri Krishna Prem Through the Eyes of a Disciple,' 30.

[6]Roy, *Yogi Sri Krishnaprem*, 289–290.

[7]Phipps, 'Sri Krishna Prem Remembered,' 278.

[8]After returning to Britain, Phipps would go on to give mantra *dīkṣā* to at least one disciple of her own. To this *śiṣya*, Tony Foster, she entrusted film footage documenting life at Mirtola in 1962–63 which includes the only known video footage of Sri Krishna Prem. The film, believed to have been shot by Walter Wiers on his home video camera, shows 'Gopalda' preparing *bhoga*, answering correspondence, and performing *ārati* with Sri Madhava Ashish. It can be viewed on the *Mirtola Reflections* YouTube channel (https://youtube.com/@mirtolareflections3816).

[9]Phipps, 'Sri Krishna Prem Remembered,' 280.

[10]Shah, 'Memoirs,' 4.

[11] Vimala Thakar, *The Art of Dying While Living (Vimalaji's Communications with Mumbai Inquirers in the Festival of Friendship Gathering in Mount Abu in November, 1994)*, (Mumbai: Vimal Parivar, 1996), 53.

[12]Singh, *Autobiography*, 299.

[13]Singh, *Letters from Mirtola*, 83.

[14]*Ibid.*

[15]'Ronald Henry Nixon' (obituary), 52.

[16]Aitken, 'Sri Krishna Prem in the Last Years,' 270.

[17]Singh, *Letters from Mirtola*, 84.

[18]Singh, *Letters from Mirtola*, 83.

[19]Penelope Phipps, 'Sri Madhava Ashish,' *The Independent*, 6 May 1997, 14.

[20]Shah, 'Memoirs,' 5.

[21]Roy, *Yogi Sri Krishnaprem*, 293.

[22]Aitken, email to the author, 24 June 2021.

[23]Pandey, *Guru by Your Bedside*, 38.

[24]Sah, 'The Guiding Hand,' 10.

[25]Eichert, 'The Last English Saint,' 5.

[26]*Ibid.*

[27]Martin Gardner, *Urantia: The Great Cult Mystery*, paperback edn, (Amherst: Prometheus, 2008), 162.

[28]Tandan, *Faith & Fire*, 25.

[29]Tandan, *Faith & Fire*, 81.

[30]Eichert, 'Sri Madhava Ashish.'

[31]Aitken, *Branch Line to Eternity*, 73.

[32]Gerald T. Carney, 'Sri Yashoda Ma,' *Journal of Vaishnava Studies*, 30.2, (2022), 79.

[33]Aitken, *Sri Sathya Sai Baba*, 150.

[34]Roy, *Yogi Sri Krishnaprem*, 134.

[35]Haberman, 'A Cross-cultural Adventure,' 222.

[36]*Ibid.*

[37]Brooks, *The Hare Krishnas in India*, 98.

[38]See, for example, Roy, *Yogi Sri Krishnaprem*, 13: "O Dilip, why did you write about me and, if at all, why so much? ... I begged you not to write about us but you just print my request and leave it at that! You are incorrigible and if you were anyone else I should hate you, but I can't!"

[39]Krishna Prem, *Initiation into Yoga: An Introduction to the Spiritual Life*, 32.

[40]Vijay K. Chavda, 'Understanding Sri Krishna Prem,' *The Aryan Path*, 49.1, (1978), 1.

[41]Promila Chitkara, instant message to the author, 9 March 2023.

[42]*Ibid.*

[43]Dilip Kumar Roy, *Yogi Sri Krishnaprem*, 1st ebook edn, (Mumbai: Bharatiya Vidya Bhavan, 2019), 6.

[44]*Ronald Henry Nixon (later known as Swami Krishna Prem)—the Unsung Hero of Department of English, LU* [online video], presenter Ranu Uniyal, Lucknow, University of Lucknow, 2020, https://www.youtube.com/watch?v=vigOj9wspiM (accessed 21 March 2023).

[45]On the superficial differences between these teachers and their respective traditions, he might have quoted what Blavatsky is said to have told Gyanendra Nath Chakravarti: "Some people like jam with their bread and some like cheese."

[46]Sen, 'Sri Krishnaprem', xv.

[47]Krishna Prem and Madhava Ashish, *Man, the Measure of All Things*, 203.

[48]Krishna Prem and Madhava Ashish, *Man, the Measure of All Things*, 216.

Afterword: 'The Still Point of a Turning World' by Chitra Iyer

One morning in 1956, prompted by a dream that night, Sri Krishna Prem broke the *chulha* (mud stove) in the temple kitchen. The evening before he had tended it carefully in a regular ritual, smoothing on a fresh coat of mud, filling the cracks, readying the stove for the next day's service. We can only guess at the compelling nocturnal instruction that caused him to shatter that heat-hardened stove, a symbol of a way of life he had dedicated himself to for thirty years. The temple is, after all, the centre of the ashram, and the kitchen is central to the temple. It is the main artery of the temple's material heart, where food is prepared with great care and devotion every day for Krishna and Radha, the presiding deities. But the *chulha*, with its strict rules of access, was also a symbol of ancient and sometimes oppressive hierarchies. That dream and its instruction, like a koan, "dark to the mind, radiant to the heart," must have been urgent, the inner impulse demanding dramatic outer action. More than six decades later, that singular event still seems of inestimable worth, for it unfolded an ongoing dialectic on the founding principles of Sri Krishna Prem's "Uttar Brindaban" ashram, also called Mirtola.

In a search for Truth that began early in his life, Sri Krishna Prem, or Gopalda as we call him, was profoundly influenced by Buddhism and Theosophy. But he readily donned the ochre robes of an Indian ascetic and devoted himself singularly to his beloved guru, Sri Yashoda Ma, following unquestioningly for years her prescribed discipline and form of worship. Impeccably honest in his surrender, on that fateful morning in 1956, over a decade after Yashoda Ma had passed on, Gopalda broke a structure which no longer served the same purpose it thus far had. Sensitive to changing times and a new generation of seekers, he kept what was essential and let go of what was not. In the years that followed,

Gopalda and his disciple and successor, Sri Madhava Ashish (Ashishda), continued to simplify daily life at the ashram, opening the temple and kitchen to all, and teaching in an increasingly direct, less religious mode. The emphasis shifted, subtly but surely, from the orthodox framework "of religious paraphernalia," as Ashishda put it, to "the natural growth of man as man," where "nothing depends on the acceptance of dogma or belief."

Those who came to Mirtola in the 1960s must have found the lack of rigid orthodoxy in the ashram refreshing. The temple *pūjā* and *ārati*, conducted three times a day, still formed the luminous heart of life at Mirtola, but the teaching was now truly comprehensive and fed by many streams—a cogent spirituality that resonated with the modern seekers and their investigations of the ultimate mystery. Uttar Brindaban, no longer an 18-mile hike up a steep slope, was now accessible by road. Gopalda's profoundly insightful commentaries on the *Bhagavat Gītā* and the *Kaṭhopanishad* drew many who sought direction beyond a traditional approach. In Gopalda and Ashishda they would discover "pupil teachers" who encouraged healthy debate and pointed to a direct enquiry into the mystery at the heart of man's being. The inner goal was reflected in every aspect of the outer routine at Mirtola—a way of work that to this day allows one to build and integrate a productive outer life with a central inner enquiry. As Gopalda said, we must "adventure for ourselves along the pathway whose gate is in our own hearts." In a letter to Dilip Kumar Roy, he wrote: "Our loyalty to this Path must overrule everything else whatsoever and must be unconditional." The Mirtola way requires nothing less than all.

In the decades that followed Gopalda's passing, Ashishda continued to teach, and embody, the simultaneous development of a meaningful inner and outer life. From the 1960s onwards, he built on Yashoda Ma's legacy of forest conservation with a series of pioneering ecological initiatives, both for Mirtola and for the Himalayan foothills that surround the ashram. To this day, it sits within a richly diverse mixed forest, and the Mirtola watershed feeds a perennial spring. In the 1980s, Ashishda permitted a small group of disciples to take up residence at the ashram, to perform the daily *pūjā* in the temple, and help with work in fields, gardens, kitchen and dairy. Unused to physical labour, stripped of all distractions, each of us struggled to quieten an unruly mind in a rebellious body. At all times we were pointed towards self-observation and self-remembering, to become and remain aware of the ceaseless vibration within, the silent thrum of being, while efficiently performing our outer duties. It was a balancing act requiring great energy, sincerity of purpose and focus of attention. As Ashishda said—referring to the automatic, mechanical nature of so much human behaviour—"nothing mechanical is of any use on the Path."

Psychological work and introspection also form a vital part of our work in Mirtola. Ashishda built on Gopalda's deep understanding of the strange yet universal symbology of dream to help us access hidden connections and patterns in the labyrinthine psyche—a steady distillation of impulses through the disciplined recording and interpretation of dreams. Gopalda and Ashishda taught that the key to real understanding lay in an honest introspection of our internal world.

My first visit to Mirtola, as a fourteen-year-old in 1976, made an impact that has lasted to this day. I watched Ashishda one morning as he performed a series of routine tasks around the temple kitchen: putting tea leaves into a bucket to be later mixed into the cow feed, sweeping the verandah, hanging laundry out on the clothesline to dry, petting Yami the temple dog. Later that evening in the temple, I saw him enveloped in a haze of incense as he offered the *ārati*, the evening worship, to Radha and Krishna, Mirtola's sovereign presences. Yet I could not say which of these many activities he conducted with more attention or reverence. He did everything, from sweeping to worship, with the same quiet and precise efficiency and focus. I was too young fully to understand then what I was witnessing, but the seed was sown. Here was a man who embodied a way of life, unlike any other person I had experienced. Today, as I offer the daily routine and service, which remains centred on the temple—on Radha and Krishna—I understand that this path always goes through undiscovered country; that no matter how many have gone before, it is new for each one who treads it. This way calls for us to cultivate faith, but live with doubt. It calls for courage, and unwavering intent and attention. Everything outside and inside is grist for the mill and must be surrendered to the work. To walk this path, one must throw every ounce of oneself into striding forward.

Like any living tradition, the story of Uttar Brindaban resists a concluding summary. Mirtola went into retreat for a decade or so after Ashishda's passing, but the seed sown by Sri Yashoda Ma and nurtured by Gopalda and Ashishda sprouts again, renewed and freshly relevant to a new generation of seekers. The light at Uttar Brindaban continues to burn steadily, directing us always inwards, to the root of our being, at the still point of the turning world. As Gopalda said: "In yourself the Truth exists. By yourself it must be striven for and tested. In yourself it will be found."

Chitra Iyer[1]
Uttar Brindaban,
Mirtola
2024

Notes

[1]Chitra Iyer is a disciple of Sri Madhava Ashish and the head of the Uttar Brindaban ashram at Mirtola.

Further Reading

By Sri Krishna Prem:

Sri Krishna Prem, *The Search for Truth*, (Calcutta: Ganesh Chandra Bose, 1938).

Sri Krishna Prem, *The Yoga of the Kaṭhopanishad*, (Allahabad: Ananda Publishing House, 1940).

Sri Krishna Prem, *The Yoga of the Bhagavat Gita*, (London: John M. Watkins, 1948).

Sri Krishna Prem and Sri Madhava Ashish, *Man, the Measure of All Things*, (Wheaton: Quest Books, 1969).

Sri Krishna Prem, *Initiation into Yoga: An Introduction to the Spiritual Life*, (Wheaton: Quest Books, 1976).

Of related interest:

Aitken, Bill, *Footloose in the Himalaya*, (Delhi: Permanent Black, 2003)

Brooks, Charles R., *The Hare Krishnas in India*, (Princeton: Princeton University Press, 1989)

Ginsburg, Seymour B., *In Search of the Unitive Vision: Letters of Sri Madhava Ashish to an American Businessman 1978–1997*, (Boca Raton: New Paradigm, 2001)

Haberman, David L., 'A Cross-cultural Adventure: The Transformation of Ronald Nixon,' *Religion*, 23(1993),3

Kapoor, OBL, *Saints of Vraja*, (New Delhi: Aravali Books International, 2015)

Kaul, Narendra Nath, *Writings of Sri Krishna Prem: An Introduction*, (Bombay: Bharatiya Vidya Bhavan, 1980)

Leary, Timothy, *Flashbacks – A Personal and Cultural History of an Era: An Autobiography*, (New York: GP Putnam's Sons, 1990)

Sri Madhava Ashish, *An Open Window: Dream as Everyman's Guide to the Spirit*, (New Delhi: Penguin Books, 2007)

Sri Madhava Ashish, *Man, Son of Man*, (Wheaton: Quest Books, 1970)

Sri Madhava Ashish and Seymour B. Ginsburg (ed), 'Mirtola: A Himalayan Ashram with Theosophical Roots,' *Quest*, 100 (2012), 3

Mooney, Brian, *Frank Baines: A Life Beyond the Sea*, (London: Thorogood Publishing, 2011)

Pandey, SD, *Guru by Your Bedside: The Teachings of a Modern Seer*, (Gurgaon: Penguin Books, 2003)

Roy, Dilip Kumar, *Yogi Sri Krishnaprem*, (Bombay: Bharatiya Vidya Bhavan, 1992)

Singh, Jyotsna, ed., *Letters from Mirtola (Written by Sri Krishnaprem and Sri Madhava Ashish to Karan Singh)*, (Mumbai: Bharatiya Vidya Bhavan, 2004)

Singh, Karan, *Autobiography*, (New Delhi: Oxford University Press, 1995)

Photo Album

Figure 1: Sri Krishna Prem the Vaiṣṇava, with *tilaka* and *tulsi* beads, late 1940s.

Figure 2: Sri Krishna Prem, late 1950s or early ’60s.

Figure 3: With disciples Benoy Banerjee (seated), Amulya Dutta, Dilip Kumar Roy (no relation to the author of *Yogi Sri Krishnaprem*) and Sri Madhava Ashish.

Figure 4: The marble *mūrti* of Krishna which was later placed in Sri Yashoda Mai's *samādhi mandir*.

Figure 5: Yashoda Mai at Uttar Brindaban.

Figure 6: Visiting the Radha-Raman Temple of Bal Krishna Goswami in Vrindavan.

Figure 7: With Ramana Maharshi at the Sri Ramana Ashram in Tiruvannamalai.

Figure 8: 2Lt RH Nixon in RFC uniform.

Figure 9: A wintry Mirtola, 1930.

Figure 10: Sri Haridas, Moti Rani, Govinda Priya (Frank Baines), Madhava Ashish, Keshab Priya and Sonny the dog at Yashoda Mai's *samādhi mandir*.

Figure 11: Monica Chakravarti, the "*dame de salon*" of 1920s Lucknow.

Figure 12: Moti Rani and Madhava Ashish, late 1940s.

Figure 13: Krishna Prem and Madhava Ashish, c. 1960.

Figure 14: Krishna Prem at Mirtola, late 1950s or early '60s.

Figure 15: Ronald Nixon at Cambridge.

Figure 16: 'Gopal' and 'Ma' (playing *esraj*), Uttar Brindaban.

Figure 17: With disciples and friends at Mirtola. From left to right: Beryl Stoneman, Savitri and Kishansinh Chavda, Madhava Ashish, Karan Singh, David Beresford (Sri Dev Ashish).

Figure 18: Relaxing at Mirtola, late 1950s or early '60s.

Figure 19: With Madhava Ashish, 1960s.

Figure 20: Krishna Prem as he would have appeared around the time of the Leary visit, 1960s.

Figure 21: A newly initiated Sri Yashoda Mai Vairagini with shaven head and *tulsi mālā*.

Appendix: The teachings of Sri Krishna Prem [As summarised by the author]

- **The spiritual life is not easy** and there are no shortcuts to the Goal. Without stickability—perseverance—there can be no chance of success. "Clench your teeth and stick it out."
- **Seek out a living master.** Yoga is the art of the soul and can only be taught by a qualified guru. When the student is ready, the teacher will appear.
- **Ego is the enemy.** There are no separate selves—apart from the All, there is nothing. As light is one, consciousness is one, and pervades all beings.
- **Man is the measure.** Human beings are unique as the vehicle through which the Divine Consciousness, the source of all existence, perceives Itself.
- **As within, so without.** Events in the outer world, like the wake from a ship far ahead, originate in those which have already played out within. As is one's thought, so one becomes.
- **Pay attention to your dreams.** As the royal road to the unconscious, dreams contain important signals from our subconscious to our conscious minds.
- **Psychic phenomena are real,** but beware superstition: belief in the occult, like any belief, should come only as a result of firsthand experience.
- **Ignore the sacroids.** The integrated man knows that earthly love, including the physical, is a shadow of the heavenly. The battle of life must be won and not run away from.
- **Books are useful—to a point.** The Eternal is beyond words, which in any case mean different things to different people. The finger that points to the moon should not be mistaken for the moon itself.

- **Doubt is the doorway to knowledge,** and he who knows Reality fears no scrutiny of the grounds of his beliefs.
- **Love is the guide.** There is no why, no wherefore—love is its own law, and nothing is greater.
- **Embody the Bodhisattva.** Having crossed over to the other shore, one is obliged, following the example of the Buddha, to help others across.
- **Religions are man-made; the Truth is eternal.** Though it has many names, the Path that leads from death to Deathlessness is one—and all who tread it will ultimately reach the same Goal.

www.ingramcontent.com/pod-product-compliance
Lightning Source LLC
Chambersburg PA
CBHW061753070526
44586CB00023B/2604
9781952232886